"Johnny, We Hardly Knew Ye"

*My very
best wishes
Dave Powers*

"JOHNNY, WE HARDLY KNEW YE"

MEMORIES OF JOHN FITZGERALD KENNEDY

by Kenneth P. O'Donnell and David F. Powers
with Joe McCarthy

Little, Brown and Company — Boston — Toronto

The authors are grateful to Robert Graves for permission to reprint
lines from *Oxford Addresses on Poetry* by Robert Graves. Copyright
© 1961, 1962 by Robert Graves.

Library of Congress Cataloging in Publication Data

O'Donnell, Kenneth P
    Johnny, we hardly knew ye.

    1. Kennedy, John Fitzgerald, Pres. U.S., 1917–1963.
I. Powers, David F., joint author. II. Title.
E842.03   973.922'092'4   [B]   72-5693
ISBN 0–316–71625–1
ISBN 0–316–63000–4 paperback

10   9   8   7   6   5

BP

*Published simultaneously in Canada
by Little, Brown & Company (Canada) Limited*

PRINTED IN THE UNITED STATES OF AMERICA

To our wives,
for their many sacrifices

We wish to thank Sander Vanocur for his help in stimulating many of our memories of President John F. Kennedy and the events of his career while we were preparing this book.

K. P. O'D.
D. F. P.

A Note about the Narrators

Kenneth P. O'Donnell and David F. Powers had a closer personal relationship with President John F. Kennedy during his years in the White House than any of the other members of his inner circle of advisers and aides, except, of course, his brother Robert. At the same time, during that colorful period in Washington when so much was written about the people around Kennedy, both O'Donnell and Powers managed to remain almost unknown to the reading public. They were always within beckoning distance of the President around his office and always at his side when he traveled, but they stayed so anonymous that they were usually mistaken for a couple of Secret Service agents. Devoted to the President and sharing his intimate confidences, but keeping out of his limelight and cloaking themselves in closed-mouth reticence, they were dubbed by the White House press corps "Kennedy's Irish Mafia."

Both of them are Massachusetts Irishmen who knew President Kennedy and all of the Kennedy family since Jack ran for Congress in Boston back in 1946. They worked for him in his Senatorial campaigns, in the primaries and at the Democratic convention and in the Presidential campaign of 1960, and they were among the first few men whom he named as special assistants to the President when he was elected. O'Donnell's official title in the White House was Appointments Secretary, but he handled a much wider variety of duties than the sensitive responsibility of deciding who would be allowed to see the President, and for how long, and who should be turned away during the course of a busy day. He was also the President's political right hand, troubleshooter, expediter and devil's advocate. ("Kenny, tell Bobby what you told me this morning about why you think it would be a disaster to appoint that fellow he suggested for the Supreme Court.") Jacqueline Kennedy called O'Donnell "the wolfhound" because when she saw his unsmiling face entering the room, she knew that the President's fun was over and it was time for him to go back to work. President Kennedy phoned O'Donnell in the morning at his home before he was awake to ask him if he had seen that item in a Detroit newspaper about a local controversy over the closing of a government warehouse, and often telephoned him again as many as six times in the evening after dinner about various problems that had just occurred to him.

In his memoirs of his service as JFK's press secretary, Pierre Salinger describes O'Donnell as the most powerful member of Kennedy's White House staff with "the greatest responsibility, influence, and accessibility to the President." A reporter who covered the White House during its brief New Frontier era puts it another way: "When everybody else around the President thought something was marvelous, and O'Donnell thought it was full of crap, he said so to the President and the President listened to him."

O'Donnell was unwilling to embark upon the writing of a book of memories of John F. Kennedy without the collaboration of his own closest companion on the White House staff, Dave Powers, who, as O'Donnell and several members of the Kennedy family believe, saw a side of President Kennedy that nobody else saw. O'Donnell says, "Outside of Bobby, President Kennedy had only one really close friend and that was Dave Powers." Powers, who is a warm and genial and completely unpretentious man, several years older than President Kennedy and Ken O'Donnell, describes himself as "a three-decker Irishman," meaning that he comes from a neighborhood of three-flat tenement houses in the Charlestown waterfront district of Boston. He likes to recall his early days when he sold newspapers at the Charlestown Navy Yard. Powers is an avid student of Democratic party politics with an incredible memory for names, faces, and poll statistics and election voting figures that President Kennedy valued highly, but his function in the White

House was not that of a political adviser. He was simply a guy that President Kennedy liked to have around him as much as possible.

In the summer when Jackie and the children were at Cape Cod, Dave and the President had dinner together alone in the White House and Dave stayed on in the evening until the President went to sleep. They swam together every day in the warm White House pool, with Dave using a breaststroke so he could carry on the joking conversation that the President liked to listen to. Their friendship dated back to a night in the winter of 1946 when the young Jack Kennedy, taking his first try at politics, climbed three flights of stairs to the tenement flat where Dave was living with his widowed sister and asked if Dave would help him in the coming Congressional primary fight. They hit it off immediately and lastingly. When Jack Kennedy was at his father's home at Palm Beach in 1955, recuperating painfully from his last serious spinal operation, he asked for Dave to come down and stay with him for a few weeks. After President Kennedy's death, his wife asked Dave to come to her house in Georgetown every day at noon so that young John could eat lunch with him. Next to his father, Dave was the man John knew best.

Dave Powers now works on the staff that is planning the museum section of the proposed John F. Kennedy Memorial Library. He has no degrees from a university to qualify him as a professional archivist, but for the Kennedy Library he has something more important. He remembers almost everything that John F. Kennedy did between 1946 and 1963, even more than Ken O'Donnell remembers, which is quite a lot.

JOE McCARTHY

A Note about the Narration

When Dave Powers and I decided to put our memories of President John F. Kennedy into a book, our first problem was to decide which of us would serve as the narrator. The editors felt that we might impose too much confusion on the reader if both of us tried to share or take turns in the telling of the story. The only solution was for one of us to take on the role of the narrator, and after some discussion it was handed to me.

Although I may appear to be the writer of this book, more than half of the incidents described in it and most of its factual information come from the voluminous personal notes and the incredible memory of Dave Powers, whose total recall of names, dates, figures and interesting small details and funny stories was a constant source of both invaluable help and fascinating entertainment for President Kennedy during the seventeen years of their close association. Without Dave Powers as a collaborator, I never would have tried to put on paper this remembrance of the greatest friend and the greatest man both of us ever knew. Like so many other things in this book, that description of our feeling for President Kennedy comes from Dave.

KENNETH P. O'DONNELL

A Note about the Title

The main title of this book is an adaptation of the recurring line from the lyric of an Irish folk song that runs, "O, Johnny, I hardly knew ye."

Contents

"Johnny, We Hardly Knew Ye"

ONE

The End of the Beginning

OUR MEMORIES of President John Fitzgerald Kennedy go back from Dallas over seventeen crowded years to the winter of 1946 in Boston, when he was a young war veteran getting into politics for the first time in a free-for-all fight for a vacant Congressional seat and liking the taste of it. But when Dave Powers and I think of John Kennedy now, we both remember him as he was on the Thursday morning of November 21, 1963, when he was leaving the White House to go to Texas. That day before he died was a good day, when he was looking forward eagerly to his best years. Everything seemed right for him, and for all of us. As he said at the time, quoting one of those obscure Victorian English poets only he seemed to know and remember, "Westward, look, the land is bright."

Later it was reported that President Kennedy was tired and irritated that day because Vice-President Lyndon Johnson had forced him, in a long and bitter argument, into making the trip to Texas against his will. With the 1964 election year coming up, the Democrats in Texas were split into two warring factions, with Governor John Connally's conservatives not speaking to Senator Ralph Yarborough's liberals, and Johnson, so the stories said, had insisted on the President going down there to patch things up. It appeared to Kennedy, one reporter wrote, that "Johnson ought to be able to resolve this petty dispute himself; the trip seemed to be an imposition."

That wasn't the trip we planned, nor was it the President Kennedy we saw boarding Air Force One that morning. "I feel great," he said to me. "My back feels better than it's felt in years." A new treatment of calisthenics had strengthened his back muscles, and he was able to play golf again for the first time since he crippled himself planting a ceremonial tree at Ottawa in the spring of 1961. Along with his good health, Dave and I never saw him in a happier mood.

His big worry of the previous two years, the threat of a nuclear war with Russia, was safely behind him. He was elated over the signing of the nuclear test ban treaty with the Soviets a few weeks earlier, which he regarded as his greatest accomplishment. Now he was doing the thing he liked even better than being President, getting away from Washington to start his campaign for reelection in a dubious and important state, with twenty-five electoral votes, where he was sure he could win the people even though many of the bosses and most of the big money were against him. It was a tough political challenge that he relished with much more enjoyment than he found in his executive duties in the White House.

If the trip to Texas was not something special for the President, not just a tiresome feud-patching chore, he would not have made it the occasion of his wife's first appearance on a Presidential campaign tour, much to his delight and to the astonishment of all of us. I almost fell over when he told me Jackie was coming with us. I knew then how much winning Texas meant to him. He regarded the Connally-Yarborough battle as a minor annoyance that he could easily straighten out, as he soon did before he reached Dallas. He was thinking of a bigger thing, his own votes. That morning when he came aboard Air Force One, he tucked into the edge of the mirror in his dressing room a card with three figures that he would use to needle the Democratic leaders in Texas. The figures reminded him that in 1960 the Kennedy-Johnson margin in Texas over Nixon-Lodge was only 46,233 votes, but Johnson, also running alone in another slot on the ticket for U.S. Senator against Republican John G. Tower, had a plurality of 379,972, while Price Daniel, the Democratic candidate for governor in the same election, won by 1,024,-792. The President was going to do some sharp talking in Texas about the big difference between his own vote and those of the other Democratic candidates. He had asked Dave Powers to get him the figures the day before while they were swimming together in the White House pool. "Great man for the small details, always the perfectionist," Dave said when he showed me the figures that morning. Nobody had to force President Kennedy to go to Texas, least of all Lyndon Johnson; he could not have been held back from going there.

Texas and Florida were the two states where President Kennedy was planning to make his strongest effort in the 1964 campaign. He had campaigned in Florida the previous weekend. Johnson had not been closely involved in the planning of the coming campaign and suspected that Bobby Kennedy was engineering a move to dump him as the Vice-Presidential candidate in 1964 because of his connection with Bobby Baker, the Johnson protégé whose scandals case had just been revealed. Johnson was sure that Bobby Kennedy had been behind the exposure of Baker, a ridiculous assumption because a scandal of any kind in Washington reflecting on the Democrats was the last thing the Kennedys wanted. Furthermore, President Kennedy never had any thought of dumping Johnson. I was sitting with the President and Senator George Smathers on the way to Florida the Saturday before we went to Texas, when Smathers asked him if he was planning to get rid of Johnson because of the Baker case.

The President glanced at Smathers and said, "George, you must be the dumbest man in the world. If I drop Lyndon, it will make it look as if we have a really bad and serious scandal on our hands in the Bobby Baker case, which we haven't, and that will reflect on me. It will look as though I made a mistake picking Lyndon in 1960, and can you imagine the mess of trying to select somebody to replace him? Lyndon stays on the ticket next year."

Actually, Lyndon Johnson was not anxious for the President to go to Texas. He did not want the President to see for himself how little prestige and influence the Vice-President then had in his own home state. Since he had joined the New Frontier ticket, his fellow conservatives in Texas had turned against him. The more liberal Texas Democrats, such as Senator Yarborough, had always been against him because he was looked upon as a conservative. As Vice-President, he felt sidetracked and ignored, and sorely missed the patronage and the power he had enjoyed back in Texas when he was the majority leader in the Senate.

Johnson blamed his fallen prestige on Bobby Kennedy. He felt that Bobby had taken over his rightful position as the number two man in the government, which was true enough. The President himself sometimes pointed out with amusement that many of Bobby's friends in the administration, who were always trying to push Bobby into running the State Department as well as the Justice Department, looked upon his younger brother as the real number one man in the government. I remember how annoyed President Kennedy was one day when he went to a meeting in the White House with Bobby and several of his assistants from the Justice Department and found a television camera and sound-recording equipment in the room. It was to be a confidential and rather sensitive discussion on the timing of the administration's proposed civil rights bill. The President and the Vice-President, who was also present, and Larry O'Brien, our Congressional liaison assistant, and myself all felt that the civil rights legislative action should follow our new tax reduction bill for political reasons. The Justice Department wanted to push first on the civil rights bill. This was to be an argument on the question, with Bobby and his aides asking for civil rights action now and the President asking them to stall it for a while. Now we discovered that Bobby's press relations people in the Justice Department had given a television network permission to tape the whole discussion as a scene in a documentary news show on Bobby's role as a champion of civil rights.

To put it mildly, the President did not feel comfortable sparring with Bobby and his Justice Department assistants over civil rights before a television camera. I don't think Bobby realized that his press people had put the President in an embarrassing position. Bobby, whose reputedly ruthless heart was actually as soft as a marshmallow, never wanted to cause anybody any embarrassment, least of all his brother. Pierre Salinger, the President's press secretary, made the mistake of assuming that anything Bobby's people wanted to do on television would be all right with the President. Pierre, anguished and shaken, learned later from the President, much the toughest of the Kennedy brothers, that the next time such a situation happened, Pierre's head would be handed to him. I was asked to take a careful look at the tape of the meeting, and when I reported back to the President, he said to me, "How did I look?"

"You looked like a frightened antelope," I said. Arrangements were made with the network to kill the tape.

As Vice-President, Johnson did a slow burn for three years as he watched the constant buildup of Bobby Kennedy in the press and on television by Bobby's aides in the Justice Department and by his many friends in the Washington press corps. Bobby himself was not too conscious of the buildup that he was getting, and he was entirely unconscious of the irritation that it was giving to Johnson. Bobby never had any particular hard feeling against Johnson, never really thought much about the Vice-President one way or another. When Jack Kennedy offered the Vice-Presidential nomination to Lyndon at the 1960 convention, Bobby was surprised but not vehemently opposed to the idea — anything that Jack wanted to do was all right with Bobby. In fact, Bobby was shocked and confused by my angry outburst when I first heard that Johnson was being offered the number two spot on the ticket. One of my jobs was keeping the labor leaders happy and all of them were then against Johnson. I thought Stuart Symington would get us as many votes in the South, and the labor people liked Symington. I went straight to Jack Kennedy, as we called him before he became President but never afterwards, and told him behind a closed door in the bathroom of his hotel suite that I thought he was making the biggest mistake in his career. "You won the nomination as President last night as a knight on a white charger," I said to him. "Now in your first move after your nomination you're going against the people who backed you." He became livid with anger, and hurt because his judgment was being questioned. After he explained to me his interesting reasons for offering Johnson the nomination, which I will go into later in this account in detail, he said something to me that I have always remembered: "Get one thing clear, Kenny, I'm forty-three years old, and I'm the healthiest candidate for President in the country, and I'm not going to die in office."

President Kennedy was always uncomfortably aware of Johnson's unhappiness in the Vice-Presidency and leaned over backwards in an effort to keep him involved in important government affairs and to give him a feeling of participation in the important affairs of the administration. He issued a firm order that everybody in the White House was to be courteous and considerate with Johnson and put me in charge of seeing to it that the order was not ignored. I became friendly with LBJ and with his aides, Walter Jenkins and Bill Moyers, and spent evenings with him, listening to his problems and complaints, which were mostly imaginary because he certainly was not being slighted as he claimed. The President always included him in the National Security Council meetings and Congressional leadership meetings and tried without much success to get him to participate in the policy discussions. Johnson was given the responsibility for directing the space program and was sent on important overseas missions. The President loved it when Johnson invited a camel driver from Pakistan to come to Washington. "If I tried that," Kennedy said, "I would have ended up with camel dung all over the White House lawn."

Only two men in the government, Johnson and Bobby Kennedy, were given the special privilege of entering the President's office at any time unseen through the back door from the garden, without following the normal route through the front door from my appointment secretary's office. Neither of them ever abused this privilege and seldom came to see the President without calling me first. Johnson called and asked to see the President often with various personal complaints, frequently about Bobby. The President and I worked out a set routine for handling Johnson's laments. The President would first hear him out alone, and then call me into his office and denounce me in front of Johnson for whatever the Vice-President was beefing about. I would humbly take the blame and promise to correct the situation, and the Vice-President would go away somewhat happier.

I remember one day when Johnson's complaint about Bobby ("That kid brother of yours") involved Sarah T. Hughes, the same lifelong Texas friend who later as a Federal judge in Dallas swore Johnson in as President in the hot and sticky cabin of Air Force One after the assassination.

"Damn it, Kenny, you've gone and done it again," the President said when he called me into his office. "Lyndon, you go ahead and tell him yourself what's happened this time."

Johnson began a long recital of woe, prefacing it, as he usually did, with a recollection of John Nance Garner describing the Vice-Presidency as a thankless office with as much prestige as a pitcher of warm spit, but Johnson used another word in place of spit. He explained that he had asked Bobby Kennedy a few months earlier for a Federal judgeship in Texas for Sarah Hughes, and when the Justice Department told him that Mrs. Hughes, then sixty-five, was too old for the position, he had offered the appointment to another well-known Texas lawyer. After Johnson explained sorrowfully to Mrs. Hughes that she couldn't have the job, the Berlin crisis broke in that August of 1961. The President and Secretary Dean Rusk decided that the American flag would have to be displayed in Berlin, and the Vice-President was sent there for a visit. When he returned, he learned to his deep embarrassment that Mrs. Hughes had been given the Federal judgeship after all, and, checking around, he found out how "ole Lyndon had been done in behind his back as usual."

One day on Capitol Hill Bobby Kennedy had encountered another prominent Texan, Sam Rayburn, the Speaker of the House, and asked the Speaker when a couple of bills that the Justice Department was especially interested in would be getting out of the judiciary committee. Rayburn ventured the opinion that the Justice Department's bills might never get out of committee if his friend, Sarah Hughes, did not get a judgeship in Texas. Bobby explained that she had been suggested by Johnson, but she was too old for the appointment. "Son, everybody looks old to you," Rayburn said. "Do you want those bills passed, or don't you?" The next day Sarah Hughes was appointed to the Federal bench.

Johnson cried, "Mr. President, you realize where this leaves me? Sarah Hughes now thinks I'm nothing. The lawyer I offered the job to after your brother turned Sarah down, he thinks I'm the biggest liar and fool in the history of the State of Texas. All on account of that brother of yours!" The President was unable to keep from laughing, and the Vice-President, seeing the humor of the situation, laughed, too.

Later we had another showdown with Johnson concerning Rayburn that was not entertaining. Sam Rayburn as Speaker of the House was the most powerful and widely respected figure in the government next to the President, and nobody wanted to cross him, especially President Kennedy, who valued his support and friendship highly. Although Rayburn and his close crony Harry Truman had tried to keep Kennedy from getting the Presidential nomination in 1960, their opposition never deeply troubled him. It was understandable. As a member of the House, in his three terms as a young Congressman, Kennedy had kept away from Rayburn, John Mc-Cormack and the other elders of the Democratic party on Capitol Hill because he did not want to be marked as a protégé of the Old Guard, so naturally he could hardly expect the backing of the Old Guard before the convention in 1960. President Truman refused to support Kennedy before the convention simply because Kennedy's father, Joseph P. Kennedy, had refused to contribute to Truman's campaign fund in 1948. He had no personal feeling against Jack Kennedy, whom he hardly knew at the time. President Truman came out for Stuart Symington for President, but that was part of a plan he had worked out with Rayburn in the hope of splitting the delegates' votes and stopping Kennedy on the first ballot so that Rayburn's man, Lyndon Johnson, might win on a later ballot. We felt that the Democrats who were supporting Adlai Stevenson at the convention, such as Senator Eugene McCarthy, were also really working for Johnson's nomination. But after Kennedy was nominated he made peace with President Truman and with Rayburn, who gave him warm support in the White House for the remaining year of his life in the Speaker's chair before his death late in 1961.

Not long before Rayburn's last illness, he requested an appointment to an important position in an executive department for a personal friend from Texas who had held the same job in the Truman administration. The Texan had been fired by Eisenhower, but now that the Democrats were back in office, Rayburn wanted to give him back his old job. We got the word from the national committee that this request from Rayburn was a must, but it was customary to clear such appointments with Lyndon Johnson. The Vice-President told the President privately that the man was an alcoholic who might be an embarrassment to the administration, and urged Kennedy to turn Rayburn's request down, although there was no mention of alcoholism in the careful security check on the man's background that had been made by the FBI.

"I don't want to turn down the Speaker," the President said to me. "And I don't want to go against Lyndon. It will only hurt him, and make him feel more strongly than ever that we're ignoring his advice. I asked him to come here and discuss it with us. It's your ball of wax. You handle it."

Johnson came to the President's office and explained to me in front of the President why Rayburn's friend should not get the job. I agreed with him, and reached for one of the telephones on the President's desk.

"Who are you calling?" the Vice-President said.

I said I was going to call Rayburn. Johnson stood up and put his hand on top of my hand to keep me from picking up the phone.

"What are you going to tell him?"

I said that I was going to explain to the Speaker that his friend could not have the job because the Vice-President would not approve the appointment.

"Don't tell him that," Johnson said. "Tell him you don't want the man to have the job."

"How can I tell him I'm disapproving the appointment?" I said to the Vice-President. "I don't approve or disapprove of anything here — I only work for the President and I don't speak for myself. I speak for the President. I can't tell the Speaker that the President doesn't want his friend to have this job. You're the one who is against the appointment, not the President, and that's what I have to tell the Speaker."

Johnson stared at me, frowning. I glanced at the President. The President was looking out a window. After a few moments of heavy silence, Johnson told me to let the matter rest and not to do anything more until we heard from him. Later Walter Jenkins called me and said the Vice-President was withdrawing his objection and wanted us to forget it. He would have liked us to tangle with Rayburn, but he wouldn't do it himself.

Along with seeking popular votes, the President was going to Texas to raise campaign money. He had been pressing the reluctant Governor Connally for months to stage a fund-raising event for the party, and Connally, who had no desire to be marked as a Kennedy supporter in Texas, had been stalling him off. Finally, on October 4, Connally came to the White House with plans for a big hundred-dollar-a-plate dinner Friday night in Austin following a midday visit to Dallas. Johnson was furious because Connally had not bothered to invite him to that White House meeting with the President.

President Kennedy also timed the trip to Texas so that he could appear on Thursday night at a testimonial dinner for Representative Albert Thomas in Houston, the Congressman's hometown. The elderly Thomas was one of the President's favorite Congressmen and had done important fiscal favors for Kennedy in his capacity as chairman of the subcommittee that approved supplementary appropriations. Thomas had raised the money for the launching of the space program. The President initiated the costly drive to put astronauts on the moon not only for national prestige, but equally because he thought that large government spending on the space project was urgently needed to stimulate the national economy. He felt deeply indebted to Thomas for his support of the program and raised no objection when NASA located its Manned Spacecraft Center in Houston, instead of somewhere in the Midwest or near Boston, where the President would have liked to have seen its huge payroll spent.

The President knew, of course, that NASA picked Houston for only one reason — Albert Thomas. It was always entertaining to watch the President listening impatiently to a visitor who was beating a long-winded path around the bush and then interrupting with one quick question which immediately brought the heart of the matter into suddenly clear focus. When James E. Webb, the director of NASA, came to the President to explain the choice of the Manned Spacecraft Center's site, he began with a lengthy technical discussion about national geography. The President's eyes strayed to a written proposal that Webb had placed on his desk, and when he saw halfway down the page the first mention of Houston, he looked up at Webb and said, "How is Albert Thomas feeling these days?"

Appearing at the Albert Thomas dinner was especially important to the President because Thomas was thinking of retiring due to poor health and the President had been urging him to stay on in Congress for at least another term. We paid no attention to it at the time, but later we remembered that the President said in his speech about Thomas, "I asked him to stay as long as I stayed — I didn't know how long that would be."

But far more important than patching up the Connally-Yarborough feud, raising money, or appearing at the Thomas dinner was the simple eagerness to get the 1964 campaign off to a strong early start. The coming election year looked good; the economy was booming and the Saturn I rocket, which the President had just inspected at Cape Canaveral a few days ago, was to be fired in December. But he cautioned us, as he did before every campaign, that there was a lot of hard work ahead. He felt that prejudice against his Catholicism, or "the canonical impediment," as we called it, was not as dead an issue as many Americans assumed it to be. This time, he ·said, the people who were voting against him because of his religion would claim they were against his stand on civil rights. He was planning to campaign hard in Texas and in Florida because he had little hope of winning the other Southern states; Barry Goldwater, carrying Alabama, Georgia, Louisiana, Mississippi and South Carolina from the South's Lyndon Johnson in 1964, proved Kennedy's prediction to be right.

It was difficult for President Kennedy to imagine that the Republicans would actually give Goldwater their nomination. One morning when Dave Powers was talking with him as he was shaving, Pierre Salinger came into the bathroom to show him a poll that named Goldwater as the probable Republican choice. The President said in surprise, "Dave Powers could beat Goldwater." He added that if he did run against Goldwater, all of us would get to bed much earlier on election night than we did in 1960. He thought that the Republicans would end up selecting a more moderate candidate, probably George Romney, who could give us more trouble.

The President was anxious to be reelected by the biggest possible landslide vote and to start his second term with a strong mandate from the people because, as he told me privately before we went to Texas, he had made up his mind that after his reelection he would take the risk of unpopularity and make a complete withdrawal of American military forces from Vietnam. He had decided that our military involvement in Vietnam's civil war would only grow steadily bigger and more costly without making a dent in the larger political problem of Communist expansion in Southeast Asia.

President Kennedy first began to have doubts about our military effort in Vietnam in 1961 when both General Douglas MacArthur and General Charles de Gaulle warned him that the Asian mainland was no place to be fighting a non-nuclear land war. There was no end to Asian manpower, MacArthur told the President, and even if we poured a million American infantry soldiers into that continent, we would still find ourselves outnumbered on every side. De Gaulle said the same thing in Paris that spring, pointing out that the French had shown us the hopelessness of trying to fight in that country.

The President's first meeting with MacArthur, a courtesy call on the general at his apartment in the Waldorf Astoria shortly after the Bay of Pigs disaster, was an agreeable surprise to Kennedy. Like most Navy veterans of the Pacific war, the President had always assumed that MacArthur was a stuffy and pompous egocentric. Instead, the President told us afterward, MacArthur turned out to be one of the most interesting men he had ever met, politically shrewd, intellectually sharp and a gifted conversationalist. Later the President invited the general to the White House for lunch and they talked for more than two hours, ruining my appointments schedule for that day. I could not drag them apart. The President later gave us a rundown of MacArthur's remarks. He was extremely critical of the military advice that the President was getting from the Pentagon, blaming it on the military leadership of the previous ten years which, he said, had advanced the wrong officers. "You were lucky to have that mistake happen in a place like Cuba, where the strategic cost was not too great," he said about the Bay of Pigs, and urged the President not to listen too carefully to advisers who favored a military buildup in Vietnam.

The President would always read up on biographical material about a special visitor before meeting him. While he was sitting with his brother Bobby and Dave Powers in his office waiting for MacArthur to arrive for lunch that day, he was reading aloud a citation for a decoration given to the general in World War I. "Dave, how would you like this to be said about you?" the President said, and quoted from the citation: " 'On a field where courage was the rule, his courage was the dominant feature.' " Bobby Kennedy said shyly in his quiet voice, "I would love to have that said about me."

During most of President Kennedy's time in office, most of 1961 and all of 1962, the situation in Southeast Asia was overshadowed by the more urgently dangerous threat of a nuclear war with Russia over the crisis in Berlin and then over the missile crisis in Cuba. When the President began to be able to pay more attention to Vietnam after the Soviet missiles were removed from Cuba late in 1962, he found himself frustrated by the conflicting reports from his own observers in Saigon. One day at a National Security Council meeting, he listened to a Marine general and a State Department officer who had just returned from South Vietnam on the same plane. The Marine general said that the war was going fine and that the Diem government, then in power, was strong and popular. The State Department man said that the Diem government was on the verge of collapse. The President said, "Were you two gentlemen in the same country?"

Ironically, it was President Kennedy's firm and successful stand against Khrushchev during the Cuban missile crisis that helped to break the alliance between Russia and China, increased the threat of a Chinese move against South Vietnam, and provoked the first sizable buildup of American advisory troops in the South Vietnamese forces to strengthen the wavering Diem government. Around this time, late in 1962, when we were accelerating shipments of reinforcements to South Vietnam, Senator Mike Mansfield visited the President at Palm Beach, where the Kennedy family had gathered for the Christmas holidays. The Senate majority leader, whose opinions the President deeply respected, had just returned from a trip to Southeast Asia, which he had made at the President's request.

Mansfield emphatically advised a curb on sending more military reinforcements to South Vietnam and then a withdrawal of U.S. troops from that country's civil war, a suggestion that shocked the President. A continued steady increase of Americans in South Vietnam, the Senator argued, would lead to sending still more forces to beef up those that were there, and soon the Americans would be dominating the combat in a civil war that was not our war. Taking over the military leadership and the fighting in the Vietnam war, Mansfield warned, would hurt American prestige in Asia and would not help the South Vietnamese to stand on their own feet, either. The President was too disturbed by the Senator's unexpected argument to reply to it. He said to me later when we talked about the discussion, "I got angry with Mike for disagreeing with our policy so completely, and I got angry with myself because I found myself agreeing with him."

Publicly over the next few months the President continued to stress the need for bolstering the South Vietnamese government of Diem, as much as he was embarrassed by Diem's terrorist brother Nhu, but we noticed that privately Kennedy complained that everybody in the State Department and the Defense Department seemed to be forgetting that our role in Vietnam should be political rather than military. When Secretary Dean Rusk recommended sending

Henry Cabot Lodge to Saigon as our ambassador, President Kennedy was astonished along with all of the Boston Irishmen of the White House staff. The President had an Irish distaste for the aloof North Shore Yankee Republican, whom he had beaten in the 1952 Senatorial race in Massachusetts, and again in 1960, when Lodge was Nixon's running mate. When we were watching Lodge on television at the Republican convention the night he accepted the Vice-Presidential nomination, Kennedy said to us, "That's the last Nixon will see of Lodge. If Nixon ever tries to visit the Lodges at Beverly, they won't let him in the door." The President told us that when Rusk suggested sending Lodge to Saigon, he decided to approve the appointment because the idea of getting Lodge mixed up in such a hopeless mess as the one in Vietnam was irresistible.

In the spring of 1963, Mike Mansfield again criticized our military involvement in the Vietnam war, this time in front of the Congressional leadership at a White House breakfast, much to the President's annoyance and embarrassment. Later the President asked me to invite Mansfield to his office for a private talk on the problem. I sat in on part of the discussion. The President told Mansfield that he had been having serious second thoughts about Mansfield's argument and that he now agreed with the Senator's thinking on the need for a complete military withdrawal from Vietnam.

"But I can't do it until 1965 — after I'm reelected," Kennedy told Mansfield.

President Kennedy explained, and Mansfield agreed with him, that if he announced a withdrawal of American military personnel from Vietnam before the 1964 election, there would be a wild conservative outcry against returning him to the Presidency for a second term.

After Mansfield left the office, the President said to me, "In 1965, I'll become one of the most unpopular Presidents in history. I'll be damned everywhere as a Communist appeaser. But I don't care. If I tried to pull out completely now from Vietnam, we would have another Joe McCarthy red scare on our hands, but I can do it after I'm reelected. So we had better make damned sure that I *am* reelected."

That fall, before he went to Dallas, the President was so disgusted with Diem and Nhu that he decided to put pressure on them to force them into liberalizing their police state government and stopping their persecution of religious and political enemies. Along with cutting off economic aid to Diem, the President issued an order, against the objections of many advisers, to reduce American military advisers in South Vietnam immediately by bringing home one thousand U.S. soldiers before the end of 1963. This was quite a considerable withdrawal at that time because the American forces in South Vietnam, which later grew to more than five hundred thousand under the Johnson administration, then numbered only about sixteen thousand. Most of our combat personnel were Green Beret "advisers" attached to South Vietnamese troops; there were not yet any complete American combat units in Vietnam.

On October 2, when Defense Secretary Robert McNamara and General Maxwell Taylor came to a meeting of the National Security Council to report on a trip to Saigon, President Kennedy asked McNamara to announce to the press after the meeting the immediate withdrawal of one thousand soldiers and to say that we would probably withdraw all American forces from Vietnam by the end of 1965. When McNamara was leaving the meeting to talk to the White House reporters, the President called to him, "And tell them that means all of the helicopter pilots, too."

McNamara discreetly softened the President's prediction of a complete 1965 withdrawal in his on-the-record statement to the press; he merely said that in his judgment "the major part of the U.S. military task" in Vietnam could be "completed by the end of 1965."

President Kennedy made no move to change or cancel his troop reduction order when he heard the news of the killing of Diem and Nhu in the uprising of South Vietnamese generals against their government on November 1, just before we went to Texas. The collapse of the Diem government and the deaths of its dictatorial leaders made President Kennedy only more skeptical of our military advice from Saigon and more determined to pull out of the Vietnam war. General Paul Harkins, then our military commander in South Vietnam, had been reporting all along that Diem had strong popular support.

The anti-Diem coup, which had been plotted for several months, came as no surprise to President Kennedy, but the brutal killings of Diem and Nhu, committed by the rebels in spur-of-the-moment anger, shocked and depressed him. The President was not averse to the idea of changing the government for a practical and useful purpose. One day when he was talking with Dave and me about pulling out of Vietnam, we asked him how he could manage a military withdrawal without losing American prestige in Southeast Asia.

"Easy," he said. "Put a government in there that will ask us to leave."

The President's order to reduce the American military personnel in Vietnam by one thousand men before the end of 1963 was still in effect on the day that he went to Texas. A few days after his death, during the mourning, the order was quietly rescinded.

On that Thursday morning when we were to leave for Texas, Dave Powers found President Kennedy in his office reading a report on the new leaders in South Vietnam in the November sixteenth issue of the *New Republic*. When he saw Dave, the President dropped the magazine and immediately began to cross-examine him about Bobby Kennedy's birthday party that Dave and I had attended at Bobby's house the night before — who was there, what did they have to say, what happened. The most insatiably curious man who ever walked the face of the earth, he always wanted to know everything about everybody. His fondness for Frank Sinatra, which perplexed a lot of people, was simply based on the fact that Sinatra told him a lot of inside gossip about celebrities and their romances in Hollywood. The President hated to miss anything like Bobby's party, but he wanted Jackie to rest that night because the next day's travel to San Antonio, Houston and Fort Worth called for five hours of jet flying and two and a half more hours on the road in motorcades.

Later on Air Force One, he quizzed me about Bobby's party to see if he could pick up something that Dave had forgotten to mention. I did not tell him that at the party Ann Brinkley, David's wife, had urged me to keep him away from Dallas, or that Bobby had asked me if I had seen a letter he had sent to me from Byron Skelton, a Democratic National Committeeman from Texas. Skelton asked us to stay away from Dallas because the anti-Kennedy feeling there seemed dangerous. Showing the letter to the President would have been a waste of his time. If I had suggested cutting such a large and important city as Dallas from the itinerary because of

[18]

Skelton's letter, the President would have thought that I had gone out of my mind.

President Kennedy was well aware of the hostility toward him and his administration in Dallas; he had only recently congratulated Adlai Stevenson for keeping cool when Stevenson was pushed around and insulted by an angry crowd there during a United Nations Day visit on October 24. The President took a fatalistic attitude about the possibility of being assassinated by a fanatic, regarding such a danger as being part of his job, and often talked about how easy it would be for somebody to shoot at him with a rifle from a high building. On a campaign trip such as this one, he was particularly annoyed by the efforts of the Secret Service to keep him from mixing in crowds. He and I were both tired of explaining to his guards that politics and protection don't mix. Elaborate escorts of police on motorcycles and in squad cars with sirens whining and red lights flashing made him uncomfortable. A week before we went to Texas, on November 14, he waved aside a police motorcycle escort and made the long trip from Idlewild Airport to the Carlyle Hotel in New York during the heavy evening rush-hour traffic without having the road ahead cleared because he did not want to cause a traffic tie-up. When we stopped for a red light at Madison Avenue and Seventy-second Street, an amateur photographer walked up to our limousine, pushed his camera against its window, and popped his flashbulb, giving the Secret Service agents a bad scare.

One day at the opening game of the baseball season at Griffith Stadium in Washington, a radio commentator made his way into the President's box without being halted or questioned by the Secret Service and shoved a microphone in front of the President's face without warning. The President later turned to Dave Powers, who was sitting beside him, and said, "What would you have done if that fellow had a grenade in his hand instead of a mike?" Dave said, "I would have said the Act of Contrition." Going to church with the President, as he always did on holy days of obligation and on Sundays while we were traveling, made Dave a nervous wreck. Dave was sure that if the President was to be killed, it would happen in a church, either by a shot from the choir loft or by a gunman walking past the President's pew in the procession of people going to the altar for communion. Instead of praying, Dave spent his time at mass eyeing the kneeling Catholics around him and glancing over his shoulder at the choir loft.

When we were in the air on the way to Texas that morning, the President checked with me on the small details of the arrangements, forgetting nothing as usual. Dave and I were to be in the Secret Service backup car, immediately behind the rear bumper of the President's limousine in the motorcades, because he wanted us to study the reaction of sidewalk crowds in Texas to the appearance of Jackie and him. Bill Moyers, the Texan who was Lyndon Johnson's aide in the 1960 campaign, had escaped from Lyndon with our help and was now serving as Sargent Shriver's deputy assistant in the Peace Corps. We decided that Moyers, with his knowledge of Texas politics, would be the ideal man to handle our interests in Austin, the state capital, where we were to end up this tour at Governor Connally's dinner on Friday night. But Shriver had protested that an official of his Peace Corps should not be lowering the dignity of his position by getting mixed up in party politics. The President had told me to tell his brother-in-law to cut out the nonsense. Right now party politics in Texas was more important than the lofty esteem of the Peace Corps. Moyers went to Austin.

Dave and I had hoped to fly back to Washington from Austin on Friday night and to spend the weekend with our families instead of staying on in Texas with the President, while he and Jackie visited the Johnsons on Saturday at the LBJ Ranch, but he had gotten wind of our plot and had put his foot down on us. "You two guys aren't running out on me and leaving me stranded with poor Jackie at Lyndon's ranch," he said. "If I've got to hang around there all day Saturday, wearing one of those big cowboy hats, you've got to be there, too."

The President was fretting because his Air Force aide, Brigadier General Godfrey McHugh, had given him a wrong weather prediction, and he was worrying that Jackie's clothes might be too warm for Texas. Already we were getting some flak from the local politicians about our schedule. Henry Gonzalez, the Democratic Congressman from San Antonio, where we would make our first stop, was complaining because I had given only two hours to his constituency and three hours to Dallas, the John Birch–Dixiecrat-Republican stronghold. Senator Yarborough had boarded Air Force One in a rage. He had just learned that Governor Connally had not invited him to the reception for the President and Jackie at the governor's mansion before the big dinner Friday night. Furthermore, although Yarborough had sold $11,300 worth of tickets for the dinner, he was not being honored with a place at the head table and his wife was not invited. When we landed in San Antonio, where the Johnsons and the Connallys were waiting for us, Yarborough refused to ride in the same car with Johnson, whom he regarded as the governor's co-conspirator.

But the President was too happy with the wild and warm reception given to him and Jackie by the big crowd at San Antonio to give much thought to Yarborough's squabble. About 125,000 people lined the streets from the airport to Brooks Air Force Base where the President spoke at the dedication of the new Air Force School of Aero-Space Medicine. At one point, we saw a nun race out of the crowd and almost throw a flying tackle on the President. I noticed one homemade sign that said, "Jackie, Come Water-Ski in Texas." We passed a school where all of the children were waving American flags. At the medical center, about twenty thousand people were fighting for the nine thousand seats before the platform where the President was to speak. I remember hearing him in his speech quoting Frank O'Connor, the Irish writer, whose story about the Irishman throwing his hat over a high wall, in order to force himself to climb the wall, was one of the President's favorites. Only Kennedy, I thought, would be telling an Irish story by an Irish writer in Texas. He applied it to our effort to conquer space travel — "This nation has tossed its cap over the wall of space, and we have no choice but to follow it." That night in Dublin, a newspaper editor telephoned O'Connor at his home and said to him, "President Kennedy is quoting from some book of yours in San Antonio, Texas."

O'Connor wrote later, "He was not a man to be afraid of quoting some Irish writer, whom most of his audience had never heard of. He was leading the Irish in America out of a ghetto of humiliation and pretense and telling them they were a people with a history and a literature as good as the best."

After his speech, the curious President ignored our time-pressed schedule and went to a building at the medical center to look at an oxygen chamber which simulated the atmospheric pressure of an altitude of thirty thousand feet. He put on a headset telephone and questioned four young men who were inside the tank, and then he asked the scientist in charge of the experiment if his work in space medicine might lead to improving oxygen chambers for premature babies. The death of his infant son, Patrick Bouvier Kennedy, was still weighing on the President's mind.

From San Antonio we flew to Houston, where a bigger and more wildly enthusiastic crowd had turned out to greet the President and to look at Jackie. When we reached the Rice Hotel, Max Peck, the hotel manager, staring at Jackie and ignoring the President, shouted, "Good evening, Mrs. President!" Upstairs in their suite, the President found a spread of champagne and caviar awaiting them and kidded Jackie about it. "If the word gets around town that you ordered champagne and caviar," he said to her, "we'll be ruined." Well aware that Nixon had carried Houston in 1960, he asked Dave how the crowd compared to the one on his last visit to the city in 1962, and he beamed when Dave gave him the reply that he wanted Jackie to hear. "Mr. President, your crowd here today was about the same as last year's," Dave said, "but a hundred thousand more people came out to cheer for Jackie." Jackie smiled, and said to her husband, "I'm looking forward to campaigning with you in 1964."

That night, before going to the Albert Thomas dinner at the Houston Coliseum, the Kennedys appeared at a gathering of Lulacs — the League of United Latin-American Citizens — in the hotel, where Jackie delivered a speech in Spanish, much to the roaring delight of the crowd. As Dave described it, when Jackie finished her talk, she and the President "exchanged eyes." Leaving the ballroom, the President grabbed one of the Spanish-speaking guests at the dinner and questioned him about how Jackie had sounded and what she had said. "The man said you were wonderful," he reported to her. After the Thomas dinner, we flew from Houston to Fort Worth where there was another big crowd of people waiting for the President, even though we did not arrive there until nearly midnight.

The President got up early the next morning at the Texas Hotel in Fort Worth because he was scheduled to give a short talk to a crowd of people in the parking lot across the street from the hotel before he and his wife appeared at a Chamber of Commerce breakfast. He was in a good mood about the successful visits to San Antonio and Houston the day before when Dave went to his room and found him shaving. "I'm glad Jackie is pleased with the trip," he said to Dave. "That's a definite plus, isn't it?"

His mood changed when he picked up the *Dallas News* and saw on one of its pages an ugly black-bordered advertisement signed by an organization calling itself the American Fact-Finding Committee and paid for by the local John Birch Society and Nelson Bunker Hunt, the son of H. L. Hunt, among other people. The ad accused President Kennedy of being pro-Communist and demanded to know "why have you ordered or permitted your brother Bobby, the Attorney General, to go soft on Communists, fellow-travelers and ultra-leftists in America, while permitting him to persecute loyal Americans who criticize you, your administration, and your leadership? Why has Gus Hall, head of the U.S. Communist Party, praised almost every one of your policies? Why have you scrapped the Monroe Doctrine in favor of the 'Spirit of Moscow'?" On its front page, the *News* played up stories of the rift between Connally and Yarborough and told how Yarborough had refused to ride in the same car with Johnson at San Antonio and Houston.

The President folded the newspaper and handed it to Dave, telling him to take it out of the room. "I don't want Jackie to see it now," he said. He called me on the telephone and told me to work on Yarborough. "Tell him if he doesn't ride with Lyndon today, he'll have to walk," the President said. He and Dave went downstairs and across the street to the parking lot where the waiting crowd of Fort Worth people was chanting, "Where's Jackie? Where's Jackie?" It was raining slightly but the President wore no hat and no raincoat. He smiled at the growing crowd and said to them, pointing up at the windows of his suite, "Mrs. Kennedy is organizing herself. It takes her a little longer, but, of course, she looks better than us when she does it." Meanwhile Larry O'Brien and I were talking to Yarborough and not getting anywhere with him; he was trying to argue that his refusal to appear with Johnson would not affect Kennedy's popularity in Texas.

From the parking lot, the President headed back into the hotel where Jackie was to appear with him at the Chamber of Commerce breakfast. In a hallway, he ran into Yarborough, backed him against the wall, and told him sharply to cut it out. Jackie was twenty minutes late getting downstairs from her room to the breakfast, but when she made her appearance, the crowd of two thousand

Texans in the ballroom went wild, standing up on their chairs to get a better look at her and cheering. "Two years ago I introduced myself in Paris by saying that I was the man who had accompanied Mrs. Kennedy to Paris," the President said when he started his talk. "I am getting somewhat the same sensation as I travel around Texas. Why is it nobody wonders what Lyndon and I will be wearing?" He was presented with a ten-gallon cowboy hat. I was convulsed watching him on television upstairs in my room while he evaded putting the hat on his head. He would never wear a funny hat. He said something about putting on the hat when he got back to Washington, and managed to push it out of sight as soon as he could.

When the Kennedys came back upstairs to their suite to rest for an hour before starting the short plane trip to Dallas, I went there to talk to the President. I found them both in a cheerful mood after the warm reception that they had been given at the Chamber of Commerce breakfast. Jackie was saying, "I'll go anywhere with you this year."

The President, laughing, said to her, "How about California in the next two weeks?"

She said, "I'll be there."

He turned to me and said, "Did you hear *that*?" I was grinning like an ape. I had thought it was a big loss when Jackie was unable to travel in the 1960 campaign because she was pregnant with young John; back in Massachusetts in 1958 when her husband was running for reelection as Senator, she was great on the road. I particularly remember one night in Chicopee when Larry O'Brien and I took her to a rally at the parish hall of a French Catholic church. Nobody showed up at the rally. Jackie saved the night with an idea of her own. She walked over to the rectory, rang the doorbell, introduced herself in French to the pastor, and sat with him for a half hour, conversing in French and drinking tea. The next Sunday at every mass, the priest practically ordered everybody in the parish to vote for Kennedy.

I had in my hand a copy of the *Dallas News*, with its black-bordered anti-Kennedy tirade, but I hesitated to show it to the President because I was reluctant to dampen his cheerful mood. I waited while he made a telephone call to Uvalde, Texas, to talk with John Nance Garner; Lyndon Johnson had reminded him that today was

Garner's ninety-fifth birthday. Then I handed him the newspaper. He said he had seen it, and he showed the black-bordered advertisement to Jackie. That night on the way back to Washington, she and I talked about what he said to her while she was reading the ad.

"We're heading into nut country today," he said. "But, Jackie, if somebody wants to shoot me from a window with a rifle, nobody can stop it, so why worry about it?"

Roy Kellerman, the Secret Service agent in charge of our detail, came into the room and said that two of his agents who were in Dallas with the President's convertible limousine wanted to know whether or not to put the clear plastic bubble-top covering over its seats. The Dallas newspapers had predicted rain, but it looked to them as if the weather would clear. The bubble top, incidentally, was neither bulletproof nor bullet-resistant, as many people assumed. Jackie loved it because it kept her hair from getting wind-blown. The President, of course, disliked it on a political appearance because it shielded him from the people.

I said, "If it's not raining, have the bubble top off."

Then Larry O'Brien called with a bit of pleasant news. Senator Yarborough had agreed to ride with the Johnsons in the motorcade at Dallas.

"Good," the President said. "Now we've got to get Connally to invite Yarborough to the reception at the governor's mansion."

"We'll keep them apart on the plane while we work on Connally," I said. "Larry can stick with Yarborough up front and I'll hold Connally back near your cabin. Maybe I'll have to lock him in with you, and let you give him the treatment."

The flight from Carswell Air Force Base in Fort Worth to Love Field, the airport in Dallas, was only a pop fly, about thirteen minutes in the air. We could have driven easily to Dallas on the expressway from Fort Worth in a half hour, but I had to veto that suggestion because it would have eliminated an airport welcome for the President and Jackie when they arrived in Dallas. The big greeting from the crowd waiting at the airport is as important in political campaigning nowadays as the whistle-stop cross-country train was in Harry Truman's day. But the short flight to Dallas left us little time in the plane to put the squeeze on Governor Connally.

It was good old Albert Thomas, the financier of the space program, who came to our aid. The President beckoned to Thomas from the doorway of his cabin and said to him, "Give Kenny a hand with Connally." Thomas said, "Certainly, Mr. President, after what you did for me last night in Houston, that's the least I can do." Thomas and I talked to Connally and the governor began to wilt.

"It was my wife who didn't want the Senator at the reception, not me," Connally protested. "She said she wouldn't let that man in her house, and when your wife says something like that, what can you do?"

I took both Thomas and Connally by the arm and pushed them into the President's cabin and closed the door. Within three minutes, the governor was agreeing to invite Yarborough to the reception at the mansion and to put him at the head table at the dinner. "How can anybody say no to that man?" Connally said to me when the President excused himself to change into a fresh shirt.

So we landed in Dallas with everybody on the plane in love with each other and the sun shining brightly. The President knotted his tie, peered out the window at the big crowd waving and jumping up and down behind the fence, and said to me, "This trip is turning out to be terrific. Here we are in Dallas, and it looks like everything in Texas is going to be fine for us."

When the President and Jackie took their place at the back door of the plane, waiting for the door to be opened, Dave looked them over approvingly and said to them, "You two look like Mr. and Mrs. America. Mr. President, remember when you're riding in the motorcade downtown to look and wave only at the people on the right side of the street. Jackie, be sure that you look only at the left side, and not to the right. If the both of you ever looked at the same voter at the same time, it would be too much for him!"

When we were riding through Dallas on our way from the airport to the Trade Mart luncheon, I said to Dave, "There's certainly nothing wrong with this crowd." We could see no sign of hostility, not even cool unfriendliness, and the throngs of people jamming the streets and hanging out of windows were all smiling, waving, and shouting excitedly. The steady roar of their cheering was deafening. It was by far the greatest and the most emotionally happy crowd that we had ever seen in Texas. Sitting on the two jump seats of the Secret Service's backup car, only about ten feet behind the President and Jackie, we could see their faces clearly when they turned to nod and wave to the screaming people pushing into the street beside them. The President seemed thrilled and fascinated by the crowd's noisy excitement. I knew he had expected nothing like this wild welcome.

When we were making the sharp left turn around Dealey Plaza in front of the School Book Depositary building, I asked Dave what time it was. Ahead of us in the back seat of the long Lincoln, the President was sitting on the right side of the car with his arm out-stretched, waving to the crowd in front of the Book Depositary. Mrs. Kennedy, in her pink suit with her matching pink pillbox hat perched on the back of her head, was beside him on his left with the red roses presented to her at the airport on the seat between them. Governor Connally was on the pull-out jump seat in front of the President and Mrs. Connally was seated in front of Jackie. In our backup car, where Dave was sitting on the right jump seat, directly behind the President, with me on his left, there were eight Secret Service agents and enough high-powered firearms to start a Latin-American revolution. Four of the agents were standing on the run-ning boards, two on each side of the car. Behind us was the Vice-Presidential car, a four-door Lincoln convertible, with Johnson and Yarborough in the back seat with Mrs. Johnson between them and Secret Service Agent Rufus Youngblood sitting in the front beside the driver, a Texas state highway patrolman named Hurchel Jacks.

"It's just twelve-thirty," Dave said, looking at his watch. "That's the time we're due to be at the Trade Mart."

"Fine," I said. "It's only five minutes from here, so we're only running five minutes behind schedule."

I had just finished speaking when we heard shots, two close to-gether and then a third one. There must have been an interval of at least five seconds before the third and last shot because, after the second shot, Dave said to me, "Kenny, I think the President's been shot."

I made a quick sign of the cross and said, "What makes you think that?"

"Look at him!" Dave said. "He was over on the right, with his arm stretched out. Now he's slumped over toward Jackie, holding his throat."

While we both stared at the President, the third shot took the side of his head off. We saw pieces of bone and brain tissue and bits of his reddish hair flying through the air. The impact lifted him and shook him limply, as if he was a rag doll, and then he dropped out of our sight, sprawled across the back seat of the car. I said to Dave, "He's dead."

A Secret Service agent beside me, probably Tim McIntyre who was standing behind Clint Hill on the left running board, pulled his gun and I reached for it, pushing it down, thinking that if he fired, he might hit somebody in the crowd. We saw Jackie in her blood-stained pink suit, crawling out of her seat, on the back of the trunk cover of the moving car with a dazed expression on her pale face. Clint Hill jumped from the front running board of our car and ran forward to keep her from falling to the street under our front wheels. Hill threw himself onto the back of the Presidential car, reaching for Jackie, and they grasped hands, clutching at each other as the driver finally realized what was going on and stepped on the accelerator, lurching the car forward at a high speed. It was hard to tell then whether Jackie was pulling Hill aboard or if he was pushing her back to safety. When the car was zooming under the railroad underpass ahead of us, Jackie slid back into the seat with her fallen husband and the crouching Connallys, and Hill was spreading his body above them as a protecting cover.

We did not realize then that Governor Connally had also been hit, apparently by the same bullet that had passed through President Kennedy's neck, one of the two fired in the opening burst of shots. The police found a bullet mark on the street pavement, indicating that one of the three shots might have missed the President's car, but Dave, who was watching the President and Connally carefully during the shooting, still thinks that the first bullet hit Kennedy in the neck, the second struck Connally and the third one ripped open the President's head.

I don't remember any of us in our car saying a word during the fast drive to Parkland Hospital. I was thinking (and Dave told me later that he was thinking about the same thing) of the interval between the first shot that hit the President and the later one that killed him — a lapse of time long enough for Dave and me to talk about whether or not there had been a shooting. As Dave says, if there was an interval of at least five seconds between the second and third shots, as it seemed, that was long enough for a man to run fifty yards. If the Secret Service men in the front seat had reacted quicker to the first two shots at the President's car, if the driver had stepped on the gas before instead of after the fatal third shot was fired, would President Kennedy be alive today?

Nobody knows what Jackie had in her mind when she almost killed herself by climbing out of the back seat and crawling on the rear deck of the moving car. On the Thanksgiving weekend after the President's funeral, when Dave was visiting Jackie and her children at Hyannis Port, he showed her the color pictures of herself on the back of the car taken at the scene by Abraham Zapruder's movie camera and published in that week's *Life*. She had no recollection of leaving the back seat after the President was shot. "Dave, what do you think I was trying to do?" she asked. Dave could only suggest that maybe she was searching for the President's doctor, Rear Admiral George G. Burkley, who was in a bus at the rear of the motorcade.

The President's car, our Secret Service car and the Vice-President's car behind us all arrived together with screeching brakes at the emergency entrance of the hospital. Everybody was running to the President's car, except Johnson, who was grabbed by a few nervous Secret Service agents and hustled into the hospital with Lady Bird trailing behind him. I could not bring myself to look at the President. I stopped near his car, and turned away from it. I was sure that he was dead. Dave, more courageous and more hopeful, went to the car, praying that he would find the President alive and talking. When he saw the President in Jackie's arms, with his eyes open, Dave thought that he was conscious and able to hear, and said to him, "Oh, my God, Mr. President, what did they do?" Jackie looked up at Dave and shook her head. She said, "Dave, he's dead." Then Dave noticed that the opened eyes were fixed in a vacant stare, and he broke down in tears.

When Dave, with Clint Hill and Roy Kellerman, first tried to lift the President from the car, Jackie clung to him and refused to let him be moved. Clint sensed what she was thinking — she did not want strangers staring at her husband's broken and bleeding head. Clint took off his jacket and wrapped it over the President's head, and Jackie drew back and allowed him to be taken from her lap. The jacket began to slip away from his head as he was being lifted, and Jackie quickly reached for it and tucked it back into place.

Jackie ran along beside the stretcher, holding the coat in place, while the President was quickly wheeled into the hospital and down a corridor to a trauma room in the emergency surgery section. Only when the doctors and nurses were taking over did Jackie give up her grasp on the coat. The doctors found that President Kennedy still had a heartbeat and his lungs were still breathing. More doctors and nurses came to work on him, and the small room became over-crowded. Jackie was asked to wait outside. She sat on a folding chair in the corridor near the trauma room's door. I paced the corridor with Dave and Larry O'Brien, watching her and feeling too numb to talk to her. Various people were stopping me and asking questions but I couldn't answer them. Curious things happen at a time like that. One of the doctors in the hospital that day was Skip Garvey from Buffalo, New York, who had played football with me at Harvard. Skip began to reminisce about various fellows on the team and asked me if I had heard from any of them lately. I realized later that he was probably trying to distract me and relax me, but at the time I was in no mood to chat about old Harvard football friends and what they were doing now.

Up until the President was brought to the trauma room, Jackie was as certain as I that he was dead. Seeing the doctors running in and out of the room, she began to wonder why they were giving him blood transfusions and so much other medical attention. She beckoned to me and Dave and whispered to us, "Do you think he still has a chance?" I did not have the heart to tell her what I was thinking. I walked down the hall with Dave and said to him, "If he's got a chance, it's a thousand to one."

I went to see Lyndon Johnson, who was waiting in a room in another section of the emergency wing with Mrs. Johnson and a group of Secret Service men. I told the Vice-President that it looked bad and that I would let him know as soon as I heard definitely whether the President was dead. "Kenny, I'm in your hands," Johnson said. "What do you think I ought to do?"

"I'll let you know as soon as I hear about the President," I said.

Coming back to the trauma room, I found Mrs. Kennedy's folding chair in the corridor empty. She had fought her way past a nurse back into the room to be with her husband. "I'm going in there," she told the nurse. "I want to be with him when he dies." A few minutes later, at one o'clock, Dr. Kemp Clark told her that the President was dead, and at about the same time, a Catholic priest from the nearby Holy Trinity Church, the Very Reverend Oscar L. Huber, C.M., arrived at the hospital and gave John Kennedy the last rites of his church. Jackie and Dave stood beside the body and joined Father Huber in the prayers. Dave was so distressed and so physically upset by the President's death that he drew the priest aside when they were leaving the trauma room and asked Father Huber to hear his confession. He thought he was having a heart attack.

When I heard that President Kennedy had been officially pronounced dead, I began to think of the responsibilities that were ahead of me. I was here in Dallas as a government servant in charge of the security and travel arrangements of the President of the United States, who was now Lyndon Johnson. According to the strict letter of the law, I should now be with Johnson, getting him safely to the airport and back to Washington as soon as possible. But I felt that my real duty was to take care of Jacqueline Kennedy, and I was sure that Johnson would agree with my feeling, as he did. I figured that Johnson, who had flown to Texas separately from the Kennedys on Air Force Two, the second 707 jet plane in our party, which was identical to Air Force One, would be taking off for Washington immediately. We did not know then whether or not President Kennedy's assassination was part of a planned conspiracy that might also threaten Johnson, and, in any case, it seemed imperative to get the new President out of Dallas right away.

I knew, however, that Jackie would not leave Dallas until she could bring her husband's body with her. This would take at least a little time, so I assumed that Johnson would be leaving for Washington ahead of us. That presented no problem; with the two planes waiting at nearby Love Field, he could take one and leave the other one for us. If Johnson wanted to use Air Force One, as more fitting to his new office as President, that would be all right with Jackie and with us. Both planes had the same equipment and facilities. The only difference between Air Force One and Air Force Two was the identification numbers on their tails.

I went to Johnson to urge him to go to Washington immediately and to explain to him that I wanted to remain in the hospital with Jackie until President Kennedy's body was ready to be moved to the airport. Johnson had already heard of the President's death. He was nervous and excited, and so were the Secret Service agents with him, Rufus Youngblood, his own guard, and Emory Roberts, one of President Kennedy's agents who had decided to switch to Johnson as soon as Kennedy was shot. Roberts jumped up when he saw me coming into the room and kept asking, "What'll we do, Kenny, what'll we do?"

"You'd better get the hell out of here," I said, "and get back to Washington right away."

"We don't know if this is a conspiracy," Johnson said. "Don't you think it might be safer if we moved the plane to Carswell Air Force Base, and took off from there?"

I vetoed that idea, pointing out that it would take time to move one of the jets from Love Field to Carswell on the other side of Fort Worth, and that it would be risky for Johnson to make a thirty-five-mile drive over the roads from Dallas to the Air Force base. "Get the police to seal off Love Field, and go there right now," I said. "And take off for Washington as soon as you get there."

Johnson agreed that I should stay behind at the hospital until Mrs. Kennedy was able to leave with the President's body. "You take good care of that fine lady," he said. He never suggested that he might wait at the airport for Jackie and the body of President Kennedy before he left for Washington. If he had made such a suggestion, I would have vetoed it for the same reason that I vetoed the idea of taking off from the Air Force base in Fort Worth — anything that would delay Johnson's departure from Texas was a bad move. He never discussed with me whether he should use Air Force One instead of Air Force Two, a question which would have seemed highly unimportant at the time.

When Johnson was leaving the hospital to go to Love Field, I went back to the corridor outside of the trauma room where Jackie was sitting on her folding chair, waiting while the nurses and the orderlies cleaned the President's body. Clint Hill, Dr. Burkley, Dave Powers, Larry O'Brien, Evelyn Lincoln, the President's secretary, and Mary Gallagher, Mrs. Kennedy's secretary, were gathered around her. When she saw me, Jackie whispered, "I'm not going to leave here without Jack."

"I know," I said, and turning to Clint Hill and Dr. Burkley, I told them to get a casket. Jackie asked me to be sure that she would be able to see her husband once more before he was put into the casket. When the nurses were finished cleaning the President's body, I took her into the room and watched her take off her wedding ring. She lifted the President's hand and slipped the ring on his finger. After we came out of the room, she said to me, "Did I do the right thing? I wanted to give him something."

"You leave it right where it is," I said. I was not going to disagree with anything she wanted to do right now. I knew we could always get back the ring for her later, as we did that night at Bethesda Naval Hospital.

Before the casket was brought to the trauma room, there was trouble. The medical examiner of Dallas County, Dr. Earl Rose, appeared on the scene and announced that President Kennedy's body could not be moved from Parkland Hospital without an autopsy. The sheriff's office and the Dallas Police Department's homicide bureau agreed with the medical examiner. The fact that this was the body of the late President of the United States, that the circumstances of his death were already known all over the world, that he had been medically examined and that there would be an official government autopsy in Washington, and that a further delay in bringing his body home would only cause more misery for his widow — all of these objections meant nothing to the tough and belligerent Dr. Rose. He was determined that nobody from the White House was going to interfere with the rules and laws of Dallas County. We had visions of the President's body being held there for another day or two, and I knew Jackie was in no condition to stand up under such an ordeal.

We took turns arguing with the medical examiner, but none of us could shake him. Phone calls were made to higher authorities, but we couldn't find anybody who would overrule him. A county judge, a young fellow named Theron Ward, was brought from a town fourteen miles away to sign a waiver that would permit us to remove the body. Ward turned out to be too timid to take a stand against Dr. Rose. By now the casket was closed and on a hand truck, ready to be wheeled through the door of the emergency ward to the outside corridor leading to the waiting hearse. We were gathered around the casket — Jackie, Dave Powers, Larry O'Brien; General McHugh and Major General Ted Clifton, the President's military aides; the Secret Service men, and myself — all of us glaring at Dr. Rose while he yelled at us that the casket could not be moved. The crazy situation was getting so preposterous that I couldn't believe it, and my Irish temper was getting hotter. We had with us on our side a great young Dallas police sergeant, Bob Dugger, who had been guarding the door of the trauma room when the President died. Dugger, big and husky, had his fists doubled and I could see that he was ready to belt Dr. Rose if the medical examiner did not get out of our way. Another local judge joined the angry crowd. When I tried to get him to overrule the medical examiner and let us go to the airport, he said he could not make any exception because the body happened to be that of the President. The judge said, "As far as I'm concerned, it's just another homicide case."

That did it. I boiled over and said to the medical examiner and the policemen who were with him, "Get the hell out of the way. We're leaving."

We shoved Dr. Rose aside and the policemen backed away, and we pushed the casket down the corridor to the outside door and lifted it into the hearse. Andy Berger, one of the Secret Service agents, got behind the wheel, and we told the surprised undertaker to follow us to the airport and to pick up his hearse there later. Jackie climbed into the back of the hearse with Clint Hill and Dr. Burkley and sat beside the casket on a jump seat. The rest of us piled into four other cars, and we took off in a rush to Love Field.

I was sure that the medical examiner and the police would follow us to the airport and try to stop us from putting the casket on the plane. When we pulled up beside Air Force One, and hauled the heavy bronze casket out of the hearse and carried it up the steep steps into the rear section of the plane, I kept looking back to see if any police cars were coming, and telling the others to hurry. After the casket was set in place in the tail of the plane, where several seats had been removed to make room for it, I told General McHugh, the Air Force aide and the ranking Air Force officer on board, to tell the pilot, Colonel Jim Swindal, to take off immediately. I was still expecting the medical examiner to appear on the runway waving an order to halt our takeoff.

Jackie left us with the casket briefly to go to her compartment to freshen up. She came back in a few minutes and told me something that left me stunned: when she opened the door of her cabin, she found Lyndon Johnson sitting on her bed, dictating messages to his secretary, Marie Fehmer. I had no idea that Johnson was on the plane. I assumed that he had left the airport at least a half-hour before and was now on his way to Washington. While we were at the hospital arguing with the medical examiner, the thought passed through my mind that Johnson had done well to leave Dallas ahead of us. If he had decided to wait for Mrs. Kennedy and the President's casket, I said to myself, God only knows how long he might be stuck here along with the rest of us. When we had been putting the casket on Air Force One, I was too excited and too worried about the police and the medical examiner to notice that the Vice-Presidential jet, Air Force Two, was still standing on the runway beside us.

I went up forward to talk with Johnson, and asked him if we could take off without any further delay. I explained to him quickly about the trouble with the medical examiner at the hospital, and urged him to get the plane off the ground before the sore-headed Dr. Rose tried again to stop us.

"We can't leave here until I take the oath of office," Johnson said. "I just talked on the phone with Bobby. He told me to wait here until Sarah Hughes gives me the oath. You must remember Sarah Hughes, my old friend, the Federal judge here in Dallas. She's on her way out here now."

I was flabbergasted. I could not imagine Bobby telling him to stay in Dallas until he had taken the Presidential oath. This was no time to be waiting around at the airport for a judge to swear him into office. It was my understanding — shared, I found out later, by Bobby and by Nick Katzenbach, the assistant Attorney General, and by a lot of other people, including President Eisenhower and Hubert Humphrey — that Johnson acquired all the powers of the Presidency when President Kennedy died. Taking the oath is just a symbolic formality and there is no need to hurry about it. Johnson could have waited until he got to Washington and spared all of us on Air Force One that day, especially Jackie, a lot of discomfort and anxiety.

Later that night Bobby gave me an entirely different version of his conversation with Johnson about taking the oath. He said Johnson had telephoned him at Hickory Hill to express his sympathy, and then said to Bobby that "a lot of people down here had advised him to be sworn in right away" and asked if Bobby had any objections.

"I was too surprised to say anything about it," Bobby told me. "I said to myself, what's the rush? Couldn't he wait until he got the President's body out of there and back to Washington? Then he began to ask me a lot of questions about who should swear him in. I was too confused and upset to talk to him about it, so I switched him over to Nick Katzenbach, who was also perplexed by the whole thing."

We waited for Sarah Hughes. After all the trouble we had gone through getting the President's body out of the hospital, waiting around like this was driving me crazy. I kept looking out the windows, expecting to see the flashing red lights of a dozen Dallas police cars, coming with a court order to stop our takeoff. The air conditioning in the cabin could not go on until the engines started, and it was hot and suffocating. Jackie was suffering badly from the heat and asking when we would be able to leave.

Finally Judge Hughes appeared, and Johnson asked all of us who were in the back of the plane with President Kennedy's casket to come up to the front to attend his oath-taking ceremony. I found everybody standing around and waiting again, although the judge was ready with President Kennedy's Bible in her hand. I asked Johnson why he was still delaying. He said he was waiting for Mrs. Kennedy, which bothered me because I felt that attending the swearing-in might be upsetting for her. "She said she wants to be here when I take the oath," Johnson said. "Why don't you see what's keeping her?"

Jackie was in her dressing room with the door closed. I hesitated about knocking on the door. Then I thought again about the medical examiner and the police, and I opened the door and looked inside. She was standing in front of the mirror, combing her hair. I asked her if she wanted to watch Johnson take the oath, explaining that it would not be necessary if she did not feel up to it. I remember that she said, "I think I ought to. In the light of history, it would be better if I was there." She was still wearing the bloodstained pink suit, and she asked me if I thought she should change her clothes. I told her not to go to all that trouble.

After Johnson was sworn into office, he and Mrs. Johnson asked Jackie if she wanted to use the President's lounge in the middle of the plane during the flight to Washington. She thanked them, and explained that she wanted to sit next to her husband's casket in the rear of the aircraft, which they understood sympathetically. Dave, Larry O'Brien and I stayed with her beside the casket until we landed in Washington. There was not much room in the rear compartment, with the casket taking up most of the space. Other members of the Kennedy staff — Pamela Turnure, Jackie's press secretary, Dr. Burkley, General McHugh, Evelyn Lincoln, Clint Hill — came back and visited with us one at a time. When the plane lifted off the runway, I felt a great relief to be getting away from Dallas at last and announced that I was going to have a stiff drink of Scotch. I made one for Jackie, too. She was unable to feel it, and switched to coffee. The rest of us drank several more Scotches but it was like drinking water. It left us cold sober.

Later descriptions of the mood in Air Force One on the flight back from Dallas by writers who were not on the plane painted a picture of open and bitter resentment toward Johnson from the Kennedy group. Some of us did feel that he was using Mrs. Kennedy and the Kennedy aura when he moved into her husband's Presidential plane so he could stage his oath-taking ceremony there with her present, and so he could arrive in Washington with her and President Kennedy's casket. I think Johnson sensed that he might be criticized for taking over Air Force One instead of going back to Washington earlier on his own plane, as we assumed he would do. This must have been why he later made a big point of insisting in his testimony before the Warren Commission, and in interviews with reporters, that I had specifically told him to take Air Force One when we talked before he left Parkland Hospital. He was trying to shift the blame for his being on Air Force One to me, just as he insisited that he waited in Dallas to take the oath on the plane because Bobby Kennedy had told him to do so, which was not true at all.

I distinctly remember that when Johnson and I talked at the hospital there was no mention of which of the two planes he should use. Nor was there any mention that he was considering waiting for Jackie and the President's casket to be on the same plane with him before he left Dallas. Later a lawyer for the Warren Commission pointed out to me that Johnson's testimony that I had told him to board Air Force One disagreed with my own testimony before the commission about our conversation at the hospital. He asked me, to my amazement, if I would change my testimony so that it would agree with the President's. "Was I under oath?" I asked him, as, of course, I was. "Certainly I wouldn't change anything I said under oath."

But whatever resentment some of us might have felt, neither Dave nor I can remember any open display of antagonism against Johnson because he was aboard Air Force One on the flight back from Dallas. Nor do we recall that we forcibly prevented him from joining Mrs. Kennedy and our group when we were carrying President Kennedy's casket from the plane at Andrews Air Base in Washington, as he claimed in later interviews.

The impression that there was a wall of coldness between us and Johnson on the plane rose simply from the fact that we remained during the flight with Jackie beside the casket, separated by a narrow passageway from the President's office and lounge, where Johnson sat with his advisers, Cliff Carter and Bill Moyers. Johnson came back once to visit with us, and told Larry and me that he wanted us to stay on with him at the White House. "I need you now more than President Kennedy needed you," he said. We heard later that he said the same thing in exactly the same words to everybody else on the White House staff during the next few days. Bill Moyers came back to us later and said that the President wanted us to come up and join him for a talk about arranging a Congressional leadership meeting. I explained that we did not want to leave Jackie, and Moyers said agreeably, "We understand perfectly."

Our talk with Jackie beside the casket that evening during the flight back to Washington was like the talk at an Irish wake, filled with warmly sentimental reminiscences. She remembered how much Jack had loved the singing of Luigi Vena, a tenor from Boston, at their wedding in Newport, and she decided then and there that Vena would sing Schubert's *Ave Maria* and Bizet's *Agnus Dei* at the President's funeral Mass, as he did. Of course, she added, their good friend Cardinal Cushing, who married them, would say the low requiem Mass, which Jack liked better than the solemn high ritual. She enjoyed it when Dave and I told her about Cardinal Cushing's meeting with the President at the North American College in Rome during our trip to Europe a few months earlier. All of the prominent Cardinals from the United States had been in Rome during the previous week, attending the coronation of the new Pope Paul VI, but Cardinal Cushing was the only one remaining to greet President

Kennedy. "They're all gone home, Jack," the Cardinal roared at the President, throwing a playful punch at his shoulder. "I'm the only one who's for ya! The rest of them are all Republicans!"

Jackie listened, entranced, while Dave described to her President Kennedy's last visit to his father at Hyannis Port on Sunday, October 20, after he had appeared at a Democratic fund-raising dinner in Boston the night before. On visits to the family compound at Cape Cod, the President usually landed in his helicopter on the big lawn in front of his father's house, where he had played touch football as a youth, because he knew that the crippled and speechless Ambassador Kennedy enjoyed watching his arrival from a wheelchair on the porch. This Sunday the President landed on the lawn in the morning and spent the whole day with his father. Early the next day, when the helicopter was waiting to take him to Air Force One at Otis Air Base and the Ambassador was on the porch in his wheelchair to see him off, the President went to his father, put his arm around the old man's shoulders, and kissed his forehead. Then he started to walk away, turned and looked at his father for a moment, and went back and kissed him a second time, something Dave had never seen him do before. It almost seemed, Dave said to Jackie that night on the way back from Dallas, as if the President had a feeling that he was seeing his father for the last time. When the President and Dave were seated in the helicopter, waiting for the takeoff, he looked out the window at the figure in the wheelchair on the porch and for the first time in all of the years that Dave had known John Kennedy, he saw his eyes filled with tears. The President said to Dave sadly, "He's the one who made all this possible, and look at him now."

Dave and I both talked with Jackie about our visit on the Saturday afternoon of that same weekend to Patrick's grave in Brookline, and told her how the President had said to us, looking at his baby son's burial place, "He seems so alone here." Jackie listened, nodded slowly, and said, "I'll bring them together now." Dave and I looked at each other, wondering if she was thinking of burying President Kennedy in Boston, but she had already decided on the Arlington National Cemetery across the Potomac from the White House, and she was planning to move Patrick's body to his father's gravesite.

Jackie talked with us that night on the plane about our trip to

Ireland with the President late in the previous June. "How I envied you being in Ireland with him," she said. "He said it was the most enjoyable experience of his whole life." Jackie remembered how impressed the President was by the drill performance of a group of Irish military cadets at Arbour Hill in Dublin when he placed a wreath on the graves of the leaders of the 1916 Easter Week Rebellion. "I must have those Irish cadets at his funeral," she said. "And he loved the Black Watch pipers. They must be at the funeral, too." A band of pipers from the Black Watch of the Royal Highlanders Regiment, who had performed for the President only nine days before his death, marched in the funeral procession from the White House to St. Matthew's Cathedral. The cadets from Ireland were at his grave at Arlington Cemetery.

Dave recalled how he and the President joked about funerals; the black limousine from the White House reminded them of an undertaker's car. When they rode in it to church on a holy day or a Sunday, President Kennedy would say to Dave, pretending that they were Knights of Columbus on the way to a funeral, "Which of our worthy brothers are we burying today?"

Jackie said to Dave, "Oh, Dave, you've been with Jack all these years. What will you do now?"

When we were landing at Andrews Air Base in Washington, we received word that a detachment of military pallbearers was waiting to carry the casket from the plane. Overcome with maudlin Irish sentiment, I said, "We'll carry him off ourselves." Mrs. Kennedy said that she wanted Bill Greer, the driver of the President's car in Dallas, to drive the casket to Bethesda Naval Hospital where the autopsy was to be performed before the body would be taken to the White House. Greer had been remorseful all day, feeling that he could have saved President Kennedy's life by swerving the car or speeding suddenly after the first shots. Jackie felt sorry for him. We grouped ourselves around the casket at the rear door of the plane — the Secret Service agents, General McHugh, Larry, Dave and I, and Mrs. Kennedy and the women in our party.

The first person to board Air Force One when it stopped at the terminal was Bobby Kennedy, who ran up the ramp to the front door and then ran from the front end of the plane, through the cabin area and the President's stateroom, to the rear compartment where Jackie was waiting beside the casket at the back door. As

Bobby said later, he had only one thing in his mind when he was running through the plane from the front door — he was trying to get to Jackie as fast as possible. According to Johnson, as told to Jim Bishop, when Bobby was dashing through the President's stateroom, Johnson stuck out his hand to shake Bobby's hand and Bobby ignored Johnson deliberately. Knowing how emotionally upset Bobby was at that moment, and how anxious he was to get to Jackie, I doubt that he even saw the outstretched hand or Johnson. If the Pope had tried to stop him to offer condolences, Bobby, a devout Catholic, would have brushed past the pontiff.

Recently I asked a formerly close associate of Johnson's why Lyndon goes to the trouble of slanting such incidents. The man said, "Lyndon himself doesn't know why he does it, but he soon convinces himself that his version of the story is the gospel truth." In any case, if Johnson felt that I caused him any embarrassment in Dallas or on the flight back to Washington, he never mentioned it to me during the year that I worked with him in the White House after President Kennedy's death.

That night, while Jackie was waiting at Bethesda Naval Hospital for the autopsy to be completed, Dave, Larry and I went with Muggsey O'Leary, the President's longtime driver and bodyguard, to Gawler's Funeral Home to select another casket for the burial. The casket we had bought in Dallas had been damaged when we were frantically loading it on Air Force One. Several months after the President's death, I learned that my fear of the Dallas police coming to Love Field to stop our takeoff had been groundless; unknown to us, as we were leaving the hospital with the casket, Judge Theron Ward had received an order to let us go from the local district attorney, Henry M. Wade. At Gawler's, we picked a mahogany casket, the second one we looked at. Dave said to us, "You know, back in that neighborhood in Charlestown where I grew up, they measured your importance by the prestige of the people who came to your funeral. I always thought my funeral would be great because President Kennedy would come to it. And now here I am, helping to pick out his casket."

We did not leave Bethesda to bring President Kennedy's body in the new casket back to the White House until after four o'clock in the morning. Dave went to his home to change his clothes, still bloodstained from lifting the President's body from the car at the

Parkland Hospital. Mrs. Kennedy invited Larry and me to sleep on the third floor of the White House with Pierre Salinger, who had been flying across the Pacific with Dean Rusk and other Cabinet members on a mission to Tokyo when he heard the news of the President's death. We sat and talked with George Thomas, the President's grief-stricken valet, until we were finally able to go to sleep at seven o'clock. Around eight, the telephone rang. Pierre answered it and heard a woman secretary's voice saying, "Mr. Salinger, the President is calling." Pierre smiled, relieved and happy, thinking that the day of President Kennedy's death had been a bad dream. Then another voice came on the telephone and brought Salinger rudely back to reality. It was a man and he said, "Pierre, this is Lyndon Johnson."

The day of the President's funeral, Monday, November 25, was the third birthday of his son, John F. Kennedy, Jr. After the funeral, and after the buffet reception for visiting dignitaries that followed it, Mrs. Kennedy staged a small birthday party for John upstairs in the family quarters of the mansion, with a three-candle cake and ice cream. Dave, one of young John's favorite people, was the only guest at the party outside of members of the family. He led the group in singing "Happy Birthday" and then joined Bobby and Ted Kennedy in "Heart of My Heart," a song that President Kennedy loved. Singing "Heart of My Heart" was too much for Bobby. It brought back to him the night of the last rally of the 1958 Senatorial campaign in Massachusetts when Jack, Bobby and Ted had climbed up on a table at the G and G Delicatessen on Blue Hill Avenue in the Dorchester section of Boston to harmonize on that song before a crowd of admirers.

TWO

Getting into Politics

THE TURN IN THE ROAD of young John F. Kennedy's life that led him into politics and onward to the White House came in August, 1944, when his older brother, Joseph P. Kennedy, Jr., was killed in a plane explosion while flying a dangerously experimental volunteer mission against a German rocket base in Europe. Young Joe was the star of the Kennedy family, a lively personality with winning charm, who had planned a political career with the determination of becoming President of the United States. His father and many other people who knew him were sure that he would make it. He had already made something of a political name for himself as a delegate to the 1940 Democratic convention when he created a stir by refusing to switch his vote from James A. Farley to make Franklin D. Roosevelt's nomination unanimous.

Because the Kennedys were so certain that Young Joe had a big career as a public figure ahead of him, his tragic sudden death came as an especially crushing blow to all of them. Along with his father, who took the loss of his high hopes for his eldest son and namesake harder than anybody in the family, Jack had been looking forward eagerly and confidently to Young Joe's climb to political prominence. At the Chelsea Naval Hospital near Boston, where he was recovering from the spinal injury that he suffered when his PT boat was wrecked in the South Pacific by a Japanese destroyer, Jack spent several months after Young Joe's death putting together and editing a privately published book of memoirs by friends and relatives, *As We Remember Joe*, which he planned as a Christmas gift to his parents. In his own contribution to the book, Jack wrote, "It is the realization that the future held the promise of great accomplishments for Joe that made his death so particularly hard for those who knew him. His worldly success was so assured and inevitable that his death seems to have cut into the natural order of things." Many years later at Hyannis Port, Ambassador Kennedy remarked to Dave Powers and me that he was never able to read *As We Remember Joe*. "I have to put it down after the first couple of pages," he said. "I never got over that boy's death."

Ambassador Kennedy's ambition to have a son in politics who might someday become the first Irish Catholic President of the United States was too strong to be discouraged completely by Young Joe's death. He urged Jack to take over that role, although, as he afterwards admitted, until Joe died, he had never been able to picture the scholarly and quiet-mannered Jack as a politician. According to a legendary story, widely told and accepted among the Boston Irish, the Ambassador dramatically summoned Jack to appear at a formal meeting of the grief-stricken Kennedy family a few days after the news of Young Joe's death had been received, and ordered Jack to pick up the political torch that had fallen from Joe's hand. Jack immediately agreed to carry on for his dead brother and the whole family pledged him their help and support.

To anybody who knew the Kennedys that tale does not hold water, mainly because such a theatrical scene, which might happen in many sentimental Irish families, hardly could have occurred in the casual atmosphere of the Ambassador's home at Hyannis Port, where emotional displays were frowned upon. Actually, Jack did not finally decide to go into politics, as a candidate for a vacant seat in Boston's Eleventh Congressional District, until more than a year after Joe's death. First he tried journalism, as a special correspondent for the Hearst newspapers at the formation of the United Nations organization in San Francisco and at the Potsdam Conference in Germany. During that year of 1945, when the war was ending and he had been discharged from the service, his father repeatedly talked with him about considering a political career, such as Joe had planned, but no great pressure was brought on him to do so and Jack took his time in thinking it over. The Ambassador himself often said that the cool and strong-minded Jack, even in those youthful years, could never be told to do anything unless he wanted to do it. As Jack explained it later in private conversations, and once in a television interview with Walter Cronkite, he did not feel obligated to go into politics to carry out Joe's unfulfilled ambitions, as his father and many other people assumed at the time, but Joe's death was indeed a decisive factor in his choice of a political career simply because it cleared that path, which had been previously reserved for the Kennedy family's eldest son. "We have heard the story many times that you got into politics sort of to take the place of your brother Joe, who was killed in the war," Cronkite said while interviewing Jack in 1960. "Was it a conscious feeling on your part of taking Joe's place?"

"No," Jack said, "but I never would have run for office if he had lived. I never would have imagined before the war that I would become active in politics."

It seems strange that Jack never thought of becoming a politician before the war because in those years, when he was in his early twenties and a student at Harvard, he seemed to be more deeply interested in politics than Joe, the family's political hopeful. Like Joe, Jack was drawn to politics as a youngster in a political-minded family where both of his grandfathers and his father had been involved in party politics. Faculty members and fellow students who knew both of the brothers at Harvard thought that Jack had a wider knowledge of current politics, political history and government. His favorite books were John Buchan's political autobiography, *Pilgrim's Way*, and David Cecil's biography of Lord Melbourne, Queen Victoria's prime minister. When he was a twenty-three-year-old Harvard senior, he wrote a best-selling political book of his own, *Why England Slept*, a study of Britain's unpreparedness for World War II, based on his own observations in London where he worked for his father in the U.S. Embassy during the outbreak of the war. As a PT-boat officer in the Pacific, he conducted lively political discussions at the nightly bull sessions.

But apparently Jack never gave a thought to entering politics himself as a candidate for an elective office, mainly because his older brother had staked a claim on that vocation, and in those days — unlike the later 1960s when three Kennedy brothers and two Kennedy brothers-in-law were all involved in politics at the same time — it was felt that one politician in the family was enough. Jack was also acutely aware that he did not have the easy hale-and-hearty personality that a politician was supposed to have, and which Joe had in abundance. Jack did not acquire a smooth and poised manner in meeting strangers until he became a Congressman; in his younger years, he was awkward and ill at ease outside of his circle of close friends. At the end of the war, during the period after Joe's death, he resisted his father's urging to try politics because the thought of shaking hands on street corners made him uncomfortable. He knew, too, that as a political candidate he would be exploited by his backers as a war hero because John Hersey's stirring account of his heroic experience in the South Pacific had received wide attention when it was reprinted from the *New Yorker* in the *Reader's Digest*. That made him squeamish. He remarked unhappily to his PT-boat companion, Red Fay, early in 1945 that he had no taste for "trying to parlay a lost PT boat and a bad back into a political advantage."

The thing that finally moved Jack Kennedy toward active politics, as he said later, was not trying to carry on for Joe or "my father's eyes on the back of my neck," but his own experience as a correspondent at the United Nations conference in San Francisco and at Potsdam, which sharpened his interest in the national and international issues of the coming postwar period. After getting a close look as a reporter at the postwar political leaders in action, he decided that he might be able to find more satisfaction and to perform more useful service as a politician than as a political writer or a teacher of government and history, the two careers that he had been considering up to that time. Dave Powers and Bill Sutton, who both knew him intimately during the winter of 1945, and the following spring when he was feeling his way into his first Congressional campaign, agree that he was drawn into politics by the same motive that drew Dwight Eisenhower and other World War II veterans, with somewhat the same reluctance, into the political arena — the realization that whether you really liked it or not, this was the place where you personally could do the most to prevent another war. John Droney, then a young law school graduate just out of the service, remembers Kennedy saying just that when he was asking for Droney's help in the campaign. Droney was protesting that he had no interest in politics and that he had to get started with his law practice. "If we're going to change things the way they should be changed," Kennedy said, "we all have to do things we don't want to do."

"I went to see him intending not to become involved, but with that little speech I went completely the other way," Droney later recalled, explaining how he became one of Jack's most active workers in 1946 and treasurer of the Kennedy campaign organization. "I thought to myself, he has a very winning way and he is obviously sincere, so I asked him immediately how I could help."

When Jack was deciding to try politics, his father's friends in Massachusetts tried to interest him in running for the state's lieutenant-governorship on the Democratic ticket with Maurice Tobin, who was then planning to try for reelection as governor. A secondary office in the State House held no appeal for Jack. Late in 1945, while he was still debating whether running for an elective office was the thing for him to do, a stroke of luck opened up just the right opportunity, too attractive to resist, a big chance to get to Washington as a Representative in Congress from a Boston constituency — a gift from James Michael Curley, of all people. Curley, the perennial roguish mayor of Boston, ran for his favorite office in City Hall once again in November, 1945, and won, giving up the seat in the House of Representatives from the Eleventh Congressional District that he had held during the war. Curley's mayoralty victory, which he celebrated at an inaugural ceremony in Symphony Hall with disabled war veterans limping across the stage while he led the audience in singing "My Buddy," left his Congressional seat to be filled in a special 1946 election. For Jack Kennedy, a newcomer to the Boston political scene but a son of a well-known local Irish Catholic political family with roots in that particular district, this was an opportunity to enter politics at the national, rather than the state or city, level that comes rarely in anybody's lifetime. With such an inviting situation before him, any last remaining doubts about becoming a politician vanished for all time.

Despite the fact that Jack Kennedy himself was a stranger in Boston, having lived as a youth in New York and at Hyannis Port on Cape Cod, the Eleventh Congressional District of Greater Boston was an ideal stage for his political debut. It included Boston's North End, the birthplace of his mother and his maternal grandfather, John F. ("Honey Fitz") Fitzgerald, who had served as a

Congressman in the same district before becoming the mayor of the city. The Eleventh District also covered East Boston, the waterfront area where his father was born and raised, and where his paternal grandfather, Patrick J. Kennedy, had been the local Democratic ward leader for many years. It was in East Boston that Jack's father became in 1914, at the age of twenty-five, the youngest bank president in the United States. He still owned the same bank, the Columbia Trust Company, in 1946 when Jack was running for Congress. As a part of their education, the three older Kennedy boys, Joe, Jack and Bobby, had worked in the bank for a few weeks during summer vacations when they were in school. On the first day that Jack began to campaign in East Boston, his father happened to be standing in front of the bank at Maverick Square, talking with a friend. He recalled later how surprised he was to see Jack across the street, shaking hands with a group of longshoremen and asking them for their vote. "I remember saying to the man who was with me that I would have given odds of five thousand to one that this thing we were seeing could never have happened," the Ambassador said. "I never thought Jack had it in him."

The North End of Boston and East Boston, once filled with Irish immigrants, had become thoroughly Italian neighborhoods. The Eleventh District also covered the waterfront community of Charlestown, still solidly Irish, with three Catholic churches within its one square mile of three-decker tenement houses on the slopes of Bunker Hill behind the Charlestown Navy Yard, where the frigate *Constitution*, "Old Ironsides," is docked. The district in Boston also includes the West End, the top of Beacon Hill around the State House, part of the South End and Chinatown and Ward 22 in Brighton. Across the Charles River, the constituency covers the whole city of Cambridge and three wards in the suburban city of Somerville. Cambridge has the most votes in the district, and in 1946 it had a favorite son, Mike Neville, a former mayor and a popular state legislator, running for the Congressional seat. Another strong candidate was Charlestown's John Cotter, who was well known throughout the district because he had handled its affairs in Washington as administrative assistant to two former Congressmen, Curley and John P. Higgins. Cotter had narrowly missed winning a special election for the seat himself a few years earlier, when Higgins retired from Congress to accept a judgeship.

Older politicians in Boston were sure that Jack Kennedy, a young and completely inexperienced outsider despite his well-known family name and enviable war record, would not stand a chance against Neville and Cotter. One evening before he formally declared his candidacy, Kennedy was introduced to Dan O'Brien, a prominent political figure in Cambridge. O'Brien looked him over scornfully, and said, "You're not going to win this fight. You're a carpetbagger. You don't belong here. I'll tell you what I'll do — if you pull out of the fight and let Neville go to Washington, I guarantee you I'll get you the job down there as Neville's secretary."

One of the few politicians in Boston who thought Kennedy would win was Curley. Too busy in 1946 getting City Hall back in order after his return as mayor, Curley took no part in the Congressional battle and supported none of the candidates. A reporter asked him before the primary, which in that solidly Democratic district was more decisively final than the routine Democratic-Republican election, what he thought about John Fitzgerald Kennedy's chances. "With those two names, Fitzgerald and Kennedy, how can he miss?" Curley said. Incidentally, Curley himself had been a carpetbagger when he ran for Congress in the Eleventh District in 1942. Massachusetts has no law that says a Congressman must live in his district. Curley's home was in Jamaica Plain on the other side of Boston. Jack Kennedy at least established a residence within the district before he filed his candidate's papers, room 308 at the Bellevue Hotel on Beacon Street next to the State House. His grandfather, John F. Fitzgerald, was then living in retirement at the Bellevue in vigorous good health at the age of eighty-three. Later, as a Congressman, Jack rented a small and rather dingy three-room apartment at 122 Bowdoin Street, near the Bellevue, which was to be his legal home and voting address for the rest of his life. On the day when he died in Dallas, he was carrying in his wallet a Massachusetts driver's license which bore the Bowdoin Street address.

When Jack decided to enter the race for Curley's vacant seat in the House of Representatives, he and his father turned first for guidance to Joe Kane, the Ambassador's first cousin and a shrewd and cynical veteran manager of Boston political wars. Kane was a gruff, bald-headed little man who spent most of his adult life sitting over a cup of coffee in one of the cafeterias near City Hall. His knowledge of local politics was extensive and his help in getting

Cousin Joe's son started was considerable. (Kane and the Ambassador always addressed each other as "Cousin Joe.") Among other things, Kane composed the winning Kennedy campaign slogan, "The New Generation Offers a Leader — John F. Kennedy." He adapted the phrase from a line written by Henry Luce in Luce's introduction to the 1940 Kennedy book, *Why England Slept*, one of the few appraisals of Jack that had appeared in print up to that time. The editor of *Time* and *Life* said, "If John Kennedy is characteristic of the younger generation, and I believe he is, many of us would be happy to have the destinies of the Republic turned over to his generation at once."

Kane's relationship with the Kennedy-Fitzgerald family over the years had its ups and downs. He was instrumental back in 1919 in getting his cousin's father-in-law, John F. Fitzgerald, removed from the same Congressional seat on charges of election frauds after Honey Fitz defeated Peter Tague, Kane's candidate, in 1918 by 238 votes. Tague had run on stickers in the election after Fitzgerald defeated him by only 50 votes in the primary. Kane and Tague convinced a Congressional investigating committee that along with using mattress voters, Martin Lomasney, the famous Boston political czar who was backing Fitzgerald, had seen to it that Tague's stickers were not gummed. The unsticky stickers fell off the ballots in the ballot boxes, leaving Tague's ballots blank and void. It was common knowledge that the mattress voters and the ungummed stickers were supplied by Lomasney, who was more interested in beating Tague, his enemy at the time, than in getting Fitzgerald elected. But Fitzgerald was unseated by the Congressional committee and Tague took his place in the House. After working for Fitzgerald's grandson in 1946, Kane said proudly, "I kept the grandfather out of the House of Representatives and I put the grandson in."

Kane, an entertaining raconteur, enjoyed recalling an earlier occasion when his Cousin Joe Kennedy enlisted his help in another political campaign. In 1942, after he was forced to resign from his post as U.S. Ambassador at the Court of Saint James's, Joe Kennedy was in a bitter anti–Franklin D. Roosevelt mood. That year FDR was strongly backing a New Deal candidate, Congressman Joseph E. Casey, who was running against the Republican Senator Henry Cabot Lodge in Massachusetts. Kennedy asked Kane if he could put up a Democrat who might be able to beat Roosevelt's man in the primary.

"You've got somebody in your own family who isn't doing anything at the moment," Kane said. "Your father-in-law almost knocked off Lodge's grandfather in the Senatorial fight in 1916. With the proper handling, he might be able to take Casey."

Honey Fitz, pushing close to eighty that year but still a tireless and convincing speaker, was doing well in the primary race against Roosevelt's candidate until a few days before the voting when Kane brought Joe Kennedy to the offices of a Boston advertising agency to look at a series of proposed full-page newspaper ads that praised Fitzgerald and savagely denounced Casey.

"These ads will cost a lot of money," Kane said, "but they'll beat Casey and give Fitz the Democratic nomination."

"Then what will happen?" Kennedy asked.

"Then Fitz will run against Lodge in the election."

"How much will that cost?"

"About two or three hundred thousand dollars," Kane said.

"Will Fitz have any chance of beating Lodge?" Kennedy asked.

"Not a chance in the world," Kane said.

Kane would bring the story to its conclusion by describing how Joe Kennedy then turned quietly away from the advertising layouts and began to button up his topcoat. "I don't know where you're going, Cousin Joe," Kennedy said, "but I'm going back to the Ritz."

It was Kane who brought Bill Sutton into the Kennedy movement one day in January, 1946, a few hours after Sutton had been discharged from the Army at Fort Devens. As Sutton tells it, he had taken a train from Fort Devens to the North Station in Boston and was walking up School Street when Kane saw him and dragged him to Kennedy's room at the Bellevue. Sutton protested that he was on his way to see his mother after being overseas for two years. "You can see your mother later," Kane said. Sutton was a prize catch. He had worked with John Cotter, a fellow native of Charlestown, on two elections in the Eleventh Congressional District and he knew everybody in the district. "I was quite impressed by Jack Kennedy," Sutton said. "We got along together immediately. He asked me for advice, and before I left to go home to see my mother, he made arrangements for me to work with him full-time. The next morning I arrived at his room very early and we started the organization. I lined up various young men throughout the district. I told him he should try to get Dave Powers in Charlestown because Dave knew every voter in Charlestown by his first name. Dave and I used to sell newspapers together in the Charlestown Navy Yard, so that was ten thousand people Dave knew to start with, and Dave ushered at five masses at Saint Catherine's Church every Sunday and he had coached the CYO teams. But when I talked to Dave, he said he had already decided to work for John Cotter because Cotter was a Charlestown guy like himself and the Charlestown guys are great for sticking together. I said to Jack, 'Why don't you go over and see him?' He said he would do that."

Dave Powers, with his precise memory for dates, names and figures, remembers that it was on the evening of January 21, 1946, that Jack Kennedy climbed the three flights of stairs to the top floor of the three-decker at 88 Ferrin Street in Charlestown and knocked on the front door. Fifteen years later, when they were swimming together in the pool at the White House, the President said to Dave, "If I had gotten tired that night when I reached the second floor, I never would have met you." Dave knew that the caller knocking on the front door of the cold-water flat must be a stranger. Three-decker families congregate in the kitchen, especially in the wintertime, to be close to the warmth of the kitchen stove, and their friends come up the back stairs to the kitchen door. Dave had just been discharged from the Army Air Force, after serving as a sergeant in China. He was living at the Ferrin Street apartment with his widowed older sister and her eight children. Like many newly discharged veterans that winter, Dave was at loose ends, drawing twenty dollars a week from the 52-20 Club, as the benefit payment for unemployed veterans was called, and helping to support his sister's family from his wartime savings.

"There was only a twenty-watt light bulb in the front hallway, and I could barely make out this tall and thin, handsome young fellow standing there alone in the semidarkness," Dave said, recalling the scene years later. "He stuck out his hand and said, 'My name is Jack Kennedy. I'm a candidate for Congress.' I said, 'Well, come on in.' While we were walking back toward the kitchen, where we could sit down and talk — my sister was listening to the radio in the parlor and the kids were in bed — he said that Bill Sutton had suggested me as somebody who might be able to help him in

Charlestown. I said, 'Gosh, if I help anyone, it should be John Cotter.' I could see that didn't discourage him. He seemed rather ill at ease and shy, but I think the word to describe him that night, and I have used it often, is to say that he seemed aggressively shy. He knew what he wanted and he wouldn't give up. We talked for about twenty minutes about the people in the district and their needs. He had then that way of talking to you, asking you questions, and listening to you attentively that made you feel as though you were important — the only person in the world who mattered to him at the moment. He was really curious about finding out your ideas and your opinions. I heard a lot of people say that he impressed them that way later on when he was a Senator and when he was the President, but he was that way with me that first night we met in our kitchen back in 1946. I remember saying to him that the people in Charlestown were only looking for a decent place to live, an opportunity to give their children an education, and knowing where their next buck was coming from. He took that in as if he was trying to memorize it. He said, 'You know, that sounds about right.' "

When Jack was leaving, he mentioned casually that he was planning to attend a meeting of a group of Gold Star Mothers two days later at the American Legion hall in Charlestown. He asked if Dave would go to the meeting with him.

"I said I'd be glad to go with him to the meeting," Dave said later. "Here I had just told him that I was with John Cotter, but he was asking me to help him out and I was agreeing to it. I said to myself, 'Oh, well, I won't be doing Cotter any harm just going to this meeting with him.' So I made a date to meet him at his room in the Bellevue. I couldn't say no to him."

The meeting of the Gold Star Mothers was an afternoon party. Arriving at the Bellevue, Dave found Kennedy with a group of newly enlisted workers, all of them recently discharged veterans like himself, including Sutton and Eddie McLaughlin, who had served in the same PT-boat squadron with Jack and later became lieutenant governor in Massachusetts. Sutton said, "Do you want some of us to go with you?" Jack said quickly, "No, just Dave and I." This was one of his first political appearances — he did not announce his candidacy until two months later — but he was already instinctively setting the style of unpretentious restraint that was to set him apart from the old familiar type of flashy hat-waving politician. Then, as later, he disliked the thought of arriving at a speaking engagement in a big limousine, surrounded by an entourage of applause-leading lieutenants. Jack and Dave went to Charlestown that day on the subway. Dave noticed with surprise that Jack, unlike every politician that Dave had ever seen, was not wearing a hat. All during the months of campaigning that followed, Joe Kane continually urged Jack to wear a hat and Jack went bareheaded, ignoring Kane's complaint that his uncovered shock of boyishly tousled hair made him look as youthful as a high school student. Dave glanced at Jack's hair as the train came out of the subway and climbed the elevated tracks across the bridge to Charlestown, and said to himself, "This guy looks awfully young to be running for Congress." From the windows of the train on the high elevated structure above the Navy Yard and the old masts of the *Constitution*, Dave pointed out the wide view of the Congressional district — the Bunker Hill Monument ahead of them, Somerville and Cambridge in the distance at the left, and behind them the North End and East Boston. "And those are the kind of people you'll represent," Dave said, pointing below at the longshoremen and freight handlers working on the docks. Jack nodded thoughtfully and said, "Those are the kind of people I want to represent."

The young candidate's talk to the Gold Star Mothers at the American Legion hall was short and earnest. He spoke for ten minutes on the sacrifices of war and the need to keep the world at peace. Then he paused, looked at the women and said to them hesitantly, "I think I know how all you mothers feel because my mother is a gold star mother, too." All of the women in the room stood up and hurried to the platform, crowding around Jack, shaking his hand and talking to him excitedly, smiling and wishing him good luck. "I had been to a lot of political talks in Charlestown, but I never saw a reaction like this one," Dave said. "I heard those women saying to each other, 'Isn't he a wonderful boy, he reminds me so much of my own John, or my Bob.' They all had stars in their eyes. It took him a half hour to pull himself away from them. They didn't want him to leave. I said to myself, I don't know what this guy's got. He's no great orator and he doesn't say much, but they certainly go crazy over him."

When Jack finally managed to make his way out of the hall, he turned to Dave and said to him, "How do you think I did?"

"How do I think you did?" Dave said. "You were terrific. I've never seen such a reaction from a crowd of people in my whole life."

"Then do you think you'll be with me?" Jack asked.

"I'm already with you," Dave said. "I've already started working for you." They shook hands. Recalling that handshake recently, Dave, always the sentimental Irishman, added sadly, "And I stayed with him from that day until November 22, 1963, when I was riding in the car behind him in Dallas."

A few weeks later Dave was the Kennedy man in Charlestown, renting a vacant store on Main Street for fifty dollars a month as the local John F. Kennedy for Congress headquarters, and rounding up friends to stuff envelopes and to arrange house parties and street-corner rallies where the candidate could meet the voters. Newspaper stories which said that Ambassador Kennedy was spending a fortune on his son's campaign in 1946 perplexed Dave. To get the fifty dollars each month for the rent on the Charlestown storefront headquarters, Dave had to visit Edward Moore, the Ambassador's long-time assistant for whom Ted Kennedy was named, and present a bill that was made out in triplicate. The only other Kennedy money that passed through Dave's hands was a few dollars for mailing expenses. Being the Kennedy man in Charlestown that spring made Dave as popular as Benedict Arnold. He was damned as a traitor for deserting Charlestown's own John Cotter and supporting a millionaire's son from Harvard, an institution in low repute among the Charlestown longshoremen who claimed that its football team was too yellow to play against Catholic Boston College. Kennedy's aides from Cambridge, Mark Dalton, John Droney and Joe Healey, were similarly damned for deserting Cambridge's Mike Neville, but the loyalty of the Irish in Charlestown to Cotter was more ferocious. Taunted for backing a stranger whose voting address was a Boston hotel room, Dave would shout, "Nobody asked him his address when he was on PT-109! Because his boat was sunk, does that mean he can vote only in the Pacific?" Well aware of the ordeal Dave was enduring in his home neighborhood, although he seldom complained about it, Jack Kennedy would say to him with a smile, "Never mind, Dave, years from now you can say you were with me on Saint Crispian's Day. We few, we happy few, we band of brothers." It was not until much later that Dave learned that Jack's reference to Saint Crispian's Day was a quotation from Shakespeare's *King Henry V*.

As inexperienced as he was in organizing a campaign, Kennedy seemed to know by intuition how to select at a glance, and with only a few words of casual conversation, a recruit for his staff of workers with no previous political background or connections who would turn out to be a conscientious and able, and usually tireless, Kennedy crusader. "I don't know where he gets them," an opposing Boston politician said at the time, "but they're good, and they're all *new*." From the start of that first campaign for Congress in 1946, he made it a point, with a few exceptions, to avoid alliances with well-known and established politicians and their followers. His theory was that an experienced politician might bring you his friends, but you would also inherit all of his old political enemies. "Get me some people who haven't been involved in politics," he would say to a newcomer who impressed him favorably. "Fellows like yourself, around your age and just out of the service. Call me when you get eight or ten of them, and we'll have a meeting." John Droney, who did such recruiting in Cambridge, says, "He had fantastic judgment in sizing people up. I got together for him one night a group of thirty-five or forty young fellows and girls. He instantly picked out the two or three of them who would be good key workers, and he proved to be right. That was how we got started."

Slowly but surely as he declared his candidacy and the campaign got underway, Jack deftly moved his father's old political cigar-smoking friends into the background and replaced them with new young faces. Red Fay, his fellow PT-boat officer in the Pacific, was summoned from San Francisco and stayed for two months at the Bellevue until a terse letter from his father warned him that he had better get back to his job in the family's construction business. Torbert Macdonald, Jack's Harvard roommate, worked in Cambridge and in Somerville, where Ted Reardon, Young Joe Kennedy's college roommate, was in charge of the local headquarters. LeMoyne Billings, Jack's roommate at Choate School, was called to help out in the Cambridge office for a week or two, and ended up working there for the whole primary and election campaign, postponing until the next year his plan to do graduate work at the

Harvard Business School. Bobby Kennedy, a youngster just out of the service as an enlisted man in the Navy, pitched in and worked hard for three months knocking on doors in East Cambridge, the most anti-Kennedy section of the district. His sister, Eunice, worked in the Boston headquarters.

For all of his quiet determination and drive, Jack Kennedy would often let important matters slide until the last minute. On the day when he was to make a formal announcement of his candidacy to the newspapers and on the radio, somebody realized that nothing had been done about preparing a press release or writing the candidate's radio speech. Shortly before noon John Dowd, a friend of the Ambassador and head of a Boston advertising agency, asked his young and newly appointed public relations director, John Galvin, if he happened to know Jack Kennedy. Galvin said he had heard of Kennedy and his survival experience in the South Pacific, where he himself had served as a Naval officer in the war, but he had never met him. "Well, he's coming in here sometime this afternoon," Dowd said. "He's going to announce today that he's running for office, either for Congress or for lieutenant governor, I'm not sure which. I told his father we would put out a story to the newspapers for him, and he also needs a speech to make his announcement on the radio tonight. Will you handle it for him?" Galvin expressed the hope that Kennedy would show up early in the afternoon. Getting out a release to the newspapers and wire services in time for that night's deadline, and writing a radio speech as well, would be rather a large order.

Kennedy was late when he arrived smiling at the Dowd office with Red Fay at his side. Taking down biographical material for the press release with one eye on the clock, Galvin realized that he would need somebody else to do the radio speech. He telephoned a friend, Mark Dalton, and quickly explained the situation. Dalton, who had gone to Boston College with Galvin and later to Harvard Law School, was also just out of the Navy and starting a law practice in Boston. He was experienced in both politics and writing, having worked as a speech writer and speaker for Paul Dever, a prominent local Democratic politician, and as a dramatic and movie critic for the *Boston Herald*. He took a taxicab and hurried to the Dowd office. It turned out that Kennedy suddenly remembered that he had in his pocket a rough draft of the radio speech. Dalton found that it was good enough and needed only a little polishing and rewriting. They made a quick dash to the WNAC radio station, arriving just in time for Kennedy to go on the air with the first radio talk of his career — political television was then a thing of the future — and the announcement of his candidacy for the Eleventh District's Congressional seat went off well.

During the hustle and bustle of the evening's fast preparation of the press release and the radio talk, Kennedy took an instant liking to both Galvin and Dalton. Galvin promptly took over the task of handling Kennedy's publicity, not only in the 1946 Congressional race, but in the later Senatorial campaigns of 1952 and 1958 as well. Dalton, thoughtful and intellectually sharp, with a keen and scholarly interest in such current issues as labor laws, housing, veterans' problems and taxation, became Kennedy's closest political adviser. "For the next six years, while Jack was in the House of Representatives," one of JFK's closest friends says, "he listened more to Mark than to anyone else." The modest and idealistic Dalton also shared Kennedy's distaste for the old clichés and the high-pressure oratory used in campaigns by the pre-World War II politicians. Kennedy made Dalton his campaign manager and the coordinator of his activities in the various communities of the district, moving Joe Kane and the Ambassador's few remaining older political cronies farther backstage. The atmosphere in Jack's crowded rooms at the Bellevue became so youthfully Ivy League, and so amateurish from the professional politician's viewpoint, that most of Kane's old-timers strayed away in disgust.

One notable figure from Boston's political past who enjoyed mingling in the youthful bustle at the Bellevue was Grandfather Fitzgerald. The elderly Honey Fitz wandered around the Kennedy rooms every day, recalling in lengthy detail his own experiences in Congressional, mayoralty and Senatorial campaigns, offering advice to speech writers, and often breaking into "Sweet Adeline," his personal theme song which he sang at public and private gatherings for more than thirty years. Jack Kennedy told us that when Honey Fitz took him and his brother Joe to visit President Franklin D. Roosevelt during the 1936 campaign, Roosevelt threw out his arms and cried, "El Dulce Adelino!" Roosevelt had once heard Fitzgerald singing "Sweet Adeline" in Spanish in South America. In the early 1920s, at a Fourth of July sandlot baseball game, Honey Fitz was run over by a truck. He insisted upon sitting up and singing "Sweet Adeline" before he was taken to the hospital so that the crowd would know that he was all right.

Honey Fitz often reminisced about his bitter fights with his old enemy, James M. Curley. After Jack Kennedy moved from the Bellevue to the Bowdoin Street apartment, he arranged to meet his brother Teddy and Honey Fitz one Friday afternoon outside of the apartment building's corner drugstore so that they could drive with him to Hyannis Port for the weekend. Jack was late, as usual. Teddy, a student at Milton Academy at the time, was carrying his schoolbooks in a Harvard-style green flannel bag. He asked his grandfather to hold his books while he went into the drugstore for an ice-cream soda. Walking up Beacon Hill along Bowdoin Street came Jim Curley. Glancing at the bulky bag of books in Fitzgerald's hands, Curley said to him, "I see that you are still carrying your burglar's tools." Fitzgerald was furious. Jack was delighted by Curley's remark when his grandfather, still sputtering with rage, reported it on the drive to Cape Cod.

Kennedy's many biographers have pointed out often that Jack's popular success in politics, from the start of his first campaign in 1946, was largely due to his disdain for the overblown rhetoric and corny style of the older politicians. Well suited to the changing times, his air of quiet refinement and his unaffected and sincere platform manner were a welcomed contrast to the hard-boiled pols of the Curley era. "Compared to the Boston Irish politicians we grew up with," Bill Sutton says, "Jack Kennedy was like a breath of spring. He never said to anybody, 'How's Mother? Tell her I said hello.' He never even went to a wake unless he knew the deceased personally." One night when he was appearing at a rally along with dozens of other candidates who were running for state legislative seats, the chairman kept Kennedy waiting impatiently until a late hour while he introduced speaker after speaker, hailing each one as "a young fellow who came up the hard way." When Kennedy was finally called upon, he said, "I seem to be the only person here tonight who didn't come up the hard way." The audience roared its approval.

"When young Jack Kennedy appeared without forewarning on the Boston political scene in 1946, the middle-class suburban Irish hailed him with joy and relief," Francis Russell wrote recently.

"After a half a century of oafishness — Honey Fitz and 'Sweet Adeline,' Southie's annual St. Patrick's Day parade enlivened by japers like 300-pound Knocko McCormack mounted on a dray horse, of deft operators and blackmailers, of silvercrossed younger pols — this attractive, well-spoken, graceful, witty, Celtic, Harvard-bred and very rich young man was what every suburban matron would like her son to be. In fact, many of them came to see Jack *as* their son."

But although Jack carefully avoided imitating the old campaign techniques and politely ignored most of the advice offered to him by the old professional ward bosses, he found their colorful personalities to be fascinating. He came to Boston with no knowledge of ward-level politics. The names of veteran pols, familiar household words among the Irish and Italians of his own age who had grown up in the city, were all new to him. "It took Jack three months before he found out that Mother Galvin wasn't a woman," says Dave Powers, referring to Bill Galvin, the prominent Charlestown politician who wore that maternal nickname because of the many kind favors he had done for his constituents. Because the old Boston Irish politicians and their world were so unknown to him, he was much more impressed by them when he discovered them at the age of twenty-nine than he might have been if he had known them from his childhood. His father was amazed to find that Jack loved listening to Joe Kane's political philosophy and campaign recollections. "When I brought Jack and Joe Kane together," the Ambassador said, "I thought Jack wouldn't put up with Kane for more than two hours." The Ambassador was more surprised to hear that Jack was getting along famously with Mike Ward, the ward boss in Brighton who had been Curley's right-hand man, and with Clem Norton, another City Hall figure who provided Edwin O'Connor with most of the material for O'Connor's Curleyesque novel, *The Last Hurrah*. Jack was entranced by Ward's account of how he imitated Curley's voice on the telephone while the mayor was out to lunch to get jobs for friends on the city payroll. Impersonating Curley, Ward once ordered a department head to hire a man whom he described as "my first cousin," not knowing that Curley's alleged cousin was a Negro. After a heavy snowstorm, Ward arranged with a crew of street department laborers to shovel snow on a probation officer whom he disliked as the officer tried to enter the Roxbury courthouse. Poles apart from Jack Kennedy's political style and outlook, Ward did him several important favors in the 1946 campaign. "He was always picking my mind, asking questions about local politics and politicians," Clem Norton said of Kennedy. "But he was the most impressive man I ever met."

"As much as he personally disagreed with their viewpoint, Jack enjoyed the Boston Irish pols and they liked him, just as fellows like Mayor Daley in Chicago, Peter Crotty in Buffalo and Charlie Buckley in the Bronx admired him in later years," Dave Powers says. "He was a completely new type of Irish politician himself, but he was very Irish and he loved everything about politics, including the old pols and their stories and political jokes."

Kennedy was delighted to hear stories that were old stuff to the rest of us in Boston, such as the one about how Curley's henchman, Up-Up Kelly, got his nickname. One of Kelly's duties was to run into a crowded rally just before Curley was to make his grand entrance, yelling at the seated people, "Up! Up! Everybody up for the governor!" During one campaign, Kelly jumped out of Curley's car in South Boston looking around frantically for the American Legion hall where a Democratic rally was in session. A couple of wags on the street corner directed him to a Methodist church where the congregation had gathered for an evening service. Kelly ran down the aisle, interrupting the minister's sermon, shouting at the astonished Methodists, "Everybody up for Governor Curley!" It took a while to restore order in the church.

One of Kennedy's favorite tales concerned Martin Lomasney, the old mahatma of Boston's West End who advised fellow politicians never to put anything in writing and never to say yes or no if they could nod or shake their heads. Kennedy was convulsed by a Lomasney story told one night at a house party by Dave Powers, and later repeated it often. The anecdote involved an Irishman, just arrived from Ireland, penniless and jobless, who dropped into Lomasney's headquarters in the West End and watched a few people working on precinct voting lists. The Irishman picked up a broom, swept the floor, found a room with a bed in it, and slept there that night. He stayed on in the headquarters for several months. One day Lomasney asked his name. "Paddy Sullivan," the Irishman said. Not knowing that Paddy was sleeping in the headquarters, Lomasney said, "You must be the hardest worker we've got. You're always the last one here at night and you're always here ahead of me in the morning. There's a vacancy in the house of representatives at the State House. I'll put you into it."

After a few years as a state legislator, Paddy ran for the state senate with Lomasney's backing and won, of course. Four years later, on a day when Lomasney happened to be in a bad mood, Paddy came to him and said that he wanted a favor. "A favor?" Lomasney roared. "I made you a state representative and then I made you a senator, and now you want a favor? What's the favor, for God's sake?"

"Martin," Paddy said, "I want you to make me an American citizen."

The Democratic primary in the 1946 campaign soon developed into a wild free-for-all, with a field of ten candidates. Along with Neville and Cotter, Kennedy was opposed by Katharine Falvey of Somerville, a WAC major in the war who campaigned in her white dress uniform, and Joseph Russo, a Boston city councillor who had a strong following among his fellow Italian-Americans in the North End and East Boston. A second candidate named Joseph Russo entered the race and it was widely suspected that Joe Kane had persuaded him to do so in order to cut into the first Russo's vote, but, as Bill Sutton said, "If Kane did actually put anybody into the fight, I am sure Jack Kennedy was never aware of it." This was not the first time that the two Russos had opposed each other. In an earlier campaign, the "real" Joe Russo, the one who served in the city council, ran against the second Russo and another namesake. He had to explain to the voters that he was the Joe Russo who was on the ballot between the two other Russos. "Vote for the one in the middle," he said. It was a common practice in the knavery of Boston politics for an obscure namesake to capitalize on a well-known political name. While Jack Kennedy was in the Senate in the 1950s, a man named John F. Kennedy, a shop foreman in the Gillette safety razor factory in South Boston, was twice elected to the thirteen-thousand-dollar position of state treasurer in Massachusetts, simply by putting his name on the ballot, with no party backing or campaigning.

A prominent Beacon Hill Proper Bostonian, Joseph Lee, was also in the Eleventh District Democratic primary, along with Mike DeLuca, Robert B. Di Fruscio and Francis X. Rooney. Kennedy had little hope of beating Neville in Cambridge or Cotter in Charlestown, but he and Mark Dalton figured that if he could win a sizable vote in those two communities and then run strongly throughout the rest of the district, he could win the primary. Neville and Cotter were unbeatable in their own wards, but they both lacked strength in the rest of the district.

From the start of the campaign, Kennedy showed the incredible stamina and zest for hard work that was to set him apart in later years from other politicians. He would spend one whole day a week in each of the district's community areas — one day in Cambridge, other days in Charlestown, Somerville, Brighton, East Boston, and the wards in downtown Boston — starting early in the morning, shaking hands at factory gates and on the waterfront docks, walking throughout the day shaking hands in shopping districts and visiting homes on residential streets, and ending up at night at local house parties and political meetings and rallies. Dave Powers' description of a typical day of campaigning in Charlestown, which was duplicated the next day and the day after that in other parts of the district:

"I would get him out of bed at the Bellevue Hotel around six-thirty in the morning and we'd rush over the bridge to Charlestown. He would stand outside the Charlestown Navy Yard from seven to eight, shaking thousands of workmen's hands as they went in to their jobs. By a quarter past eight, most of them were inside the yard and we would stop for breakfast. At nine o'clock we began a street tour, walking up Bunker Hill Street knocking on every door in that three-decker neighborhood. Most politicians are inclined to be lazy about campaigning. They go to rallies and meetings and dinners and luncheons, but they don't knock on peoples' doors. The housewives were startled to see Jack Kennedy standing on their porches because most of them had never seen a politician that closely before. He was the first one who took the trouble to come to them. He would talk to the Dohertys on the first floor, to the O'Briens on the second floor and the Murphys on the third floor.

"Those Irish mothers loved him. I could picture them, telling their sons that night that Jack Kennedy was there today and the family should vote for him. In an Irish home, the mother's word is law. The son doesn't argue with his mother.

"We'd stop for lunch — a frappe and a hamburger. A frappe is

Boston for a milk shake with the ice cream beaten up in it. In the afternoon, we'd hit the barber shops, the neighborhood candy or variety stores and the taverns, the fire stations and the police stations. At four o'clock, back at the Navy Yard, catching the workers coming out of a different gate from the one where we worked that morning. They had three gates for their ten thousand workers. Then to the Bellevue for a shower and a change of clothes.

"In the evening there would be a rally or a political forum with all the candidates invited, and the house parties. We would arrange with young girls, schoolteachers or telephone operators or nurses, to invite their friends to a party at their house to meet Jack. The parties would range from small ones, with about fifteen people, to big ones that might take up two or three floors of a three-decker house. A wonderful girl named Ronnie Murphy gave a party at her house at 296 Bunker Hill Street one night where they must have had seventy people. Jack would go to three or four house parties in a night, one around seven-thirty and the later ones at eight or nine or nine-thirty.

"These people who met Jack at the house parties would turn out to be his workers. The next night they would be at our headquarters on Main Street, addressing envelopes or calling people on the telephone. We did a lot of work on getting young veterans just out of the service to register. Boys were coming home, just turning twenty-one, and we knew that with Jack Kennedy's great record in the war they would vote for him. The other guys who were working for Jack in other parts of the district — Teddy Reardon in Somerville, John Droney in Cambridge, Billy Kelly in East Boston, Tom Broderick in Brighton, Billy De Marco in the North End — they would call me and say, 'We heard you had fifty people working in your place last night. Where do you get them?' I would say, 'Well, they meet Jack at the house parties and they become very enthusiastic.' "

The success of the house parties led to the famous Kennedy teas, formal receptions for women only, which later played an effective role in the statewide campaign for the Senate against Henry Cabot Lodge in 1952. Engraved invitations were sent to every woman on the locality's voting list, asking her to meet the candidate and his parents. For older women, the chance to get a close look at Rose Kennedy and the former Ambassador to the Court of Saint James's, the most celebrated couple to emerge from their generation of Boston Irish Catholics, was irresistible. Younger unmarried girls were thrilled to shake hands with Jack. As Patsy Mulkern, Joe Kane's precinct worker in Boston, observed at the time, "Before the teas, the hairdressers were working overtime and the dressmakers were taking dresses in and letting dresses out. Every girl in the district was dreaming and hoping that maybe lightning would strike." When the teas were first suggested, John Droney and others were against the idea, arguing that it seemed too effeminate in such a tough district.

"I was dead wrong," Droney says. "More than a thousand women turned out for the first tea at the Hotel Commander in Cambridge. They filed across the ballroom and passed along the reception line, each one shaking hands with Jack and his mother and father. I heard several of the women telling Jack that he would be President of the United States some day. An old Cambridge politician who was with me looked at the turnout and said, 'This kid will walk in.' I remember watching one elderly lady who marched up to the head of the receiving line, instead of waiting for her turn, and somebody took her by the arm to lead her away. Jack saw her, and excused himself from the people he was talking with and followed her across the ballroom floor, shook hands with her, asked who she was, and thanked her for coming. The old lady walked over to the table where they were serving tea and everybody could see that she was on cloud nine. The little scene made a nice impression on everybody there. In a situation like that you could count on Jack to do the right thing."

Ambassador Kennedy's appearance at the first reception and tea party in Cambridge was his only public appearance in the 1946 campaign. Then, as in the Presidential campaign of 1960, he was afraid that his reputation as a prewar isolationist and his falling out with the New Deal might do Jack some harm. Behind the scenes, he was always busy, fretting over small details, worrying whether Jack's unpoliticianlike style of campaigning was wrong for the Boston scene. He hired the *New York Daily News* straw ballot crew to make a private poll of the district; they predicted that Jack would get as many votes as his nine opponents' combined total. One night the Ambassador dropped in unexpectedly at Dave Powers' Charlestown headquarters and was surprised to find it crowded with volunteers working on the telephones and on mailing *Reader's Digest* reprints of John Hersey's article on the PT-109 crew's survival to every veteran on the voting list. "Dave," the Ambassador said to Powers, "I won't worry about Charlestown any more."

Blanketing the district with copies of Hersey's account of Kennedy's wartime heroism was an obvious but highly effective promotional move. It was a year when the vote of the veterans was to be a big factor. None of Kennedy's opponents had a war record worth talking about, and his well-known display of incredible courage in the South Pacific gave him an aura of glamour that overshadowed his political inexperience and the charges that he was a carpetbagger whose wealthy father was trying to buy him a seat in Congress. I remember that when Bobby Kennedy, my friend at Harvard, took me to the Bellevue that spring to introduce me to Jack, I was much more interested in meeting Bobby's war-hero brother than I was interested in meeting Bobby's brother who was running for Congress.

Although Kennedy's supporters played up his war record during the primary campaign, Jack himself seldom mentioned it and squirmed uncomfortably when he was introduced at rallies as a war hero. In one speech that he delivered to a few veteran organizations that year, he talked at length about the heroism of Patrick McMahon, the forty-one-year-old engineer of the PT-109 who was badly burned when the torpedo boat was run down and wrecked by a Japanese destroyer. Kennedy referred to himself only once and very briefly as McMahon's commanding officer, and never mentioned in the speech that he himself had saved McMahon's life by swimming for five hours with a strap on the crippled engineer's life belt clenched between his teeth. Dave Powers found a carbon copy of Kennedy's speech on McMahon's bravery last year in his attic among some 1946 campaign papers. It brings back Kennedy's thinking about heroism and America's postwar problems at that time, and expresses the disillusionment of the many newly discharged veterans who found at home none of the comradeship and loyalty to each other that they knew in combat overseas.

After describing the rescue of the PT-109 survivors, Kennedy goes on in his speech to tell how McMahon turned down a medical discharge and stayed on in the South Pacific for several more months to work with his painfully burned hands on repairing PT-boat engines. "I felt that his courage was the result of his loyalty to the men around him," Kennedy said. "Most of the courage shown in the war came from men's understanding of their interdependence on each other. Men were saving other men's lives at the risk of their own simply because they realized that perhaps the next day their lives would be saved in turn. And so there was built up during the war a great feeling of comradeship and fellowship and loyalty.

"Now McMahon and the others are coming home. They miss the close comradeship, the feeling of interdependence, that sense of working together for a common cause. In civilian life, they feel alone, they feel that they have only themselves to depend on. They miss their wartime friends, and the understanding of their wartime friendships. One veteran told me that when he brought one of his Army friends to his home, his wife said, "What can you possibly see in O'Brien?' The veteran remembered O'Brien in Italy, walking with him from Sicily to the Po Valley, every bloody mile of the way. He knew what he could see in O'Brien.

"We forget that dependence on other people is with us in civilian life just as it was in the war. We are dependent on other people nearly every minute of our lives. In a larger sense, each one of us is dependent on all the other people in this country — on their obedience to our laws, for their rejection of the siren calls of ambitious demagogues. In fact, if we only realized it, we are in time of peace as interdependent as the soldiers were in the time of war.

"The institutions and principles for which we fought will be under a growing fire in the years ahead. We, in this country, must be willing to do battle for old ideas that have proved their value with the same enthusiasm that people do for new ideas and creeds. The tremendous vote in England last year for socialistic collectivism was largely the result of the tremendous enthusiasm that the socialists whipped up with their vigorous propaganda. If you wish to combat a similar move here — because, mark you, you may be sure there will be such a movement — you must be willing to match your enthusiasm and interest and belief in the old with their interest and enthusiasm and belief in the new and novel.

"We must work together. We must recognize that we face great dangers. We must recognize how interdependent we are. We must have the same unity that we had during the war. For years we enjoyed certain blessings, just laws, freedom to speak and believe and write as we please, a government for and by the people. We came to accept these blessings not as privileges for which we must fight but as our rights. They had lost their glamour — we had had them too long.

"Now, however, in recent years we have seen these institutions challenged by new doctrines supported by great armies. We have found that these privileges that we had accepted so casually were indeed worth fighting for. The dictators did us a profound service in awakening us to their value. Now we know these principles are never secure. We must work continually to keep them alive."

In a lighter vein, the young John F. Kennedy delivered another notable speech during the 1946 campaign to a much different kind of audience, the Proper Bostonian debutantes of the Junior League who invited him to discuss the question, "Why I Am a Democrat." Taking his place on the rostrum, and looking over the smiling throng of almost solidly Yankee Republican young ladies, Kennedy began his explanation by admitting that his party affiliation was largely due to his having been born in a Democratic family. "Accident of birth," he added, wryly eyeing the assembly of family-conscious Back Bay Brahmins, "explains much more than the purely physical and intellectual differences in individuals. It is useful also in analyzing basic differences in social philosophy, economic outlook and politics. I would venture to guess that some ninety-five percent of this group here tonight adhere to the general political beliefs of their immediate forebears."

After comparing the doctrines and history of the Republicans and the Democrats, Kennedy argued that in recent times "the Democratic Party understood the economic and political forces raging through the world far better than the Republicans." He ended urging the Junior League girls to follow the advice of John W. Davis:

"First, then, make choice of your political party, on grounds that satisfy your reason if you can, by tradition or by environment or sentiment or impulse if you have not the wit to do better. In any event, make choice. Do not wait until you find an aggregation of demi-gods or angels; they are scarce — some people think they are even scarcer than they used to be. Perhaps even you might not be comfortable in their midst. And do not expect to find a party that has always been right, or wise, or even consistent; that would be scarcer still. Independent judgment and opinion is a glorious thing, on no account to be surrendered by any man, but when one seeks companionship on a large scale he must be content to join with those who agree with him in most things and not to hope to find a company that will agree with him in all things."

The primary voting day in Massachusetts that year was June 18 instead of in September, the usual primary time, in order to allow the men in the armed forces more time before the November election to mail absentee ballots. When the primary campaign was reaching its peak late in May, the Jack Kennedy who had been hesitant about running for office back in January had developed into an assured and eager candidate, loving every minute of the fight. He became more than able to hold his own in the often rough give-and-take of the meetings in the American Legion halls and armories and ward rooms. One night in Charlestown a heckler tried to question him about his father's money. "I don't have to apologize for my father or any of the Kennedys," Jack said with his eyes blazing. "I'm running for Congress. Let's stick to that. If you want to talk to me about my family, I'll meet you outside." At another rally, Kennedy entered the hall when Mike Neville was speaking on the stage. "Here comes the opposition," Neville said to the crowd. "Maybe he's going to talk to you about money and how to manage a bank." Kennedy said, "I'm not going to talk about banking, Mike. I'm going to talk about you." Even Neville joined in the laughter.

"He was a great competitor," Dave Powers says. "If we were in Charlestown and he heard that one of his rivals was appearing at a meeting in Somerville or Brighton, he would say, 'Let's get a car and go over there right away.' When he saw a Kennedy-for-Congress sticker on a window, he would ring the doorbell and thank the people for their support. One day we were driving to Brighton and a car passed us with a Kennedy sticker on its back window. Jack said to Bob Morey, who was driving our car, 'Turn around and follow him.' It took us several miles to catch up with the man, who was driving with his wife and children. We pulled up beside him at a traffic light, and Jack rolled down his window and said to him, 'I want to thank you for wearing my sticker.' The man stared at him as if he was stunned, and finally pulled himself together and said, 'It's an honor to have your sticker, Mr. Kennedy.'

A fellow in Cambridge, a close friend of Mike Neville's, wanted to bet John Droney a thousand dollars that Neville would beat Kennedy in Cambridge two to one. Droney told the Neville supporter that Kennedy would be in the Cambridge headquarters the next day, and asked him to come in and meet Kennedy. The next day Droney introduced the man to Jack Kennedy, and said, 'He can't be with you. He's an old friend of Mike Neville.' Jack said to him, 'If you were with me, I wouldn't think much of you. Never leave your friends. Some day there may be another campaign and then maybe you will help me.' He talked to Neville's friend for about ten minutes. The next day I saw the fellow again and I said to him, 'How about that bet?' He said, 'No bet.' That's the way it went."

Mark Dalton remembers that once or twice during the campaign Jack mentioned his dead older brother Joe, as if he was remembering that Joe's death had brought him into politics. "One day we went to mass together," Dalton said. "When we were leaving, he said to me, 'Would you mind waiting a minute? I want to light a candle for Joe.' I was amazed. It was totally unlike him. He rarely showed any such sentimental feeling."

The grand climax of the Kennedy campaign was the appearance of the candidate and his followers in the annual Bunker Hill Day parade in Charlestown. Bunker Hill Day, the June seventeenth anniversary celebration of the Battle of Bunker Hill — the day before that year's primary voting — is a big holiday with fireworks in Boston, and its parade on Bunker Hill Street in Charlestown is an event among the Boston Irish rivaled only by the Saint Patrick's Day parade in South Boston. Dave Powers and his workers had placed Kennedy banners on every other house along the parade route. The Kennedy contingent marched as representatives of the Lieutenant Joseph P. Kennedy, Jr., Post 5880 of the Veterans of Foreign Wars, which Jack and his veteran friends had recently organized. Jack led the group, hatless in a dark flannel suit, with all of his youthful followers in white shirts. "People to this day tell me there were a thousand of us with Jack Kennedy in that parade," Dave Powers says. "Actually there were one hundred twenty-eight of us, but we marched only three abreast, stretching out the formation as long as we could. Up in front, Bill Sutton and Frank Dobie carried a big sign, 'John F. Kennedy for Congress,' about twenty feet wide and five feet high. People were running out into the street, shaking hands with him. I said to him, 'It's all over now.' But that last night, after the parade, he was still working. He went all over Charlestown, to the American Legion's open house, to the Veterans of

Foreign Wars' open house, to the Amvets' open house and to the big dance at the Armory."

In the next day's primary, Kennedy led the field of ten candidates on the Democratic ballot with 42 percent of the total votes, 22,183 against Neville's 11,341 and Cotter's 6,671. As he expected, Kennedy was defeated by Neville in Cambridge by a slim margin of some 1,500 votes and in Charlestown he was 337 votes behind Cotter, but he ran far ahead of both Neville and Cotter throughout the rest of the Congressional district. The other seven candidates trailed far behind. That night at the victory celebration in the Kennedy headquarters in Boston, Grandfather Fitzgerald climbed up on a table and sang "Sweet Adeline."

The next day Jack went to Cape Cod for some swimming and sailing. The election in November in that Democratic Congressional district was a mere formality. Kennedy buried the Republican candidate, Lester Bowen, with 69,000 votes to Bowen's 26,000, despite the fact that the Republicans swept Massachusetts that year. In his district, Kennedy received 13,000 votes more than the well-known Democratic governor, Maurice Tobin, who lost to the Republican Robert Bradford in his bid for reelection. The grandson of John F. Fitzgerald and Patrick J. Kennedy, soon to become the most successful Irish American politician of them all, was on his way to Washington.

THREE

The Lodge Fight

BOSTON SEEMS to be full of people who now claim that they knew for certain when they first saw John F. Kennedy running for Congress in 1946 that he would become the President of the United States within the next fifteen years. The same people, and many others who never knew him then, also assume that back there at the age of twenty-nine when Kennedy was elected to the House of Representatives, he was already carefully aiming at the White House. One of the many curious misbeliefs about Kennedy is this strange notion that his whole career was marked out for him when he first went into politics — apparently by a council of strategists on his father's payroll — and he only had to follow his prearranged plan and take advantage of the opportunities it brought to him until all the pieces fell into place and he became the Democratic party's Presidential candidate in 1960.

Actually, Jack Kennedy did not begin to think seriously about running for President until 1956, after he suddenly emerged on the national scene as a popular political figure at that year's Democratic convention, much to his own surprise and to the even greater surprise of the party leaders. During the ten years before that rise to prominence — while he served three terms in the House, fought a hard fight against Henry Cabot Lodge to move up to the Senate, married Jacqueline Bouvier, survived critical spinal surgery, and endured a long, painful and lonely recuperation — he went through many political, as well as personal, frustrations and depressions. I can remember a group of supposedly shrewd Boston politicians, who now say that they knew all along that Kennedy was headed for the Presidency, offering to bet me a considerable sum of money in 1954 that he would never be reelected to the Senate. There were very few people in 1946 who really thought of him as a Presidential possibility, outside of his father and his grandfather and a few admiring Boston Irish mothers. When I first met him that year, I did not think that he would even be elected to the House of Representatives. Bobby Kennedy, my closest friend in the locker room at Harvard, brought me to Jack's rooms at the Bellevue Hotel one afternoon after spring football practice, and introduced me to him. He seemed too boyish and shy to be running against experienced politicians like Mike Neville and John Cotter in that tough Congressional district. Later when Bobby asked me if I would do some work for Jack in Cambridge, I said to him, "I'll do it as a favor for you, but he'll never make it." I was still not particularly impressed by him when he did make it to Congress. Like many young war veterans of my age in Massachusetts who were interested in the political situation, I did not begin to pay much attention to Jack Kennedy as a Congressman until he refused to sign a petition for a Presidential pardon for James M. Curley and attacked the American Legion for its opposition to low-cost public housing projects.

These two bold acts of political independence made him something of a symbol of hope for the veterans who were home from the service feeling left out of the establishment and ignored by the older politicians who were trying to keep things as they were before the war. Here is a guy, we thought, who is one of us and who may be able to take them on. Kennedy's refusal to sign the petition for Curley's pardon, when it was handed to him on the floor of the House, was a startling display of political courage in 1947. Curley, then doing time in the Federal penitentiary at Danbury, Connecticut, for wartime construction-contract frauds, was such a popular figure in Boston that he continued in office as mayor while serving his prison sentence. He had made a dramatic appeal, appearing in court in a wheelchair, pleading that he was suffering from nine ailments, including an "impending cerebral hemorrhage," and wearing a collar too large for his neck, but the judge refused to suspend his sentence.

Curley was regarded as a martyred hero in Kennedy's Congressional district, where he had served as the previous representative and where, as his followers loudly recalled, his retirement from the House seat had made Kennedy's election possible. Furthermore, Kennedy was the only Massachusetts Democrat in Congress who declined to sign his predecessor's pardon petition, which had the endorsement not only of McCormack, who controlled Federal patronage in the state, but also the backing of the Democratic National Committee and the blessing of President Truman himself. Despite this pressure, Kennedy held back his signature because he doubted that the imprisoned mayor was as ill as he claimed to be, a suspicion that later appeared to be justified. When Curley was finally released after five months in the penitentiary, he made a sudden recovery, returned immediately to his office at City Hall, and announced to crowds of jubilant well-wishers that he was feeling better than he had felt in the past ten years.

Kennedy's attack on the American Legion in 1949 stunned his fellow Congressmen, none of whom would have dared at that time to oppose the conservative brass of the Legion in public any more than they would have spoken against J. Edgar Hoover, the Boy Scouts or Billy Graham. For two years Kennedy had been trying to organize veteran groups in a united front to support a low-cost housing bill, so urgently needed in that postwar period that even the conservative Senator Robert Taft sponsored it. But the American Legion, supporting the private real estate and construction interests, had fought against the bill all the way.

Finally Kennedy's temper boiled over one day during a debate in the House on a bonus bill, which the Legion was backing as a diversion while opposing his bill to provide Federal funds for local low-rent public housing projects. Among other heated remarks, he said in his outburst, "The leadership of the American Legion has not had a constructive thought for the benefit of this country since 1918."

A ripple of nervous shock swept through the House and various members jumped up to put themselves on the record against Kennedy's blast. John Rankin of Mississippi declared that the American Legion was the most patriotic organization in the United States. The gentle Edith Nourse Rogers, apologizing for her fellow representative from Massachusetts, reminded the members that the Kennedy family had suffered in the war. Kennedy's friends in the House rushed to him and urged him to make an immediate retraction to save his political future from ruin. He asked for the floor, but instead of retracting, he calmly denounced the Legion again for its opposition to Federal housing for veterans.

Jack went back to his office and told his assistant, Ted Reardon, what had happened. "Well, Ted, I guess we're gone," he said with a smile. "That finishes us down here." Reardon pointed out that attacking the leadership of the American Legion was not quite as bad as attacking the membership. As it turned out, Kennedy's attack against the Legion on the housing issue did him more good politically than any other single stand that he took on a legislative controversy during his six years in the House of Representatives. The public reaction was strongly in his favor; the heavy mail response, mostly from veterans, supported him ten to one.

Like the Curley petition rumpus, which did Kennedy more good outside of the Democratic party's Old Guard than harm within it, the American Legion fracas showed him that following his own instincts and taking a political risk instead of playing it safe at the showdown usually pays off in the long run and seldom brings any lasting damage. More often than not, Kennedy used to say, the right thing to do is also the right thing politically. Even the American Legion itself soon forgot his sharp slap at its leaders; he was given a warm welcome at the next state convention of the Legion in Massachusetts. Talking about the Legion dispute in later years, Kennedy remarked that if he had retracted his statement in the House, as his friends urged him to do, he would have done himself much more harm than he could have suffered by sticking to his guns. "But my friends didn't realize that at the time," he said. "And neither did I."

From the first day that he arrived in Washington to take up his freshman's seat in Congress, January 3, 1947, Jack Kennedy was determined to be his own man and nobody's protégé. He was well aware that the kind and courtly John McCormack, then the minority whip of that Republican Congress, as well as the leader of the Massachusetts Democrats and a good friend of President Truman, would have been delighted to tutor him and open doors for him on Capitol Hill. But Kennedy had decided to steer his own course. He was late, as usual, getting to Washington on that January morning from Palm Beach, where the Kennedys had spent the holidays. When Ted Reardon and Billy Sutton met him in the lobby of the Statler Hotel, after driving from Boston in a snowstorm in Eunice Kennedy's Chrysler, Jack announced that he was starving and needed breakfast. "Breakfast will have to wait," Sutton said. "John McCormack's been calling for you on the phone every ten minutes. He wants you on the Hill right away for a party caucus."

"Mr. McCormack has been getting along all right without me here in Washington for twenty-eight years," Kennedy said. "He can get along without me for another fifteen minutes. Let's go into the drugstore and get some eggs."

A few days later at the Capitol a prominent Boston Irish politician, Patrick J. ("Sonny") McDonough, a good friend of McCormack's, saw Kennedy in a corridor and said to him, "Jack, if I were you, starting in down here, I'd *marry* John McCormack. I would hang around with him, eat dinner with him a couple of nights a week, ask him questions and listen to his advice." Recalling Kennedy's reaction, McDonough says, "You know what Jack did when I told him that? He backed away from me in horror as if I had pointed a gun at him."

One of Kennedy's first moves as a freshman Congressman in the spring of 1947 was a display of independence that amused his elders. As a member of the House Labor Committee, he filed a separate report of his own opinion on the proposed Hartley labor reform bill which disagreed with both the Republican majority report and the dissenting Democratic minority report. He also annoyed McCormack, Speaker Sam Rayburn and President Truman by delivering on the floor of the House a speech against the State Department's China policy and by criticizing the administration's trade agreements and civil defense planning. He spoke out often against Truman's defense policies and budget appropriations.

Any young Congressman who tries to play the role of an active independent legislator with no close ties to his own party's leadership soon begins to feel lost and ignored in the large membership of the House of Representatives. Dave Powers remembers one day at the Kennedy family's dinner table at Hyannis Port when Jack was feeling disenchanted with his work in general and particularly depressed over his fellow Congressmen's recent disapproval of his lonely attack on the American Legion. "I feel that nobody outside of Washington pays much attention to what I'm doing down there," he said.

"People who follow Congress know what you're doing," Ambassador Kennedy said encouragingly. "And everybody knows your stand on the American Legion."

"Sometimes I wish the American Legion didn't," Jack said.

If Jack Kennedy had been happier in the House of Representatives and willing to make a career there, he could have stayed on indefinitely in the Boston-Cambridge-Somerville Eleventh Congressional District's seat; he was unopposed for reelection in 1948, and while running in 1950 for his third term against the Republican Vincent J. Celeste, he received 87,000 votes, more than the winning Democratic candidate for governor, Paul Dever, received in the district in that same election. Dave Powers and Jack often speculated on whether he could have won a race for the United States Senate against Leverett Saltonstall in 1948, the year when Truman upset Dewey. A comparatively unknown Boston politician, John I. Fitzgerald, who was not related to the Kennedys, received an astonishing 954,000 votes while running on the Democratic ticket against Saltonstall that November, and it could be assumed that in such a Democratic landslide Jack Kennedy could have done much better.

But Kennedy realized before he had finished his first two-year term in the House that the career of a Congressman was not for him. While campaigning in Massachusetts for the Democrats in the Presidential election drive of 1948, he began to plan for a statewide campaign of his own in 1952, either against the incumbent Republican Senator Henry Cabot Lodge, or for the governorship. Which of those two offices Kennedy would seek depended on the 1952 choice made by Paul Dever, the leading Democrat in Massachusetts at the time. Dever was elected as governor in 1948 and reelected in 1950. If he decided to run against Lodge for the Senate in 1952, Kennedy would be in no position to oppose him for the party's nomination. But if Dever decided not to risk a fight against the powerfully entrenched Lodge and to run for a third term as governor instead, as seemed likely, Kennedy could have the Democratic nomination for Senator. Nobody else in the party, except Dever, was able or willing to take on Lodge.

Kennedy prepared for a statewide campaign in 1952 in the characteristic hard-working Kennedy manner, spending the previous four years trying to make himself known all over the state by systematically planning speaking engagements and appearances at social events in each of the thirty-nine cities and three hundred and twelve towns. He followed a set routine every weekend, flying to Boston on Friday afternoon from Washington, driving to various civic, fraternal, political or veteran group meetings on Friday night and Saturday, appearing at Catholic communion breakfasts or Protestant church socials on Sunday and then hurrying back to Boston to catch the Federal at Back Bay Station on Sunday night and crawling into a sleeping-car berth for the trip to Washington. Dave Powers was then working as a rental director for the state's public housing authority, traveling to housing projects for veterans in eighty-eight communities. "Jack told me to let everybody know he was available as a speaker on weekends, and I talked Kennedy to the local Elks, VFW's, Amvets, Holy Name Societies and volunteer fire departments wherever I went," Dave says. "I became his booking agent. No town was too small or too Republican for him. He was willing to go anywhere, and every group was glad to have him, not only because he was an interesting political figure and a well-known war hero, but because he never charged a dime for expenses."

The speaking tours were often rough ordeals for Kennedy and the companions who traveled with him, Bob Morey from Charlestown who did most of the driving, John Galvin, Dave Powers or Frank Morrissey, who managed the Congressman's Boston office. Back in 1949 and 1950 there were no fast expressways in most of Massachusetts and few nice motels. "We usually ended up sleeping in a crummy small-town hotel, with a single electric light bulb hanging from the ceiling over the bed and a questionable bathtub down at the far end of the hall," Galvin recalls. "I remember one night watching the future President of the United States shaving at a sink in the men's room of a bowling alley at Danvers, wearing his topcoat and squinting at himself in the dirty mirror. We were hurrying from a meeting of the Loyal Order of Moose to a Knights of Columbus affair when he decided that his chin felt stubbly. I went to a drugstore for a razor and shaving cream while he found the men's room in the bowling alley which had only one water faucet with cold water in it. He was the only guy I ever knew who could shave while wearing his topcoat."

In those years Jack Kennedy's wartime spinal injury was causing him constant pain. He traveled with crutches, which he concealed in his car when he arrived at the hall where the audience was waiting. Dave would notice him gritting his teeth when he walked with a determined effort from the car to the door where the chairman or the committee members were waiting to greet him, but then when he came into the room where the crowd was gathered, he was erect and smiling, looking as fit and healthy as the light-heavyweight champion of the world. "Then after he finished his speech, and answered questions from the floor, and shook hands with every-body, we would help him into the car and he would lean back on the seat and close his eyes in pain," Dave says. "When we got to the hotel, out would come the crutches from the floor of the back seat and he would use them to get upstairs, where I would fill the bath-tub with hot water, and he would soak himself in the tub for an hour before going to bed."

The pain often made him tense and irritable with his fellow trav-elers. "You're driving with Jack at eighty miles an hour because he's already ten minutes late at the next town," Frank Morrissey once said. "A motorcycle cop chases you, and you stop and get out, and miraculously, you manage to fast-talk the cop into letting you go on. Naturally, you're feeling proud of yourself for accomplishing such a feat. A few miles farther on, you come to a railroad crossing where the red light is flashing and the bell is ringing. Jack says, 'Come on, we've got to beat that train.' So you step on it, and race to the crossing, but the locomotive gets there a few inches ahead of you, and you just miss hitting it. Jack grits his teeth in disgust. 'If you hadn't wasted so much time back there talking to that cop, we would have made it,' he says."

Dave tacked a state housing authority map of Massachusetts on the bedroom wall in the Bowdoin Street apartment where Jack stayed in Boston, and began to put colored pins on each city and town where Jack had made a speaking appearance. Jack would study the map and point to an area of the state where there were not many pins. "Dave, you've got to get me some dates around there," he would say. "When we've got this map completely covered with pins, that's when I'll announce that I'm going to run statewide."

It was during the weekend speaking tours that Kennedy began to accumulate the card index file on young people in various Massachusetts communities who impressed him favorably and who might be likely to work for him in future political campaigns. At a communion breakfast or a testimonial dinner for a high school football coach, he would jot down a name and address with a few words of comment. ("Good speaker" or "Active in electrical workers' union.") He would hand the notes to Grace Burke, the secretary in his Boston office, who typed the data on a card and filed it for future reference, along with cards on people whom he had met in his earlier Congressional campaigns or in the course of his work as a Congressman. Out of the new names and new faces in this file came the workers in the Kennedy organization in 1952, which was to be completely separate from the Paul Dever organization with its familiar older Democrat politicians. Kennedy was determined to identify himself in every city and town with younger people new to politics. As he gained more experience in politics, both in Washington and on the campaign trail in Massachusetts, his distaste for the image of the stereotyped party politician grew even stronger than it was in 1946, and he tried harder to disassociate himself from the bosses in the large hats who loudly dominated the Democratic party in those Truman years.

When President Truman came to Boston during his 1948 election campaign, a gala rally was staged in his honor at Mechanics Building with elaborate fanfare. Along with Dever, Curley, John McCormack and other Democratic Congressmen, Kennedy was to be a speaker. Each speaker was to make a grand entrance down the middle aisle through the roaring crowd with band music. Jack Kennedy squirmed at the thought of such hoopla. Instead of arriving at the hall in a limousine, surrounded by an entourage of cronies, like all of the other dignitaries, he walked to the rally from his Bowdoin Street apartment with Dave Powers. While they were crossing Boston Common, he said to Dave, "Don't you think we could find a back door where I could sneak into the building quietly? I don't want all that stuff with the spotlight playing on me and the band leading me down the aisle." Avoiding the greeters at the front door, Jack and Dave went through an alley to the back of the building where they suddenly found themselves surrounded by five Secret Service agents, who grabbed them both and brought them to Jim Rowley, the agent in charge of President Truman's protection detail. "This is Congressman Kennedy," Rowley said. "You can let him in, and I guess the fellow with him must be all right, too." The encounter in the alley behind Mechanics Building in 1948 was Rowley's first meeting with the President of the United States who appointed him Director of the U.S. Secret Service in 1961.

By the end of 1951 the map of Massachusetts on the bedroom wall in the Bowdoin Street apartment was almost completely covered with colored pins; Jack had appeared in each of the thirty-nine cities more than once and in most of the three hundred and twelve towns. In that year of 1951, as a matter of fact, he had made speaking appearances in seventy different communities. The card index file had grown enormously. But he still did not know whether he was running for the Senate or the governorship because Paul Dever, the Democratic governor, had not yet made up his mind about which office to seek. Dever was still undecided in February, 1952, when Bobby Kennedy telephoned me from New York and asked me to take a full-time job on Jack's campaign staff.

I scarcely knew Jack Kennedy at that time, although I had seen him and talked with him occasionally when I visited Bobby at Hyannis Port. Bobby and I had been close friends since we played football together at Harvard. When he was studying law at the University of Virginia and later when he became a lawyer in the Justice Department, Bobby called me on the phone once a week just to chat about things in general. He arranged for me to work with Jack because he knew I was bored with the job I had in a paper company and had been anxious for a long time to get into politics. Bobby himself had no interest whatever at that point in Jack's political situation in Massachusetts and knew nothing about it. He was deeply involved in his own work as a government lawyer, out of touch with Jack and unaware of Jack's problems.

I found myself sharing a small office at 10 Post Office Square in Boston with Mark Dalton, the Boston lawyer who had been Jack Kennedy's closest political adviser since the day he announced his candidacy for Congress in 1946. Mark was to manage the Kennedy campaign when Kennedy found out from Paul Dever what office he was to campaign for. Dalton was strongly in favor of running against Henry Cabot Lodge for the Senate. A few of the other people around Kennedy were trying to talk him into a primary fight against Dever for the governor's nomination, which would have been disastrous, but Kennedy was in no mood to oppose Dever, the strong man in the Democratic party, for either nomination; he would take the one that Dever didn't want.

Finally on April 6, Palm Sunday, Kennedy met with Dever and learned that the governor had decided to run for reelection, leaving the unenviable Senate nomination open to Kennedy. Dever told us later that private polls throughout the state showed that he had no chance against Lodge but gave Kennedy at least an even chance in that race. Jack announced his candidacy for the Senate in the next morning's newspapers, after consulting Archbishop Cushing to make sure that such an announcement would not be inappropriate on the Monday of Holy Week. The Archbishop, who was then not yet a Cardinal, roared his approval, declaring that Jack could not have picked a better day.

But during the two months after Kennedy announced that he was entering the Senatorial race, his campaign was so disorganized that it almost never got off the ground. Although he had done a splendid job of making himself known throughout the state over the previous four years, he had done nothing about forming a statewide Kennedy organization at the time when he announced his candidacy. Nobody had gone to his card index file to pick and appoint local Kennedy-for-Senator organizers in various cities and towns. Jack himself was busy with other things, apparently either reluctant to give anybody else, such as Mark Dalton, the authority to select local Kennedy managers, or "secretaries" as we later called them, or casually assuming that the rather delicate work of putting together a statewide organization was being done without his supervision. Jack did like to have things done for him without hearing about the problems and difficulties involved. But in this particular situation, Dalton was hesitant about naming a secretary in Fall River or Springfield without knowing which of the five or six prospects in those cities Jack preferred. As a newcomer to politics, whose judgment could be questioned later, I wasn't about to make such a choice, either. So nothing was being done and time was marching on.

Meanwhile, to add to the confusion, the candidate's forceful father, Ambassador Joseph P. Kennedy, was moving in strong behind the scenes. Our basic problem with Joe Kennedy, not only in 1952 but in the Presidential campaign of 1960, was that he firmly believed that Jack's political affairs should have been handled by the same type of old Democratic pols who worked for Jim Farley and

Ed Flynn on the Roosevelt campaign of 1932. The Ambassador could never quite understand why Jack avoided those veteran politicians, with their valuable experience and connections, and surrounded himself with young college graduates from the station-wagon set with no political background. If Jack had known about some of the telephone calls his father made on his behalf to Tammany-type bosses during the 1960 campaign, Jack's hair would have turned white.

During that hectic spring of 1952, the Ambassador and his political friends were trying to take over the management of the campaign, sniping at Dalton with petty complaints about the money he was spending. Dalton, a quiet and sensitive man, was unable to cope with the Ambassador. Apparently Jack Kennedy did not know what was going on, or, if he was aware of it, he did not seem to be talking to his father. Then one day during a heated argument with the Ambassador, Dalton walked out of the office. I found him later in the quiet reading room of the Boston Athenaeum, Beacon Hill's stately private library, still upset and trying to cool off. He said he was quitting his job as the campaign manager. The Ambassador was surprised when I told him that Dalton was leaving. "What's he getting so hot and bothered about?" the Ambassador said. "We were only having a conversation. I didn't mean to offend him."

Viewing the chaos around me, I decided that nobody could talk about it to the Ambassador and to Jack except another member of the Kennedy family. I went to a telephone and called Bobby in New York, where he was working for the Justice Department on a Federal tax case.

Bobby did not want to get involved. He said that he was too busy with his own work to be thinking of Jack's political problems and he particularly did not want to get into an argument with his father. "Don't drag me into it," he said. I called him again twice the next day, explaining to him once more that the campaign organization was in a mess with nobody to run it the way Jack wanted it and that Jack was doing nothing to straighten it out. Then Bobby began to get aroused. He said he would talk to his father.

I don't know what transpired between Bobby and his father, or between the Ambassador and Jack. I did not hear from Bobby until a few days later. I remember the circumstances well, because I was on the golf course at Winthrop, playing the best round of golf I ever shot in my life. I was on the ninth green, putting for a birdie, when somebody came out of the clubhouse and told me that Bobby Kennedy was on the telephone.

"There you are, playing golf," he said. "And here I am with Jack and my mother and my sisters at a big tea party with a couple of thousand women in Quincy, thanks to you. I hope you're satisfied. Get down here right away. I want you to tell Jack some of that stuff you've been telling me."

Bobby Kennedy, twenty-six years old and knowing nothing about Massachusetts politics, and not particularly caring much about politics, had given up his job in the Justice Department to manage his brother's campaign for the Senate. Those of us who worked with him over the next few months are convinced that if Bobby had not arrived on the scene and taken charge when he did, Jack Kennedy most certainly would have lost the election.

The tea party reception in Quincy, and two earlier ones in Worcester and Springfield attended by thousands of women, had been the only successful accomplishments of the campaign up to that time. When I arrived there, I could see from the expression on Jack's face that he was furious with me for talking to Bobby about our lack of a statewide organization. The reception was over, and Jack told me to ride back to Boston with him and Bobby and Bob Morey, who was driving. Frank Morrissey, the manager of Jack's Congressional office in Boston who was the Ambassador's right-hand man, and the Ambassador's right eye in the campaign, started to get into the car with us. "Get a ride with somebody else," Jack said to Morrissey. This was to be a conversation that Jack and Bobby did not want reported back to Old Joe.

"What have you been telling Bobby?" Jack said when we pulled away from the disappointed Morrissey.

"I told him I've been waiting for three months for us to get started on putting together a statewide Kennedy organization, and we haven't got one yet," I said to him. "You know we're not supposed to use Dever's people — you don't want them, and he doesn't want you to use them. You announced that you were running for the Senate the first Monday in April. Here it is the end of May, and we haven't appointed a single Kennedy chairman or organizer in any city in Massachusetts."

I realized while I was talking that this was the first time since I came to work for him that I was speaking to him about the campaign.

"You're supposed to be doing those things," Jack said. "As far as I'm concerned, you can go ahead and start naming anybody you want. That's what we hired you for. It's not my job."

Both of us were getting heated. "All right," I said. "As of tomorrow morning, we start naming chairmen of local Kennedy for Senator committees all over the state."

"I thought you were doing that all along," Jack said. "I don't know what the hell else you've been doing."

That was the supposedly smooth, efficient and powerful Kennedy political machine. Jack knew very well that no organizing had been done, because he had given nobody the authority to do it. In any case, after Bobby took over the management of the campaign, there was no more lack of administrative authority. When you wanted something done, Bobby would say to go ahead and do it and it was done, period. Even though Bobby knew nobody in Fitchburg or Fall River, and not many people in Boston, either, you could suggest to him the name of somebody as a local chairman in those towns and that man was opening a Kennedy headquarters there the next day. Under Bobby's direction, the confusion disappeared and everything fell into place. He saved the campaign and made it click.

Around the same time that Bobby arrived, Larry O'Brien joined us as an organizer, and he was another strong plus factor because he had more practical political experience than any of us. He had grown up in Democratic politics in Springfield and had worked for three years as administrative assistant to Foster Furcolo, then the Congressman in Springfield. Furcolo and O'Brien had a falling out, the details of which Larry never discussed. Furcolo was so mad at Kennedy for taking on O'Brien that he refused later to support Kennedy in western Massachusetts, which was a blow to us because Furcolo was the most prominent Italian-American Democratic politician in the state. "In return for one Irishman, I lose all the Italians," Kennedy remarked. "And I need another Irishman around here like I need a fur hat." As it turned out, O'Brien's organizational know-how was much more valuable to us than Furcolo's support.

From then on, Kennedy took a dim view of Furcolo. They had a bitter argument in 1954 when Furcolo was running against Leverett

Saltonstall for the Senate. Kennedy appeared on television with Furcolo and Bob Murphy, the Democratic candidate for governor, and endorsed Murphy and the Democratic ticket without mentioning Furcolo's name. It was probably the only wrong political move Jack Kennedy ever made, but he was in intense pain at the time — he went to the hospital for his spinal operation a few days later— and his political acumen was not hitting on its usual twelve cylinders. Rumors started circulating a report that Kennedy wanted Saltonstall instead of a Democrat as his fellow Senator. The next morning Frank Morrissey was quoted on the radio as saying that Kennedy did not want Furcolo elected. I met Morrissey at the Bowdoin Street apartment and he admitted that he had been quoted correctly. "I didn't think they would use it on the air," Morrissey said. "What do you think I ought to do now?" I opened a window and said to him, "Jump."

As the campaign manager in 1952, Bobby worked from eight in the morning until midnight. When he could not get somebody to do something, he did it himself. One day he decided that he wanted a huge Kennedy-for-Senator poster on the side of a building where it could be seen by everybody crossing the heavily traveled bridge between Charlestown and the North End of Boston. The longest ladder that could be found would not reach the high place on the building where Bobby wanted the sign. "Drive me over there, Dave," he said to Powers. "I'll put up the sign myself." To reach the height where he wanted to nail the sign to the building, Bobby had to balance himself on the top rung of the long ladder. "While I was holding the ladder," Dave says, "I was wondering how I could explain it to the Ambassador and Jack when Bobby fell and broke his neck. I also said to myself, if I had his money I would be sitting at home in a rocking chair instead of being up there on the top of that ladder."

With Bobby in charge of the campaign, Ambassador Kennedy was content to remain in the background where he played a valuable role trying to keep a peaceful relationship between his two sons and the Democratic politicians in Governor Dever's campaign organizations. The Ambassador and Dever were old friends who understood each other and spoke the same language. Bobby did not endear himself to Dever's Boston Irish political hangers-on. Seeing them sitting around and reminiscing at the Kennedy headquarters on Kilby Street in Boston, he was likely to ask them to address envelopes. "All they want to do is talk and give you advice and pose for pictures," he said. A prominent Boston politician, who had once campaigned for mayor by singing "Danny Boy" from a sound truck, paid a call to the Kilby Street offices and was astounded to discover that nobody in the headquarters, including Bobby, knew who he was. "You mean to say you don't know me?" he shouted. "And you call this a political headquarters?" Annoyed because the political celebrity was using profane language in the presence of several girl volunteer workers, Bobby threw him out.

In the spring when Kennedy and Dever planned their respective campaigns, it was agreed that each candidate would work separately with his own statewide organization, except in Suffolk County, the City of Boston, and Chelsea, Winthrop and Revere, where the Democrats would make a joint effort. Kennedy, of course, was anxious to have his own organization of new and younger people, not closely identified with the old Democratic organization, which was solidly behind Dever. Dever and his associates were also eager to avoid being involved in Kennedy's campaign against Lodge. They thought that Lodge would be the winner and they regarded Kennedy's followers as inept and inexperienced, likely to be a hindrance to their fight to retain Dever in the governorship. So it was decided that the two organizations would have not only separate groups of workers, but separate campaign headquarters in every city and town except Boston, where John E. Powers, the Democrat leader of the state senate, would direct both the Senatorial and gubernatorial campaigns. This was the first campaign for the U.S. Senate, incidentally, in which the candidate had a statewide organization with headquarters of his own in the various cities and towns. Previous Senatorial campaigns in Massachusetts were managed from a single headquarters in Boston.

During the summer and early fall, when the Kennedy organization was functioning smoothly and drawing strong support from people who had not been previously involved in Democratic politics, the Dever people began to wonder if the separation of the campaigns was working to their disadvantage. Dever's stock fell badly after a disastrous appearance on television as the keynote speaker at the Democratic National Convention; he lost his voice and spoke in a hoarse whisper, while the television cameras showed the bored delegates in the audience talking among themselves and reading newspapers. Then in the September primary voting, Kennedy ran far ahead of Dever. Although they were both unopposed, Kennedy drew 75 percent of the total primary vote while Dever, the party leader, received 60 percent. The heavily Republican press in Massachusetts, which was against Dever, played up Kennedy's bigger vote. At the same time it was becoming obvious that Dwight Eisenhower, as the favored Republican candidate in the Presidential election of 1952, was sure to carry Massachusetts and might carry the rest of the Republican ticket into office with him, including Christian Herter, who was opposing Dever for the governorship.

Dever's organization panicked, and tried to move into the local Kennedy headquarters in several cities, hoping to change the Kennedy movement to a Kennedy-Dever campaign so that the governor might be reelected on the Congressman's coattails. Two days after the primary, without a word to any of us in Boston, the Dever people in Fall River sent a truck to our headquarters there with a huge Dever sign that they planned to put up on our building. Our man in Fall River phoned me and said, "They've got a picture of Dever as big as City Hall and they want to turn our headquarters into a Dever headquarters. It will blow our whole operation. A lot of our people say they won't work in the same office with them." I told him to send the Dever people away. The same thing happened in other cities.

Ambassador Kennedy called Bobby and told him to let the Dever organization work with us, arguing that we could not fight Dever and risk a split in the party ranks. We decided to stand fast to our original plan of a separate organization and to keep the Dever people out of our headquarters. Bobby called his father, battled with him, and then called Jack, who agreed with us totally. "Don't give in to them," Jack said, "but don't get me involved in it. Treat it as an organizational problem." Bobby went to Dever and told him flatly that there would be no joint Kennedy-Dever headquarters outside of Boston. Dever was furious with Bobby, and so was the Ambassador, but Bobby stuck to his guns and his decision stood firm. Thanks to the Ambassador's efforts, there was no open warfare between Dever and the Kennedy brothers, but the governor sent out word that he would deal with our organization only through the candidate's father. "Keep that young kid out of here," he said about Bobby.

Late one night at the Kilby Street headquarters, when Bobby was allowing Dave and me to have our first beer of the evening, after checking to make sure that the door was locked, Dave remarked that Bobby was not too popular with the Democratic pols in Boston. "I don't care if anybody around here likes me, as long as they like Jack," Bobby said. Bobby's insistence on keeping the Kennedy campaign separate and independent from the regular Democratic state organization over his father's objections was the thing that gave Jack an image of his own, different from the rest of the losing Democratic ticket in that Eisenhower year.

Kennedy's surprising survival in that 1952 nationwide Republican landslide is too often lightly described as a tea-party victory. He became very tired of hearing himself introduced at dinners for years afterwards as "the man who drowned Henry Cabot Lodge in seventy-five thousand cups of tea." The tea party receptions were indeed very effective. Many of the seventy-five thousand women who turned out in their best dresses to get a look at the charming Congressman and his mother and sisters became devoted Kennedy workers. Polly Fitzgerald and Helen Keyes, the girls who staged the tea receptions, were quick to point out to us after the election that Kennedy's majority over Lodge, 70,737 votes, was almost the same figure as the number of ladies attending their thirty-five parties. Even in the low-brow Irish stronghold of South Boston, where Bobby was warned by local politicians that such a "highfaluting" social event would be a big mistake, the tea reception was a smash hit. But the teas were only a small part of the campaign work and careful planning that went into our hard-earned defeat of Lodge, a candidate who had everything going for him.

Lodge's big advantage, of course, was his close identification with Eisenhower, the popular political personality of that election year. Lodge had persuaded Eisenhower to leave the NATO command and run for President, and Lodge had led the fight against Senator Robert Taft for Eisenhower's nomination at the Republican National Convention. There was a theory that Lodge's opposition to Taft might have cost him some conservative votes in Massachusetts, but this was a ridiculous argument. Eisenhower was much more popular than Taft in Massachusetts. People were saying, "What's the point in electing Kennedy to the Senate, as good as he is, when we are going to have a Republican President, Eisenhower, in the White House? Eisenhower will make Lodge the majority leader in the Senate." On the other hand, Adlai Stevenson, the Democratic Presidential candidate, did nothing for us. Stevenson was not popular among the Democrats in the state. When he slipped badly late in the campaign, Kennedy and Dever both slipped with him. We figured that we lost 100,000 votes in the last few days before the election when Eisenhower made his final campaign appearance in Boston and delivered a strong plea for Lodge.

Lodge's mistake, of course, was underestimating Kennedy and spending too much time that summer promoting Eisenhower instead of working on his own campaign at home. He predicted that he would win by 300,000 votes and sent word to Ambassador Kennedy, through their mutual friend Arthur Krock of the *New York Times*, that Jack's campaign would be a waste of money. Dave Powers likes to recall the day in July when he delivered to the State House ten thousand sheets of Kennedy nomination papers with 262,324 signatures from all over the state, the greatest number of nominating signatures ever collected by a candidate for elective office. Only 2,500 names are required by law. Senator Lodge's son, George Lodge, then a reporter for the *Boston Herald*, was at the State House covering the filing of the papers. He stared at the bales of signed nominations, an incredible sight to anybody familiar with politics, and ran his hand over them as if he doubted that they were real. "I could see from the expression on George's face what he was thinking," Dave says. "Here it is, only the twenty-eighth of July. They've done all this work and my father hasn't even started yet."

Each of the 262,324 people who signed Kennedy's nomination papers received a personal thank-you letter from him later. We were learning that the worst mistake you can make in running a political campaign is to gather a crowd of enthusiastic supporters who are eager to help the candidate and not give them any work to do. To keep up their interest and enthusiasm, they must have something to do. Sending out thank-you letters, Dave's idea, served that purpose, just as later in the campaign we had teams of workers delivering Kennedy literature from door to door by hand instead of sending it through the mail. Jack Kennedy was dubious about the mailing of 262,324 thank-you letters. "This will cost us a lot of money," he complained. One evening when he was in Charlestown with Dave, he stopped to visit Matty Loftus, the proprietor of Dave's favorite neighborhood tavern, who had been an enthusiastic Kennedy supporter in 1946. A longshoreman at the bar shook Kennedy's hand warmly and showed him a thank-you letter which he was carrying in the pocket of his denim work shirt.

"I've been signing nomination papers for politicians around here for the last twenty years," the dock worker said. "You're the first son of a bitch who ever wrote me a letter thanking me for it."

Jack and Dave went out of the saloon and walked down the street for a few blocks. "Dave," the Congressman said, "maybe you better keep on sending out those thank-you letters."

Lodge was hard to attack on issues. We were unable to find any vote of his on any particular issue that really irritated us; in fact, it was often difficult to figure out where he stood on several controversial questions. The two candidates had a face-to-face confrontation only once in the campaign, at a debate in Waltham in October staged by the ladies of the League of Women Voters. The debate was very similar to Kennedy's first debate against Richard Nixon in 1960 — against the more experienced and distinguished-looking Yankee blue blood who had been in the Senate for twelve years, the younger Irishman was quicker, smarter, more sure of himself. You could feel the air going out of the Lodge people in the audience. I stood backstage watching Lodge nervously squeezing and flexing his hands behind his back, and I imagined him thinking, "Why did I have to get a Democrat like this fellow?" We were expecting a planted question from the audience on aid to Israel. The Lodge people had been circulating in the Jewish neighborhoods of Boston and Brookline an exaggerated story about Kennedy voting in Congress against funds for Israel. (Actually he had voted against aid to the entire Middle East, including the Arab nations.) When the question came, from a youngster who had obviously memorized it, Kennedy knocked it out of the ball park with a flash of humor that left the audience laughing and applauding. Lodge left the hall alone after the debate while a crowd of people gathered around Kennedy, congratulating him and shaking his hand.

But generally speaking the voters in that election were not interested in issues. Kennedy won on his personality — apparently he was the new kind of political figure that the people were looking for that year, dignified and gentlemanly and well-educated and intelligent, without the air of superior condescension that other cultured politicians, such as Lodge and Adlai Stevenson, too often displayed before audiences. I remember my mother listening to him give a talk on Southeast Asia and hanging on every word that he said. I asked her if she understood what he was talking about. "No," she said. "But he talks so nicely." My Irish father, who disagreed with the Congressman on most issues, heard him give a speech in Worcester and said later, "That's a very classy boy." Dever would put on a show of derisive oratory in the Curley manner, getting a laugh by referring to his opponent, Christian Herter, as "Christian *Archibald* Herter." Kennedy would never resort to that. His air of respectability and good manners was such a novelty in the arena of Democratic party politics that it was almost a sensation.

A factor as decisive in Kennedy's win as his personality was the four years of travel throughout the state which made him and his personality known everywhere. Larry O'Brien and I were amazed during the campaign to find so many non-political-minded people in such out-of-the-way towns as Webster and Palmer who not only had shaken hands with Kennedy back in 1949 or 1950 but had also discussed Korea and Indo-China with him over a cup of coffee.

Eisenhower's strong support of Lodge made the vote so close that as late as midnight on election night the television and radio commentators were naming Lodge as the winner. Kennedy was so calmly sure of himself that night, however, that he remarked to his Harvard friend Torbert Macdonald, "I wonder what kind of a job Eisenhower will give Lodge." Eisenhower carried Massachusetts by 208,800 votes, a much bigger majority than the Democrats expected. As the heavy Eisenhower returns were reported in the early hours of the morning, most of the politicians assumed that he would carry Lodge into office with him. Around two o'clock the well-wishers who had crowded our headquarters earlier in the evening had all drifted away and the place was almost empty, except for the Congressman and Bobby and a few others. Then the word spread that Kennedy was holding his own. At five o'clock the headquarters began to fill up with people, cheerful faces that we had seldom seen during the campaign. Photographers appeared, and the new Kennedy admirers struggled to get into pictures with the candidate as the flashbulbs popped. Lodge's headquarters was directly across the street from our offices. At seven-twenty-five the watchers at our windows saw Lodge coming out of his headquarters, getting into his car and driving away, and a few minutes later Bobby was standing on top of a desk reading Lodge's telegram of congratulations to the cheering mob. All of us were so exhausted that the victory party was postponed until the following night. It wasn't until later in the day that we learned that Herter had beaten Dever for the governorship by 14,456 votes.

Jack Kennedy was happy to be leaving the House of Representatives, where he felt that seeking a course of advancement as a Congressman under the guidance of such party leaders as John McCormack and Sam Rayburn did not fit his style. Too independent and too impatient to serve such an apprenticeship, he was glad to give his seat as the Eleventh District's representative to a newly elected successor, Thomas P. O'Neill, Jr., of Cambridge, better known as "Tip" O'Neill, a former Speaker of the House in the Massachusetts legislature, who seemed to Kennedy more capable of establishing a successful career as a Congressman. O'Neill went on to prominence on the Hill, as Kennedy expected, and is now the Democratic party's whip in the House. On the day when Kennedy was moving out of his office in the House Office Building and O'Neill was moving into it, the Senator-elect said to the new Congressman, "Tip, don't do what I did down here in Washington. Be nice to John McCormack."

O'Neill passed on Kennedy's interesting piece of advice to McCormack, who beamed with pleasure and surprise and said, "Did *he* say that? Did that young man say that?" Some years later, in a discussion about the relationship between Kennedy and McCormack, always a topic of interest among Democratic politicians, O'Neill related the story to one of Kennedy's journalist friends. The next time the friend found himself alone with Kennedy, he said to the Senator, "Did you tell Tip O'Neill not to do what you did when you were in the House, and that he should be nice to John McCormack?"

Kennedy smiled.

"That's exactly what I told him," he said. "But you must remember that the thing I think Tip O'Neill should do in Washington isn't necessarily the thing that would have been right for me to do in Washington."

FOUR

Onions Burke and the
1956 Convention

DURING THE SENATORIAL CAMPAIGN in 1952, the Congressman, as we then called our candidate, was carrying on another intensive campaign of his own in Washington with Jacqueline Bouvier, but none of us who were working with him in Massachusetts knew about it at the time. Jack Kennedy kept his personal affairs, his various friendships, his political activities, and other interests in separate compartments; when he was with Dave Powers, Larry O'Brien and me, he talked Massachusetts politics and very little else — he seldom mentioned his social and political life in Washington, his family, his health problems or his wartime experiences. Getting to know him intimately was not easy. There were many parts of him, many of his private opinions, emotional feelings and intellectual convictions, that he never revealed to anybody. Unlike Bobby, who was making close friends up until the time of his death, Jack's close personal friends during the last ten years of his life were all old friends whom he knew in the 1930s and 1940s — Lem Billings, Torbert Macdonald, Dave Powers, Red Fay, Chuck Spalding, Ben Smith, David Ormsby-Gore. I worked with him for almost ten years, on three election campaigns and then as his assistant in the White House, before I began to feel a relationship of complete trust and understanding between us.

Dave Powers picked up the first inkling that the Senator was seriously considering marriage one day in the spring of 1953 when Jack said to him, "Do you think there is really much of a problem in getting married to a girl twelve years younger than you are?" Dave pointed out that his own wife, Jo, was twelve years younger than her husband. Kennedy beamed and said, "You two get along fine, don't you?" A few weeks later when the Senator came to Boston to keep a Memorial Day speaking engagement, he lunched on cream of chicken soup in the Powers kitchen and showed Jo and Dave a picture of Jackie. He told them that the announcement of the engagement had to be delayed, somewhat to Jackie's annoyance, until after June 13, because the *Saturday Evening Post* of that date had an article entitled, "Jack Kennedy: The Senate's Gay Young Bachelor." That summer when Jackie paid her first visit to Hyannis Port, looking forward to a weekend of sailing with Jack, she found a third sailor in the boat, a photographer from *Life* who was doing a picture story on their courtship.

We presented to Jack an oil painting reproduction of the cover of that issue of *Life*, a picture of him and Jackie in their sailboat, at a bachelor party in the Parker House in Boston a few days before their Newport wedding. The party was a happy reunion of all the secretaries in the Massachusetts cities and towns who organized the local Kennedy committees in the 1952 campaign. There was a great deal of kidding during the evening about Jack's selection of a bride with French ancestry, which we claimed was politically motivated. Compared to Lodge, who traveled with a well-known French Canadian priest from Lowell in his entourage, we were weak in the French communities. The wedding reception at Hammersmith Farm, the Auchincloss estate at Newport overlooking Narragansett Bay, was one of those dream-perfect parties that you seldom see in real life — a lovely bride and a handsome bridegroom, a gorgeous seaside setting, more than twelve hundred distinguished guests, happy dance music, flowing champagne. The Senator made a huge fuss over each of our wives when they came to him in the reception line, introducing them to Jackie and telling her that without their husbands he would never have been elected. From that day on, Jack Kennedy could do no wrong in our wives' eyes — which, of course, was what he had in mind at the time. After a honeymoon at Acapulco, where Jack caught a massive sailfish that he proudly hung on the wall of his Senator's office and later brought with him to the White House, they moved into the late Justice Robert Jackson's big and handsome Georgian Colonial brick house at Hickory Hill in McLean, Virginia, where they looked forward to having a large family.

But after this bright beginning the first year of their marriage, 1954, turned out to be the unhappiest year of their life together. Jackie suffered a miscarriage and learned that carrying and delivering a child would always be difficult for her. Jack's spinal injury became almost unbearably painful, forcing him to use crutches constantly. He hated being seen on crutches more than he hated the pain. On top of his physical trouble, he was harassed by political trouble both in the Senate and back in Massachusetts. It was the year of the prolonged Army-McCarthy hearings when the Senate was facing a jittery showdown on the question of whether it should censure its troublesome member from Wisconsin. Any stand taken by Kennedy on the Joe McCarthy issue would be blasted in Boston, either by the Harvard liberals, whose respect he valued, or by the ferocious Irish Catholics. As Paul Dever remarked at the time, "Joe McCarthy is the only man I know who could beat Archbishop Cushing in a two-man election fight in South Boston." South Boston was Archbishop Cushing's birthplace.

At the same time Kennedy was being damned by Democrats and Republicans alike in Massachusetts for favoring President Eisenhower's proposal to develop the Saint Lawrence Seaway, which would bring ocean shipping through the Great Lakes to Chicago, bypassing such East coast ports as Boston. Kennedy was the only Massachusetts member of Congress who voted for the Seaway. His thoughtful and courageous stand on the issue against the overwhelming opposition of his constituents was applauded by such distinguished Senators as New York's Herbert Lehman, but the Boston newspapers accused him of "ruining New England." He was also openly charged with supporting the Seaway to benefit his father's Merchandise Mart in Chicago. The labor unions in Boston, particularly the longshoremen who had been his strongest supporters, turned against him violently. One night when Dave Powers and I were having a drink at Matty Loftus's Horseshoe Tavern in Charlestown, Powers graciously handed over to me the task of defending Kennedy's position on the Seaway against the arguments of the assembled dock workers in the saloon. During the course of the discussion, I almost had my head pushed through the bar. While he was embroiled in the McCarthy and the Seaway controversies, Kennedy was being attacked by Democratic politicians in Massachusetts for his lukewarm attitude toward Foster Furcolo, the party's candidate against Leverett Saltonstall in that year's Senate fight. At a time when he was painfully crippled and unable to move without crutches, his political popularity was never lower.

Kennedy told me then that his personal position on the McCarthy issue was complicated by the well-known fact that his brother Bobby had worked for McCarthy in 1953. After the 1952 campaign, Larry O'Brien and I were both distressed when we realized that our excellent Kennedy organization, with its enthusiastic workers in every Massachusetts city and town, would probably never be put to any good political use again until the Senator ran for reelection in 1958. That was six long years away, long enough for the organization to fall apart. I wondered why the Kennedy people could not be held together by putting them to work for Kennedy-sponsored statewide candidates in the elections of 1954 and 1956. I also frowned on the thought of Bobby Kennedy leaving Massachusetts, where he had built up considerable popularity as Jack's campaign manager, and tried to talk him into running for governor or for attorney general in 1954. But Bobby was not particularly enchanted by the idea. Although he was a great political campaign organizer, he did not care much for politics. In fact, I don't think that Bobby ever really acquired a taste for politics and political campaigning until he became involved in the Presidential primaries as a candidate himself in 1968, just before his death. So Bobby turned a deaf ear on my pleas, and went back to his lawyer's job in the Justice Department. A few months later he joined the McCarthy subcommittee as a counsel, working under Roy Cohn but mostly directly with McCarthy himself on one of the more worthwhile investigations conducted by the Senator — the exposure of shipping companies in United Nations countries receiving American financial aid that were transporting supplies and Communist troops to Red China during the Korean War.

Bobby soon left the McCarthy office because he could not endure working with Roy Cohn, who assumed more authority on the subcommittee than McCarthy himself. In the winter of 1954 he returned, not to work for McCarthy and Cohn, but as counsel for the subcommittee's Democratic minority who fought against McCarthy during the televised hearings on the Senator's battle with the Army, which charged that McCarthy and Cohn had tried to use their authority as Senate investigators to get preferential treatment for their soldier friend, Private G. David Schine. There was not much doubt about where Bobby stood on the McCarthy issue during the 1954 hearings; he and Cohn almost came to blows one day before the nationwide television audience watching the proceedings. But the fact remained that Bobby had indeed been closely associated with McCarthy and Cohn a year earlier. "How could I demand that Joe McCarthy be censured for things he did when my own brother was on his staff?" Jack Kennedy said. Actually, Jack had been strongly opposed to Bobby joining McCarthy's staff in 1953 but his father, who was friendly with McCarthy, was all for it.

Nevertheless, Jack decided to make a speech on the Senate floor in favor of the censure motion, but for a different and more limited reason than the broad disapproval of McCarthy's Red-hunting methods stated in the resolution under debate. Kennedy made it clear in his speech, which was written but never delivered, that he was for confining the censure action specifically to McCarthy's abuse of Senatorial privileges in allowing and supporting Roy Cohn's threats of reprisals against the Army to get preferential treatment for Schine. But the Senate voted to curtail further debate on the question before Kennedy had a chance to give his speech. When the McCarthy censure motion finally came up for a vote in the Senate on December 2, 1954, Kennedy was in the Hospital for Special Surgery in New York, fighting to recover from infection after a spinal fusion operation that almost took his life.

Strangely enough, although Kennedy was at the point of death when the censure vote was taken, and unconscious or too ill during the previous five weeks to be told what was going on in the Senate, he was often accused in later years of deliberately avoiding casting a vote against McCarthy. His opponents, notably Eleanor Roosevelt, claimed that despite his serious illness he could have put himself on the record for or against the censure. That charge was so unfair that it was ridiculous; everybody in the Senate knew that Kennedy had been planning to vote for the McCarthy censure. None of the Democrats voted against it — the one-sided count was sixty-seven to twenty-two with only a few Republicans supporting McCarthy. Kennedy most certainly would not have been the only Senator in his party to take a stand in favor of McCarthy, who had stopped speaking to Jack after Kennedy voted that year against McCarthy on several of the Wisconsin Senator's pet issues. Among other things, Kennedy had ignored a personal plea from McCarthy and voted for confirmation of Harvard's James B. Conant as Ambassador to West Germany. McCarthy had accused Conant of harboring Reds on the faculty at Harvard. Kennedy fought continually against McCarthy while serving on his Government Operations Committee and stopped his henchman, Owen Brewster, from becoming the committee's counsel. Kennedy also infuriated McCarthy by supporting the appointment of Charles Bohlen as Ambassador to the Soviet Union and by blocking McCarthy's friend Robert Lee from the Federal Communications Commission. Even Kennedy's fellow Senator from Massachusetts, Leverett Saltonstall, with his November reelection safely behind him, voted for the censure of McCarthy.

Later on, after he recovered his health, Kennedy might have tried to save some face by issuing a statement approving the censure of McCarthy, but that was not Kennedy. As he told us at the time, McCarthyism was then dead and McCarthy was finished. "If I had made a big thing about giving McCarthy an extra kick after he was censured," he said, "I would have looked cheap."

All of that summer of 1954, when he was forced to sit on the sidelines with his despised crutches, watching, instead of playing in, the touch football and baseball games at Hyannis Port, Jack argued with his doctors about whether he should undergo the spinal fusion surgery. His only hope of getting relief from pain was a removal of the metal disc that had been placed in his spine by Navy surgeons in 1944 and a remending of the separated vertebrae. The Kennedy family's physician, Dr. Sara Jordan, and her colleagues at Boston's Lahey Clinic were opposed to such an operation, or any kind of an operation, because he was suffering from an adrenal insufficiency, which increases the possibility of shock and infection during surgery. He was warned that his chances of surviving the operation were no better than fifty-fifty. He was determined to take the risk. Pounding his fist on his crutches, he said, "I'd rather be dead than spend the rest of my life on these things."

He entered the Hospital for Special Surgery in New York where he went through a long and difficult operation on October 21. As expected, infection set in, and twice during the next month he was so close to death that his family was summoned and he was given the last rites of his church. Then he rallied, and on December 20 with Jackie at his side he was taken to a plane on a stretcher and flown to the Kennedy home at Palm Beach for the Christmas holidays, with the hope that he might improve in those pleasant surroundings. But within a month he was back in the same hospital again, undergoing a second operation, which was more successful. Late in February, Ambassador Kennedy called Dave Powers and asked him to come to the hospital and to fly to Palm Beach with Jack, Jackie and Ted. Before Jack was taken from the hospital, Dave watched the dressing on the surgical wound being changed. "He had a hole in his back big enough for me to put my fist in it up to the wrist," Dave says.

Dave spent the next five weeks at the Palm Beach waterfront home with Jack and Jackie. "He never said one word about what he went through at the hospital," Dave says. "He was in constant pain all the time I was there, unable to sleep for more than an hour or two at a time, but he never complained about the pain, never mentioned it. The Ambassador, who was there with us all the time, would say to me often, 'Dave, don't try to give him anything for the pain — it's something he has to go through.' I suppose he was afraid I might try to slip him a dose of sedative or a drink of whiskey. Jackie was with him all day and all night. He was in a room off the patio beside the swimming pool, and she had a room next to it, but it seemed as though she never went to bed. We would beg her to go out beside the pool to get a little sun. Jack would say, 'Dave is here if I need anything.' But she seldom left his bedside. Every Thursday, the cook's day off, the Ambassador would go into the kitchen and make a terrific lamb stew for our dinner."

When the Senator arrived at Palm Beach, Dave noticed that his room was crowded with several cartons of books from the Library of Congress. Back in January, before he returned to New York for the second operation, he had worked to pass the time in bed on a magazine article on political courage which he had been thinking about for more than a year. The idea for the article first came to him when he became interested in John Quincy Adams, who lost his seat as a Senator from Massachusetts because he took a brave and lonely stand against his own pro-British Federalist party and against the merchants and working people of New England by supporting President Thomas Jefferson's Embargo Act. Early in 1954, when Kennedy himself was being attacked by Boston newspapers and business interests for his own unpopular support of the Saint Lawrence Seaway, he began to collect material on other political figures who defied pressure from their constituents on unpopular issues — George W. Norris, Daniel Webster, Sam Houston, Lucius Lamar, Thomas Hart Benton, Edmund G. Ross, and Robert Taft, whose opposition to the Nuremberg Trials cost him the Republican Presidential nomination in 1948. When Kennedy returned to Palm Beach for his long convalescence after the second spinal operation in February, he decided to expand the magazine article into a book, which became his Pulitzer Prize–winning *Profiles in Courage*. The plan for the book that he had in mind called for an enormous amount of reading and research, because he wanted to include in it not only biographical sketches of the eight political figures he selected to illustrate his theme and detailed accounts of the crises in which they stood up for their principles against popular disapproval, but a full picture of the background and the mood of the time when each incident took place.

Unable to sleep for more than an hour or two at a stretch, Jack worked on the book day and night, reading, and writing notes and then drafts of the chapters on long yellow legal pads. He clung to the research work doggedly, keeping his mind on it to distract himself from his pain. When he was too tired to write or read, Jackie and Dave read to him. "I would be reading to him from a book about Texas in Sam Houston's time, and he would be stretched out flat on his back with his eyes closed for a couple of hours, listening to every word I said," Dave says. "I would think he had fallen asleep, and I'd stop reading. He would open his eyes and tell me to keep going. When I came to a line that he liked, he would stop me and tell me to read it again. I remember reading to him Sam Houston's farewell speech in the Senate after the Texas Legislature kicked him out of office for refusing to repeal the Missouri Compromise. When I came to Houston saying, 'I wish no prouder epitaph to mark the board or slab that may lie on my tomb than this: "He loved his country, he was a patriot; he was devoted to the Union." If it was for this that I have suffered martyrdom, it is sufficient that I stand at quits with those who have wielded the sacrificial knife,' Jack was delighted. He loved those words, and he repeated them over and over."

Early in March, about a week after his return to Palm Beach, Jack was able to get out of his bed and walk without his crutches for a distance of fifty feet from his room to a chair on the patio outside beside the pool with Jackie and Dave beside him. "You never saw anybody more pleased," Dave says. "Then, the next day, he walked all the way from the pool across the lawn to the beach and down to the edge of the water. He stood there, feeling the warm salt water on his bare feet, and broke into a big smile. The Ambassador was watching us from a window when Jack walked back to the house, leaning on Jackie and me. The Ambassador said to me later when we were eating lunch, 'God, Dave, he's getting stronger all the time. Did you see the legs on him? He's got the legs of a fighter or a swimming champion.' Then the Ambassador said, and I often thought of it later, 'I know nothing can happen to him now, because I've stood by his deathbed three times and each time I said good-bye to him, and each time he came back stronger.' "

On May 23, 1955, seven months after his first spinal surgery in New York, Kennedy arrived back in Washington from Palm Beach. He waved aside the crutches and the wheelchair that were waiting for him at the airport, went to the Capitol to pose for newspaper and television cameramen, and then walked unaided from the Capitol to his office in the Senate Office Building. The next day he was on the floor of the Senate, getting a big welcome from the two party leaders, Lyndon Johnson and William Knowland, and voting for an increase in pay for postal workers over President Eisenhower's veto. Determined to show everybody how well he was feeling, Jack plunged into a busy schedule, went back to Boston for a Jackson-Jefferson Day dinner, where he made peace with Foster Furcolo, and entertained the whole state legislature at a clambake at Hyannis Port. That fall, on a trip to Europe, he strained his back, and was furious when he was forced to use crutches in public again for a short time.

For the remaining eight years of his life, he was never completely free from pain but never again as crippled as he was in 1954 before the two spinal fusion operations. In his later years as a Senator and after he became President, Dr. Janet Travell and White House physician Admiral George Burkley gave him periodic injections of Novocain, which deadened his back pains. The Novocain injections relieved his discomfort but brought no real improvement to the muscular condition that was causing it. In 1963 he began calisthenics to strengthen his back muscles. This treatment worked so well that he announced to us on the day that he went to Dallas, of all days, that his back was feeling well for the first time in many years.

Kennedy's history of adrenal insufficiency, which made his spinal surgery dangerous, started reports when he was running for the Presidency that he was suffering from Addison's disease, a tubercular breakdown of the adrenal gland. The outstanding symptoms of Addison's disease are weakness and easy fatigue, so the rumor was demolished by Kennedy's obviously tireless energy and stamina which wore out everybody following him on an average eighteen-hour day of campaigning. But up until the 1960 Democratic convention rival candidates did their best to keep the myth of his illness in circulation, much to Jack's irritation. In the spring of 1959, during a weekend speaking tour in California, he had his first private meeting with Governor Pat Brown. Brown was hoping for a place on the 1960 ticket himself, possibly as a Vice-Presidential candidate paired with Lyndon Johnson. As a Catholic, he could hardly expect to benefit from Kennedy's nomination. We asked Jack later how he had gotten along with Brown. Jack sighed and said, "Do you know the first thing he said to me when we were alone? Here's a fellow I never met before in my whole life, and I am sitting down to have breakfast with him, just the two of us in the room, and he looks at me and the first thing that comes out of his mouth is, 'I understand you've got Addison's disease.' "

Some of Kennedy's liberal critics tried to contend later that he wrote *Profiles in Courage* as a sort of act of contrition for his own failure to take a more outspoken stand against Senator Joe McCarthy. That is not much of a theory because Kennedy felt no guilt about his position on McCarthy. His failure to vote on McCarthy's censure was not his fault, and he gave McCarthy more trouble and more opposition during the short time he and McCarthy served together in the Senate than most of his fellow Democrats did. But there was a noticeable change in Jack Kennedy after his serious illness and long convalescence. The months that he spent in bed, reflecting on his own role in politics and studying the courage of great men in political history, made him deeper, stronger, and more intellectually and emotionally mature and secure. The Jack Kennedy who went into the pits and fought Onions Burke and Congressman John McCormack for the leadership and control of the Democratic organization in Massachusetts in 1956 was much tougher and more sure of himself than the charming young Senatorial candidate of 1952.

Those of us who were closely associated with Kennedy regard his fight with Burke and McCormack as his coming of age as a party politician and a turning point in his career as decisive as the Presidential primary victory in West Virginia in 1960. If Kennedy had not gained control of the Democratic party in Massachusetts in the spring of 1956 by personally ousting Burke, McCormack's man, from the chairmanship of the party's state committee, McCormack would have gone to that summer's Democratic National Convention in Chicago as the leader of the Massachusetts delegation. Kennedy would have been just another delegate on the floor. Instead, Kennedy arrived in Chicago as a new figure of stature in the party because he had beaten the Old Guard's John McCormack, a crony of Harry Truman and Sam Rayburn, in a power struggle in McCormack's own state. Kennedy was sought after as a speaker at luncheons and delegation meetings and invited by Adlai Stevenson, the Presidential nominee, to give the principal speech of nomination for Stevenson. He became so popular that he almost won the Vice-Presidential nomination and was talked up as the next Presidential choice in 1960. This rise to national prominence at the 1956 convention was entirely due to his hard fight against an onion farmer back in Massachusetts a few months earlier.

William H. Burke, the onion farmer from Hatfield in the Connecticut River Valley, had been more involved for many years in Democratic party politics than in agriculture. Onions Burke, as he was called, was a good friend of James M. Curley and a tough and loud pol of the Curley type, big, bald-headed and flashy. He was devoted to John McCormack, who had secured for him the Federal appointment as Collector of the Port of Boston during the Roosevelt and Truman administrations. In 1955, Burke engineered a move to give McCormack control of the state's official Democratic organization, which had been controlled by Paul Dever up to that time. Dever's influence had declined since he was defeated for reelection as governor in 1952 and had later suffered a heart attack which discouraged him from running again for office. Burke managed to get himself elected as chairman of the state's Democratic committee, the governing body of the party organization, replacing John Carr, Dever's man in that position. Dever was not inclined to hand over the party leadership to McCormack; even though he was no longer interested in running for office himself, he wanted to hold onto the prestige and power of being the Democratic boss in the state. He appealed to Jack Kennedy for help, but Kennedy at that time was not anxious to oppose McCormack in an intraparty battle as much as he disliked Onions Burke being the chairman of the state committee.

Meanwhile we were eyeing the leadership vacuum in the state organization that was being created by Dever's waning influence. Ever since our successful campaign in 1952, we had been trying to persuade Kennedy to move in and take over the state organization and to fill it with our own people who had worked so well independently from the regular party machinery of Dever in the battle against Henry Cabot Lodge. We saw no reason why we should sit back and let McCormack and Onions Burke and Burke's eager friends take over the party in Massachusetts, especially when there were so many available older Democratic politicians in Dever's following who did not care for McCormack and Burke but quietly idolized Kennedy. While we were pointing this opportunity out to Kennedy, and while he was listening to us with growing interest, his father and some of his friends in Washington were strongly advising him to keep out of the Irish fight for control of the party in Massachusetts. "Leave it alone and don't get into the gutter with those bums up there in Boston," the Ambassador was saying to him. "Don't listen to O'Brien and O'Donnell — they're only trying to feather their own nest." Which, of course, was partly true.

Without consulting Kennedy or getting his approval, O'Brien and I began to line up Kennedy admirers all over the state to run for the Democratic state committee in the coming April primary election of 1956. The state committee was the key to controlling the party apparatus. It consisted of eighty members, forty men and forty women, one man and one woman selected by the voters in each of the state legislature's forty senatorial districts. We figured that if we could elect enough Kennedy and Dever people to the committee in the April primary, we might be able to vote Burke out of the chairmanship of the committee when he came up for reelection in May.

Because the Ambassador was strongly opposed to a fight against McCormack and Burke, we had to provide our own base of operations and keep our activities concealed from the Kennedy family. Judge James J. Mellen, friend and Kennedy supporter in the Boston area, came to our aid, turning over to us his law office and his telephones and secretarial help, and it was from Jim Mellen's office that we organized and directed the beginning of the fight to give Kennedy control of the state committee — the first step toward winning him national prominence at the 1956 convention — with the Ambassador and the other Kennedys knowing nothing about our drive.

Finally we reached the point where we had to let Kennedy know what we were doing. The news of our operation came as no great surprise to him — we were sure that he knew about it all along — but he warned us that we had to hold our cards close to the vest. Kennedy, as usual, was a couple of steps ahead of us. He had learned that Burke and McCormack were trying to get control of the state organization so that they could control the vote of the Massachusetts delegation at the national convention. Kennedy was for Stevenson, and so was Dever. McCormack, guided by his friends Harry Truman and Sam Rayburn, was against Stevenson and in favor of Averell Harriman. McCormack was planning to run in the Massachusetts primary as a favorite son, and then he would go to Chicago with a delegation that would vote against Stevenson, Kennedy's candidate, after the first ballot.

Kennedy went to McCormack and Burke and warned them that he would run as a favorite son himself against McCormack if they did not agree to give him and Paul Dever approval of the members in the Massachusetts delegation. In return, he would let McCormack run as a favorite son and he would also allow Burke to continue as chairman of the state committee. McCormack and Burke agreed to the deal. Kennedy, Dever and McCormack, after some vigorous haggling, selected a slate of delegates to the national convention that was divided equally between their choices.

"So we can't let Burke or McCormack know that we're trying to get our people on the state committee," Kennedy told us. "At least, not for the time being. Keep working on it, but don't let Burke know about it, and don't mention my name to anybody."

Trying to persuade people to run for the state committee without letting them know why, or whom you were for and against, was rather difficult, especially for me because everybody in Massachusetts knew I was a Kennedy man and realized that Onions Burke was not my type of Democrat. I talked one night with a certain city councillor in Boston, an old friend whom I thought I could trust, about getting an anti-Burke candidate to run in Ward 20. The following Saturday morning I was summoned to appear in the bathroom of the Kennedy apartment at Bowdoin Street where the Senator was soaking his back in the tub.

"Did you talk to Freddy Blip about the state committee?" he said. "And did you use my name?"

"I talked to him," I said. "I might have sort of used your name, but only indirectly."

"You stupid bastard," Kennedy said. "He went right back to McCormack and told him. A half hour ago Burke called me and said, 'Now we can prove you are putting people in against the McCormack people all over the state.'"

He climbed out of the steaming tub and wrapped himself in a towel.

"Now I'm going to get Burke back on the phone," he said. "You can tell him that he's wrong."

He called Burke and handed the phone to me. Burke said, "Did you talk to Freddy Blip and tell him to get you a candidate in Ward Twenty?"

"Why, Bill, who told you that?" I said.

"Freddy Blip told me that."

"Bill, one of us is a liar," I said. "Either Freddy Blip or me, and you can make your choice."

"Are you calling Freddy Blip a liar?" Burke said.

"Absolutely," I said. "I did not talk to him."

I hung up the telephone and saw Jack Kennedy smiling at me.

"That was pretty good," he said. "A nice performance. Not bad at all."

Another ruction arose a few weeks later when we concocted a dramatic scheme to put up a Kennedy candidate against Onions Burke himself in Burke's own district in Hampden County. This was to be a strictly subterranean operation. Not even the Senator was to know about it. Our first choice was Sebastian Ruggieri, a prominent Kennedy supporter in Greenfield, who decided after a few days of deliberation that he did not care to antagonize Burke and McCormack. Ruggieri suggested instead Peter Sullivan, another Kennedy backer who was delighted to run against Burke. Sullivan's papers were filed. I received a telephone call from Kennedy, who was in his Washington office, and I could gather from the way he was talking that John McCormack was sitting beside him.

"You two fellows are a couple of amateurs," he said. "Where did you get the great idea of filing a candidate against Burke in his own hometown? Congressman McCormack just told me you've got Buster Ruggieri, a well-known Kennedy guy, running against Burke and now it's war."

"Wait a minute," I said. "You can tell McCormack positively that Buster Ruggieri is not running for the state committee and anybody who says so is full of bull."

"You're sure about that?"

"Absolutely sure," I said.

The next time I saw Kennedy in Boston, he said, "Well, I told McCormack that he was wrong about Ruggieri and he apologized for getting me upset."

Then Kennedy looked at me for a moment.

"By the way," he said. "Who is Peter Sullivan?"

Naturally the pact of harmony between the Senator and Onions Burke did not last long. Although the slate of delegates to the convention could not be changed, Burke and John Fox, the violently Red-hating, pro–Joe McCarthy and anti-Stevenson and anti-Kennedy publisher of the *Boston Post*, turned the favorite-son candidacy of McCormack into a crusade against Stevenson and Kennedy. The ballot in the April primary provided space for the voter to express his Presidential preference. Declaring that a vote for McCormack was a vote against Stevenson and Kennedy, the *Post* ran daily front page editorials urging write-ins for the Congressman and citing Kennedy's support of Stevenson as proof of his pink socialism. The publisher of the *Post* had supported Kennedy in 1952, because Lodge had opposed Taft's candidacy for President, but turned against the Senator later because Kennedy failed to support Joe McCarthy. Fox, a Harvard man himself, had tried to get Kennedy to join him in organizing an alumni committee to withhold alumni financial gifts to the university until it removed "left-wingers" from its faculty. Kennedy had refused and had been on Fox's black list ever since. The campaign for write-in votes for McCormack was a huge success, mainly because Stevenson was never particularly popular in Massachusetts anyway, and most of the voting in the primary was in Boston where McCormack was strong. He topped Stevenson by 10,000 votes statewide.

Beating his chest after the great victory, Onions Burke went a few words too far. Alger Hiss was in the newspapers that week, making a speaking appearance at Princeton University after his release from prison. "Anybody who's for Stevenson," Burke said, making it plain that he was referring to Kennedy, "ought to be down at Princeton listening to Alger Hiss."

Then we saw a side of Jack Kennedy that none of us had seen before. The gloves came off. The morning after the April 24 primary, when we had a good number of our people elected to the state committee, he called me on the telephone and said, "How do we stand?" I told him that Burke now had about thirty sure votes, or "suries" as we called them, and we had twenty, which left about thirty others who could go either way. "Get up a list of those thirty others," he said, "and find out everything about them — who do we know who knows them, what time do they get home from work at night. I'm going to ring their doorbells and talk to each one of them personally." He was now out to destroy Burke. I tried to explain to him that our chances of getting the uncommitted or neutral committee members to vote Burke out of the chairmanship would depend on whether they liked the candidate we were putting up to oppose him — and we had not yet picked our chairman. He was in no mood for delays or excuses. "We can pick our chairman later," he said. "In the meantime, let's get to work on getting those members they haven't got."

The next day he was driving to the western part of the state, Burke's home territory, to talk to newly elected committee members. He surprised me by calling Burke himself, and making a date to have breakfast with him in Northampton so he could tell him bluntly to his face that he was finished as chairman of the committee. He then offered Burke a chance to bow out gracefully by resigning. Burke, of course, replied that if Kennedy tried to remove him, Kennedy would have his brains knocked out.

After the breakfast the Senator surprised us again by announcing to a startled newspaper reporter that he was planning to remove Burke from the state committee. This open declaration of war was not to be expected from the Jack Kennedy we knew. Dave Powers thinks he made the statement on the spur of a moment when he was still furious over Burke's Alger Hiss remark. I am inclined to think it was a coldly deliberate move to make his stand known so that the party politicians would be forced to take sides and the newly elected committee members would have to make a choice between Kennedy or Burke.

If that was his intention, he succeeded sensationally. The Kennedy-Burke war was splashed across front pages all over the state. Paul Dever and several other prominent Democrats backed Kennedy. McCormack said he was standing behind Burke "one thousand percent." Burke made headlines of his own with a phony charge that at the Northampton meeting Kennedy had offered him James M. Curley's seat on the Democratic National Committee if he would resign from the chairmanship of the state committee. Already primed by Burke, Curley immediately fabricated a story about Kennedy attempting to bribe him into retiring from the national committee to make room on it for Burke. "He hasn't got enough money to buy me," Curley told the press. "I never took any money from him, or from his family, and I never will."

For the first time in his career, Kennedy was caught in a mudslinging Boston Irish political brawl. We never saw him so angry and frustrated. His father was saying, "I told you so." Yet it never occurred to him to pull out of the dirty fight, or to turn on us and blame us for getting him into such a mess. I reminded him again that he had made a mistake moving against Burke without selecting a candidate to offer to the committee members as Burke's replacement. "All right, let's get a chairman," he said. "Who do you have in mind?" He was in for a surprise. I knew he was thinking of putting up a new chairman of his own Ivy League type and style. "If we're going to rebuild the party in Massachusetts," he had been saying, "let's put a bright, new, young face in there to run it." The chairman I suggested, John M. ("Pat") Lynch, the longtime mayor of the suburban city of Somerville, was neither new nor young. He wore the wide-brimmed hat of the veteran Boston Irish politician.

"Pat Lynch?" Kennedy said. "When I was running in 1946, Joe

Leahy took me over to Somerville to meet him and he refused to support me because Mike Neville was an old friend of his. At least he told me to my face where he stood, instead of knifing me behind my back like the rest of them. Why Pat Lynch?"

I explained to him that it was going to be a tough and close fight and we needed a candidate who would get the votes of the Dever people on the committee, the older Democratic party-line regulars. Lynch was one of their own kind and an old friend of Dever's.

"They'll buy Lynch," I said. "But they won't buy an out-and-out Kennedy candidate, a new Harvard Irishman like Kenny O'Donnell or a young Dartmouth Irishman like Dick Donahue. They don't want you pushing one of your bright new faces down their throats. They want an old familiar face. Besides, Pat Lynch is straight and honest, and I happen to know he admires you and will stand by you."

I told him how Bobby and I had gone to Somerville to get Lynch's support for Kennedy in 1952. Lynch said to Bobby, "I've got a lot of enemies in this town. I win a mayoralty by fifty-five to forty-five, so if I'm for your brother, you get forty-five percent of the Somerville voters against you. Pick somebody my enemies like to run your campaign here, and I'll pass the word quietly among my friends that I'm for Kennedy and then you'll get everybody."

Kennedy listened and said, "Bring him in here so I can get a look at him. I don't remember what he looks like."

When I brought Pat Lynch to Kennedy's apartment on Bowdoin Street, we met John E. Powers coming out. Johnny Powers, also a friend of Dever's and the Democratic leader in the state senate, was from South Boston in McCormack's Congressional district so Lynch was surprised to find him leaving Kennedy's apartment. When I asked Powers a month earlier to help Kennedy, he said, "Of course, you know John McCormack is my Congressman and my old friend — when do we start?" I watched the two Boston Irish pols in their large hats and velvet-collared coats shaking hands in Kennedy's doorway and eyeing each other, and I thought about how broadening an experience this political adventure was for the Senator. When Powers made his way to the elevator, Lynch turned to me and said, "What's that fellow doing here? I suppose he must be having income tax troubles."

All of the Kennedys, and especially Jack, judged people by their appearance. I saw the shock on Jack's face when he looked at Pat Lynch, a small and bald-headed man, about five feet six and one hundred thirty pounds and well along into his fifties, exactly the type of crusty old-fashioned Irish politician that Jack always frowned upon. I had told Kennedy that Lynch played football at Holy Cross when my father was coaching there in the twenties, but I neglected to mention that he was a tiny and lightweight end, so Jack was probably expecting somebody tall and distinguished looking, like Henry Fonda. Instead I had brought him a leprechaun. He said to me, "Can I speak to you for a minute, Kenny?" He led me into the bathroom and closed the door.

"You didn't make any commitment to this guy, did you?" he said.

"Not yet," I said.

"Well, don't," he said.

Four days later he called me and said that he wanted Dick Donahue to be the chairman of the state committee. I said, "Dick Donahue would be my candidate if you could elect him. He's young and clean-cut, everything that we want, but he's not electable." Kennedy said, "He's the guy. See how many votes you can get for him." I began to hear rumbles from all over Boston, many of them from Kennedy people. Johnny Powers called me to the State House, where a group of Democratic legislators on the state committee told me that they were switching to Burke. I called Kennedy. He had already gotten the message. "I know what you're calling about," he said. "Pass the word that Pat Lynch is our candidate." The news that Kennedy had selected Lynch was in the next day's newspapers. Dever and Dever's people on the committee were delighted. McCormack and Burke were dumbfounded. They had been telling everybody that Kennedy would put up one of his own boys, either Donahue or me, and the news of Lynch's nomination caught them flat-footed. It was hard for McCormack to rap Lynch because he and Lynch had been good friends for years.

Lynch brought us several new votes, but we still needed to win at least twenty more of the uncommitted committee members during the few weeks that remained before the chairmanship election, which was to take place at the Hotel Bradford in Boston on May 19. The tug of war between us and the Burke group over those undecided members, and the pressure from both sides on the committed men and women on the committee in an effort to change their votes, developed into the most vicious fight I have ever experienced in all the years I have worked in politics. The abuse and the insults hurled at Kennedy when he tried to talk politely to some of the McCormack people now seem unbelievable. The Senator asked us to give him a list of every committee member whose vote seemed questionable. He drove to their homes in the old battered Chrysler that he used for traveling in Massachusetts — no shining new Cadillac for him — and rang their doorbells, sat down in the living rooms, and explained why he was interested in reorganizing the committee. One day we sent him to a man in Lynn named George O'Shea, who we thought was a friend of Dever's. We didn't know that O'Shea had had a falling out with Dever and his best friend was a friend of McCormack's. Kennedy came back from the interview laughing. "I never thought at this stage of my political career," he said, "that I'd have to sit and listen to somebody calling me a stupe. But where do I go tomorrow?"

I sat one afternoon with Paul Dever, listening to him pleading on the telephone with five committee members who were supposed to be his friends; he had done favors for all of them when he was the governor. Each one of them flatly turned him down. Campaigning against McCormack's chairman, Burke, was particularly difficult because McCormack had personally controlled all of the Federal patronage in Massachusetts during the years of the Truman administration. Every committee member, including those pledged to us, seemed to have an uncle or a brother who had gotten a job in the post office through McCormack. Kennedy had not gotten a crumb of patronage when he was a Congressman and when he was a Senator the Eisenhower Republican administration was in office. He was known as a politician who couldn't get a job for his own cousin. The only argument we could use was that McCormack was an elderly man while Kennedy was young and healthy and would be able to repay favors for the next twenty-five years, and that didn't cut much ice. Kennedy's declared support of Adlai Stevenson was no help, because the rank and file Democrats in Massachusetts were cool toward Stevenson.

McCormack tried to make the battle appear to be a fight between Kennedy and Burke, playing the role of the dignified elder statesman who would not stoop to such unseemly tactics and pretending not to be personally involved. But the Congressman issued one strong statement, declaring that he would consider it a personal affront if his great friend William Burke was not retained as the chairman. He also made many phone calls to the committee members.

There were many rumors that Kennedy was buying votes, which worked to our disadvantage. A few rogues on the committee, hearing from the Burke people that Kennedy was paying five hundred dollars for a vote, suddenly became doubtful about their choice because we had not offered them five hundred dollars. As far as I know, nobody received as much as five cents for a Kennedy vote. The usual stories, circulated loudly by Burke himself, about the wealthy Kennedy family buying control of the state committee were particularly ridiculous because Ambassador Kennedy, who held the family purse, sternly disapproved of Jack's involvement in the whole affair. We even had trouble scraping up expense money when it was urgently needed. One night, when we had to send out a very important telegram to every member of the committee, legally setting the time and place for the election of the chairman, we discovered that the supposedly heavily financed Kennedy organization had no money to pay for the telegrams. The banks were closed, because it was almost midnight, and Western Union was demanding cash — no checks, no credit cards. Dick Maguire went somewhere in Boston and came back with the several hundred dollars required to wire the messages. Then I had to deliver the press releases, announcing the election meeting, to the newspaper offices myself because we did not have enough money left over to pay a messenger.

On the other side, the Burke workers were dangling jobs and favors before wavering committee members. There was one fellow on the committee who switched to Burke at the last minute because he was hard pressed financially and he was offered a lifetime job as a bartender at the Otis Air Force Base on Cape Cod, which he desperately needed. He was one of our own men. In fact, we had arranged for him to run for his place on the committee. Kennedy met him face to face in an elevator at the Hotel Bradford when he was going upstairs to the election meeting. The Senator said to him, "Tom, you wouldn't go back on me now, would you?" Tom broke into tears. "No, I won't," he said. "The hell with them." He voted for Pat Lynch.

Kennedy's appearance that Saturday in the hotel, where the election meeting was taking place in an atmosphere charged with open hostility and hot tempers, astonished the Burke and McCormack people. McCormack was carefully hiding himself in Washington. Jean Kennedy, the Senator's sister, was being married that morning in New York to Steve Smith, but not even a family wedding could keep Jack away from the big showdown with Onions Burke. He had to be there for the kill. The Senator escorted his wife to the wedding in New York, slipped out of Saint Patrick's Cathedral after the ceremony, rushed to the airport and flew to Boston. When he walked into the crowded lobby at the Bradford, getting cheers from his friends, and glares and a few boos from the Burke contingent, Kennedy shook hands with Edward "Knocko" McCormack, the Congressman's hard-boiled and three hundred-pound brother who always rode an enormous white truck horse in South Boston's Saint Patrick's Day parade. We thought Knocko was going to have a stroke. Kennedy did not go into the meeting itself, but he stayed in the hotel, keeping in touch with everything and eagerly wanting to know every word that was said and every move that was made, until after the votes were safely counted. Then he hurried to the Logan Airport in East Boston, flew back to New York, and casually sat down beside Jackie at Jean's reception.

We went into the meeting figuring that we had forty-seven votes, six more than we needed to beat Burke, but we were afraid that Burke might pull some kind of illegal move or even take over the counting of the votes by force. We hired two brawny off-duty policemen from Charlestown to look after our interests. They almost came to blows with Burke in a scramble with much heavy pushing and shoving that nearly turned into a free-for-all. Pat Lynch, who had jumped into the last two hectic weeks of the fight battling like a bantam rooster, turned out to be a tower of parliamentary strength during the election itself and won Kennedy's lasting admiration. Pat succeeded in getting himself elected as the meeting's temporary chairman after sparring with Burke for more than an hour. "Paddy, I ought to knock you right on your ass," Burke said to Lynch at one point.

"Here's my card, Bill," Lynch said calmly. "You know where you can find me."

With Lynch in the chair, the seventy-eight eligible committee members who were present then proceeded to vote exactly as we expected, forty-seven for Lynch and thirty-one for Burke, who became livid with rage when the count was announced. We had picked up almost all of the previously uncommitted votes, largely because of the Senator's door-to-door campaigning. When I brought the news to Kennedy, who was waiting impatiently in an upstairs room during the voting, he said, "Well, this has been a brawl of monumental proportions. We ought to seize what we can out of it. Get Pat Lynch to put out a statement hailing it as a great victory in Massachusetts for Adlai Stevenson."

I gave the message to Lynch, who gave me a cold and steady Irish stare. "Let's not try to kid anybody," Pat said. "This is no victory for Adlai Stevenson or Averell Harriman or any other Presidential candidate. This is a victory for John F. Kennedy and nobody else. If I put out a statement about this being a victory for Stevenson, it will look like I'm being Kennedy's stooge. Most of these people who voted for us today don't care much for Stevenson and neither do I. Tell that to the Senator."

I told that to the Senator and the Senator smiled. "Very independent fellow, isn't he?" Kennedy said.

"Of course he's independent," I said. "That's why we ran against Burke and that's why forty-seven members of the committee voted for him — because they know he's nobody's stooge."

"Well, he's right," Kennedy said. "Let's just say this is the beginning of a new era for the Democratic party in Massachusetts, and let it go at that."

Later that afternoon the Senator called us from his sister's wedding reception in New York and asked if anything else was new. We took pleasure in telling him that Onions Burke had just announced that he would run against John F. Kennedy for Kennedy's seat in the Senate in 1958 and that Kennedy would not be able to buy that election like he bought the state committee's election.

"Gosh," Kennedy said. "If that's all the opposition I get in 1958, I'll be very thankful." When 1958 arrived, incidentally, Burke was not heard from.

Kennedy took command of the party in Massachusetts with a firm hand. He called a meeting of the delegation to the coming national convention and had himself elected as its leader. One of his first moves was to dump from the delegation and from the Democratic National Committee a grand old dame of Boston ward politics, Margaret O'Riordan, a close friend of Curley's. When Curley was governor, he appointed Mrs. O'Riordan as the state librarian, although she admitted in an interview at the time that she had no books in her home and read only two magazines, *Spy Stories* and *True Romances*. Mrs. O'Riordan had told off Senator Kennedy with some very shocking language when he called on her during the state committee chairmanship fight. It was agreed that she did not fit into a delegation to the national convention that had the Senator as its new leader. Kennedy referred privately to the removal of Mrs. O'Riordan as "Operation Big Splash" because she made a big splash when she went over the side.

Curley himself was allowed to remain in the delegation and on the national committee, because of his old age. Kennedy made peace with John McCormack and gave his blessing to nominating the House majority leader as the Massachusetts favorite-son candidate for the Presidency on the first ballot, but McCormack agreed that the state's delegation would switch to Adlai Stevenson if the voting between Stevenson and Harriman became close.

The young Senator Kennedy's sudden rise to nationwide political prominence and personal popularity at the Democratic National Convention at Chicago in 1956, which caught Adlai Stevenson and the party leaders by surprise and nearly overturned their previously arranged Stevenson–Estes Kefauver ticket, was largely their own doing — one of those backfires that make politics interesting. Stevenson came to the convention needing support from the big city Democratic bosses, many of them Irish Catholics. He found in Kennedy, the attractive new boss of the party in Massachusetts, an interesting personality who could be built up and exploited as a Stevenson enthusiast to win him Irish Catholic backing. The buildup of Kennedy made him much more popular with the delegates than Stevenson had wanted him to be. It reminded us of the story about the Irish girl who worked so hard at converting her Jewish boyfriend to Catholicism that he became a priest.

Kennedy became a widely and wildly acclaimed choice for the Vice-Presidential nomination, backed by Northern bosses who disliked Kefauver and by Southerners who regarded both Kefauver and Hubert Humphrey as too liberal. One thing we learned about convention politics in 1956 is that the delegates, who are local party leaders back home, and the state bosses, who influence the delegates, are mainly interested in getting candidates on the national ticket who will get votes for their own local candidates in the November elections. Whether or not John J. Smith will make a good President or Vice-President is beside the point — will his name on the ticket help Joe Blow, my candidate for governor in Maryland or North Dakota? In the early days of the convention, when the then unknown John F. Kennedy came across strong on television as the narrator of the party's historical documentary propaganda film and then as the nominator of Stevenson, the delegates decided that he would be a national candidate who would do good for their state and county party tickets. The 1956 conventions were the first ones powerfully influenced by television. The delegates were watching television constantly in Chicago and they were getting telephone calls from their wives and friends who were watching the convention on TV at home. "Who is this young Kennedy?" they were hearing on the telephone. "He's marvelous on television. You better vote for him." Kennedy happened to come along when political television was looking for a Jack Kennedy. There was not much that the party leaders could do about that.

After allowing Kennedy too much prominence on television, and thereby starting a Kennedy-for-Vice-President boom, Stevenson was in a predicament. Stevenson was firmly committed to Kefauver, who had withdrawn from the Presidential race in return for a promise of the second place on the ticket. But if Stevenson now named Kefauver as his choice and turned down Kennedy, he would be accused of being anti-Catholic, a charge that he could hardly afford in the coming campaign. There was only one alternative. He was forced to leave the selection of a Vice-Presidential candidate to the delegates, probably assuring Kefauver privately that Kennedy would be too unprepared to win the open floor fight.

Kennedy certainly was unprepared to run for the Vice-Presidential nomination and more astonished by the Kennedy boom that any of us who were with him in Chicago. If he had any serious intention of trying to win the Vice-Presidential nomination before the convention, Bobby would have known of it and the Ambassador would have been in Chicago that week, pacing back and forth in a room in the Conrad Hilton and telephoning every older Democratic politician in town. Bobby invited me to go to the All-Star game in Chicago and to attend the convention with him as his guest, and it was understood that we were to view the spectacle strictly as spectators. No work. Just a week of relaxation, because our man was playing no competitive role and there would be nothing for us to do. On the plane trip to Chicago, Bobby never mentioned that there was even a remote possibility of Jack getting into a fight for a place on the ticket. When we landed in Chicago, we saw a story in the *Sun-Times* mentioning Jack as one of the many dark horses under consideration for the Vice-Presidential nomination but both of us laughed at it. Jack's father was far from Chicago, basking in the sun on the French Riviera, where Jack was planning to join him for a brief sailing holiday on the Mediterranean as soon as the convention was over. The Ambassador's last words to Jack before he went to Europe were a stern warning not to accept the Vice-Presidential spot on the Stevenson ticket even if it were offered to him. The elder Kennedy was convinced, along with everybody else, that Eisenhower would beat Stevenson and that the defeat of the Democratic candidates would be blamed on Kennedy's Catholicism if Kennedy was Stevenson's running mate, which was sound reasoning.

Jackie Kennedy, uncomfortable in the advanced stages of pregnancy, had come to the convention, expecting to share some of it with her husband. If she or Jack had suspected that he would turn out to be the star of show, busy day and night at meetings and caucuses, she would have watched it on television at her mother's home in Newport. Jackie stayed with Eunice at the Shrivers' Chicago apartment and never had a chance to talk with Jack all week. His room at the Conrad Hilton was always filled with politicians and cigar smoke. Bobby and I shared a room at the Ambassador East. When we checked in, the manager showed us to a penthouse suite, explaining that it would cost us nothing because Peter Lawford, Bobby's brother-in-law, rented it by the year. Bobby was so horrified by the thought of Lawford paying a year's rent for a penthouse seldom used that he refused to sleep there.

Talk about Kennedy as a Vice-Presidential candidate did not begin to spread through the convention until after his narration of the opening night's documentary film on the party's glorious history. He had recorded the narration several weeks earlier, but after the film was shown in the convention hall, he was brought to the platform to take a bow and received a much bigger ovation than the one given to Frank Clement's keynote speech. At the same time opposition to Kefauver was growing. Several Southerners and a few influential Northerners, notably Chicago's Mayor Richard Daley, were arguing that a Stevenson-Kennedy ticket would be more effective than a Stevenson-Kefauver ticket. On the other hand, a few influential Catholics, James A. Farley, David Lawrence of Pennsylvania and Mike DiSalle of Ohio, were afraid to risk putting a Catholic on the ticket.

Lawrence was also committed to Kefauver. His insistence on holding the Pennsylvania delegation against a switch to Kennedy turned out to be a crucial stumbling block. I was with Pat Lynch when Pat tried to persuade Jim Farley to back Kennedy and Farley refused on the grounds that this was the wrong year to put the religious issue into the Presidential campaign. "You've got one hell of a nerve being against Jack Kennedy," Lynch said to Farley, "after the way young Joe Kennedy stuck with you in 1940 when you were flat on your back." Farley became exceedingly flustered and embarrassed by this reminder that Jack's brother had refused to switch his vote at the 1940 convention, after Farley's defeat, to make Franklin D. Roosevelt's nomination unanimous.

On the poor advice of a well-meaning friend, Jack arranged to see Eleanor Roosevelt in the hope that she might put in a kind word for him with Stevenson. Instead Mrs. Roosevelt berated him before a room of people for not taking a firmer stand against Joe McCarthy. Bobby talked the Senator into putting the question up to Stevenson himself. Adlai was evasive, but made it plain that he was still planning to name Kefauver by asking Kennedy to deliver the principal speech nominating Stevenson as the Presidential candidate. According to the book, you don't ask a man to nominate you for the Presidency if you have any intention of selecting him as your Vice-Presidential candidate. So Kennedy came back from his meeting with Stevenson, carrying the nominator's assignment, which meant that he had been kissed off the party's ticket. He did not take his dismissal calmly. He had come to Chicago with no thoughts of getting the second place on the ticket, but now, after listening to so much talk against Kefauver and for his own candidacy, his hopes had been built up. Like any ambitious politician, he was finding it hard to believe that the opening door had been suddenly pushed closed again. I was with Bobby when he told us not to bother any more about the Vice-Presidential thing, that it was all decided against him and that was it. He was very chagrined, and had a few grim words to say about Stevenson.

But Jack decided to make the most of his nominating speech, which was only twenty-four hours away. He threw away the prepared script that the Stevenson people had handed to him and sat up all night with Ted Sorensen writing a new one of his own. It made a big hit and started the Kennedy-for-Vice-President boom all over again with one line that the delegates loved, a slam at Eisenhower and Nixon as a team of one candidate who took the high road while the other followed the low road. Mayor Daley told me later that it was this nominating speech for Stevenson that convinced him that Kennedy had to be on the ticket.

Now the pressure against Kefauver and for Kennedy was so strong that Stevenson was forced to announce after he was nominated that he was throwing the selection of a Vice-Presidential candidate open to the convention the next day. Stevenson's late-night announcement caught all of us completely by surprise. Bobby and I rushed from the convention hall with Pat Lynch, trying to get downtown to see Jack in his room at the Conrad Hilton to find out what we would do next. The street outside the hall was in an uproar — everybody yelling for a taxicab with no cabs in sight — but we managed to hitch a ride from a private citizen. Or rather, I should say, Bobby practically commandeered the car, much to Pat Lynch's admiration. When the driver found out that Bobby was Jack Kennedy's brother, he wanted Bobby's autograph and insisted upon driving us to the door of the Conrad Hilton; Jack had become that well known in Chicago in a few days. We found a crowd gathered around Jack, everybody talking at once, trying to get organized, and nobody knowing what to do. Abe Ribicoff and Dennis Roberts, the governor of Rhode Island, along with Paul Dever and various delegates from New England, were all trying to figure out if any of them knew any influential figures in the party outside of New England. Senator Kennedy himself was taking a cool and detached view of the confusion. At one point he said, "Why don't each one of you talk to somebody and report back to me about what progress you've made? Abe, you talk to Denny Roberts. Bobby, you talk to Kenny. I'll talk to Sarge Shriver." It was said later that at this point in the late evening or early morning, Carmine DeSapio, the Tammany

Hall leader, came to Kennedy's room to offer him New York's support, but nobody in the room recognized him. I doubt it, because DeSapio's face was well known to all of us, but that night anything like that might have happened. Kennedy learned that Pat Lynch knew more important party leaders in Chicago than any of us.

Kennedy was in no great hurry to rush into an open fight for the Vice-Presidential nomination against Kefauver, knowing that Stevenson and many of the party bosses were still committed to Kefauver and realizing that all of the opposition to Kefauver was by no means sold on Kennedy. Hubert Humphrey, also in the running, would be backed in farm states and by the Walter Reuther labor-union liberal types. Albert Gore would get some of the anti-Kefauver votes in the Southern delegations. New York had decided to vote for Robert Wagner on the first ballot. Kennedy waited to get an idea of just how much support he could count on before declaring himself, particularly in the Protestant Southern states. He was still waiting, leaning in the direction of running but not yet quite decided, when a delegate from Louisiana came to him and pleaded that he had to run. The Louisiana delegation had voted against their governor in favor of supporting Kennedy. "We went out on the limb for you, and you can't leave us hanging there," the Louisiana man argued. "You've *got* to run." That gave Jack the push that he needed. He turned to Bobby and said, "Call Dad and tell him I'm going for it." Bobby placed a telephone call to the Ambassador's home on the French Riviera, by no means an enviable assignment. Jack disappeared from the room, leaving me alone with Bobby when the call came through. The Ambassador's blue language flashed all over the room. The connection was broken before he was finished denouncing Jack as an idiot who was ruining his political career. Bobby quickly hung up the telephone and made no effort to get his father back on the line. "Whew!" Bobby said. "Is he mad!"

We were so unprepared that when Abe Ribicoff was nominating Kennedy for the Vice-Presidential candidacy that we had nobody to second the nomination. While Ribicoff was delivering the nomination speech, Peter Cloherty, one of the delegates from Boston, came to me on the floor where I was standing with Bobby and pointed at John McCormack, who was sitting with the Massachusetts delegation. "Why don't you ask McCormack to second him?" Cloherty said. I stared at Cloherty, who can be a mischievous rogue at times, and said, "Are you serious?"

"Of course I'm serious," Cloherty said. "Forget that Onions Burke fight, and remember that John McCormack happens to be the majority leader in the House of Representatives. You can use him right now, and he'll do it."

I spoke to Bobby, who was standing ten feet away from McCormack, and Bobby told the Congressman that Jack would feel honored if he seconded the nomination. "Well, now, that's nice of him," McCormack said. Before McCormack had a chance to change his mind, Bobby practically carried him to the platform. Jack was in a room at the adjoining Stock Yard Inn, watching the proceedings on television. He must have been surprised when he saw McCormack appearing on the screen to second his nomination.

We were hoping to give Kefauver a good run, but we thought the prearranged deal between Stevenson and the leaders who favored Kefauver was too well set to allow an upset. I left the convention floor with a fellow Massachusetts Irishman, James Patrick Boyle, to watch the voting on TV in a neighborhood bar across the street. During the first ballot, when states like Virginia, Georgia and Nevada began to go for Kennedy, Boyle and I began to be amazed. Even more amazing was the assembled crowd of Chicago truck drivers, policemen and stock yard workers around us, all of them cheering, pounding on the bar and waving their beer glasses when another Kennedy vote was announced. I said to Boyle, "We had better get back over there. This is an entirely different ball game." On the first ballot, Kennedy had 304 against Kefauver's 483½, while Albert Gore, Kefauver's rival in Tennessee and a strong backer of Kennedy before the convention, ran third with 178. Behind Gore was Bob Wagner, with 162¼, running as a New York favorite son with many of his second-ballot votes promised to Kennedy, and far behind and well out of it was Hubert Humphrey with 134½ votes from Minnesota and Missouri.

On the second ballot the Gore and Wagner voters started to switch to Kennedy, who came within 33½ votes of the needed majority. The Senator was convinced, and so were most of us on the floor, that he had more than enough votes to win the nomination. But several delegations that wanted to switch to Kennedy were not recognized by Sam Rayburn, the chairman, and delegates in such states as California, Pennsylvania and Tennessee who wanted to switch to him were prevented from doing so by their leaders. I remember watching the bitter scene that took place in the Tennessee delegation when Senator Gore and Governor Clement, both against Kefauver and ready to go for Kennedy, received the word from high, through an influential newspaper publisher, that they were to switch the delegation to Kefauver or else. "My God!" Clement roared. "Not Estes!" Kennedy had some choice words to say later about David Lawrence, who kept Wagner's anti-Kefauver votes in Pennsylvania from switching to Kennedy. The dismantling of the electric tote board in the convention hall was a bad break for Kennedy; it kept wavering delegates from seeing how close he was to a winning majority. But his biggest handicap was lack of time to get organized for the floor fight. He only had a few hours between Stevenson's throwing the Vice-Presidential nomination open and the start of the balloting, hardly enough time to get a few Kennedy-for-Vice-President banners printed. Stevenson, never much of a politician, made a terrible political mistake when he did not pick Kennedy as his Vice-Presidential candidate instead of throwing the nomination open. During the campaign that followed, Kennedy was much more in demand as a speaker than Kefauver all over the country.

The prevailing view, of course, was that Kennedy gained more national popularity from the 1956 convention than either Stevenson or Kefauver, and that losing the Vice-Presidential nomination was a lucky break because it saved him from sharing the blame for the defeat of the Democratic ticket in that year's election. Kennedy himself later took that cheerful view of his defeat, but when the delegates were filing out of the convention hall and we gathered around him and Jackie in his room at the Stock Yard Inn, he was still furious over losing to Kefauver. He hated to lose anything, and he glared at us when we tried to console him by telling him that he was the luckiest man in the world.

"This morning all of you were telling me to get into this thing," he said, "and now you're telling me I should feel happy because I lost it."

His anger and frustration were intensified by the conviction that he had been jobbed and double-crossed by the party's bosses. Moreover, this had been his first political encounter outside of Massachusetts, and for the first time he had been hit by religious prejudice, which disgusted him. He was in no mood for conversational post mortems. He quickly made arrangements for Jackie to go to her mother's home in Newport to await her baby, as they had planned, and he flew directly from Chicago to the French Riviera to join his father for a sailing trip, which had been arranged months before the convention.

My wife and I went to Hyannis Port to spend a few days with Ethel and Bobby. While we were there, we received word that Jackie had gone into labor a month prematurely and the baby, a girl, was born dead. I drove Bobby to Newport, where Jackie was in critical condition. We had trouble trying to reach Jack, who was on a sailboat on the Mediterranean, out of touch with his father. When we finally managed to get a message to him, he flew back to Newport immediately.

A few weeks later, after Jackie had recovered, Jack brought her to Hyannis Port. Sitting in the sun on the porch of his father's house, he talked politics one morning with Bobby and me, our first discussion since the convention. It was a memorable conversation. Jack told us that his experience that year in the state committee fight with Onions Burke in Massachusetts and in the floor fight at Chicago had changed his thinking on his role as a politician.

As we all knew, Jack had gone into politics assuming that he could run for office simply by presenting himself to the voters as a conscientious and hard-working candidate who was concerned with their interests, without getting himself deeply involved in the party machinery or becoming entangled in the behind-the-scenes wheeling and dealing of the organization politicians. He had managed to follow such an independent course — making his appeal to the voter and keeping the party bosses at arm's length — in running for Congress and even in the statewide Senatorial race in 1952, which he won while practically ignoring the regular Democratic state organization, a feat that Paul Dever and other experienced politicians had regarded as impossible. Then he was drawn, more or less against his will, by Onions Burke into a bloody party leadership fight and found it to be a broadening and rewarding experience. Winning the backstage battle against John McCormack in Massachusetts had brought him valuable support from big city bosses,

Southern governors, and county leaders in Chicago that he never would have won if he had continued to play the Lone Ranger.

"I've learned that you don't get far in politics until you become a total politician," he said on the porch at Hyannis Port. "That means you've got to deal with the party leaders as well as with the voters. From now on, I'm going to be a total politician."

None of us mentioned 1960 that morning but the Senator made it plain, by outlining his plan to become deeply involved, at Stevenson's urgent request, in the coming campaign, that he had already decided to run for the Presidency at the next Democratic convention. He asked Bobby to travel with Stevenson in order to learn what should be done, and what shouldn't be done, in arranging a Presidential campaign. "You do what you can for Adlai in Massachusetts," Jack said to me. "You won't be able to do much for him, but keep your eyes open."

Jack spent the next two months on the road constantly, crisscrossing the country speaking for Stevenson, while Bobby traveled with the candidate, doing nothing because nobody in the Stevenson organization asked him to do anything. I had a drink with Bobby when he came to Boston with Stevenson. "You wouldn't believe it," Bobby said. "This is the most disastrous operation you ever saw. He gives an elaborate speech on world affairs to a group of twenty-five coal miners standing on a railroad track in West Virginia." Adlai's basic problem was that he had an intense distaste for politics and politicians.

Two days after his candidate went down in defeat, Senator Kennedy gave an informal, and strictly off the record, account of his own experiences on the campaign trail to the members of the Tavern Club in Boston: "Some of you may have some day the ill luck to participate in a national political campaign to the same extent that I did in this one," he said. "I offer you some advice that can be summed up in those immortal if not original words, be prepared. Be prepared to travel day and night, east and west, in an overheated limousine in ninety-three-degree weather in Fort Lauderdale, Florida, and in an open-car motorcade in raw thirty-degree temperature in Bellows Falls, Vermont, and Twin Falls, Idaho. Twin Falls, one of the more important metropolises I visited in my search for Democratic voters, is located between Dry Creek and Sawtooth going east and west, and Kimama and Mud Lake going north and south. Despite the ill effects of that freezing ride on my health and morale, there was at least no danger to my person in that Republican stronghold, for there were more of us in the motorcade than there were on the streets to greet us.

"Be prepared if you are a candidate, to hear your reputation slandered, your record distorted and your remarks twisted. As some of you may recall, I was a candidate for one brief moment of glory in the race for the Vice-Presidential nomination at Chicago. Socrates once said that it was the duty of a man of real principle to avoid high national office, and evidently the delegates at Chicago recognized my principles even before I did. I was not misled, I should add, by those who constantly told me that Senator Kefauver could not win because the better element in the party were against him. For I well remembered the words of Will Rogers in respect to a notorious candidate in Pennsylvania — 'They told me that the better element were all against him. I knew that, but I also knew that there are very few of the better element in Pennsylvania. I warned them three months ago to procure more better element.' Someone was lying like the devil about me in Chicago. I could hardly recognize the vicious, reactionary Junior Senator from Massachusetts who was being described as anti-farmer, anti-labor, an irregular Democrat, a slave to the Pope, a dying man — and that most damning indictment of them all — my father's son. Finally, you must be prepared to speak at an intellectual level that will be comprehended by all of your audience, regardless of education, I.Q., or literacy. In this, I might add, we Democrats had the all-time champion in our Vice-Presidential nominee. He and the American people got along well together because they demanded so little of each other. And a Texas colleague expressed it a little differently when he said that Senator Kefauver's success was due to the fact that he made the poorest, most ignorant white man in Texas feel superior. There were times, I understand, when the Republican Vice-Presidential nominee displayed finesse at the same art, and even Mr. Stevenson found it necessary to mispronounce the word 'elite.'"

But the 1956 Presidential campaign gave Jack Kennedy his first taste of nationwide politics and he found it to his liking. Dave Powers spent the Thanksgiving weekend at Hyannis Port with the Kennedys and heard from Jack what all of us had been expecting — he had now definitely decided to run for the Presidential nomination in 1960.

"With only about four hours of work and a handful of supporters, I came within thirty-three and a half votes of winning the Vice-Presidential nomination," he said to Dave. "If I work hard for four years, I ought to be able to pick up all the marbles."

FIVE

Going Nationwide

NINETEEN FIFTY-SEVEN, the year that John F. Kennedy started his run for the Presidency, was one of his happiest and most exciting years. That spring a Democratic National Committeeman was quoted as saying, "If we held a national convention next month, it would be Kennedy, period." More than 2,500 speaking invitations from all over the country poured into Kennedy's office and he accepted 144 of them, in Georgia, Oklahoma, Nevada, Colorado, Arkansas, Florida, Pennsylvania and New York, among many other places. *Time* magazine did its first cover story on him, reporting that "Jack Kennedy has left panting politicians and swooning women across a large spread of the U.S." He won the Pulitzer Prize for *Profiles in Courage* and edged out Estes Kefauver to win a cherished seat on the Senate's Foreign Relations Committee. The 1957 accomplishment that impressed Ambassador Kennedy most of all was Jack's election to Harvard's Board of Overseers. "Now I know his religion won't keep him out of the White House," Jack's father said to us at the time. "If an Irish Catholic can get elected as an Overseer at Harvard, he can get elected to anything." The Ambassador was greeted that year at the Hialeah race track in Florida by a friend who said to him, "How will it feel to be the father of the first Irish Catholic President of the United States?"

"That's nothing," Joe Kennedy said. "If my daughter Kathleen and her husband had lived, I would also be the father of the Duchess of Devonshire and the father-in-law of the head of all the Masons in the world."

That same memorable year brought the beginning of a new happiness to Jackie and Jack Kennedy's marriage, which had been under a strain during his long illness and her two difficult and unsuccessful pregnancies. After the loss of their stillborn child in 1956, they decided to move out of the large estate at Hickory Hill in Virginia which seemed to bring them no luck, and where Jack had been driven to distraction by the morning and evening commuting through slow and heavy traffic. They sold the big house to Ethel and Bobby, who then had five children, and rented a smaller one in Georgetown, near their Washington friends and within walking distance of the movies, where they were much more contented. On November 27, 1957, their daughter, Caroline, was born. When Caroline was three weeks old, they moved again, into a Georgetown home of their own, the red brick Federalist period house on N Street with a pleasant back garden, where they lived until they moved to the White House. When Jack was buying the N Street house, he said to Dave Powers, "How much would I have to pay for one of those nice old red brick houses on the top of Bunker Hill in Charlestown, next to the monument?"

"You could pick up one of them for about twelve-five," Dave said.

"Gosh!" Jack said. "Practically the same kind of a place in Georgetown is costing me eighty-two thousand dollars, plus another eighteen thousand for remodeling it!"

The Senator's four year campaign for the 1960 Presidential nomination was a rerun of his four year campaign in Massachusetts for the 1952 Senatorial election; once again he simply aimed to make himself known in as many places as possible across the country by accepting as many speaking engagements as possible, by meeting people at such gatherings and getting personally acquainted with them, just as he had done statewide in Massachusetts between 1948 and 1952. The card index file system was used nationwide the same way it had been used statewide ten years earlier. At a Young Democrats convention in Reno or at an American Jewish Congress dinner in New York or a Polish gathering in Milwaukee, the name of a likely supporter would be jotted down by the Senator or by one of his traveling companions and filed for future use. The one difference was that Kennedy was now much more concerned with local politicians, whom he had practically ignored in his younger days. After his experience at the 1956 convention and after watching the mistakes of Stevenson's campaign, he arrived at a Democratic dinner at Kansas City or Atlanta wanting to know which politicians in the hall counted, and which ones didn't, which county leader was worth courting as an ally and how much strength he represented. Gathering this local intelligence into his ever-curious mind, relishing the latest gossip from his dinner partner at the head table, weighing it and checking it with somebody else on his way to the airport later in the evening, he became intimately knowledgeable about the current political situation in every big city and most of the states, and so fascinated by it that he needed no notes to remember all of it.

Later on, when we were beginning to get his Presidential campaign plans organized, we were amazed by the amount of detailed information that he had picked up in his travels. From memory, he was able to give us a complete rundown on every state, and Puerto Rico, Alaska and Hawaii, not only naming local politicians who were friendly, hostile or on the fence and how many convention delegates they were likely to control, but telling us which states had primaries, which primaries were binding, which delegations would have unit rule, which ones would be under instruction from a state convention and which ones would be free to vote for anybody who appealed to them. He knew, for example, that the Democratic chairman in Puerto Rico, José Benitez, controlled more delegates than Governor Muñoz-Marin, and he had already enlisted key contact men in several states who were comparatively unknown before 1960 but turned out to be invaluable during the campaign, such as John Reynolds in Wisconsin, Bob McDonough in West Virginia and Teno Roncalio in Wyoming.

The Senator's constant nationwide traveling accustomed him to regard a trip from Washington to Idaho as casually as a drive from Boston to New Bedford. One day he called Dave Powers and said, "I want you to take a little trip with me." When Dave was leaving his house, Jo, his wife, asked if he would be home that night for dinner. "Oh, sure," Dave said. That night Dave telephoned Jo. "I'm still keeping the dinner waiting," she said. "Where are you?" Dave said, "I'm at a Jefferson-Jackson Day dinner in Des Moines, Iowa."

The important stepping-stone before the 1960 Democratic primaries and the national convention at Los Angeles was Kennedy's reelection as Senator in Massachusetts in 1958. He had to make an impressive show of vote-getting strength in being reelected to the Senate in order to remain in the running as a leading contender for the Presidency two years later. He began to plan the 1958 campaign long in advance, detailing us to work with Pat Lynch, our state committee chairman, in getting the fences mended in Massachusetts. But one day in the spring of 1957, when I was busy in the state committee office in Boston, Bobby telephoned me from Washington where he was then in the thick of investigating Dave Beck and Jimmy Hoffa and the Teamsters' Union as chief counsel of Senator John L. McClellan's Senate Select Committee on Improper Activities in the Labor or Management Field, better known as the Senate Rackets Committee. Or, as Jimmy Hoffa called the televised hearings, McClellan's *Playhouse 90*. Bobby needed help. He wanted me to move to Washington and to serve as his administrative assistant.

Thinking of Jack and 1960, I was not anxious to join Bobby on the McClellan committee; the 1958 campaign was going to be an exceptionally tough one because Jack wanted to roll up a tremendous popular vote and there would be nobody of importance willing to run against him. Getting a big vote with no real contest in the election to bring out the voters meant plenty of hard staff work and organizing for us, and I felt that this was no time for me to be leaving Massachusetts. I tried to point this out to Bobby, but he wouldn't listen to me. He wanted me with him on the McClellan committee for at least a year, until the following June of 1958. Then I could go back to Massachusetts and work on Jack's reelection campaign. "If this investigation flops, it will hurt Jack in 1958 and in 1960, too," Bobby argued. "He's on the committee, and a lot of people think he's the Kennedy who's running the investigation, not me. As far as the public is concerned, one Kennedy is the same as another Kennedy." Which was true enough; in those days Bobby was often confused with Jack, and Jack was frequently blamed, or praised, for the exposure of Beck and Hoffa. Anyway, it was always impossible to say no to Bobby when he wanted you to do something, so I went to Washington as his assistant. I assumed that he had already discussed my departure from Massachusetts with Jack and that Jack had agreed to it.

Later on, after I arrived in Washington, I found out that Jack knew nothing about my new assignment until Bobby mentioned it to him casually one night at a party at Hickory Hill. Jack blew up and there were several heated words between him and Bobby. The next day Jack asked me to come to his office and said to me, "I thought you were supposed to be working for me, not for Bobby. I need you up in Massachusetts. Nobody tells me anything."

"This wasn't my idea," I said. "I'd rather be in Massachusetts. There's a lot of work to do there."

"Well, don't go getting any ideas of making a career for yourself working for the McClellan committee," the Senator said. "Bobby can have you until next June, and no later. Then you go back to Boston and start working on the campaign schedule."

Bobby wrote a book about our experiences on the McClellan committee, *The Enemy Within*, which still makes good reading today, so there is no need to go into those memories in detail here. When I think back to that year I spent with Bobby in investigative travels all over the country, and with both Bobby and Jack in the long closed meetings and public hearings of the committee, I remember particularly the investigation of the deadlock strike of the United Automobile Workers against the Kohler Manufacturing Company of Sheboygan, Wisconsin, a difficult test of the integrity of the Kennedy brothers in which they both carried themselves like champions. Because Jack was a leading candidate for the Presidency, he and Bobby were constantly accused of using the McClellan committee to build up his political future. Jimmy Hoffa and his Republican-oriented Teamsters' Union, the main target of Bobby's investigations in his role of trying to show Congress that a change in labor laws was needed to prevent union graft and corruption, charged that the Kennedys were plotting with Walter Reuther and his UAW leadership to destroy the Teamsters, well-known enemies of the UAW in the labor movement. In return, Hoffa's people claimed, the Kennedys would get the support of the UAW in 1960. One of the Teamsters' Union lawyers told Bobby and me in 1957 that Hoffa was saying that the whole plot against him had been planned at a secret meeting between Reuther, Adlai Stevenson and Bobby in the fall of 1956.

That story of course was ridiculous. Reuther did not even know Bobby or Jack Kennedy at that time; moreover, in 1956 he had been against Kennedy's bid for the Vice-Presidential nomination because, like Eleanor Roosevelt, his close friend, he and his fellow leaders of the UAW were convinced that the rich and Catholic Kennedys were pro–Joe McCarthy and anti–labor conservatives. Far from being in a conspiracy with Bobby Kennedy when he was investigating the Teamsters in 1957, the UAW leaders were certain, they told us later, that his exposure of Beck and Hoffa was merely the beginning of an attempt to discredit the whole labor movement in the United States, both Democrat and Republican unions alike.

That spring when I joined Bobby's staff in Washington, the Republican Senators on the McClellan committee, led by Senator Karl Mundt, were pushing for an investigation of the UAW's prolonged and bitter strike against the Kohler Company. They made no secret of their hope that such an investigation would "get Walter Reuther." Bobby did an extensive study of the charges and counter-charges by both the union and the company management to see if such a probe by the McClellan committee was warranted. He asked me to study the reports, which clearly indicated that the whole trouble behind the four-year dispute was the company's fourteenth-century attitude toward labor unions. The Kohler management, still living in the past, simply refused to listen to requests for better working conditions. One bone of contention, for example, was the union's demand for a twenty-minute lunch period for employees working an eight-hour day in the hundred-degree heat of an enamaling furnace room, where bathtubs and other plumbing fixtures were made. The company insisted that a laborer had ample time to eat in the interval of two to five minutes while a piece of enamel was being baked in the oven. I felt that the whole controversy was a labor-management dispute that could be settled at the bargaining table — if management made reasonable concessions — and that it was not a proper matter for a Congressional committee investigation. Bobby agreed with me. Our function as a Congressional committee was to look into evasion of labor laws by labor and management so that we could recommend legislative action to change or strengthen such laws. We were not supposed to be butting into labor-management disagreements.

Bobby and Jack took that stand, and opposed the Kohler investigation, even though it laid them open to charges that they were supporting Reuther and the UAW for their own political interests. The Republican Senators on the committee, Mundt, Barry Goldwater and Carl T. Curtis, insisted on going ahead with the inquiry, and hired their own investigator to do the investigating. Senator McClellan gave in to the Republicans.

Then Bobby had no choice, as the committee's chief counsel, except to order the investigation. He appointed a staff member, Vern Johnson, to assist the Republican-appointed Jack McGovern in doing the research. "This will make the committee look silly, because McGovern won't come up with anything against the UAW," Bobby said to me. "Mundt and Goldwater think that if you investigate any labor union the union leader will come out looking as dirty as Beck and Hoffa, but that won't work with Reuther. But if the public gets the idea that I won't investigate Reuther because he's a big force in the Democratic party, that will ruin the McClellan committee. It would ruin Jack Kennedy, too, so let's go ahead with the investigation and see what happens."

The investigation conducted by McGovern and Johnson was a farce. Their first reports were turned in to Senator Mundt instead of Counsel Kennedy because, as Johnson later told us, McGovern was afraid that Bobby would show them to the UAW. The reports consisted mostly of rehashed excerpts from National Labor Relations Board hearings on the strike, with testimony unfavorable to the Kohler Company left out. McGovern told newspaper reporters that he had uncovered "sensational developments" against the UAW. One of the sensational developments was one hundred thousand dollars which McGovern found missing from the union's treasury. Our staff accountant, Carmine Bellino, found the one hundred thousand accounted for in less than an hour's study of the books. McGovern had been looking for it in the wrong column of figures. Johnson reported that a man named Brotz had made arrangements in 1956 with a UAW official named McCluskey to bring terrorist goons to the Kohler plant to attack strikebreakers. We spent three weeks looking for McCluskey in Florida and Louisiana and finally decided there was no such man. Brotz had died in 1951.

The Republicans began to realize themselves that they had little or no material to conduct hearings. They stalled off the scheduled date for the start of the public hearings, while the newspaper editorial writers and columnists kept hurling charges that the Kennedys were trying to stop the investigation to protect Walter Reuther. Barry Goldwater came to Bobby late in 1957, asking him to remove McGovern and to conduct the investigation himself. Bobby explained that in view of the public charges that he was trying to protect Reuther and the UAW, any findings he came up with would be labeled as a whitewash of the union. Goldwater then admitted to Bobby that he no longer wanted to investigate the UAW-Kohler dispute and he had no interest in calling Reuther before the committee for questioning. He agreed that he and Mundt and Curtis had been barking up the wrong tree, and were ready to drop the whole thing.

But the Kennedys were in no mood to let the Republican members of the committee bow out of the now shaky predicament, leaving Jack and Bobby suspected of squashing the case. They were determined to go on with the hearing that the Republicans no longer wanted, to give the rumored charges against the UAW a complete airing. With McClellan's consent, Bobby went to the Kohler Company towns in Wisconsin, Sheboygan and Kohler Village, with two of our staff men, Carmine Bellino and La Vern Duffy, and spent a few days there, talking with both company officials and union people to check on the eight months of so-called investigations that had been carried on by McGovern and Johnson. He found their research incomplete and full of holes. Then, at a closed session of the McClellan committee on January 8, 1958, Jack asked for the hearings to get underway as soon as possible after the first week of February, the time when McGovern and Johnson had promised that their investigation material would be ready. Mundt, Goldwater and Curtis were taken aback, flustered, and complained that they didn't want to rush into it so soon. Jack let them have it; for eight months, he said, the Kennedy brothers had been accused of dodging the Kohler case and shielding Reuther and the UAW. He was surprised at the reluctance of the Republican members to open the hearings in view of the press comments that the Kennedys were trying to cover up for Reuther. The Republicans had to give in to Senator Kennedy — and after five hot executive meetings on the question of whether Reuther should be called as the first witness for the UAW, the hearings finally started. But not until McClellan agreed to let the Republicans call the witnesses in the order they decided upon. And then Goldwater announced at a closed committee meeting a month later that he saw no reason to call Reuther at all. Furious, McClellan saw to it that Reuther appeared as a witness.

Reuther dissolved the Republicans. Reading from a newspaper clipping to show that labor unionists were violent, Goldwater cited to Reuther a strike demonstration in which thirty people were killed. "Read a little farther," Reuther said, "and you'll see that all the dead people were strikers." "Oh, my God, you're right," Goldwater said. Senator Kennedy interrupted a few minutes later when Goldwater was saying that both the Communists and the CIO used violent tactics. "There is no more significant relationship there," Jack said, "than there is in the fact that I had a brother named Joe and Stalin's first name was Joe." On the last day of the hearings, Mundt said to Reuther, "Certainly there is no evidence on the records we have before us of corruption insofar as your activities are concerned." Goldwater turned to Bobby and said, "You were right. We never should have gotten into this thing."

The real star of the UAW-Kohler hearings, in my biased opinion, was Senator Kennedy. Sharp and penetrating, fair and objective, he never hesitated in pinning down a piece of evidence against the company management and in favor of the union, even though he was well aware of the political risk he was taking in making such a stand. As it turned out, once again, doing what he thought was the right thing at that time proved in the long run to be the right thing for him politically, too. Before the Kohler investigation and the hearings, the UAW leadership — not only Reuther, but his political adviser, Jack Conway, and Leonard Woodcock — viewed Kennedy as a lightweight opportunist, not as liberal at heart as he pretended to be on the surface, and not as intellectual as he sounded. His performance at the hearings brought a complete turnabout in their attitude toward him. From then on, these tough-minded and demanding labor leaders, who exerted a strong influence within the Democratic party, respected Kennedy as a solid and intelligently grounded liberal. They backed him firmly at the 1960 convention against their former favorites, Adlai Stevenson and Hubert Humphrey. When the Republicans on the McClellan committee pushed the investigation of the UAW, thinking that it would bring a political embarrassment to Bobby Kennedy's brother, they were actually doing him a big political favor.

And yet several months after the whole UAW-Kohler investigation was all over and done with, the *New York Daily News* ran an editorial asking when the McClellan committee was going to stop protecting the Kennedys and start looking into the UAW's activities in the Kohler strike in Wisconsin.

A year later, just before the committee officially disbanded, Senators Mundt and Curtis made one more last attempt to discredit Reuther with a six-day hearing on a UAW intramural controversy in Toledo, which amounted to nothing. When McClellan announced that the committee's work was finished and accepted Bobby's resignation, Goldwater issued a statement to the press, accusing Robert F. Kennedy of running out on an investigation of Reuther. Bobby reached Barry on the telephone and asked him, "Why did you say a thing like that?"

"Oh, that's politics," Goldwater said.

"But I'm not in politics," Bobby said.

"You're in politics, Bob, whether you like it or not," Goldwater said.

Truer words were never spoken by a Republican.

One of Bobby's stories about his hectic pace of work as Chief Counsel of the McClellan committee well illustrates his father's attitude toward the duties of life. Bobby labored day and night, for seven days a week and for several weeks, on one particular investigation. Exhausted, he decided to slip away to Hyannis Port for a weekend. By Sunday afternoon he was beginning to feel better, but he decided to take one more day of rest. On Monday morning when Ambassador Kennedy came home from his daily horseback ride and saw Bobby sitting in the living room, he stared at him and shouted, "What's the big idea of sitting around up here on the Cape when you should be at your job in Washington?"

On the last day of Walter Reuther's appearances before the McClellan committee, Senator Kennedy beckoned to me during a lull in the proceedings. "Get back to Massachusetts," he said. "You should have been there six months ago instead of wasting your time in all this nonsense." I started packing immediately.

The 1958 Senatorial reelection campaign was the hardest of all the Kennedy campaigns to manage because, as I have mentioned earlier, the candidate wanted to get a record-breaking number of votes to impress the national leaders of his party, and there was no competition in the race to interest the voters. The Republican party in Massachusetts regarded Kennedy as such an unbeatable winner that they considered letting him run unopposed. Finally Vincent J. Celeste, the same obscure East Boston lawyer who ran against Jack for Congress in 1950, came forward to serve as the G.O.P. sacrificial goat, claiming that he was seeking revenge for his previous defeat. If Celeste was hoping that the publicity to be gained in opposing Kennedy's reelection might bring him a few new legal clients, he was mistaken. Even the arch-Republican newspaper, the *Boston Herald*, endorsed Kennedy, having no desire to be associated with a sure loser, and scarcely mentioned Celeste's name during the campaign.

To make our task of getting a tremendous popular vote more difficult, the Senator was determined to spend as little money as possible on the campaign, being sensitive to the constant charges that his political success was largely due to his family's wealth. Instead of setting up Kennedy-for-Senator local headquarters all over the state, as we did in 1952, we were to work out of a single headquarters on Tremont Street in Boston, manned by Ted Kennedy, who was getting his political baptism in that fight, and Steve Smith, newly married to Jack's sister Jean, and also a newcomer to the organization that year. Our advertising budget was cut to the bone. No money was to be spent, for example, on billboards beside the highways, a blow to Foster Furcolo, that year's Democratic candidate for reelection as governor, who had been hoping to share the cost of outdoor advertising, as well as statewide local headquarters rent, with Kennedy. Furcolo was so eager to capitalize on Kennedy's popularity, however, that he paid the whole expense for covering the state with billboards on which he gave Kennedy equal space.

While he was running for reelection as Senator in Massachusetts, Kennedy was still carrying on his national campaign for the 1960 Presidential nomination, making appearances at political gatherings all over the rest of the nation. That meant that the time he could give to personal campaigning in Massachusetts was limited; actually he spent only seventeen days in the state between the September primary and the November election.

To make the most of those seventeen available days, we, with the help of Arthur Garrity, now a Federal judge, who is something of a genius at figuring routing and timing of public appearances, and Dick Donahue, another able strategist, collaborated on working out a campaign schedule for the candidate that would have been physically and emotionally impossible for anybody but Jack Kennedy. Incidentally, Bobby Kennedy had no part in running the 1958 campaign because he was still tied up that year in his duties with the McClellan committee in Washington. To put it briefly, the schedule called for the Senator to spend each day covering a specific limited area of the state completely, appearing in as many cities and towns within that area as possible from early morning until late at night. Staying within a strictly confined area, we avoided wasting time on long drives between speaking engagements in widely separated cities, the annoying bug in most campaign schedules. But the short intervals between frequent stops on our condensed tour made it a punishing physical grind. After one such barnstorming trip through the North Shore of Massachusetts in October, Larry O'Brien was quoted in the newspapers as saying proudly, "We ran the Senator in one day through fifteen speaking appearances in fifteen cities and towns, from Chelsea to Gloucester, and had him back in bed by eleven o'clock at night." Reading O'Brien's boast, Kennedy called him on the phone and said, "You couldn't have done it."

We worked out the campaign schedule during the summer while the Senator and Jackie were in Europe on a Senate Foreign Relations Committee tour. He was due to return on a ship that would arrive in New York on the day after the primary voting in Massachusetts, in which both Kennedy and Foster Furcolo were running unopposed on the Democratic ballot. O'Brien and I planned to meet the Senator in New York when his ship docked to show him the schedule, which was so tough that we were afraid to hand it to him. We had already given the Ambassador a look at it, and the Ambassador had exploded. "What are you trying to do to him?" he roared. "Kill him?" But as it turned out, on the morning when we met Jack's ship, we had a bigger worry than the schedule weighing us down.

In the previous day's primary in Boston, our golden candidate's ancestral home, Foster Furcolo, an outsider from Springfield in the western part of the state, and not one of our favorite Democrats, had pulled a bigger vote than Kennedy in eighteen of the city's twenty-two wards. Furcolo had won a total of 94,303 citywide votes against Kennedy's 87,231. To say the least, we were stunned. As Dave Powers says, the only misfortune that blackened the happy first year of Caroline Kennedy's childhood was Furcolo's Boston vote in the 1958 primary.

It was not actually all that bad, but it seemed so to us at the time. The primary vote is always light, and it was especially light in that off-year because the one-sidedness of the coming November election made the primary very uninteresting. Most Kennedy voters did not vote in the primary, and many who did were mainly concerned with the contested nominations for minor state and city offices lower down on the party ballot and neglected, or ignored, the unopposed major nominees at the top of the list. It was really not so much a matter of Furcolo getting more votes than Kennedy as it was of Kennedy drawing more blanks than Furcolo. But there were many Democratic voters who had blanked Kennedy deliberately, and these were the ones who concerned us.

Some of them were disgruntled followers of James M. Curley and Onions Burke, labor union members who resented Bobby's attack on the Teamsters, longshoremen still angry over Jack's support of the Saint Lawrence Seaway. The antagonism between Kennedy and Furcolo was still alive and well known, so a large number of Italian-Bostonians and people with relatives on Furcolo's state payroll had blanked Kennedy and voted for Furcolo. Kennedy, and other candidates with Irish names, never did well against an Italian primary opponent in the solidly Italian wards in the North End and East Boston, although he would generally score heavily against a Republican in the same district's election vote. On the day before his 1950 Congressional primary contest, Jack saw in the newspapers a picture of his father presenting a check from the Joseph P. Kennedy, Jr., Foundation for five hundred thousand dollars to a group of Italians for the building of a home for elderly Italian people at Orient Heights in East Boston. "Gosh," Jack said. "This ought to get me some votes tomorrow in the North End and East Boston." The next day in the primary an opponent named Frank Bevilacqua led Kennedy in both of those districts.

However the 1958 vote in the Boston primary could be explained, it was hardly an auspicious showing for a candidate with

Presidential ambitions. The Senator and Jackie had already heard the news when we boarded the ship to meet them that morning in New York. He was obviously troubled, but he looked at us with a wry smile and said only, "I guess we didn't do as well as you fellows thought we would." From the ship we went to his father's New York apartment, where the Ambassador was in the throes of "the itch," as he called his fits of nervous irritation. The elder Kennedy had been on the telephone to Dave Powers in Boston, his favorite election statistician, demanding to know what had happened. Dave had given him a variety of explanations. The Furcolo vote in Boston had done O'Brien and me one big favor. It removed our apprehension about showing the Senator our campaign schedule. We knew that after hearing about his showing in the Boston primary, he would be glad to take a dive from the top of the Bunker Hill Monument if it might improve his vote in the election.

"Have you seen the schedule these two guys cooked up for you?" the Ambassador said to him. "It's outrageous!"

Jack took a brief and cursory glance at the schedule. "It looks fine to me," he said, and walked out of the room. The Ambassador looked at us, and threw up his hands.

The busy statewide campaign that followed, really a small-scale model of what we did nationwide in 1960, had one attractive feature that was unfortunately lacking in the later Presidential campaign: Jackie Kennedy was able that fall to accompany her husband on several of his long day's journeys. I am sure that many Democratic state legislators in Massachusetts have pictures of themselves and Jackie Kennedy, taken during the 1958 campaign, on their living room pianos today. She was always cheerful and obliging, never complaining, and to me a very refreshing change from the usual campaigning candidate's wife because she did not bother to put on a phony show of enthusiasm about everything that she saw and every local politician whom she met. The crowds sensed that and it impressed them. When Jackie was traveling with us, the size of the crowd at every stop was twice as big as it would have been if Jack was alone.

We made a point of halting the tour every day for a quiet and quite leisurely lunch, because Ambassador Kennedy insisted upon it. "You've got to see to it that he eats," Jack's father ordered. I remember one day when we were having lunch in the back room of a restaurant in Haverhill, with the Senator as usual giving me instructions on twenty-five different things that he wanted me to do that afternoon. I was hurriedly jotting down notes on a pad of note paper, while Jackie watched me quizzically. "You're always writing things down," she said, "but I never see you looking at that pad after we leave the restaurant. Do you ever do anything about all these things he tells you to do?"

"Never," I said. "I wait until he calms down, and then I rip these notes off the pad and throw them away."

Jackie laughed, but Jack looked at me with a straight and serious face. "You son of a bitch," he said. "I bet that's exactly what you do."

On another day, in the morning around eleven o'clock, he made a tour of a sausage factory in Boston where all of the workers were blacks. He stopped and talked with each of them, asking them where they lived. One man was from Georgia, the next one just moved from North Carolina, and another one was from Alabama. The Senator became interested, and spent more time talking to each of the workers than usual. He left the factory in a din of cheering and applause. When we were driving away, he turned to me and said, "Well, you just wasted an hour of my time. They gave me a great reception but not one of them is a registered voter in Massachusetts who can vote for me." The incident stayed in his mind, and he talked about it often after he became the President of the United States, about the millions of American citizens who could cheer for a candidate but could not vote for him. At the time of his death, he was determined that the Democratic National Committee in the election year of 1964 would have two primary functions — to raise money and to spend it mainly on a drive to register the country's unregistered voters, particularly those in the black population.

On the day before the election, we were in South Boston with State Senator John E. Powers, who was managing our Boston campaign again as he did in 1952. Senator Kennedy saw an elderly woman, about to cross the street alone. He yelled at Bob Morey, our driver, to stop the car. He got out of the car, introduced himself to the woman, took her arm and escorted her across the street. Powers stared at me and I stared at him, and when the Senator came back to the car, Powers said to him, "You really want *all* of the votes, don't you?"

Jack said, "How would you feel if you lost South Boston by one vote, and then remembered that you didn't bother to help this lady across the street?"

At the next corner, Powers asked Bob Morey to make a turn so that he could show us the house where he was born. Kennedy looked at the Powers house with interest. "John, you're always talking about your humble origin," he said to Powers quite seriously. "This house is a much nicer house than the one I was born in on Beals Street in Brookline. I came up the hard way."

"Oh, sure," Powers said. "You came up the hard way. One morning they didn't bring you your breakfast in bed."

Jack collapsed. He told the story for years afterwards.

Bobby came up from Washington a few days before the election to be there for the returns. On the night before the voting day, the candidate did a quick tour of Boston in the rain and ended up at the traditional place for ending an election campaign in the city, the G and G delicatessan on Blue Hill Avenue, the Jewish section of Dorchester, where he climbed up on top of a table with his two brothers and sang, off-key, the Kennedy family anthem, "Heart of My Heart."

In Massachusetts there are two very small communities, Washington, a hilltop town in the Berkshires, and Mashpee on Cape Cod, where the citizens follow a traditional practice of voting early in the morning so that their towns can be the first to complete and report their votes. The returns from Washington and Mashpee thus appear on the front pages of the newspapers early on the afternoon of Election Day. Both of the little towns are staunchly Republican so their returns always put the Republican candidates into an early lead.

Ted Kennedy decided to convert Washington and Mashpee to voting for John F. Kennedy. We tried to tell him that he was wasting his time, that both places would vote for Mao Tse-tung if Mao was running on the Republican ticket in Massachusetts, but Ted was determined. "Think how great it will look if the papers come out on Election Day with Jack beating Celeste in Washington and Mashpee," he said. Ted staged a personal crusade for his brother in the two towns, visiting the homes of the people, becoming personally friendly with all of them, and then announcing to us that he had both Washington and Mashpee sewed up. To Jack's amazement the returns from Washington and Mashpee on Election Day showed Celeste trailing Kennedy in both towns by 181 to 90.

The returns from all over the state that night began to show us at an early hour what we had been feeling for the past month, namely that the Kennedy campaign for reelection to the Senate was probably as nearly perfect in planning and operation as an election campaign in an off-year could be.

"If we don't get a majority of more than five hundred thousand," the Senator had said, "Vincent J. Celeste will be the real winner." That meant we had to get close to two million people to go to the polls, which seemed impossible in an off-year election so one-sided, with no real rivalry in it. Of course, we had a strong plus-factor in the personal appeal of our candidate. Nearly everybody in Massachusetts, Republicans and Democrats alike, had been thrilled by Jack Kennedy's performance at the 1956 Democratic convention in Chicago. They wanted him to be a candidate for President in 1960 and they were well aware that he needed a huge vote in this Senatorial election to win the Presidential nomination. To keep the average citizen's interest in Kennedy alive and throbbing and to get him to go to the polls and vote, we directed all of our campaign effort into two channels — personal appearances of the Senator in as many cities and towns as possible, and enlisting large numbers of volunteer workers for door-to-door canvassing in every community. Our workers obtained 300,000 signed pledges to vote for Kennedy and delivered personally to homes in 351 communities 1,240,000 copies of tabloid newspaper–style literature describing the Senator's past accomplishments and future aims. In other words, plenty of hard work in personal contacts with the people.

The figures that came in on election night showed how well this personal contact drive worked: close to two million people — 1,952,855, to be exact — actually went to the polls and voted, an incredible record-breaking number for an off-year election with no Presidential race. Kennedy received 73.6 percent of the votes, 1,362,926, giving him a majority of 874,608 over Celeste, the biggest majority ever won by a candidate for any office in Massachusetts, and the biggest majority won by any Senatorial candidate in the United States that year. His showing in the returns, even stronger than he hoped it would be, naturally attracted much attention all over the country, and he came out of the 1958 election a much more prominent candidate for the Presidency.

At his father's apartment in Boston, where we gathered that night to get the returns by telephone from our precinct workers, the Senator listened to the good news quietly, with little to say. He watched his father, who was eagerly answering the telephones, talking to the precinct workers, and repeating their figures to Dave Powers, who was working out percentages on a calculating machine.

"Here's Ward Two, Precinct Five," the Ambassador said at one point. "Where's that, Dave?"

"That's in Charlestown, the upper side of Bunker Hill Street," Dave said.

"Well, here's the vote — Kennedy twelve hundred seventy-one, Celeste eighty-five," Joe Kennedy said. He looked at Dave and frowned. "Say, Dave, that's your neighborhood. Have you got any idea who those eighty-five are?"

The Senator and Jackie said good night and left before two o'clock, which is early for an election night. The rest of us left soon after them, none of us particularly excited. We were already thinking about the next ball game.

SIX

Wisconsin and West Virginia

RELAXING ONE EVENING at the White House after a busy day that had gone well, President Kennedy leaned back in his chair with a smile and said to us, "Just think — if I had buried Hubert in Wisconsin, we might not be sitting here now." Like his fortunate defeat in the floor fight for the Vice-Presidential nomination in 1956, Kennedy's less than decisive win over Hubert Humphrey in the 1960 Wisconsin primary was a disappointment that later turned out to be a blessing. It was the lure that encouraged the happy Humphrey to challenge Kennedy once more in the West Virginia primary, forcing Kennedy to run against a Protestant opponent in a Bible belt state, 95 percent Protestant, where Kennedy's Catholicism was the burning issue. Kennedy faced the religious issue head-on, fought the greatest campaign of his career, and won 61 percent of the vote, carrying forty-eight of the fifty-five counties — much to our astonishment, and to the even greater astonishment of most of the Democratic leaders around the country who then made haste to climb on the Kennedy bandwagon. Kennedy won the Democratic Presidential nomination in West Virginia, rather than at the national convention in Los Angeles two months later, so you could say that Hubert Humphrey nominated Jack by running against him in that primary and giving him that opportunity to lick the religious issue in a showdown test that certainly must be a monument in American political history.

Politics, of course, is a very iffy business. What would have happened if Humphrey had not run against us in West Virginia? Perhaps Kennedy would have lost the nomination in Los Angeles, or at least he would have had a hard time winning it. If Hubert had won that primary, as seemed highly likely before the voting, Kennedy would have been finished as a Presidential candidate, and Humphrey himself would have been no better off politically. He was already out of the running for the Presidential nomination because he had failed the primary test in Wisconsin, next to his home state of Minnesota; any contender who cannot carry a state in his home territory stands little chance of nomination for national office. So Hubert had nothing to gain, except heavy financial debts, when he rushed into West Virginia. At our urging, his liberal friends, notably Walter Reuther, tried to talk him out of it, pointing out that if he knocked Kennedy out of the box, he would only be helping Lyndon B. Johnson. But happily for Kennedy, as it finally turned out, Hubert refused to listen.

There were hard and perplexing decisions in the earlier chain of moves and deals that led Kennedy into the primary at Wisconsin and from there to the all-decisive religious confrontation in West Virginia, which neither JFK nor any of the rest of us relished at the time. In fact, we dreaded it. We had not been anxious to run in Wisconsin, either. The most important decision facing Kennedy when he declared his candidacy for the Presidential nomination on January 2, 1960, was whether to enter the primary in Wisconsin or Ohio. It had to be one of those states or the other. He did not have the resources to run in both of them.

Our first choice was Ohio. Kennedy had agreed not to oppose Governor Pat Brown in the California primary in return for a promise of Brown's support at the convention if Jack came to Los Angeles as the leading candidate. But Kennedy was in no mood to make a similar tentative deal with Governor Mike DiSalle, who was running as a favorite-son candidate in the Ohio primary. DiSalle, a friend of Harry Truman's, could be expected to throw Ohio's sixty-four delegate votes to Stuart Symington, Truman's candidate, or to Lyndon Johnson, another old friend of Truman's. Moreover, DiSalle was one of the Catholic leaders who had opposed Kennedy in the 1956 Vice-Presidential fight.

To get Ohio's delegates, Kennedy was ready to run a campaign with strong backing from Ray Miller, the Democratic leader in Cleveland who was anxious to beat DiSalle and the Toledo organization in such a battle for party control in the state. Miller is a staunch Notre Dame alumnus and a brother of Don Miller, one of Knute Rockne's Four Horsemen. Dave Powers accompanied Kennedy to a meeting at Miller's home when the Senator was enlisting his support in Ohio, and came back with the report that "They take their politics as seriously as Notre Dame plays football."

The prospect of entering such a primary brawl in Ohio was naturally much more attractive to the Senator, and to Bobby and O'Brien and O'Donnell, than a campaign in March and April in the chilly farmlands of Wisconsin, where we would be facing Hubert Humphrey in his own Northern backyard. To recall the primary situation that year for those whose memory of it may be dim, Hubert was the only other contender for the Democratic nomination willing to run in the primaries. Lyndon Johnson was staying in Washington, campaigning in the cloakrooms of the Senate, convinced that he and Sam Rayburn, the Speaker of the House, could gain enough delegate votes by exerting pressure on Democratic Congressmen. Kennedy knew that the really influential figures in the various state delegations were county leaders and state legislators rather than the Senators and Congressmen in Washington, and he sought out the local politicians in extended speaking tours and primary campaigns. He expressed surprise that Lyndon was not competing in at least a few Northern primaries to show that he was capable of getting votes outside of Texas.

We felt that Stuart Symington, more acceptable to labor and Northern liberals than Johnson and also favored by the Old Guard Democrats and the Southerners, could have been our strongest opponent in 1960 if he had built up a bigger organization and had worked earlier and harder. Kennedy thought he could have been beaten by Symington in the Indiana primary, and perhaps knocked out of contention by such a defeat, if Symington had chosen to make a fight there. But Symington played coy, avoiding primary tests and hoping to capitalize on a deadlock at the convention. Adlai Stevenson was waiting for the nomination to be handed to him on a platter.

Kennedy's leading supporter in Wisconsin, Ivan Nestingen, the mayor of Madison, advised us that we would be much better off running in the primary in Ohio than in Wisconsin, where delegates are elected in each separate Congressional district and where Republicans can cross over in a primary and vote for or against a Democratic candidate. Kennedy could thus gain a big popular total vote and still lose delegates in rural and Protestant districts. Humphrey was strong with organized labor as well as with farmers in Wisconsin, where he was practically regarded as a native and often called "Wisconsin's third Senator." Humphrey was as well known and well liked in Wisconsin as Kennedy was in New Hampshire or Connecticut, and, as Nestingen pointed out, Kennedy was not well known in Wisconsin.

But Kennedy was more anxious to get unified Democratic support behind him in Ohio than he was eager to back Ray Miller's feud against DiSalle. There would be no point in making a costly primary fight if he could get DiSalle's backing and endorsement. Besides, a declaration of support from the Democratic governor of an important Midwestern state, coming out early in January before the primaries, would be a priceless boost for Kennedy's whole national campaign. Kennedy offered to stay out of the Ohio primary, and to let DiSalle run as a favorite-son candidate, if the governor would announce such an early endorsement.

DiSalle agreed to talk it over at a secret meeting with Kennedy in a motel at the airport at Pittsburgh, where Steve Smith reserved two rooms, one under the name of Smith and the other in the name of Brown, to hide the identity of the guests. John Bailey, our experienced politician from Connecticut who knew DiSalle well, made the trip to Pittsburgh with the Senator and me in the *Caroline*, the Kennedy family's Convair prop plane which we had been using in our travels since the previous September. Because of head winds, we were an hour late arriving at Pittsburgh. Then we went to the wrong motel. The desk clerk had never heard of reservations for Smith or Brown. I remembered that DiSalle had been planning to drive to Pittsburgh instead of flying there, so Bailey and I ran around the crowded parking lot, getting down on our knees to search in the darkness for an Ohio license plate. The smoothly organized and highly efficient Kennedy political machine had collapsed again.

"This is great," the Senator said. "Now you guys have ruined me in Ohio."

After we waited in the motel lobby, hoping that DiSalle might make a late appearance, the desk clerk remembered to mention that the airport had another motel. To reach it, we ran to the terminal and took an escalator up to the higher level of the building. While we were riding on the upbound escalator, we saw DiSalle with his secretary, Millie Cunningham, and his administrative assistant, Maurice Connell, coming down past us on the adjoining descending escalator. We waved to each other. As Jack remarked later, the whole situation was like a scene in a Mack Sennett movie comedy. DiSalle had given up waiting for us in the room reserved for Mr. Smith and was starting back to Ohio. He returned with us to the motel, where he and the Senator talked for an hour while Miss Cunningham, Connell, Bailey and I waited in the other room.

DiSalle was evasive in that first meeting, stalling for time against Kennedy's stipulation that he must come out immediately with an endorsement to avoid a primary fight with Ray Miller. Remembering the wrath of Harry Truman, whom he had served in Washington as head of the OPA, he had no desire to be the first big state governor to come out for Jack Kennedy, whose father was despised by Truman because Ambassador Kennedy had refused to contribute to Truman's 1948 campaign. ("I'm not against the Pope," Truman said of JFK's candidacy. "I'm against the Pop.") DiSalle argued that as a Catholic he was the wrong governor to support Kennedy first. "Get a couple of important Protestants to announce for you, and then I'll endorse you," he said. Kennedy argued that there was no time for a delay. The closing date in Ohio for the filing of a slate of Kennedy candidates was only a few weeks away, and he had to make an immediate decision. DiSalle warned that if Kennedy ran against him, Senator Frank Lausche, another potential favorite-son candidate, might go into the primary and beat both of them, but that possibility failed to upset Jack. He came out of the meeting knowing that he had DiSalle hooked, and he had no intention of letting the governor get off the hook.

Bobby Kennedy went to Ohio with John Bailey to put more pressure on DiSalle. Bailey, a veteran politician who does not shock easily, told me later that he was startled by the going-over that Bobby had given DiSalle. Jack had been allowing Mike a few inches of leeway to slide around in, understanding his political predicament, but Bobby closed up those few inches. Bobby made it coldly clear that DiSalle could avoid a showdown fight from Ray Miller for party leadership in Ohio, with the Kennedys backing Miller, only by agreeing to be the first governor of an important state to announce an endorsement of Jack Kennedy. We were sure that DiSalle was getting similar threats of primary opposition from Hubert Humphrey, and perhaps from Johnson and Symington, but since none of those candidates had an alliance with Ray Miller to wave before the governor, he could safely laugh at them, or tell them to go to hell.

I received word of DiSalle's capitulation from our candidate on New Year's Day, the day before his formal announcement that he was running for the Presidential nomination. He did not mention DiSalle or Ohio. All he said was, "You're going to Wisconsin." Which meant, of course, that Ohio was all wrapped up. Ray Miller was furious. A week later, to the great surprise of everyone in Washington, the newspaper headlines announced that Governor Michael DiSalle was pledging all of Ohio's delegate votes to John F. Kennedy.

The shrewd toughness used by the Kennedy brothers in wringing this all-important endorsement out of the reluctant governor so early in their campaign seemed to escape notice generally. Hubert Humphrey was probably unaware of it and Adlai Stevenson could not have appreciated such a power play if it was explained to him. But it did not escape Lyndon Johnson and it was noted with interest by Mayor Richard J. Daley in Chicago, by Carmine DeSapio and Charlie Buckley in New York, and other such old pros as Bill Green in Philadelphia and Frank McKinney in Indianapolis who were becoming more aware that the rising prominence of the Kennedys was based on something more substantial than boyish good looks, charm and money.

During the period when we were in the throes of trying to decide whether to run in the primary in Ohio or in the one against Humphrey in Wisconsin, Jack and Bobby worked out a contingency plan which they could use to explain why we were taking one or the other of those two routes. In December of 1959, Bobby called a press conference to announce to nobody's surprise that Jack would be running in the March primary in New Hampshire. (In that opening primary, close to home, the Senator opposed a local ball-point pen manufacturer named Paul Fisher and received 45,000 votes, including 2,000 write-ins on the Republican ballots, twice as many as the previous all-time record.) Bobby arranged to be asked during the discussion of the New Hampshire primary if his brother would also run in Wisconsin against Humphrey. Bobby ventured the opinion that Wisconsin, next door to Humphrey's home state of Minnesota, would not be a fair place for Hubert to challenge the Senator from Massachusetts, just as Jack Kennedy would never expect Humphrey to face him in New Hampshire. If Humphrey wanted to meet Kennedy in a primary bout, Bobby said, it should be on more neutral ground, such as Nebraska, Maryland, Ohio or California. This was Contingency Explanation Number One, prepared to cover our invasion of Ohio instead of Wisconsin, in case the deal with Mike DiSalle did not jell. If DiSalle gave in, Contingency Explanation Number Two was ready to go into a press release, with Jack announcing that on second thought he was overruling his brother's demand for a challenge on neutral territory — he was ready to meet Humphrey in any arena anywhere, even in Humphrey's own neighborhood. When DiSalle agreed to give his delegates' votes to Kennedy and we were forced unhappily to go into Wisconsin instead of Ohio, Jack played up the switch in plans with that dramatic flourish.

Our memories of Jack Kennedy are filled with scenes and incidents in Wisconsin, most of them seeming more amusing now in retrospect than then in that winter of cold winds, cold towns and many cold people. Campaigning in rural areas of the state where nobody seemed to care about the Presidential election was a strange and frustrating experience. When Dave Powers woke up the Senator on the seventeenth of March for a day of touring the unfriendly Ninth District, Kennedy eyed Dave's Kelly green necktie and said, "That tie won't get us any votes where we're going today." In some towns, it was difficult to find anybody who was willing to shake hands, and most of the people who did talk to Kennedy were schoolchildren, too young to vote. He went into a tavern and approached a booth where a man and a woman were sitting over two glasses of beer, saying to them, "My name is John Kennedy and I'm running for President." The man turned his head toward Kennedy, looked him over slowly and said, "President of what?" At six o'clock that evening, he climbed into the waiting car, facing a drive of fifty more miles on empty roads before visiting a factory in Ashland, an ice-locked port on Lake Superior. He said to Dave, "What a hell of a way to spend Saint Patrick's Day."

Dave and I recalled recently one terribly cold morning when we had to get the Senator out of bed at five-thirty to shake hands with workers at a meat-packing plant. The night before he did not get to sleep until after two o'clock. Dave and I were having a beer when we noticed a note on the next day's schedule reminding us to call him at five-thirty so he would be able to meet an incoming crowd of fifteen hundred employees at the nearby plant. The blue-collar workers arrived between six and eight o'clock and the white-collar people between eight and nine. I said, "God, Dave, I don't have the guts to wake him at that hour." We thought about it and had another beer. Dave said, "Well, fifteen hundred people are hard to get in this damned part of Wisconsin. If we let him sleep until nine, he'll be mad at us for letting him miss a crowd like that. I'll walk into his room at five-thirty." He would go to sleep as soon as his head touched the pillow, but he would usually wake up immediately if a mouse walked through his bedroom.

At five-thirty that morning it was about fifteen above zero outside, and cold in the Senator's bedroom with frost on the window. Dave tiptoed into the room and Jack sat up in bed, saying "Who's that?" Dave said, "It's Dave Powers, Senator. It's five-thirty."

"What the hell are you doing in here at five-thirty, Dave?"

Dave began to explain about the suggested visit to the meat-packing plant. While he was talking, Jack was getting dressed, pulling on the heavy pants and shirt of long underwear. As much as he hated to wear heavy clothing, he agreed to wear long johns under his suit and shirt in that freezing weather. When we went outside, he wore a fur-lined glove on his left hand but his right hand was bare, for handshaking. Dave, Ivan Nestingen and I stood beside him in the darkness at the plant gate, passing out Kennedy buttons and literature, while he shook hands with each arriving worker. For the first hour it was so dark that we could hardly see him. We could only hear his voice, saying over and over again, "I'm John Kennedy, candidate for President, and I'd like to have your vote in the primary. . . . I'm John Kennedy, candidate for President . . ." My ears were numb from the cold and I was trying to rub them. Dave said to me, "God, if I had his money, I'd be down there on the patio at Palm Beach." It was so cold that even Jack was wearing a hat, pulled down over his ears, a strange sight to see. When the office workers began to dwindle at nine o'clock, we hurried into a nearby luncheonette and ordered coffee, which was served in tall paper cups.

Then we noticed that Jack's bare right hand, swollen and blue from the cold, was scratched and bleeding. Its flesh had been torn in many places by the fingernails scraped against it in hurried handshakes. Jack picked up his steaming cup of coffee, took a sip of it, and put it down on the counter.

"You know, Dave," he said to Powers cheerfully, "they have pretty good coffee here, don't they?"

Dave enjoys recalling another night in Oshkosh when Jack delivered a speech declaring that the nation needed a change in administration in 1960 after eight drab years of Eisenhower Republicanism as much as it yearned for the new dynamic drive of Franklin D. Roosevelt's New Deal in 1933. Contrasting Herbert Hoover's "hesitant and moribund" outgoing administration of the Depression with the bold spirit brought to Washington by Roosevelt, Kennedy quoted from a poem written at the time by Robert E. Sherwood:

> *Plodding feet*
> *Tramp — tramp*
> *The Grand Old Party's*
> *Breaking camp.*
> *Blare of bugles, din-din*
> *The New Deal is moving in.*

After the speech Jack stopped in the bar of the hotel where we were spending the night and talked with some of the newsmen who were covering the primary campaign. Austin Weirwein of the *New York Times* said to him, "You were a little off in that speech tonight."

"A little off?" Kennedy said.

"That line of verse," Weirwein said. " 'The blare of bugles, din-din, the New Deal is moving in.' There should be another 'din' in there. 'The blare of bugles, din-*din*-din.' "

Jack stared at him for moment, without saying anything, and went upstairs to bed. The next morning when he was shaving, he said to Dave, "Haven't we got enough troubles without that Weirwein complaining because he thinks there ought to be another din? What am I supposed to do? Put it to music and play it for him?"

Jackie Kennedy was unable to join the later campaign, after her

husband won the nomination at Los Angeles, because of her pregnancy, but she worked hard in Wisconsin, not only in March and
April when we brought in everybody in the family and all of their
friends to help in the final drive before the voting, but on weekends
in January and February when the rough winter weather was at its
worst. Getting out of the car into the snow and wind, Jackie would
shake hands and talk with people on one sidewalk on the main
street of a small town while her husband worked his way along the
opposite side of the street. He kept his eyes on her, and often muttered to one of us, "Jackie's drawing more people than I am, as
usual."

With his total recall of dates, names and places, Dave tells a story
about Jackie and Jack in Fort Atkinson, Wisconsin, in which the
date is significant. I remember the incident well, but I cannot swear to
the authenticity of the date that Dave ascribes to it. When we arrived in Fort Atkinson, a town noted for manufacturing sausages
and musical saws, the wife of the local Lutheran minister was waiting outside the Blackhawk Hotel with her thirteen children, eager to
introduce them to the Senator. She had read *Profiles in Courage* and
admired it deeply. Jack shook hands with the beaming mother and
each of her children, posed for pictures with them, and then said to
me, "Get Jackie and bring her over here." I escorted Jackie across
the street from the opposite sidewalk where she had been charming
a crowd of her own admirers. Jack introduced her to the mother of
thirteen children and said to her, "Shake hands with this lady,
Jackie. Maybe it will rub off on you." Dave pauses dramatically at
this point in the story before delivering the punch line.

"That was on February 15, 1960," he says. "Nine months later
John F. Kennedy, Junior, was born."

Jackie had her own ideas about campaigning, and often carried
them out calmly and coolly without consulting any of us. One day
in Kenosha she walked into a busy supermarket and listened to the
manager announcing bargain sale items over a loudspeaker system.
She located the microphone, gave the manager a dazzling smile, and
asked if she could say a few words. The next voice heard throughout
the crowded store was the soft tones of Jacqueline Kennedy. "Just
keep on with your shopping while I tell you about my husband,
John F. Kennedy," she said. She talked briefly about his service in
the Navy and in Congress and then closed with, "He cares deeply

about the welfare of his country — please vote for him." We never heard about the speech in the supermarket from Jackie. Helen Keyes, who was traveling with her that day, told us about it later and said, "While she was talking, you could have heard a pin drop."

On the evening of that same day in Kenosha, Jackie was trying to keep a crowd entertained until her husband arrived. "Let's sing a song," she said. "Does anybody here know 'Southie Is My Home Town'?" Needless to say, nobody in Kenosha had ever heard the favorite Saint Patrick's Day marching song of the South Boston Irish.

All of the Kennedys — except the Ambassador — were actively involved in the Wisconsin primary. Squeamish about his conservative image, Joe Kennedy made no public appearances with his son during the entire 1960 Presidential campaign, and did not appear in a newspaper photograph with Jack until the day after Election Day. But the Ambassador was very busy at home on the telephone. Rose and her daughters, Eunice, Pat and Jean, appeared at receptions and house parties and rang doorbells. Teddy risked his neck making a publicized ski jump on his brother's behalf, and Bobby, as usual, worked a twenty-hour day every day. Hubert Humphrey complained about the Kennedy invasion. "They're all over the state, and they look alike and sound alike," Humphrey said. "Teddy or Eunice talks to a crowd, wearing a raccoon coat and a stocking cap, and people think they're listening to Jack. I get reports that Jack is appearing in three or four different places at the same time."

All of Jack's college and PT-boat friends, and many of the men and women who worked for us in Massachusetts in 1952 and 1958, came to Wisconsin and pitched in for the cause. The assignments given to some of them seemed not only unreasonable but impossible. Helen Keyes, whose father was the Kennedy family's Boston dentist, went into the small towns in the anti-Kennedy and anti-Catholic districts, where she knew nobody, and asked housewives to arrange tea parties and receptions in their homes for Eunice, Pat and Jean Kennedy. And not just a few house parties. Bobby told her that he wanted each of his three sisters to attend nine house parties a day, or a total of twenty-seven parties a day in every town, over a period of two weeks. We sent Paul Corbin, one of our Wisconsinite workers, to help Helen get started on her rounds. Corbin admired

Bobby Kennedy so much that he became a Catholic so he could have Bobby as his godfather.

The first prospective house party hostess approached by Corbin and Helen was the waitress who served them breakfast in Wisconsin Springs, the first town they visited. They found out that the waitress was a Democrat, and asked if she would vote for Kennedy. "I can't vote for him," she said. "He's a Catholic."

"How about inviting some of your friends to your house to meet one of his sisters?" Helen asked.

"Well, I'll ask my father," the waitress said. "But I don't think he'll like it. Aren't Kennedy's sisters Catholics, too?"

Paul Corbin pointed at Helen Keyes, a very devout Catholic, and said to the waitress, "This lady is a Baptist from Boston and *she's* for Kennedy." Helen remarked later that she was so nervous about hiding her religion that she expected to hear a cock crowing three times. The waitress called her father and agreed to have a Kennedy party at her house.

"Then I went to a local drugstore," Helen says, "and I asked the druggist if his wife would give a party for one of the Kennedy girls. He said he was afraid to do it because his father lost his business in that town because he came out for Al Smith in 1928. But after some soul-searching the druggist decided to take a chance on letting us have a party in his house, and it was a big success. In another town we talked the wife of a funeral director into giving a party in her living quarters, in the rear of the funeral home. When she gave the party, with Jean as the honored guest, there was a wake going on in the funeral parlor down the hall. The mourners left the wake and came to the party, and after Jean talked with them and drank a cup of tea with them, they went back to the wake. That afternoon I got Jean to give a talk at a cattle auction. We found out that it was easier to talk a housewife into giving a party if we told her that Peter Lawford's wife, Pat Lawford, would be coming to her house. Peter Lawford had a weekly comedy show on television then, and he was a much bigger celebrity in Wisconsin than Jack Kennedy. After a big crowd of women gathered at the party to get a peek at Pat Lawford, I would appear with Eunice or Jean, and explain with profuse apologies that Pat couldn't make it. Of course I didn't mention that Pat couldn't be there because she was at another party in the next block."

Since Wisconsin has a considerable Catholic population, Kennedy's religion was not as bad a problem there as it was later in totally Protestant West Virginia, but it was bad enough. The Senator was irritated by the heavy play given to the religious issue in the local newspapers. He counted twenty mentions of the word "Catholic" in one story about the primary contest that ran only fifteen paragraphs in length. The *Milwaukee Journal* on the Sunday before the voting day listed the numbers of voters in each county, dividing the figures into three columns, Democrat, Republican and Catholic. When he was discussing the religious issue with local politicians, Kennedy would surprise them by showing them that Al Smith had carried more states in 1928 than Adlai Stevenson won in 1956. Despite the Ku Klux Klan, Smith defeated Herbert Hoover in Alabama, Arkansas, Georgia, Mississippi, South Carolina and Louisiana, as well as in Massachusetts and Rhode Island, a total of eight states, one more than Stevenson won in 1956 and three more than Barry Goldwater won in 1964.

In the primaries and in the later election campaign, Kennedy often kidded the religious issue in a speech opening that he had used to wake up a sleepy audience at the annual Alfred E. Smith memorial dinner in New York the year before. With an air of seriousness, he would say, "I think it well that we recall what happened to a great governor when he became a Presidential nominee. Despite his successful record as a governor, despite his plain-spoken voice, the campaign was a debacle. His views were distorted. He carried fewer states than any candidate in his party's history." The listeners assumed that he was talking about Al Smith. Then he would say, "To top it off, he lost his own state that he had served so well as a governor. You all know his name and his religion — Alfred M. Landon, Protestant."

Kennedy won in Wisconsin with more popular votes than any candidate in the history of the state's primary, carrying six of the ten Congressional districts and getting two-thirds of the delegate votes. That seemed good enough to me, but it was not good enough to satisfy the experts, because Kennedy failed to carry the three so-called Protestant districts in the western part of the state and lost to Humphrey in the Second District, around Madison, where we had expected to win. Kennedy's big popular vote was belittled because it came from strongly Catholic districts. In the hotel room at Milwaukee, when Dave was getting returns on the telephone from Bobby and me and handing them to the candidate, Eunice Kennedy was puzzled to see her brother glancing at the impressive popular-vote figures with a glum expression on his face. "What does it all mean, Johnny?" she said to him.

"It means that we've got to go to West Virginia in the morning and do it all over again," Jack said. "And then we've got to go on to Maryland and Indiana and Oregon, and win all of them."

Humphrey was claiming a moral victory and announcing that he would take on Jack again in West Virginia. "Maybe I can hitch a ride down there in Jack's private plane," he was saying. That night the *Caroline* dropped off Jackie and Jack and Dave in Washington, and came back to Milwaukee and flew Bobby and Larry O'Brien and me to West Virginia the next morning. We arrived in Charleston rather tired from the last hard week of work in Wisconsin, and rather hung over from the previous night's quiet victory party, but all of us were looking forward to the primary campaign in West Virginia in a reasonably cheerful and optimistic mood. One of the most skillful and knowledgeable Democratic politicians in the state, Bob McDonough, had been putting together a Kennedy organization there for the past year. A poll of voters, taken by Lou Harris four months before, showed that Kennedy could beat Humphrey in West Virginia by a comfortable seventy to thirty margin.

McDonough met us at the airport and took us directly to a meeting of his key workers at the Kanawha Hotel which he had arranged in anticipation of our coming. The room was crowded. When we took our seats at the head table, we did not notice that everybody was silent and none of them was smiling. McDonough introduced Bobby, whom many of the people had met before in our previous visits. "Well," Bobby said to them pleasantly, "what are our problems?"

A man stood up and shouted, "There's only one problem. He's a Catholic. That's our God-damned problem!"

The room broke into an uproar with everybody yelling at us that nobody in the state would vote for a Catholic in a contested Presidential primary, or even in an election for dogcatcher. We were stunned by the suddenness of this wild emotional outburst from a group of people who had been working enthusiastically for Kennedy over the past several months, and who had never shown much concern about the religious issue up to this time. Now all of them were saying that in the last week, all over West Virginia, they were getting abuse and ridicule from their own friends and neighbors because they were supporting a Catholic. I began to gather that apparently Kennedy's Catholicism was not well known to most West Virginians until the recent reports of his religious problems in the Wisconsin primary were given widespread coverage by local newspapers and television news shows. Overnight our whole situation in West Virginia had changed, and all of the careful and hopeful planning for a successful campaign in this Southern border state, which would bring Kennedy into the Los Angeles convention as the leading contender, was on the brink of going down the drain. I looked at Bobby. He seemed to be in a state of shock. His face was as pale as ashes.

When we left the meeting, Bobby went to a telephone booth and called Jack in Washington. Our only hope of avoiding an ugly religious brawl, Bobby told Jack, was to persuade Hubert Humphrey to withdraw. It was a reasonable request to make because we had defeated Hubert in a fair and square contest in Wisconsin and he had nothing to gain in West Virginia anyway. He was already out of the running for the nomination. If he persisted in getting involved in a Protestant-Catholic battle with Kennedy in West Virginia, he might only destroy himself and Kennedy politically. As our own workers had warned us that morning, Kennedy was likely to lose such a contested primary race against a Protestant. Even if Humphrey won, he would be charged with stirring up a revival of 1928 bigotry and denounced as a tool of the anti-Catholics. That would finish him as a crusading liberal, and damage the Democratic party.

Jack was taken aback by Bobby's discouragement. "It can't be that bad," he said, and reminded Bobby of the seventy-thirty Harris poll. Bobby said, "The people who voted for you in that poll have just found out that you're a Catholic."

"Come back to Washington for a few days," Jack said, "and we'll see what we can do with Hubert."

We called Humphrey's friends and they called Humphrey. I called Jack Conway, Walter Reuther's top man, and described to him the angry scene at the meeting in the Kanawha Hotel. He called Reuther, who urged Hubert to withdraw. Jim Rowe, Humphrey's close adviser, reminded him that he had lost in Wisconsin and that he could do himself more good politically by staying out of West Virginia than by getting into a religious bloodbath there with Kennedy. Orville Freeman and Alex Rose and many other liberals called Humphrey, but the more calls Hubert received, the more determined he became to stay in the primary fight. He declared that he could not appear to be a paid tool of the Kennedys. But at the same time he was getting promises of financial backing from supporters of Adlai Stevenson who wanted him to knock Kennedy out of contention in West Virginia so that Stevenson could get the nomination at Los Angeles.

We waited for a few days, hoping that Jack might come up with some sort of magic solution to the whole depressing situation, but the only solution, he decided, was to go into West Virginia and make a hard fight of it. Any remote possibility of Jack himself withdrawing from the primary was dispelled by the growing encouragement that Humphrey was getting from other Democratic candidates, particularly Lyndon Johnson, who wanted him to stop Kennedy in order to help their own chances of winning the nomination. West Virginia's Senator Robert Byrd, an active supporter of Johnson, made no secret of the fact that he was endorsing Hubert in the primary only to stop Kennedy. Byrd issued an appeal to the voters in West Virginia in which he said, "If you are for Adlai Stevenson, Senator Stuart Symington, Senator Johnson or John Doe, this primary may be your last chance to stop Kennedy." Lyndon Johnson himself made a speech for Humphrey in Clarksburg, West Virginia, which was certainly a curious move for a rival seeking the same Democratic Presidential nomination that Humphrey was supposed to be seeking. Aside from the challenge of the religious issue, the primary in West Virginia became such a blatantly open effort on the part of all the other contenders to stop Kennedy that Jack's aroused Irish temper made him eager to plunge into it.

We went into the campaign in a gloomy mood, figuring that odds were stacked against us and praying that Jack might at least be able to keep Humphrey from winning more than 60 percent of the votes, so that we could claim the moral victory that Hubert had claimed in Wisconsin. Bob McDonough, our calm and always resourceful organizer who seemed to know everybody in the state, was more optimistic and kept assuring us that the Senator's straightforward and engaging ease in approaching people would gain him respect in

West Virginia and overcome the bigotry. "They're against Catholics in theory," Bob said, "but wait until they meet *this* Catholic." Jack admired Bob's unruffled disregard for the hostility in the atmosphere and began to call him "our man in Havana."

Jack himself, always at his best when the going was roughest, was more confident and more determined to win than any of us. I remember how chipper he was on the day when he and I flew into Charleston from Washington for the more or less official opening of the primary campaign. He was to make his first appearance at our new headquarters and go to the county clerk's office to file his candidate's papers. On the flight from Washington, I was in a dismal state of mind, certain that we were getting into a disastrous situation, and, for the first time in all the years that we had worked together in politics, he was trying to cheer me up instead of listening skeptically to my usual locker-room-type pep talks. We had just heard that on top of everything else the United Mineworkers, the big labor union in West Virginia, had strongly endorsed Humphrey in retaliation for Bobby and Jack's work on the McClellan committee. But Jack was cheerfully unperturbed. I was thinking, here we are, starting an entirely new kind of fight against emotional prejudice, with nothing working for us except the courage and personality of this fellow with the unruly hair sitting beside me in the back cabin of the *Caroline*.

We went to our headquarters in Charleston where the candidate shook hands with everybody, and then we walked to the county clerk's office with McDonough leading the way and O'Brien and me following along like a couple of Pinkerton agents. There was a good-sized crowd gathered around the county office building, waiting to get a look at the Presidential candidate, but it was the first crowd I had ever seen around Kennedy that stayed away from him, watching him quietly from the sidewalk on the opposite side of the street. Only two men approached him and reached out to shake his hand. When we were going into the building, he turned to me and said, "Those two guys must have been a couple of visiting Catholics from Pennsylvania." A few people whom we met in the corridor of the building on our way to the clerk's office shrank back against the wall to let him pass, as if they were afraid of being touched by him. McDonough introduced him to a few county officials who were waiting in the clerk's office to meet him. The Senator was given a polite welcome and everybody expressed pleasure to have him in the primary but it was explained that since most of the officials present would be on the ballot themselves — a list of the various candidates running for various county offices in Kanawha County fills three newspaper pages — none of them would be able to help him.

We went back to our hotel. When the door was closed, Kennedy looked at us and said, "Well, I guess you guys weren't exaggerating."

All of the old troopers were summoned to duty in West Virginia, along with a few new ones whom we had picked up in Wisconsin, such as Jerry Bruno, who did our advance work there and stayed on with us as an advance man until we went to Dallas. Bob McDonough and his able and tough West Virginian right-hand man, big Matt Reese, were understandably perplexed by some of Jack's Ivy League friends and Boston Irish Catholics, who were hardly the type to mingle well with voters in the impoverished coal-mining towns and the firmly anti-Catholic industrial cities. One of Jack's PT-boat buddies had to be pulled out of the town that he was supposed to be organizing because he was antagonizing the Democrats in the area by spending all of his time socializing with coal mine owners who were enrolled Republicans. But most of our imported helpers got along famously with the down-to-earth people in West Virginia. Ted Reardon, the Senator's administrative assistant in Washington, organized the northern section of the state, around Wheeling and Parkersburg, which became a Kennedy stronghold in the closing weeks of the campaign. Bill Walton, the artist who was a close friend of both the Kennedys and Ernest Hemingway, worked in the mountain villages of McDowell County. Our girls from Massachusetts, Polly Fitzgerald, Eunice Ford, Helen Lempart, Pat Twohig and Helen Keyes, staged highly successful hot dog roasts and barbecues in mining towns and country club receptions in the more affluent cities. Ethel, Jean and Joan Kennedy came to West Virginia on their own, with no invitation, and demanded work. They were sent out to ring doorbells. Jackie, then in the early stages of pregnancy, insisted on traveling throughout the state with Ed King as her driver, and visited miners' wives in their ramshackle company houses, handed out bumper stickers at shopping centers, and shook hands on street corners. One day, driving alongside a stretch of railroad tracks, Jackie saw a gang of railroad laborers sitting on the tracks, eating lunch. She asked King to stop the car, got out and sat down with the workmen and chatted with them for a half hour.

Kennedy's most valuable campaigner in West Virginia was Franklin D. Roosevelt, Jr., whose famous name is held in reverence in the coal-mining state. As President during the early Depression years, Roosevelt's father pushed NRA legislation that gave coal miners the right to organize and to get decent living wages for the first time in history. Recruiting Franklin Roosevelt for duty in West Virginia was Ambassador Kennedy's idea. The Ambassador also saw to it that letters to voters in West Virginia, praising Senator Kennedy and signed by Roosevelt, were shipped to Hyde Park, New York, to be postmarked and mailed from there.

Roosevelt spoke for Kennedy all over the state and was mobbed by admirers wherever he went. Appealing to the militant patriotism of the West Virginians, he heavily emphasized the Senator's war record, sometimes making it seem as if his own destroyer and PT-109 had fought in the same battles. "You know why I'm here in West Virginia today?" Frank would say. "Because Jack Kennedy and I fought side by side in the Pacific. He was on the PT boats and I was on the destroyers." One day when introducing Jack to a crowd in Bluefield, Roosevelt delivered one of his often-used and most effective lines. Holding up two fingers tightly pressed together, he said, "My daddy and Jack Kennedy's daddy were just like that!"

Kennedy turned to Dave Powers and me and muttered, "This is a hard act to follow."

At the beginning of the primary campaign in West Virginia, the religious issue was treated rather gingerly in private meetings and scarcely mentioned in public. Then Jack made the crucial decision, on his own, to speak out openly to the voters about the religious prejudice against him. Several of his advisers in Washington were against it, arguing that talking about his religion would embarrass the listeners, and might only increase the anti-Catholic feeling in the state. I was against it for a different reason. I was afraid that bringing the religious problem into the open might antagonize important Catholic leaders in other states, particularly Governor David Lawrence in Pennsylvania, who was oversensitive on the subject and reluctant to back Kennedy because of his Catholicism.

As a matter of fact, Kennedy had been roundly criticized in the

Catholic press and by Catholic clergymen a year earlier when he aired his views on the issue in an interview in *Look* magazine, firmly stating his belief in the separation of the church from the state. The criticism was based on the mere fact that Kennedy submitted to such an interview. The Jesuit weekly, *America*, argued that there was no need for Kennedy to defend his religious beliefs. Cardinal Cushing in Boston and Bishop John Wright in Pittsburgh, two old friends, came to Kennedy's defense, but Cardinal Spellman in New York remained silent.

But when Kennedy made up his mind to meet the religious issue in West Virginia openly and head-on, none of us could change his mind. "Let's face it," he said. "It's the most important and the biggest issue in this campaign. Hubert can't talk about it, although he uses the music of 'Give Us That Oldtime Religion' in his campaign song. So if I talk about it, I'll be the only candidate talking about the most important issue that all the voters are thinking about."

The first time Kennedy spoke out on the religious question before a big crowd was at a noon rally on the main street in Morgantown. I was with him that day and I had no idea that he was going to do it. I had assumed that when he did make his first speech on that topic it would be carefully prepared and planned for either a special occasion or a television appearance, and not in an informal talk to a street crowd like this one. I am sure that he did not plan to go into a defense of his religion that day but did it on the spur of the moment, talking off the cuff with no preparation. He had started his speech with the usual discussion about why a change was needed in the government. I was watching the crowd without paying much attention to his words. Then I saw the interest of the people around me tightening and I heard him saying, "Nobody asked me if I was a Catholic when I joined the United States Navy." It was so unexpected, and such a strange experience for me to hear him talking about his Catholicism before a Protestant audience, that I felt as if a bucket of cold water had been thrown at my face. I could see that the crowd was as stunned as I was. He went on with a fire and dash that I had seldom seen in him, asking if forty million Americans lost their right to run for the Presidency on the day when they were baptized as Catholics. "That wasn't the country my brother died for in Europe," he said, "and nobody asked my brother if he was a

Catholic or a Protestant before he climbed into an American bomber plane to fly his last mission."

Whether or not the people in that West Virginian town agreed with what he was saying, it was the kind of bold and lively fighting talk that they liked to hear. Two men standing near me in the back of the crowd looked at each other. One of the men said, "Pretty good talker." The other man nodded, and said, "Good-looking feller, isn't he?" I said to myself, here is another new side of John Kennedy that I have not seen before. He surprised me in 1956 when he took on Onions Burke in the Massachusetts state committee fight, and he surprised me when he put the squeeze on Mike DiSalle. Now he was surprising me again.

When we got into the car to drive to the next town on our schedule, Kennedy said, "How did it go?" I was still too shaken up to say much except, "Very good. Keep it up." I could see that he was pleased with himself. He talked again about his religion and the right of a Catholic to run for the Presidency at every other stop that day, and in almost every speech that he made from then on until the primary.

We felt that Kennedy probably broke the religious barrier in West Virginia on the Sunday evening before the voting day, when he appeared on a television broadcast and delivered a serious and moving plea for tolerance, explaining that a Catholic President who allowed his decisions to be influenced by his church would be breaking his oath of office and could be impeached. Some of us who were close to Kennedy, including Dick Donahue, a diligent student of JFK's politics who was with him in the television studio, still consider that talk to be one of the greatest speaking performances of his entire career. Theodore H. White, who covered the West Virginia campaign while doing research for the 1960 volume of his *The Making of the President* books, wrote that it was "the finest TV broadcast I have ever heard any political candidate make."

Kennedy gave the talk extemporaneously during a question-and-answer discussion, with Franklin Roosevelt asking the questions. There was no written script, and unfortunately nobody made a recording or a transcript of the broadcast. If there was a copy of it available today, it might not make impressive reading. The way that Kennedy talked, holding the television audience spellbound for more than ten minutes, was more stirring and dramatic than the words he was using. Teddy White, who made notes during the broadcast, says, "Later the same phrases were to grow sterile, but at this moment Kennedy spoke from the gut. He reviewed the long war of church on state and state on church and that greatest of all constitutional decisions: to separate church from state. Then, peering into the camera and talking directly to the people of West Virginia, he proceeded, as I remember, thus:

". . . so when any man stands on the steps of the Capitol and takes the oath of office as President, he is swearing to support the separation of church and state. He puts one hand on the Bible and raises the other hand to God as he takes the oath. And if he breaks his oath, he is not only committing a crime against the Constitution, for which the Congress can impeach him, and should impeach him, but he is committing a sin against God."

When he was breaking down the prejudice against his religion, Kennedy was winning warm approval and respect from the West Virginians in the poverty-stricken mining areas by going into their villages in the mountain range hollows, listening sympathetically to their complaints, and promising to make their troubles known in Washington. The crowds of miners cheered wildly when he said, "President Eisenhower should take Vice-President Nixon by the hand and lead him into these homes in McDowell County and Mingo County and Logan County so he can see how the families of West Virginia are trying to live." Then he would ask the miners, who were all Democrats, "And if Lyndon Johnson wants to be your candidate for President, why isn't he here today?"

Johnson's support of Humphrey, and Senator Byrd's foolish admission that he was working for Humphrey in West Virginia only to stop Kennedy so that Johnson could get the nomination, shifted many votes from Humphrey to Kennedy in the closing days of the campaign. "Will my real opponent for the Presidential nomination in West Virginia please stand up?" Kennedy said in his speeches. "Hubert Humphrey has no chance to win the Democratic nomination for President, and he knows it, so why is he running against me in this primary? To stop me and give the nomination to Johnson or Stevenson or Symington. If Johnson and the other candidates want your vote in the November election, why don't they have enough respect for you to come here and ask for your vote in the primary?" This attack on Humphrey as a straw candidate appealed to the West Virginians' strong sense of fair play, and built up an attractive image of Kennedy as the one and only genuine contender for the Presidential nomination who was concerned enough about the state and its unemployment problems to become involved in its primary.

Meanwhile Humphrey's own campaign was floundering. Since he and Kennedy agreed on the basic issues, unemployment, medical care, and the need for Federal aid to schools and housing, Humphrey's aids resorted frantically to charges that Kennedy's money was buying the election. That argument stirred up no great excitement among the earthy and realistic people of West Virginia, who were accustomed to seeing the local candidate for sheriff carrying a little black bag that contained something other than a few bottles of Bourbon whiskey. Nixon's close friend, William P. Rogers, who was then the Attorney General, ordered an FBI investigation of the West Virginia primary campaign, which failed to turn up any evidence of vote-buying, excessive spending or any other wrongdoing. On the day before the voting Humphrey staged a telethon that was a disaster. He tried to answer telephone calls that could be heard on the air along with his replies, and failed to take the necessary precaution of screening out calls from nuts and fanatics. One of the first incoming voices heard on the show was that of an elderly woman who screamed at him, "You git out of West Virginia, Mr. Humphrey! You git out, do you hear?" Then while Hubert was talking with somebody on a party line in a rural area, the operator interrupted the call and told him to hang up and get off the wire because she had to put through an emergency call. Obviously, somebody on the party line needed a doctor in a hurry, but Humphrey tried to argue with the operator and his program turned into a shambles. Jack said to us later, "If I had known Hubert wasn't screening those calls, I would have called him up myself and asked him a few embarrassing questions. Or, better still, I might have gotten Bobby to call him."

Humphrey made a display of challenging Kennedy to a debate on television, and was somewhat flustered when Kennedy accepted. The debate itself was inconclusive because of the similarity of the liberal stands of both candidates on the campaign issues, but Kennedy's poise and cool wit showed to advantage on the television screen as it did in the later debates against Nixon. Kennedy came to the studio carrying in his hand a government food-ration package, one of the containers of canned soup, powdered milk and other rations then being distributed daily to families in the impoverished areas of the state. Humphrey looked at the food package, and knew that Kennedy would use it before the television camera to illustrate the plight of West Virginia's unemployed people. Hubert shook his head with sad envy and said, "This guy thinks of *everything*."

Although Humphrey was obviously slipping in the last week of the hard campaign and Kennedy was reported to be picking up new supporters all over the state, Bobby and I were both unconvinced that Jack was gaining enough ground to overcome the religious prejudice against him. The day before the voting we sat in our headquarters at the Kanawha Hotel with Bob McDonough and Lou Harris, each of us trying to figure on yellow pads of paper what the vote would be. I made the most optimistic prediction, and I gave Jack a margin of only fifty-one to forty-nine, mainly because I was trying to cheer up Bobby and O'Brien, who were both in the depths of gloom. McDonough, who could predict the vote with more authority than anybody, gave Jack an even fifty-fifty chance. Harris, our supposedly peerless pollster, was in a dither. A few weeks after the campaign opened Harris had made another poll in the state which showed Humphrey ahead, seventy to thirty, just exactly the reverse of his poll of the previous December, which had Kennedy leading Humphrey, seventy to thirty. We accused Harris of making a typing error in the first poll and getting his figures transposed into the wrong columns. Now he seemed to be changing his figures every hour, according to the latest rumors of switching votes, and we were paying no attention to his soundings. On the Saturday before the primary Tuesday, Harris decided that Humphrey was ahead forty-five to forty-two with 13 percent of the voters undecided, and after Kennedy's Sunday night television broadcast on the religious question the Harris poll gave him a slight lead. That estimate, of course, was just as wrong as the first Harris poll had been in December. When the returns began to come in on Tuesday night, Harris was more astounded than any of us.

On the morning of the primary voting day, Jack flew to Washington to spend the day with Jackie and to appear with her at a Democratic women's luncheon. When Bobby and I drove back into

Charleston after watching the *Caroline* take off, we felt that our Presidential campaign was all over. Jack had won the primary in Indiana a week before and was running, and winning by a big vote, that same day in Nebraska. He was scheduled to run in the primaries in Maryland and Oregon. But thanks to the unexpected opposition from Hubert Humphrey and the sudden rise with it of the religious issue in this Protestant state, the West Virginia primary, which we regarded as unimportant up until a month ago, was now the barrier blocking Kennedy from the party's nomination. "If we lose here today," Bobby said, "we might as well stay home and watch the convention on television. Damn that Hubert Humphrey."

That night at nine o'clock the first returns came in from a precinct in Hardy County in the northern panhandle where there were twenty-five Catholic voters. It gave Kennedy ninety-six votes to Humphrey's thirty-six. We tried not to seem too excited, because we had expected to do well in the northern part of the state, but soon there were more returns showing that Kennedy was running well ahead, by a sixty to forty margin, all over West Virginia, and even carrying Sophia, the hometown of Senator Robert Byrd.

We were unable to reach Jack on the telephone to give him the news, because he and Jackie had gone to a movie in Georgetown with Tony and Ben Bradlee. When they came home around eleven-thirty, Jack found a note from his maid posted on the bannister in his front hallway, telling him to call Bobby. He talked with Bobby, let out a whoop of joy, opened a bottle of champagne, drank a quiet toast with Jackie and the Bradlees, and flew back to Charleston in the *Caroline* to thank his workers, particularly Bob McDonough, who had directed the strategy and the tactical moves in the campaign. If there was any one man, outside of the candidate himself, who was largely responsible for Kennedy winning the Democratic nomination for the Presidency in 1960, it was Robert P. McDonough, a quiet fellow who runs a printing business in Parkersburg, West Virginia.

Bobby Kennedy looked at Humphrey's gracious telegram message of concession, and said to us, "God, this must be awful for poor Hubert, ending up this way after working so hard in two states." Bobby quietly left our headquarters and walked alone through the rain to Hubert's hotel to put his arm around him and console him.

That spectacular performance in West Virginia wrapped up the nomination for Kennedy. It settled finally the one big question about his candidacy in the minds of the party leaders who controlled the delegates in the larger states — whether a Catholic could be elected. With that obstacle behind him, Kennedy could spend the remaining two months before the convention putting together the political bits and pieces that he needed to form a solid bloc of support in Los Angeles. He won the last two primaries on his list in Maryland and Oregon easily, visited state conventions and state committee meetings, talked to governors and state leaders. The log of the *Caroline* during the five-week period between the Oregon primary on May 20 and the Montana state convention on June 27 shows an unbelievable grind of daily traveling. Kennedy flew from Oregon to Libertyville, Illinois, where he talked to Adlai Stevenson, then to Hyannis Port, Washington, D.C., New Jersey, New York, Washington State, New Mexico, San Francisco, Chicago, northern Michigan, where he received the backing of Governor G. Mennen Williams at a meeting on Mackinac Island, Colorado, Minnesota, Colorado again, New Jersey again, up to Boston to attend an Overseers' meeting at Harvard, back to New York and New Jersey, Pennsylvania, Washington, D.C., Massachusetts and then to Montana before returning to Hyannis Port for a brief rest before the trip to the Los Angeles convention. But this hard round of checking and rechecking on delegate support and leadership backing here and there was largely routine work. Thanks to his win in West Virginia, most of the leaders and delegates in the big states that he needed had already decided in their own minds that Kennedy was the Presidential candidate who would do their local Democratic tickets the most good.

As we had learned in 1956, this is the only consideration that counts. If the state leader or the leader in a big city decides that you are the Presidential candidate whose name at the top of the party ticket will bring the most votes to his local candidates for governor, Senator, Congress, and the state legislature and county judgeships, you will get his support at the national convention. It makes no difference, after he has arrived at that decision, whether he likes you personally or whether you have less national prestige or popularity in Washington than one of the other candidates. In the local leader's view of the question, even your qualifications for the Presidency are a secondary consideration. Once he makes up his mind that you are the one who will do his local ticket the most good, that is it — he needs no further persuasion or salesmanship from you, and no amount of pressure or appeals from another contender will change his decision. Usually, if he is a shrewd and able politician, he selects his Presidential candidate on his own cold and objective judgment, paying little or no attention to any attempt to influence him, just as a skillful horse player picks his own horse on his own handicapping figures without listening to touts or hot inside information from the stable hands.

Two key figures in organizing the Kennedy effort in the East before the convention were John Bailey and New York's Congressman Eugene Keough, both shrewd and resourceful political experts whose experience was vitally needed in the JFK camp. Bailey guided our Massachusetts state chairman, Pat Lynch, in consolidating the New England states, and played the same important role as the Ambassador in winning over the veteran Democrat leaders who were inclined to look upon such green Ivy Leaguers as Bobby and myself with a leery skepticism. Brooklyn's Gene Keough, working with Charles A. Buckley in the Bronx and Peter Crotty in the Buffalo area, delivered most of New York's delegates to Kennedy long before our victory in West Virginia brought Carmine DeSapio and Mike Prendergast aboard the bandwagon. Keough was also mainly responsible for swinging Pennsylvania into supporting Kennedy at Los Angeles. It was through Keough's efforts that Billy Green, his close friend and fellow Congressman from Philadelphia, and an influential power in the Pennsylvania delegation, threw his support to JFK when Governor David Lawrence was still playing hard to get. Another valuable early backer was John V. Kenny, the mayor and Democratic leader in Jersey City, who stood ready to deliver his state to Kennedy if Governor Robert Meyner tried to bolt to Stevenson or Johnson on a second ballot.

Richard J. Daley, the mayor of Chicago, who controlled the Illinois delegation at the Los Angeles convention, made up his mind to back Kennedy with no courtship from the candidate, and very few words of conversation with any of us before the convention. There had been so little contact between Daley and Kennedy over the previous two years that Pat Lynch and I became alarmed by the apparently careless neglect of Daley, who had been one of Kennedy's leading supporters in the Vice-Presidential nomination fight in 1956. One morning in September, 1959, Pat and Daley, both devout Catholics, attended Mass at five o'clock in a town in New York State where they had been guests at a testimonial dinner the night before. When they were leaving the church, Lynch said to Daley, "How is our boy doing out there in Chicago?"

Daley stared at Lynch innocently and said, "Who's our boy?"

Lynch said, "Jack Kennedy. Who else?"

"I don't know how he's doing," Daley said. "I haven't heard from him in six months."

Pat telephoned me in a frenzy and told me about the conversation. "I know he wasn't lying," Pat said, "because I met him at the five o'clock mass. We don't tell lies to each other at a five o'clock mass. Maybe at an eleven o'clock mass or a twelve o'clock mass, but not at a five o'clock mass. It sounds to me like we might no longer have Dick Daley."

I passed Pat's message on to the Senator, who seemed unperturbed by it. We arranged for Kennedy and Daley to attend a World Series ball game together, but they hardly spoke to each other during the game. "He doesn't talk much, does he?" Daley said to me afterward. "All he did was watch the game." Kennedy remarked later, "Dick didn't mention politics. He was too busy watching the game." But at least Daley had made a public appearance with Kennedy, which was enough to indicate to his followers that he was still well disposed toward the Senator. Both Kennedy and Daley knew that if nothing happened in the meantime to change Kennedy's popularity in Illinois, Kennedy would have Daley's support, and if something did happen to make Kennedy unpopular in Illinois — such as a defeat in the West Virginia primary — no amount of pleading from Kennedy could hold that support. Lyndon Johnson told me in later years that after the West Virginia primary he went to Daley in Chicago and asked for his help at the convention. Daley said to him, "Lyndon, all of us out here like you. We think you've done a great job as our majority leader in the Senate, and you would make a fine President. But Jack Kennedy will get more votes for us in Illinois than you can get, so we've got to be for Kennedy."

But Daley did not come out publicly for Kennedy before the convention. Quietly, however, he showed me every kindness when I was working in Illinois before the delegates went to Los Angeles, arranging for his assistant, Matthew Danaher, to open the doors of his lieutenants to me all over the state. Daley's and Danaher's courtesy to me was almost as good as an endorsement, because the news of their cooperation was passed on quickly to Democratic circles in other states with large delegations where Daley's leanings were watched with respect and interest. Actually, the mayor did not tell any of the Illinois delegates that he favored Kennedy until the delegation met in a caucus at Los Angeles to vote on which candidate they would back. On his way to the rostrum to act as chairman of the caucus, Daley paused in the aisle beside Congressman Daniel Rostenkowski and said to the Congressman, as if the thought had just occurred to him, "Danny, why don't you nominate Kennedy?"

Up until that moment, Rostenkowski told me later, he had no definite idea of which candidate Daley and the Illinois delegation would support for the Presidential nomination. "I was for Kennedy," Rostenkowski said, "and most of my friends were for Kennedy. But if the mayor asks me to nominate somebody else, I would have nominated somebody else." When Rostenkowski, Daley's close friend, nominated Kennedy, everybody in the room knew that Daley was for Kennedy and the delegation voted for Kennedy, 59½ to 2. The two holdouts were for Stevenson. Later, when Stevenson was deciding to make a run for the nomination, he asked Daley if he could get any support in his home state.

"Governor, you're going to look foolish running for this nomination, because you'll get no support from Illinois," Daley said to him. "These delegates weren't for you in 1956 either, but I made them vote for you then. I can't do that again."

Despite his strong and invaluable support of Kennedy at Los Angeles, in all of the three years that Kennedy was serving as President we received only one call from Daley asking for a favor. That was a request for our help in getting a Chicago boy, the only son of a widowed mother, admitted to Harvard. I called the admissions office at Harvard, talked to the dean, who was a classmate of mine, and learned that the boy had already been admitted on his own merit and needed no recommendation from the President. After he was graduated from Harvard, cum laude, the young man was killed in action in Vietnam.

On the other hand, Governor David Lawrence, the Democratic leader in Pennsylvania, made a big show of public fanfare in going through the motions of handing his delegation over to Kennedy at the last minute in Los Angeles. Kennedy pretended to take the governor's grand gesture seriously, but he knew, as we all knew, that Lawrence had no other choice. A Stevenson backer himself, he had already lost control of the Pennsylvania delegates who were ready to vote for Kennedy anyway. Lawrence was an example of a leader who makes the political error of being influenced by his personal feelings and prejudices in selecting a Presidential candidate instead of making an objective decision based on the prevailing opinion among the county and city organizations and the voters in his state, as Daley had done. An astute state leader in Pennsylvania that year would have backed Kennedy long before the convention. Kennedy had open support from Bill Green, the Democratic leader in Philadelphia, and other influential Pennsylvanians. Moreover, Kennedy had received a huge popular write-in vote in the Pennsylvania primary without having his name on the ballot.

But Lawrence stubbornly refused to read the handwriting on the wall until it was too late to do anything else. A Catholic himself, he lost votes because of the religious issue in his Pennsylvania election campaigns. He had a fetish about insisting that the United States was not yet ready to accept a Catholic President. Kennedy was deeply amused to read in the *New York Times* how shocked and puzzled Lawrence was when he was greeted on his return from a European trip with the news of Kennedy's smashing win in the West Virginia primary.

A few weeks later Lawrence invited Kennedy to speak at a private and off-the-record meeting of Pennsylvania county leaders at Harrisburg. When we were flying to Harrisburg on the *Caroline*, Kennedy said to me, "How do you think I ought to handle this one?" I reminded him that Lawrence had been complaining for years about Kennedy's religion, and suggested that he could speak out against Lawrence's trepidation before his own leaders. When Kennedy was introduced at the meeting, he attacked the Democrats who were timid on the religious issue. "If I am denied the nomination because I'm a Catholic," he said, "the party will be going on the record as opposing the political rights of forty percent of its own membership."

Lawrence was furious. When Kennedy finished his talk, the governor turned to me and said, "Whoever was responsible for that speech has done a great disservice to the party. He shouldn't be talking about religion."

"Why shouldn't he?" I said to Lawrence. "I understand that you've been talking about religion every time Kennedy's name is mentioned. I think it's only fair that he should point out to your people that the party can't deny a Catholic the right to run for President when forty percent of all the Democrats in the country are Catholics."

Lawrence stalked off in a rage. Bill Green, whom I did not know at that time, had been standing beside me, taking in the conversation with the governor. He introduced himself and asked my name. "You handled that pretty well," Green said. "Come and see me."

Before Governor Lawrence arrived in Los Angeles, and when the Pennsylvania delegation was supposed to be still uncommitted, Green and Jim Clark, another prominent Philadelphia Democrat, paid a visit to Bobby and me in our room. Green rubbed his hands together briskly and said to us, "Well, what can we do for you? Is there anybody you want us to call?" Bobby looked at me and I looked at Bobby and we both looked at Green. "You mean Pennsylvania will be for Jack?" Bobby asked. Green said to him, "Are you kidding? Pennsylvania is already for Jack." Bobby rushed to the telephone and called Jack to break the big news to him. Jack said quietly, "I already know all about it. Gene Keough and Bill Green talked it all over with me." Bobby said to his brother, "Why didn't you tell us? Kenny and I have been wasting a lot of time romancing everybody in that delegation." Jack said, "I didn't tell you because I think the both of you talk too much." Bobby hung up the phone, shook his head, and laughed.

So Jack Kennedy was less than astonished when Governor Lawrence came to him directly from the airport with John Bailey and broke the news that he was giving the Pennsylvania delegation to Kennedy. In return, the Governor said, he wanted John Bailey to be named as chairman of the Democratic National Committee after the election, an appointment that Kennedy had already planned. "My brother Bobby has been talking with Bill Green," Jack told Lawrence with a straight face. "Maybe you could get together with both of them."

As the convention opened, the only big state that we wanted and had not yet locked up was California, where Governor Pat Brown, still a hopeful candidate himself, had implied that he would be with us, but had made no promises and was doing nothing for us. We turned over our entire campaign activities in California to Jesse Unruh, who did an outstanding job for us in that state under difficult conditions. The one other state leader giving us trouble was New Jersey's Governor Robert Meyner, who was determined to remain uncommitted as a favorite-son candidate until after the first ballot, much to the anger of his own pro-Kennedy delegation. "I am entitled to my twenty minutes on television," Meyner told a reporter. Earlier we had heard that Meyner and Lawrence had tried to work out an arrangement to keep both of their delegations uncommitted so that their votes could be thrown to Stevenson if Kennedy failed on the first two ballots.

We gathered that many, if not most, of the new Stevenson backers were hoping to create a deadlock that would benefit Lyndon Johnson. The candidacy of Symington was faltering. Kennedy was beginning to feel before the convention that Stevenson himself was collaborating in a maneuver to give the nomination to Johnson. Lester Carpenter, a friend of Johnson's and husband of Liz Carpenter, Lady Bird's press attaché, wrote an article after the election which said that Eugene McCarthy, who delivered the stirring nomination speech for Stevenson, was really working for Johnson. During the primary campaign in Oregon, Kennedy told me that Stevenson had promised to endorse him and to nominate him at the convention if Kennedy won all of his primary contests. After completing his primary sweep in Oregon, Kennedy stopped off at Libertyville to see Stevenson while flying home to Hyannis Port. He came back from the meeting and rejoined us on the *Caroline* muttering unkind words about Stevenson. "The same old double-talk," Jack said. "He's got to be playing Lyndon." If Stevenson ever had a remote chance of becoming the Secretary of State in Kennedy's cabinet, he blew it that afternoon in Libertyville.

Kennedy also felt that Harry Truman was playing up Lyndon Johnson, at the behest of his old friend Sam Rayburn, when Truman staged a televised press conference on July 2, just before the convention, and blasted Kennedy as too young and "not quite ready" for the Presidency. Truman said he preferred several other Democrats — including Symington, Johnson, Meyner and Chester Bowles, but pointedly excluding Stevenson — and charged that

Kennedy had the convention controlled and "prearranged." Kennedy asked for equal time to reply to Truman on the Fourth of July, and delivered a stirring rebuttal that undoubtedly did him more good than Truman's original attack did him harm. Kennedy said, among other things, that Truman's idea of an open convention was one "that studies all the candidates, reviews their records, and then takes his advice." Kennedy pointed out that his fourteen years in the House and the Senate gave him more experience in national public elective office than any President in the twentieth century had when elected to the White House, and that included Woodrow Wilson, Franklin D. Roosevelt and Harry Truman. He added that his age, forty-three, made him older than George Washington when Washington commanded the Continental Army, older than Thomas Jefferson when Jefferson wrote the Declaration of Independence, and even older than Christopher Columbus when Columbus discovered America.

The relationship between Kennedy and his leading opponent at Los Angeles, Lyndon Johnson, had always been rather wary on both sides. Arthur Schlesinger talked over the coming election early in the year with Johnson, who was then saying that he had not yet made up his mind about becoming a candidate. "I would support Stevenson with enthusiasm," Johnson said to Schlesinger, a Stevenson man himself. "I would support Humphrey with enthusiasm. I would support Kennedy." Among Kennedy's voluminous political speeches there is an interesting introduction that he delivered before Johnson spoke at the Harry Truman Diamond Jubilee Dinner in Boston on May 8, 1959 — interesting, and quite revealing, because of the changes and deletions made by Kennedy in the original copy of the introduction, written by a staff member who had composed a glowing tribute to Johnson. Dave Powers was sitting with Kennedy in his Bowdoin Street apartment on Beacon Hill while he reworked the introduction on the afternoon before the dinner. Powers noted the revisions that Kennedy made with a certain amusement, and managed to save for posterity the copy of the talk that bears the changes made by Kennedy in Kennedy's own handwriting.

In the opening of the introduction, Kennedy's ghost-writer hailed Johnson as "a Democratic leader without peer or precedent." Kennedy crossed that out and wrote instead "the most skillful parliamentarian leader since Henry Clay." On the next page, Kennedy found himself declaring that he would "always cherish" Johnson's personal friendship. Kennedy doubted that Johnson's personal friendship was something that he would always cherish. He changed "always cherish" to "value," making the sentence say "a man whose personal friendship I value." Another ghost-written burst of enthusiasm, in which Kennedy was supposed to declare that Massachusetts Democrats "will like our speaker," met with disapproval. "These Boston Irish politicians will give Lyndon a big hand," Kennedy said to Powers, "but God knows they will never like him." He changed the line from "Massachusetts Democrats will like our speaker" to "Massachusetts Democrats will give him a great welcome."

Kennedy in 1960 regarded Johnson's identity as a Southerner who had never tried to run for office outside of Texas as an obstacle bigger in the North than his own Catholicism was that year in the South. He scoffed at the assumption that Johnson might win the Presidential nomination if the convention was deadlocked. "Do you think that Dick Daley or Bill Green and Charlie Buckley or Mennen Williams would ever accept Johnson?" he said. "They know he would never get them any votes in the North in a fight against Nixon."

Despite the rumblings about Johnson and the fervent talk from liberals about a draft of Stevenson, Kennedy went to Los Angeles knowing that he had enough delegate votes to win on the first ballot. All of us in the Kennedy contingent were amused by the speculation that he might lose if there had to be a second ballot. We knew that we could get at least one hundred more votes on a second ballot than we figured to get on the first ballot. There were that many delegates committed to other candidates on the first ballot, who were ready and eager to switch later to Kennedy if he needed their help. John M. Patterson, then the governor of Alabama and a more outspoken admirer of Kennedy than we sometimes wanted a Deep Southern governor to be, recalled recently in an interview an interesting message that he received from Kennedy before the balloting. Kennedy sent Steve Smith to Patterson asking if a few of the Kennedy admirers in the Alabama delegation would refrain from voting for JFK until the second ballot, if there was a second ballot. Alabama, the first state on the roll call, would then come out with a larger Kennedy vote on the second ballot than it had shown on the first ballot, and the psychological impact on the convention might be considerable. Jack Kennedy, as usual, was figuring all the angles. As a matter of fact, we made the same request to delegations in several other states. Our wealth of supporters on emergency stand-by reminded Dave Powers of the college quarterback who noticed that he had a team of twelve football players in his huddle. He told them that he would run the next play to the sidelines so that one of them could roll off the field and not return to the lineup. When the team gathered again for the next huddle, there were only eight players. But it is highly unlikely that Kennedy would have found himself shorthanded the second time around.

As satisfying as it was, Kennedy's nomination on the first ballot, working out even more smoothly than we had expected, with 806 votes to Johnson's 409, seemed almost too easy and automatic, rather an anticlimactic letdown after our four years of fighting and struggling to get it. There was much more excitement in the next day's behind-the-scenes battle over the Vice-Presidential nomination, which almost started an open floor fight that could have torn the party apart.

SEVEN

How Lyndon Got on the Ticket

DAVE POWERS went to Los Angeles a week before the convention to find a hideaway apartment where Senator Kennedy would be able to sleep and eat a quiet breakfast, away from the turmoil at the Biltmore, the center of activities, where all of the candidates and the Democratic National Committee were establishing their command posts and meeting rooms. Kennedy had a suite at the Biltmore, 9333, on the floor above our main center of operations, suite 8315, where Bobby, Larry O'Brien, Pierre Salinger and I were working, but we figured that Jack might not be able to survive unless he had a secret retreat for nightly rest and relaxation, unknown by the press, the politicians, or any of us, except Dave, Bobby and Evelyn Lincoln, his secretary.

Dave found the place he was looking for at 522 North Rossmore Avenue, a small three-floor pink and white stucco apartment house owned by Jack Haley, the comic actor, and his wife Flo, who rented the Senator their penthouse suite, which had three bedrooms, a living room and a kitchen. William Gargan, the actor who played Martin Kane, the private eye of early television, occupied the apartment below on the second floor with his wife. The Haleys and the Gargans agreed to be sworn to secrecy about the identity of their temporary neighbor in the penthouse. The location was ideal, only a ten-minute drive from both the Biltmore and the Los Angeles Sports Arena, where the convention was to be held. Dave was particularly pleased with the entrance to the building. The Senator could step from his car in a secluded driveway into an elevator that took him up to the top floor penthouse, unseen by anybody on the street. Dave stocked the kitchen's refrigerator with eggs, bacon and oranges. Four telephone lines were installed in the apartment, one to Evelyn Lincoln's desk in the Senator's suite at the Biltmore, another to suite 8315 where he could talk with Bobby or me, and two open lines for various calls around the city and around the country, including nightly talks with Jackie in Hyannis Port.

Jack and Dave stayed at the hideaway apartment for the first four nights of the convention week, with its address remaining a safely kept secret. They left there every morning, in a telephone-equipped car, driven by Buz Sawyer, a local man who knew every shortcut in the city, to begin a daily round of meetings, appearances at state caucuses, social gatherings and dinners. There were no major problems for any of us to iron out before the day of the nominations, although Kennedy became increasingly annoyed by Adlai Stevenson's reluctance to come to his support. Kennedy made one last attempt to get Stevenson to deliver a speech of nomination, as Jack had done for him in 1956, but Adlai protested that he had to remain "neutral."

"Neutral for Johnson?" Kennedy said to us later. "He's got a short memory. He's forgetting that I was for him in '56 when Johnson and Rayburn were both against him."

The day of the Presidential nominations, Wednesday, July 13, began as usual at the North Rossmore Avenue penthouse with Dave waking Jack at seven and Jack saying as he opened his eyes, "Dave, get Bobby on the phone for me." While the brothers talked about the day's schedule, Dave prepared the breakfast that never varied except on Fridays — freshly squeezed orange juice to wash down the vitamin pill, two four-and-a-half-minute boiled eggs, four strips of broiled bacon, toast and coffee. On Fridays, the bacon was omitted. "Dave, you're getting to do the bacon even better than Margaret Ambrose," Jack said, referring to the housekeeper who had cooked for him in Georgetown before his marriage. "Does your wife know you can cook like this?" Dave said, "No, and don't tell her." During breakfast, Dave was unable to resist making a short speech:

"Well, this is the day you've been waiting for for four years. This is the day you'll pick up all of the marbles."

Jack glanced at him, and said, "Let's hope the breakfast tastes as good as this tomorrow morning."

They drove to a breakfast meeting of the Indiana delegation at the Roosevelt Hotel and then to a visit with the South Dakota delegation, where Kennedy was rather pleased to learn that he would pick up four votes originally pledged to Hubert Humphrey, now out of the running and backing Stevenson. The next stop was at the Colorado caucus at the Chancellor Hotel, where Kennedy received a happy welcome and a pledge of 13½ votes, to Stevenson's 5½ and Symington's 2. From the Colorado meeting, Kennedy went to his suite at the Biltmore, where Bobby and I showed him our latest count of first-ballot votes. We had then 739½ sure votes, and we were certain that later in the day we would pick up the additional 21½ votes needed for the total of 761 that would give him the nomination on the first ballot.

Bobby and I told him that he could reach us during the afternoon at our communications center in a model cottage home, being exhibited on the grounds of the Sports Arena, that the Kennedys had rented for the week of the convention. Jack said that he and Dave would be spending the rest of the day with his father and mother at Marion Davies' home in Beverly Hills, which the Ambassador, an old friend of Miss Davies and William Randolph Hearst, had borrowed for that week. Jack was planning to watch the nominating speeches and demonstrations on television between swims in the Davies pool, and to eat dinner there with his parents before returning to his hideaway to follow the first-ballot voting on TV.

Before Jack could leave his suite at the Biltmore, he found himself engulfed by an invasion of delegates from Hawaii. One of the women delegates insisted on draping a white lei around his neck and tried to kiss him. While he was fending off her advances, he noticed that the men in the group were wearing Stevenson hats, and asked them how they had voted in their caucus. They admitted that the delegation had given Stevenson 3½ votes to 3 for Johnson and 1½ for Kennedy. For the first time that week, Kennedy became so annoyed that he chastised a delegation openly and told them that neither Stevenson nor Johnson had a chance to win. He ticked off on his fingers the names of the big states that were for him, New York, Pennsylvania, Illinois and Ohio.

While Kennedy was talking to the Hawaiians, Dave noticed an

envelope being slipped under the Golden Door, as we called the door from the suite's living room to the outside corridor, which was unlocked only to admit special visitors. It was a message from John V. Kenny, New Jersey's Hudson County leader, telling Kennedy that after a long and bitter caucus that morning Governor Meyner was still insisting on holding New Jersey's 41 votes committed to his own favorite-son candidacy on the first ballot. Kenny assured Kennedy, however, that he could count on 31 votes from New Jersey on a second ballot.

During the confusion of the Hawaiian visit, Pierre Salinger was pleading with Dave for the address of the hideaway apartment, arguing that its secrecy was no longer necessary and that the television and news cameramen wanted to make arrangements to photograph Kennedy there after the balloting that night. Dave was trying to stall off disclosing the address until after Kennedy had a chance to return to North Rossmore Avenue in privacy that afternoon to pick up his swimming trunks before joining his parents at Marion Davies' villa. Kennedy retreated to the bedroom of the suite for a quick lunch, a chicken sandwich and a glass of milk, saying impatiently to Dave, "Oh, for God's sake, give him the address. Anything for a little quiet around here. Give it to him." Pat Lawford dropped in to wish her brother well before she went to the convention hall. Chewing on his sandwich, Jack talked with Pat about the split in the California delegation over Stevenson. "Maybe I shouldn't have listened to Pat Brown," he said. "I should have entered that primary."

Hoping that Jack would be able to pick up his swimming trunks at the hideaway before it was surrounded by newsmen and photographers, Dave watched with dismay while Franklin Roosevelt, Jr., came into the suite and persuaded the candidate to go with him to a garden party of delegates at the Sheraton-West. "The delegates at the party were people we already had," Dave recalled later. "But Jack had to waste fifteen valuable minutes there." By the time Kennedy and Dave reached North Rossmore Avenue, the street in front of the apartment building was crowded with television equipment trucks, cameramen, reporters and a large throng of curious spectators. One of the NBC television technicians was installing a cable to the outside wall of the stucco building while the Haley's superintendent begged him to be careful about defacing the stucco. Jack glared at Dave and said, "Well, this is one hell of a hideaway, isn't it?"

They had to struggle to get into the driveway and upstairs on the elevator to the penthouse apartment. "Now that we're in here," Jack asked, "how can we get out, without having that crowd follow us to Marion Davies' house?" Dave consulted Mrs. Haley and Bill Gargan, who suggested the fire escape on the back of the building which could not be seen from the front of the driveway. Dave and the next President of the United States came down the fire escape, carrying their swimming trunks, climbed over the back fence into a neighbor's garden, and went to the next street in the block where Buz Sawyer was waiting with their car. Chuck Roche, Pierre's press relations assistant, was left behind at the hideaway apartment to assure the newsmen waiting outside that Kennedy was spending the rest of the afternoon and evening in the penthouse. "What is he doing now?" the reporters would ask Roche when he made a periodic appearance before the crowd. "He's still watching the convention and drinking a Coke," Roche would announce.

Jack and Dave arrived at the Marion Davies house in time to see Sam Rayburn on TV nominating Lyndon Johnson. They took a swim in the pool, watched Orville Freeman nominating Kennedy, and called Bobby at the communications cottage to compare probable votes again. Jack went over the figures with his father and talked with the Ambassador about the holdout of Meyner. "You'll win on the first ballot," the Ambassador said, "and that will make a goat out of Meyner. He'll be left standing there, high and dry." Jack and Dave joined the Ambassador and Mrs. Kennedy and her niece, Ann Gargan, for dinner — beef stew, hot rolls, salad and milk. Then Mrs. Kennedy and Ann went to the convention hall while the men sat down again before the television screen and listened to Eugene McCarthy nominating Stevenson, the best speech of the convention, Jack said, even though McCarthy was really backing Johnson. ("Do not reject this man who has made us all proud to be Democrats. Do not leave this prophet without honor in his own party.") During the wild demonstration for Stevenson that followed, Jack phoned Bobby again for another rundown on vote figures and learned that despite the enthusiastic display of sentiment for Stevenson on the television screen, Adlai's delegate count in California was running far behind earlier expectations. "Don't worry, Dad," Jack said to his father, as he left him to go back to the North Rossmore Avenue apartment. "Stevenson has everything but delegates."

Dave called Chuck Roche to alert him for Jack's arrival over the back fence. Chuck had been joined by Evelyn Lincoln, Torbert Macdonald, Jack's Harvard roommate and close friend, and Jim McShane, who was handling security arrangements. McShane and two Los Angeles detectives went into the backyard with flashlights to guide the Senator and Dave over the fence and up the steps of the fire escape to the apartment. Dave and Torby arranged a table in front of the television screen where Jack sat with a pencil and the cardboard tally sheet, marked with each state's delegate votes, that he had been carrying all day, ready to keep the score as the roll call began.

The chairman of the convention, Governor LeRoy Collins of Florida, called upon Alabama. As the chairman of that first state delegation was reporting, "Alabama casts twenty votes for Johnson, three and a half for Kennedy, and —" the light in the television screen and all of the lights in the apartment went out.

"God Almighty!" Kennedy said in the darkness. "I slave and I knock my brains out for four years to get this nomination, and now I can't even sit here and see it."

One of the detectives in the kitchen was already at the fuse box, lighting a match to find the blown fuse and replacing it. The television screen lit up again in time for Kennedy to hear himself getting seventeen votes in Arizona. Then the electricity in the apartment blew out a second time. Cursing and muttering, Kennedy stumbled out of the dark room and ran downstairs to the Gargan apartment where Bill Gargan and his wife, both in pajamas, were watching the roll call. "Do you mind, Bill?" he said to Gargan. "Both of our sets upstairs blew out." Mrs. Gargan, startled by the sudden appearance of Kennedy, tried to leave the room to get a dressing gown. Jack called her back. "Please don't worry about your pajamas," he said to her. "Sit down and be comfortable." They watched California giving Kennedy three more votes than he had expected on his tally sheet, and listened to Abe Ribicoff delivering all of Connecticut's 21 votes. Chuck Roche came downstairs and reported that the lights were on again. The circuit had been overloaded by a new air-conditioning unit in Jack's bedroom, not by Evelyn Lincoln's electric typewriter as she had remorsefully assumed.

"Bill, leave the door open," Jack said. "We might be back."

He sat calmly through the rest of the balloting, marking his tally board as each state reported. When the roll call reached Wyoming, he had 750 of the 761 votes that he needed to win. Regardless of how Wyoming divided its 15 votes, he knew that he had enough supporters in the remaining delegations at the end of the list — the Virgin Islands, Puerto Rico and the District of Columbia — to put him over the top. But when he saw his brother Teddy crouching in the middle of the Wyoming delegation with a wide grin on his face, Jack said, "This may be it." All of Wyoming's 15 votes went to Kennedy, giving him the nomination.

Jack stood up smiling, shook hands with Dave, Torby McDonald, Chuck Roche and Jim McShane, and said to Evelyn Lincoln, "Get Jackie at the Cape." While Evelyn was making the connection to Hyannis Port, he called his father, who was sitting alone in the Marion Davies house, and talked with him happily. "I told you Meyner would be left high and dry," the Ambassador said, "and, by God, he was. Those guys from New Jersey must be furious with him." They were furious indeed. I was standing with Meyner and John Kenny on the floor before the balloting when his delegates were yelling at him to vote for Kennedy. I thought that a few of them were going to take a punch at him.

After the newly nominated candidate talked with Jackie, he hurried downstairs to the car that was waiting to take him to the Sports Arena to make a brief appearance at the convention. He stopped first at the model cottage outside the arena to see Bobby, drawing his brother aside and talking with him seriously for a few minutes, the two of them standing alone and apart from the crowd of gathering friends and party leaders, who respectfully kept their distance until the brothers finished their private conversation. Then Jack turned away from Bobby and shook hands with John Bailey and me, and greeted Abe Ribicoff, Soapy Williams, Bill Green, Mike DiSalle, Averill Harriman, Dick Daley, David Lawrence and many others. From the cottage Jack went to the convention hall, making his entrance while the band played the Irish melody, "Toora-Loora-Loora," and "Happy Days Are Here Again." He stood on the platform with his mother and sisters, waving to the cheering delegates, said a few words of thanks, and then rode back to the apartment on North Rossmore Avenue.

All of us who were with Jack at the convention, including Dave Powers, who spent almost every waking minute of that week at his side, are almost certain that he did not begin to give any serious thought to the selection of a Vice-Presidential candidate until after he returned to his ex-hideaway apartment that night of his nomination. Before that time, not only during the previous few days when he was completely concerned with rounding up delegates to support him in the Presidential balloting but over the earlier months of countrywide campaigning, the choice of a second name on the ticket seemed far from his mind. We knew that when he arrived in Los Angeles on the Saturday before the convention week he had made no promises or definite offers to anybody. From the little he had said on the question, we gathered that he was thinking of Stuart Symington, Orville Freeman and Senator Henry M. Jackson of Washington, whom Bobby liked. We knew that Lyndon Johnson was on his list of possible Vice-Presidents. But none of us ever thought that Jack Kennedy would pick Johnson, whom he regarded as a conservative Old Guardsman, opposed to the moderate liberalism of Kennedy. (In Kennedy's files, there was a copy of a speech that Johnson had once delivered in praise of the Taft-Hartley labor law.) One of my jobs, before and during the convention, was to maintain a good working relationship with the labor leaders, particularly Walter Reuther and Alex Rose, who shared with David Dubinsky the leadership of the New York Liberal party, which had a slate of its own approved candidates on the New York ballot. The labor people had warned me repeatedly that they did not want Johnson on the Kennedy ticket. I had promised them that there was no chance of such a choice. We had given the same assurance, with Kennedy's knowledge, to wavering liberal delegates during the movement earlier in the week to draft Stevenson.

When Johnson was battling for the Presidential nomination in the opening days of the convention, his close friend Philip Graham, the publisher of the *Washington Post* and *Newsweek*, decided that Johnson did not have a prayer of getting the first place on the ticket and began on his own to promote Lyndon for the Vice-Presidential nomination. On Monday, Graham visited Kennedy at the Biltmore with Joseph Alsop, the columnist who was one of Kennedy's closest friends. When Graham broached the idea of a Kennedy-Johnson ticket, Jack agreed so quickly and casually — asking Joe Alsop in the same sentence about a party Alsop was giving that night at Perino's — that Graham assumed correctly that he was being given a fast brush-off. Later that day, Jack mentioned Graham's proposal to Bobby and me, dismissing it so lightly that neither of us paid any attention to it at the time. I was assuming then that Kennedy would probably end up selecting Symington, who was acceptable to both the labor leaders and the Southerners, but I did not really care whom he picked as long as it wasn't Johnson.

When Kennedy came back to the apartment on North Rossmore Avenue after visiting the convention on the night of his nomination, Ann Gargan, Evelyn Lincoln, Torby McDonald and a few other people were waiting to greet him. Evelyn played "When Irish Eyes Are Smiling" on the piano. Jack said to Dave, "I'll have that beer now, Dave." When Dave poured the beer, the first alcoholic drink accepted by Kennedy that day, the group drank a toast to the Democratic party's new standard-bearer. Then Jack ate his victory supper, two eggs fried in butter by Dave and served with toast, jelly and milk. He looked at a few of the congratulatory telegrams that had been received at the apartment, and read aloud a warm and cordial message from Lyndon Johnson. After the guests left, Kennedy sat at the kitchen table, drinking a second glass of milk, and read again to Dave one of the lines in Johnson's telegram, which said, "LBJ now means Let's Back Jack."

Apparently the telegram started Kennedy thinking favorably about Johnson as a Vice-Presidential candidate. Although it was then after two o'clock in the morning, Kennedy asked Dave to see if he could reach Johnson on the telephone. A sleepy aide in Johnson's suite at the Biltmore said that Johnson was in bed and could not be disturbed. Kennedy then called Evelyn Lincoln's room at the Biltmore. Since Evelyn had only left him a few minutes earlier, she had not yet reached the Biltmore. Kennedy's call awoke her husband, Abe. Jack dictated over the telephone a message which Abe typed and delivered by hand to Johnson's suite. It said that Kennedy wanted to see Johnson at ten o'clock that morning.

"Set the alarm early, Dave," Kennedy said when he was getting into his bed. "I want to be up by seven-fifteen. I wish I had asked Lyndon and George Smathers to be at that meeting of Southern governors we've got scheduled for eleven-thirty."

Getting into his own bed, Dave said to himself, my God, he's going to offer it to Lyndon Johnson.

In the morning, when Dave was serving breakfast, Jack asked him how many votes he had received from Southern states the night before. Dave rattled off the total Southern vote on the first ballot, 307 for Johnson and only 13 for Kennedy out of 409, the rest being divided between local native-son candidates and Symington. Now I know he's going to offer it to Johnson, Dave thought, and there's going to be hell to pay when this gets out.

"Dave, wasn't that a nice telegram Lyndon sent last night?" Kennedy said as he finished his coffee. "Will you call Bobby and tell him to meet me at the Biltmore at eight o'clock?"

When Kennedy arrived with Dave at his suite in the Biltmore, he asked Evelyn Lincoln to see if Johnson was awake yet. Lady Bird answered the telephone, woke her husband, and arranged for Kennedy to see him at ten o'clock. Bobby came to the suite. Jack led him into a bedroom and closed the door behind them. When they came out of the bedroom, Dave, now well aware of what was going on, heard Bobby saying to Jack, "if you're sure it's what you want to do, go ahead and see him." Dave was taken aback to see Bobby accepting the news so calmly. Then Dave realized that anything Jack wanted to do was usually acceptable to Bobby. "Even if Jack wanted to give the Vice-Presidency to Eleanor Roosevelt," Dave remarked later, "Bobby probably would have said all right."

About a half hour after Jack had broken the news to Bobby, Pierre Salinger asked me to come to Bobby's bedroom in the Biltmore. I found Pierre looking glum. He nodded his head toward the bathroom, where Bobby was soaking himself in the tub, tired after the long night before. Pierre said to me, "He just asked me to add up the electoral votes in the states we're sure of, and to add Texas."

I stared at Salinger and said, "You must be kidding."

"I wish I was," Salinger said.

We went into the bathroom. I said to Bobby, "Don't tell me it's Johnson."

"I guess it is," Bobby said. "He's seeing him now."

I was so furious that I could hardly talk. I thought of the promises we had made to the labor leaders and the civil rights groups, the assurances we had given that Johnson would not be on the ticket if

Kennedy won the nomination. I felt that we had been double-crossed.

"Do you realize this is a disaster?" I said to Bobby. "Nixon will love this. Now Nixon can say Kennedy is just another phony politician who will do anything to get elected. I want to talk to your brother myself on this one."

"All right," Bobby said, climbing out of the tub. "As soon I get dressed, we'll go and see him."

The Kennedy suite upstairs was filled with a throng of Northern Democratic leaders, David Lawrence, Mike DiSalle, John Bailey, Abe Ribicoff, Dick Daley, all of them milling around Jack Kennedy and congratulating him for offering the Vice-Presidency to Johnson. Jack was saying that he had just talked with Lyndon, who wanted a little time to think it over, but it looked as though Johnson would take it. Dave Lawrence was acting as if the whole thing was his idea. "Johnson has the strength where you need it most," he was saying to Kennedy. I could have belted him. While Bobby and I waited to catch Jack's eye, I talked with Sarge Shriver, who was feeling as terrible as I was.

When Jack Kennedy saw the expression on my face, he beckoned to Bobby and me to follow him into the bedroom. The bedroom was crowded with people, too, and realizing that I was about to explode, Jack said to Bobby, "I'd better talk to Kenny alone in the bathroom." We went into the bathroom and closed the door behind us.

"This is the worst mistake you ever made," I said to him. "You came out here to this convention like a knight on a white charger, the clean-cut young Ivy League college guy who's promising to get rid of the old hack machine politicians. And now, in your first move after you get the nomination, you go against all the people who supported you. Are we going to spend the campaign apologizing for Lyndon Johnson and trying to explain why he voted against everything you ever stood for?"

He became pale, livid with anger, so upset and hurt that it took him a while before he was able to collect himself.

"Wait a minute," he said. "I've offered it to him, but he hasn't accepted it yet and maybe he won't. If he does accept it, let's get one thing clear."

I never forgot what he said next.

"I'm forty-three years old, and I'm the healthiest candidate for President in the United States. You've traveled with me enough to know that. I'm not going to die in office. So the Vice-Presidency doesn't mean anything. I'm thinking of something else, the leadership in the Senate. If we win, it will be by a small margin and I won't be able to live with Lyndon Johnson as the leader of a small majority in the Senate. Did it occur to you that if Lyndon becomes the Vice-President, I'll have Mike Mansfield as the leader in the Senate, somebody I can trust and depend on?"

I began to soften and see things differently. Kennedy then reminded me that Congress was still in session and that he had to go back to the Senate after the convention closed and put on a fight for the issues in his platform — housing, urban renewal, Medicare, relief for depressed areas. Johnson and Sam Rayburn had not adjourned the Congress before the convention, figuring that they could pressure various members of Congress in the state delegations into supporting Johnson for President at Los Angeles if the House and the Senate remained in session for the rest of the summer.

"If Johnson and Rayburn leave here mad at me," Kennedy said, "they'll ruin me in Congress next month. Then I'll be the laughingstock of the country. Nixon will say I haven't any power in my own party, and I'll lose the election before Labor Day. So I've got to make peace now with Johnson and Rayburn, and offering Lyndon the Vice-Presidency, whether he accepts it or not, is one way of keeping him friendly until Congress adjourns. Explain that to your labor leaders and their liberal friends. All of this is more important to me than Southern votes, which I won't get anyway with the Catholic thing working against me. I doubt if Lyndon will even be able to carry Texas, as Dave Lawrence and all those other pols out in the other room claim we will."

Kennedy opened the bathroom door and called Bobby in to join us. "Now the two of you can go and see Walter Reuther and George Meany and get to work on them," he said. "But don't tell anybody what I told you about giving Lyndon the Vice-Presidency so that we can have Mike Mansfield as the leader in the Senate. Lyndon wouldn't like that."

Reuther and Meany were waiting to chew Bobby and me into bits. They had been to see Jack Kennedy earlier in the morning with Arthur Goldberg, then their lawyer, and had been infuriated by the news of his choice of Johnson, although Goldberg had tried to convince them that Johnson in the Vice-Presidency could cause them no trouble. I don't think that Bobby Kennedy fully realized the predicament that Jack had put us into until we walked into the room at the Statler Hilton where the labor leaders were assembled and saw their violently angry mood. Bobby was shaken when he watched Jack Conway, Reuther's right-hand man who had been our warmest friend the day before, coming at me as if he was about to slug me. Alex Rose pointed his finger at Bobby and roared that if Johnson's name was on the ticket, Kennedy would not be on the ballot as the Liberal party's candidate in New York.

All of the labor people in the room were shouting that they would put up a Vice-Presidential candidate of their own and humiliate Kennedy that night with a wild floor fight which would split the Democratic party. The noise finally died down when Rose went to a telephone and announced that he was calling David Dubinsky in New York. All of us listened while the call was put through and Rose yelled into the telephone. "Hello, David? David, do you know what they're doing out here? Who do you think Kennedy picked as his Vice-President? Lyndon Johnson!"

The room was silent as Rose listened to Dubinsky's reply with a look of astonishment on his face and his eyes opening wide in surprise.

"All right, David," Rose said and hung up. He turned to Reuther and exclaimed, "You know what he said? He said Kennedy is making a smart move! He said picking Johnson is a political masterstroke!"

The noise and the shouts of "sellout" and "double cross" broke out again, despite Dubinsky. We were warned once more that there would be a strong floor fight against Johnson's nomination at the convention that night. When Bobby and I went back to the Biltmore, he said to me, "Maybe Lyndon won't want to face a floor fight. Do you think he might pull out?"

"At this stage of the game," I said, "it would take a lot of nerve to ask him that."

"If Jack wants me to ask him, I'll ask him," Bobby said.

Meanwhile, back in the Kennedy suite at the Biltmore, the selection of Johnson was getting conflicting reactions. Adlai Stevenson dropped in to see Jack about it, and observed that in his opinion

Johnson would never settle for the number two spot. Sam Rayburn, who had been against his fellow Texan taking the Vice-Presidency the night before, changed his mind after talking to Kennedy and urged Johnson to go on the ticket. Rayburn reminded Lyndon that Nixon had once called Sam a traitor. "I don't want a man who calls me a traitor to be President of the United States," Rayburn said. Bedlam broke out in the bedroom of the suite when Governor G. Mennen ("Soapy") Williams, the Michigan liberal, accidentally walked into a meeting between Kennedy and a group of Southern governors who were approving Johnson as Vice-President. Williams listened to the discussion for a moment and then shouted that if Johnson was nominated, he would personally lead a floor fight against the nomination. A few of the Southerners jumped up to take a punch at Williams, but Abe Ribicoff stepped in and pacified the situation. Jack Kennedy, sitting in an armchair with one leg hanging over the arm of the chair, watched the whole scene without saying a word.

Early in the afternoon, Phil Graham, calling from Johnson's rooms downstairs, reached Jack Kennedy and said that Lyndon was ready to take the nomination. "Tell him it's all set," Kennedy said. "I'll make a statement, and I'll arrange to have Dave Lawrence nominate him."

Before the selection of Johnson was announced to the press, Bobby and I went to Jack and told him what we had been through with the labor leaders, how they were threatening to put on a floor fight against Johnson and put up a candidate of their own. We also reported to him Alex Rose's threat to remove the Kennedy-Johnson ticket from the Liberal party ballot in New York.

"Do you want me to tell Lyndon that there's a possibility of a floor fight?" Bobby asked.

"Maybe you better go downstairs and tell him that right now," Jack said. "I doubt that it will bother him, but we ought to let him know that there might be a floor fight against him, in case he doesn't feel up to facing it."

Bobby went to Johnson's suite and talked with Sam Rayburn and John Connally, explaining to them that there was a threat of a floor fight against Johnson, and suggesting that Lyndon might want to withdraw if he didn't want to get involved in such a battle. "Do you think he might be interested in being chairman of the national committee?" Bobby said to Rayburn. Rayburn stared at Bobby and said, "Shit!"

Bobby's errand was completely misinterpreted by Rayburn, who assumed that Bobby was asking Johnson to withdraw. While Bobby waited patiently in another room, panic broke out behind the scenes in Johnson's quarters. Phil Graham, Lyndon's go-between man, called Jack on the phone and said, "Bobby's down here telling Rayburn and Lyndon that there's opposition and that he ought to withdraw for the sake of the party."

The implication was that Bobby had gone to Johnson on his own to persuade Lyndon to pull out of the Vice-Presidency, which, of course, was entirely wrong. Jack had sent Bobby to Johnson to let Lyndon know that there was a strong possibility of a floor fight against him before a nationwide television audience. If Johnson wanted the Vice-Presidency enough to try for it under such conditions, Kennedy could hardly dissuade him, but if he had then decided that being the second candidate on the ticket was hardly worth so much embarrassment and strife, nobody could have disagreed with him either.

Graham later wrote a widely circulated memorandum in which he quoted Jack Kennedy as saying in reply to his complaint about Bobby asking Johnson to withdraw, "Bobby's been out of touch, and doesn't know what's happening." Dave Powers, who was with Kennedy when he received Graham's call, remembers it differently.

Jack said to Graham, "I've announced that Lyndon will be the Vice-Presidential candidate, and Dave Lawrence has agreed to nominate him. Can you put Lyndon on the phone?"

Kennedy then reassured Johnson that if he was willing to face a floor fight the Vice-Presidency was his and that Lawrence would nominate him. Johnson agreed to this. Bobby was called into Johnson's room and was put on the phone with Jack. By this time, Bobby told me later, he was exhausted by the whole mix-up. He was sorry that he had volunteered to tell Johnson about the labor and liberal opposition and the possibility of a floor fight, and he felt like knocking his head against the nearest wall. Jack told him to forget Johnson because it was now too late for Johnson to pull out anyway. When he hung up the telephone, Johnson said to him solemnly, "If the candidate will have me, I'll join with him in making a fight for it." Bobby said to himself wearily, why didn't you tell me this a half hour ago and we all could have saved ourselves a lot of trouble.

The possibility of a messy floor fight over Johnson's nomination to the Vice-Presidential candidacy was very strong and real that afternoon. At four-thirty I called Jack Conway, who had been trying to calm down Reuther, and asked him how it looked. He said that the labor people and liberals in Mennen Williams' Michigan delegation were still set on putting up a Vice-Presidential candidate of their own, and were definitely planning a fight to the finish against the Kennedy-Johnson ticket. It looked like a bad night for all of us.

I tried to get in touch with Jack Kennedy to pass on to him Conway's warning but I could not reach him, and then I decided to let him rest for a few hours; there was not much that he could do to make peace now, anyway. Around seven o'clock I went to the convention hall, prepared for trouble.

At seven-thirty when I was on the convention floor, taking soundings of the delegate votes, Jack Conway reached me by telephone. He told me quickly that I could stop worrying, that there would be no floor fight and that no candidate would be put up in opposition to Johnson.

Conway hung up without telling me what had happened between four-thirty in the afternoon, when things were looking black, and seven that evening when the floor fight was called off. I wondered if Kennedy had somehow managed to work his charm on the labor leaders and the Michigan liberals. Later I found out that Reuther and his people had made their own peace pact with Johnson. They offered to drop their opposition to his nomination if he promised to support the convention's civil rights platform. Johnson agreed and wrote a letter giving that assurance, which Leonard Woodcock, then vice-president of the United Automobile Workers, presented to a caucus of the Michigan delegation.

Despite the letter of agreement, Soapy Williams was still against Johnson's nomination. That night on the floor of the convention there were ominous rumblings among the delegations from Michigan and the District of Columbia, where Joe Rauh, the Americans for Democratic Action leader, wanted to put up Orville Freeman for the Vice-Presidential nomination. To be on the safe side, we arranged with Governor Collins, the chairman of the convention, to allow a move to make Johnson's nomination declared unanimous before the roll call reached Michigan. When Massachusetts was called upon, John McCormack rushed to the platform and moved that Johnson should be nominated by acclamation. Collins quickly called for a voice vote and announced that it had carried. So the possibility of a floor fight was finally averted.

Later on Kennedy would evade with a quizzical smile the question often asked about his selection of Johnson — did he offer the Vice-Presidential nomination to Johnson half expecting that Lyndon would refuse it, as he intimated to me in the bathroom that morning? Kennedy did admit, however, on more than one occasion, that when he held up the Vice-Presidency before Johnson, he did not expect Johnson to grab at it quite so quickly. Incidentally, Tom Wicker, the *New York Times* correspondent in Washington, has suggested that Kennedy told me in the bathroom that he wanted Mike Mansfield instead of Johnson as the majority leader in the Senate only because he wanted to pacify me. According to Wicker, Kennedy knew that I was a friendly admirer of Mansfield and he calculated that using the argument that he wanted Mansfield as the Senate majority leader would have a soothing effect on me. The only trouble with Wicker's theory is that I did not know Mike Mansfield at that time, although I later grew to admire him. I had seen Mansfield only once before the Los Angeles convention, on June 27 at the Montana state Democratic convention, and on that day Mansfield was wearing on his lapel a large Lyndon B. Johnson button. I do think now that Kennedy's desire to make a peaceful alliance with Johnson and Rayburn after beating them in the fight for the Presidential nomination was as strong a factor in his offer of the Vice-Presidency to Johnson as his desire to remove Lyndon from the majority leadership in the Senate.

On Friday, the day after the Vice-Presidential nomination was settled and sealed, Kennedy delivered his formal speech of acceptance before an audience of eighty thousand people at the Los Angeles Coliseum and a television audience of some thirty-five million. It was not one of his better speeches — he was tired after the grind of the convention and the setting sun was shining into his eyes — but it was a speech that all of us remember because in it he made his first mention of the New Frontier. That phrase, which came to mean so much to our generation, was all his own. He did not find it in a book and nobody suggested it to him. He used it not as a mere campaign slogan, because he hated slogans as much as he hated to put on a funny hat, but as a sincere expression of his appreciation of the hard challenge of the Presidency at that time, a challenge that seemed as hard to him as the challenge faced by the settlers when America was a new and rough frontier. "We stand today on the edge of a New Frontier, the frontier of the 1960s, a frontier of unknown opportunities and perils, a frontier of unfulfilled hopes and threats," he said in his acceptance speech. "But the New Frontier of which I speak is not a set of promises — it is a set of challenges. It sums up not what I intend to offer the American people, but what I intend to ask of them. It appeals to their pride, not their pocketbook — it holds out the promise of more sacrifice instead of more security."

After listening to the speech at the Coliseum, Bobby and I went back to the Biltmore to talk about the coming campaign. We quickly agreed that Dave and I would travel with the candidate and work on his schedule, that Bobby would work with the chairman of the Democratic National Committee on directing the overall operation, and that there should be a national Citizens-for-Kennedy organization with a less partisan tone to it than the national committee. The question was the choice of a national committee chairman. John Bailey could not be appointed as national chairman of the party until after the election. Which of the available well-experienced Democratic politicians could we put into the national chairmanship? Bobby Kennedy displayed a naïveté at times that was downright astonishing. This was one of those times. He said to me very seriously, "I think Whizzer White would make an excellent national chairman."

I looked at him, wondering if he had been affected by the sun during the acceptance speech at the Coliseum. Byron R. White was admired by the Kennedys because he had been an All-American halfback at the University of Colorado and a Rhodes Scholar. He was then working as a lawyer in Denver and had had no experience in politics until Jack asked him to help Teddy in rounding up delegates in the Mountain States during the previous month of June. Here was Bobby suggesting him as national chairman of the Democratic party.

"Whizzer White?" I said to Bobby. "Are you serious?"

"Why not?" Bobby said.

"Whizzer White didn't know anything about politics until three weeks ago last Sunday," I said. "Are you expecting him to be the head of the party during a Presidential campaign?"

"I guess maybe you're right," Bobby said.

The next day Senator Kennedy announced in Los Angeles that he was nominating Senator Henry M. ("Scoop") Jackson as national chairman. Then, on Sunday, the Kennedys and the many people from Massachusetts who had worked for Jack's nomination at the convention boarded a chartered airliner and flew back to Boston. On the flight, Helen Keyes came to visit Jack and said to him, "What will I say to all my friends in Boston when they ask me why you picked Lyndon Johnson?"

Jack smiled, and said, "Pretend you know something they don't know."

EIGHT

The Big One

THAT SUNDAY when we landed at Logan Airport in Boston, the newly nominated Democratic candidate for the Presidency managed to talk his way out of a triumphal march through the city that the mayor and the assorted local Irish politicians had planned for him, and headed for Hyannis Port, where he spent all of two days resting with Jackie and Caroline before planning the coming campaign. Ten days later we were sitting with him at the Ambassador's house while he watched Richard Nixon accepting the nomination at the Republican convention, with both arms held high above his head. Kennedy turned away from the television screen with a grimace, and said, "If I have to stand up before a crowd and wave my arms over my head like that in order to become the President of the United States, I'll never make it."

If Kennedy had his way, he would have started to campaign for election the day after he was nominated in Los Angeles. But because Congress spent August in the special session called by Johnson and Rayburn before the convention, in the hope of pressuring members of Congress into supporting Johnson's Presidential bid, Kennedy had to spend that month answering roll calls in Washington. Meanwhile Nixon got off to a head start with campaign trips to the South, the Midwest and Hawaii. While he waited impatiently to launch his own campaign on the Labor Day weekend, Kennedy managed to get away from Washington during August long enough to attend to what he called "fence-mending chores" — making peace with Eleanor Roosevelt and Harry Truman, the two influential Democrats who had been against his nomination.

Kennedy was still deeply irritated with President Truman when he sent Abe Ribicoff to Missouri early in August to arrange a peace conference at the Truman Library. (The choice of Ribicoff, the Jewish governor of Connecticut, as his emissary to call upon the Masonic and Baptist Truman was not accidental and gave JFK a certain satisfaction.) Kennedy was impatient with anybody who allowed disapproval of Ambassador Kennedy to prejudice him against the political ambitions of the Ambassador's son, as Truman openly admitted. "I'm not asking anybody to vote for my father," he often said. He also bitterly resented Truman's personal attack on him before the convention. As hurt and angry as he was, Kennedy was still too much of a practical politician not to turn the other cheek, particularly when he was facing a hard campaign on the religious issue and needed Baptist votes badly. He faced Truman calmly but politely in their private meeting at the library at Independence, and not much was said on either side. Later when they announced their peace pact to the waiting reporters, one of the newsmen asked Truman what had made him decide that Kennedy was now ready for the Presidency after being so positive, back in July, that Kennedy was not yet ready. "When the Democratic convention decided to nominate him, that's when I decided," Truman said with a grin.

Jack went to visit Eleanor Roosevelt at Hyde Park expecting her to demand Adlai Stevenson's appointment as Secretary of State as a price for her support. Not only did she make no such suggestion — she even made a point of telling Kennedy that he should choose his own Cabinet members without making any preelection promises or commitments to anybody. On the day before his Sunday visit to Mrs. Roosevelt's cottage at Hyde Park, one of her granddaughters was killed in a fall from a horse. Kennedy offered to postpone the meeting, but Mrs. Roosevelt insisted on keeping the appointment, apologizing to him because her mourning would keep her from meeting him at the airport. Dave Powers made the trip to Hyde Park with him. When we asked Dave later how Jack had gotten along with the First Lady of the party, he said, "The Senator came out of there like a boy who has just made a good confession. It was a great load off his mind."

The trip to Hyde Park marked Dave's return to duty after he had been given a week off to celebrate the birth and baptism of his daughter, Diane. The next time Dave saw Diane, on Election Day when he came home to Massachusetts to vote, she was three months old. From late in August until the first Tuesday in November, Dave and I traveled with our candidate from Maine to Alaska and down to Texas to speaking appearances at rallies in 237 cities. Nixon went to 168 cities. Kennedy worked eighteen hours a day, almost every day, during the campaign. I remember Dave saying to me one morning, when we were going to bed in a small town hotel at two-thirty and leaving a call for seven, "Gosh, we do things for this guy that we wouldn't do for our own mothers." Every stop on the crowded schedule seemed to follow the same noisy and frantic pattern — the wild welcome at the airport with the high school bands and the homemade hand-lettered signs ("Baptists for Kennedy," "Let's put a new John in the White House") and the red-faced police trying to hold back the people, the motorcade through the cheering crowds in the downtown streets, the luncheons, the dinners, the receptions, the speeches at local colleges and civic auditoriums. The similarity between the apparently spontaneous demonstrations in so many different and widely separated places was understandable. Each welcome was arranged well ahead of time by one of our advance men, according to the same mimeographed manual of instructions issued to our other advance men in the other cities across the country.

The role of the advance man, a key factor in the campaign, had been studied and developed in our 1958 Senatorial race in Massachusetts and then perfected in the Wisconsin and West Virginia primaries. The advance man goes to the scene several days before the arrival of the candidate to make the necessary arrangements with local party leaders, city officials, the police department, the local newspapers and television stations. He selects the best motorcade routes, sees to such logistical matters as reserving hotel rooms and automobiles and busses for the candidate's party and the accompanying press corps, and even recruits the high school bands and suggests slogans for the homemade signs. His main function, however, is to get out the crowds. Jerry Bruno, who shared with

John Treanor the brunt of our important advance work, arranged an appearance of Kennedy at Superior, Wisconsin, in the fall of 1959 that drew only a small crowd. Kennedy said to him quietly, "Jerry, what happened?"

"Everybody went to the football game," Bruno said.

"What football game?"

"There was a big high school football game rained out here last night, and they postponed it until tonight, so everybody went to the football game," Bruno said.

The excuse was not good enough for Jack Kennedy.

"Jerry," he said, "we don't want anything like this to happen again." Evidently he felt that Bruno should have prevented the football game's postponement to that Saturday night, or prevented the storm that rained it out the night before.

Before the opening of the campaign, we conducted a school for advance men. One of the lecturers was Jim Rowe, an old hand at Presidential election campaigning who joined our camp in August after working for Humphrey and Johnson. Jim discussed the many mistakes in advance work made by the Stevenson organization in 1956. The main lesson emphasized during the course was that the advance man must never act like the candidate; he was to avoid personal publicity, steer clear of making comments to the press about Kennedy or the local political problems, make no promises or commitments of any kind to local politicians, and stick to his job of handling the mechanical details of the prearranged schedule. Most of our advance men learned that lesson well, but there were a few exceptions, the law of averages prevailing as usual, who came upon the scene trying to give the natives the impression that they were the chief strategists in Kennedy's brain trust. One of these limelight-lovers was a self-assured Boston Irishman whom we shall call Pete Reynolds because that is not his real name. Reynolds was assigned to be the advance man in El Paso, where Kennedy was to start the important early September tour of Texas that would take him to his crucial discussion of the religious issue at the Greater Houston Ministerial Association's meeting of Protestant clergymen. Reynolds paved the way for Kennedy's sensitive mission to the Lone Star State by announcing to a group of local newspaper reporters at a cocktail party in El Paso before his arrival that Kennedy needed no help from Lyndon Johnson in Texas. "Kennedy is more popular down here than Johnson," Reynolds explained to the newsmen, "and he needs us in Texas more than we need him." The story appeared promptly on the next day's front pages. Lovely.

Kennedy arrived at the airport in El Paso late at night, exhausted from a tour of California. He had a tough day ahead of him, with the Houston ministerial meeting weighing on his mind, and he wanted to go straight to the hotel and to bed, with no speech at the airport. But to the amazement of Sam Rayburn, who was with us, there was a crowd of more than twenty thousand wildly enthusiastic people surrounding the plane at the airport despite the lateness of the hour. So the Senator had to make a speech. Then Lyndon Johnson appeared on the plane, waving a handful of newspaper clippings, complaining about Reynolds. Kennedy glanced at the clippings, glared at me, and handed me the clippings. I drew Reynolds aside, and said to him, "The next plane out of here, no matter how early in the morning it leaves, you're on it." That was the end of Reynolds.

Johnson talked about Reynolds all the way to the hotel and continued to talk about Reynolds while we had a few drinks with him and Rayburn. He was still talking about Reynolds when Kennedy excused himself and went to bed, and he talked to me about Reynolds until five o'clock in the morning. The next day when Lyndon came to the hotel room to have breakfast with us, Jack asked him how he was feeling.

"I didn't get much sleep last night," Johnson said. "I was too busy thinking about that feller you brought down here from Boston."

Kennedy made his most difficult, and probably the most important, decision of the campaign one day while he was shaving. While we were making a memorable whistle-stop tour of California by train, our only train trip of the campaign, we received word from our advance man in Houston, Tim May, that the ministers there wanted Kennedy to defend the right of a Catholic to be President at their association's meeting during his scheduled visit to that city a week later. All of us, including the candidate and Bobby, were dubious about accepting the invitation. We thought it might be a trap to embarrass Kennedy. On the other hand, avoiding the invitation might be even more embarrassing. Nixon had been invited to appear before the same group but had declined.

While we stalled a reply to the Houston ministers, the religious issue was stirred up strongly by an attack on Kennedy from Dr. Norman Vincent Peale's newly organized group of Protestant ministers, the National Conference of Citizens for Religious Freedom, who issued a statement that no Catholic President could be free from influence of his church's hierarchy. The Peale group revived as proof of this charge a claim by Dr. Daniel Poling of Philadelphia that Kennedy, as a young Congressman, had turned down an invitation to appear as a Catholic spokesman at a fund-raising dinner for a proposed memorial chapel in a Baptist church, honoring the four chaplains who went down with the S.S. *Dorchester* in World War II, because the Catholic archdiocese of Philadelphia was opposed to the memorial project.

When we ended our train trip in Bakersfield, and flew from there to Los Angeles on the *Caroline*, Kennedy was still debating with us over the question of whether or not to accept the Houston invitation. At the airport in Los Angeles, where he had a speaking engagement that night, he was hit at a press conference by the Peale group's charges and the Poling story about Cardinal Dougherty's disapproval of his invitation to the memorial chapel dinner. Kennedy boiled over and had some angry words to say about churchmen injecting their religious prejudices into a political campaign. He explained once again, as he had done many times before, that he had declined Poling's invitation because he did not feel qualified to appear at the fund-raising dinner as a spokesman for the Roman Catholics. "If I had been invited as a Congressman, or as a Navy veteran, or as a private citizen, I would have accepted," he said, "but not as a spokesman for the Catholics." He was still steaming when we drove from the airport to the hotel. "I'm getting tired of these people who think I want to replace the gold at Fort Knox with a supply of holy water," he said to us.

It was no time to bring it up, but I had to tell him then and there that we could wait no longer for a decision on whether to change the schedule to allow for an appearance at the ministers' meeting in Houston. Tim May, the advance man, was under severe pressure from the clergymen, who were demanding an immediate answer. Bobby was calling me constantly from Washington, asking me when Jack was going to make up his mind. By now Tim was against it, on the advice of Democratic leaders in Houston who regarded the ministers as a hostile group, and Bobby felt the same way. Lyndon

Johnson and Sam Rayburn both told us to avoid the confrontation. "They're mostly Republicans, and they're out to get you," Rayburn said.

When we reached his hotel room, the Senator began to change his clothes for that evening's speech at the Shrine Temple. He said to me, "What do you think?"

"You know what I think," I said. "I think it would be a mistake. If you have to meet the religious issue, Houston is not the place to do it."

He went into the bathroom to shave. When he finished shaving, he came back into the bedroom and said to me, "Tell them I'm going to do it. This is as good a time as any to get it over with. I've got to face it sooner or later."

I could see that his mind was made up so there was no point in further arguments. When he came to a decision, there were no second thoughts, no more wavering questions in his mind, and he wanted no continued speculation about whether or not it was the right thing for him to do. When we checked into the Rice Hotel in Houston, where the meeting was to take place in the downstairs ballroom, he was tense and nervous, well aware that most of us around him, and most of his Texas friends, were still convinced that he was making a dangerous move and exposing himself to a possibility of a humilating harassment that might cost him the election.

Luckily there was a happy accident a few minutes before he faced the ministers that broke his tension and sent him into the meeting in a more relaxed and calmer mood. I tried to keep away from him in our suite while he was dressing because he seemed as restless as a caged tiger. As I was pouring a Bourbon for Sam Rayburn, I heard the Senator in the bedroom calling, first quietly and then louder, "Dave? Where are you, Dave? Dave, come in here!" I went looking for Powers, who was nowhere to be found, and returned to report that Dave was missing. I asked if there was anything I could do for him.

"Have you got a pair of black shoes that I could borrow?" he said. He was dressed appropriately for the occasion in a dark blue suit, blue shirt and blue and white striped tie, but the only pair of his shoes in the room were brown. I had no black shoes to give him.

"Well, it's too late now," he said. "I ought to send Powers back to Charlestown for this one."

He got into the brown shoes and we headed for the elevator. In the elevator, holding the door open for the Senator, was Powers, trying to act as though nothing had happened The Senator stared at Powers, and then looked down at his blue suit and his brown shoes and looked at Dave again. Dave stared off into space innocently as the elevator descended.

"Dave, do you notice anything out of place in my attire?" Kennedy asked.

Dave cleared his throat nervously and said, "Are those brown shoes?"

"Yes," Kennedy said. "Those are brown shoes. Brown shoes with a dark blue suit. Thanks very much, Dave."

"Well, Senator," Dave said, "they won't see your shoes on television. Besides, you know that most of the men in this country wear brown shoes. Do you realize that tonight, by wearing these shoes, you'll be sewing up the brown-shoe voters?"

Kennedy broke up laughing, and went off to face the Houston ministers in a much more relaxed frame of mind. Dave called after him, "I hope all those nuns who pray for the Notre Dame football team are rubbing their beads for you tonight."

The program called for an opening statement by Kennedy and then a period of answering questions from the floor. The ballroom was crowded with the ministers and about three hundred spectators, including many nationally known political columnists and television commentators from New York and Washington who had come down to watch the historic confrontation. Because the discussion was to be televised, there was to be no speaking in the room until the chairman introduced Kennedy on the air at nine o'clock. Kennedy took his seat on the platform about five minutes before nine, so there was a long and uneasy period of silence, with Kennedy eyeing the ministers and the stiff and sullen ministers staring at Kennedy, while they waited for the program to begin. I was not there because I had decided to watch it upstairs in our suite on television with Sam Rayburn and Dave, but Pierre Salinger said later that the atmosphere in the ballroom during the silent waiting was strained and uncomfortable. "Then he got up and started to talk," Pierre said, "and he took complete command of the situation."

Kennedy's opening statement was by far the best speech of the campaign, and probably the best speech he ever delivered in his lifetime, precise, intelligent, forceful and sharply pointed, without a wasted word. The real issues of the campaign, he told the audience, were not religious issues, but more critical problems — the humiliation of Eisenhower and Nixon by those foreign nations that no longer respect the United States, the hungry children in West Virginia, the old people unable to pay their doctor's bills, too many slums, too few schools.

"These are the real issues," he said. "But because I am a Catholic, and no Catholic has ever been elected President, the real issues in this campaign have been obscured. So it is apparently necessary for me to state once again — not what kind of a church I believe in, for that should be important only to me — but what kind of America I believe in. I believe in an America where the separation of the church and state is absolute — where no Catholic prelate would tell the President (should he be a Catholic) how to act and no Protestant minister would tell his parishioners for whom to vote . . . where no man is denied public office merely because his religion differs from the President who might appoint him or the people who might elect him."

He went on from there to state his views on every aspect of the religious issue so clearly and uncompromisingly that he left no important questions for the ministers to put to him during the question-and-answer period that followed. Kennedy's poise and his forceful arguments seemed to leave the ministers so overawed and confused, with all the starch taken out of them, that they were in no mood to ask him embarrassing questions anyway. The questions that they did come up with were hesitant and routine, and not particularly memorable. Kennedy handled each one as quickly and calmly as a major-league shortstop handles an easy grounder, and often drew spirited applause from the Texas spectators in the ballroom when he threw back his firm and fast answer.

I could see how well he was doing by watching Sam Rayburn in our room upstairs as Rayburn watched him on television. Mr. Sam, of course, had been against Kennedy before the convention and lukewarm toward him afterwards. He began to be impressed by the Senator's popularity when he saw the size of the crowds that had turned out for him earlier that day at El Paso, Fort Worth and San Antonio. I reminded Mr. Sam that El Paso, after all, had a large

Catholic population. "Hell, it always had a large Catholic population," Rayburn said, "but no politician, Catholic or Protestant, ever drew a crowd like this one." Kennedy's performance at the ministers' meeting in Houston not only delighted Rayburn — it made him a staunch and enthusiastic admirer of Kennedy for the rest of his days. "By God, look at him — and listen to him!" Rayburn shouted while he watched Kennedy tear into the ministers. "He's eating 'em blood raw! This young feller will be a great President!" The next day at Austin and Dallas, Rayburn delivered a hot and fiery speech for Kennedy, hailing him as the greatest Northern Democrat since Franklin D. Roosevelt. "And you people who complain about income taxes," Rayburn yelled at the Texans, "you should remember you didn't have any incomes to pay a tax on before Roosevelt came into office."

Once again, in deciding to accept the invitation from the Houston ministers, Kennedy had instinctively done the right thing against the advice of all of his advisers. "I didn't change any votes in that room," he said afterwards, "but I didn't lose any elsewhere." The success of his appearance at Houston boosted his stock considerably among such previously doubtful Democratic leaders as Rayburn and Price Daniel, the Texas governor. It also gave Kennedy himself a stimulating psychological boost and an added confidence at a point in the early stages of the campaign, two weeks before the first debate against Nixon, when he needed it.

After that trip to Texas, the hoarseness in his voice that had been bothering him in California miraculously disappeared. He renewed his campaign with such relish in the Midwest that he even rode a horse at the Sioux City stockyards and, more incredible, allowed an Indian chief's headdress to be placed briefly on his head when he was inducted into the Sioux tribe in South Dakota. Usually Kennedy avoided such photographic gimmicks. He would grab at a construction man's hard hat or a cowboy sombrero before it could be clamped on his head, and tuck it under his arm before the camera was snapped. He often remarked that he had probably been frightened as a child by that famous picture of Calvin Coolidge in Indian chief's feathers. When Kennedy was faced with the same crowning ritual at the Indian gathering in South Dakota, he stood tensely with his arms at his sides while the chief, Hollow Horn Bear, lifted the feathered bonnet and lowered it gently over his head. His arms began to move up swiftly as the crown touched his forehead, and almost at the very second that the chief settled the feathers in place on his reddish brown shock of hair, Kennedy lifted it off. He turned to shake hands with the grinning chief and said to him, "From here on in, when we're looking at Westerns on TV I'll be rooting for *our* side."

As everybody knows, the real turning point in the campaign was the first debate with Nixon in Chicago. The contrast on the television screen between Nixon's nervous anxiety and Kennedy's cool composure wiped away the Republican contention that Kennedy was too immature and inexperienced for the Presidency and established him as a potential winner. It also brought several more reluctant Democratic notables scurrying to get under Kennedy's umbrella. We were annoyed by later reports that Kennedy had spent three days resting and studying the issues before the decisive first debate, while the exhausted Nixon campaigned until the moment before they went on the air. Kennedy spent the previous two weeks on a back-breaking tour of the middle of the country, ending up in Utah and flying from there to Chicago, where he landed at four-fifteen on Saturday morning. The next day, Sunday, the day before the debate, he was up at six o'clock to go to Cleveland, where he spent a strenuous day at a steer-roast outing attended by a crowd of more than one hundred thousand people. The steer roast, arranged by Ray Miller's Cleveland Democratic organization a year in advance, was a commitment that Kennedy had promised to attend long before the debate was arranged. It marked a gala reuniting of Mike DiSalle and Ray Miller's dissidents, but one prominent Ohio Democrat who did not attend the festivities was Senator Frank Lausche, obviously because he considered Kennedy to be a loser.

That Sunday night Kennedy went back to his hotel in Chicago. His rest and study before the debate on Monday night were interrupted again on Monday afternoon when he spent two hours or more making a speech and shaking many hands at a session of the Carpenters' Union convention at the Hotel Morrison. After the debate, we flew back to Ohio to begin a tour of that state the next day, spending the night at a motel in Paynesville.

At seven-thirty the following morning when Kennedy was eating his breakfast in the motel room, Jerry Bruno, the advance man, came in and said, "The Senator is waiting outside. He wants to know if he can travel through the state today with you and Mike DiSalle."

"Senator Who?" Kennedy asked.

"Senator Frank Lausche," Bruno said. "He wants to join our party."

The day before the debate Lausche refused to appear with Kennedy at the steer roast in Cleveland. The day after the debate Lausche was waiting outside Kennedy's motel room at seven-thirty in the morning. If we had any lingering doubts about Kennedy's success in the debate, Lausche removed them.

Bobby Kennedy and I both remarked at the time that the first impressive debate with Nixon in Chicago — hardly anybody remembers the other three — seemed to be a rerun of Jack's debate with Henry Cabot Lodge in Waltham, Massachusetts, back in the 1952 Senatorial campaign. Lodge was the debonair and experienced Republican statesman who should have eaten up the youthful Jack Kennedy. Instead it was Kennedy who showed more poise, coolness, wit and a firmer grasp of the issues that came up for discussion. The situation was much the same in the first Chicago debate eight years later. The Republicans were stressing Kennedy's "immaturity" and depicting him as too green to stand up to Khrushchev. Nixon had been Vice-President and Eisenhower's traveling emissary abroad for eight years, the champion of free enterprise who stood up against Khrushchev in the "kitchen debate" at Moscow. But before the television cameras in Chicago the myth of Kennedy's alleged immaturity was demolished. Nixon, like Lodge back in Waltham, was unnerved by Kennedy's cool nonchalance and his quick and easy confidence in handling every question that came up. More impressive than what each man had to say was how each of them appeared on the TV screen. In contrast to Kennedy's trim and well-tanned look, Nixon seemed haggard, hesitant and unsure of himself, and so strained that during the following week several Republican leaders asked if he was really as sick as he appeared that night. Herbert Klein, Nixon's press secretary, had to issue a statement that said Nixon was well and "looked good in person."

Kennedy had lost respect for Nixon as a political adversary, and paid little serious attention to anything he said. His disregard for Nixon came across strongly to the television audiences during the debates, and it often was more devastating than any verbal attack could ever be. While Nixon was earnestly arguing a point, the camera would show Kennedy glancing at him with an expression of mixed boredom and amusement that made whatever Nixon was saying seem silly. Kennedy's dislike for Nixon did not stem from the differences in their political views. He had a deep respect and liking for Barry Goldwater and other conservative Republicans. Nixon was simply too dull and coy for Kennedy's taste. After the first debate, Nixon drew Kennedy aside in the studio and talked to him quietly for several minutes. After their conversation, we noticed that Kennedy was burning with irritation. I asked him what Nixon had said.

"Oh, I don't know," Kennedy said. "Just the usual small talk. I wasn't listening to him. But while he was talking about the weather and about how hard it was to get a good night's sleep in the campaign, he was watching the photographers out of the corner of his eye. When one of them was taking a picture of us, he would put a stern expression on his face and start jabbing his finger into my chest, so he would look as if he was laying down the law to me about foreign policy or Communism. Nice fellow."

Later that night Kennedy remarked rather lightly, but perhaps not too lightly, that he owed it to the country to win the election in order to keep Nixon out of the White House.

The first Kennedy-Nixon debate marked the first time in history that a Presidential election campaign was significantly changed and affected by the appearance of the two candidates on television. It stirred up some interesting discussions about how television differed from radio as a political campaign communications medium, making the candidate's visual image and physical appearance as important, if not more important, than his words. Would Franklin D. Roosevelt's campaigns be successful in a television era when all of the voters would see that he was unable to walk? Henry Steele Commager, the historian, ventured the opinion that George Washington would have lost a television debate because of his personality defects. Earl Mazo, the political reporter, was covering the Southern Governors' Conference at Hot Springs, Arkansas, on the night of the first Kennedy-Nixon debate. At that time Hot Springs did not have a television station on a national network. The telecast of the debate shown there was a replay, seen one hour after the discussion was heard locally on radio. When the governors and the reporters at the conference first listened to the debate on radio, without seeing it, Nixon seemed to be the easy winner.

"Nixon was best on radio," Mazo wrote later, "simply because his deep, resonant voice carried more conviction, command and determination than Kennedy's higher-pitched voice and his Boston-Harvard accent. But on television, Kennedy looked sharper, more in control, more firm — his was the image of the man who could stand up to Khrushchev."

The nine Democratic Southern governors who watched the television rebroadcast at Hot Springs sent Kennedy a telegram of warm congratulations. Most of them had been either against Kennedy up to that point or lukewarm, so their message was a very pleasant surprise.

After the first debate, the 1960 campaign was an entirely different ball game. We heard reports from our organizers all over the country that were similar to the one written by James Michener, the novelist, who served as the Kennedy chairman in the strongly Republican Bucks County district of Pennsylvania. Before the first debate, Michener had difficulty trying to get people in Bucks County to work for Kennedy. Contributions were few and slim. He could afford only one office with one paid secretary. "Immediately after the first debate," Michener wrote later, "we received funds to open four additional offices, each with at least one paid secretary and some with three. We got phone calls volunteering services. We got automobiles and posters. We received checks through the mail. In Bucks County, where it used to take courage to be a Democrat, we had five thriving offices open seven days a week."

Our schedule, which had been planned and arranged back in August, was working well, and we all agreed that it should stand unchanged for the rest of the campaign. Jack and Bobby and I had resolved that we would avoid the big mistake in schedule planning that Bobby had noticed in Adlai Stevenson's 1956 campaign. Stevenson's people had arranged their own itineraries, without consulting local politicians, in states where they were strangers and knew nothing about local political problems. They wasted time, sending Stevenson to areas where he had no chance of getting votes or where the prevailing sentiment was so thoroughly Democratic and anti-Republican that his appearance was unnecessary. They stirred up resentment by ignoring the advice of local party leaders. To avoid such blunders,

I suggested, and the Kennedys immediately agreed, that in any state where Jack was planning to spend more than two days, we should turn him over to the local party leaders and let them plan his public appearances.

I don't think that any previous Presidential candidate followed such a procedure. It worked very well for us and made a major contribution to the success of the campaign. During August I traveled to the large states of the Northeast and Midwest with Dick Maguire, who served along with another Massachusetts Irishman, Dick O'Hare, as the schedule department's coordinator and troubleshooter in our Washington headquarters while I was on the road with our candidate. We visited such Democratic leaders as Dick Daley, Mike DiSalle, Dave Lawrence, Bill Green, Charlie Buckley and Carmine DeSapio. I remember that DeSapio received us at a vacation resort in upper New York State, wearing only his usual dark glasses and a pair of tight white swimming shorts. To each of them I said the same thing: our candidate can spend so many days here on these dates and he wants you to decide where he should go on each of those days. The leaders were surprised and delighted to be given the selection of a schedule that, in their opinion, would do both Kennedy and their own local Democratic candidates the most good.

We planned to avoid time-wasting travel between widely separated speaking engagements by giving saturation coverage to one area in one day, as we had done in Massachusetts in the 1958 Senatorial campaign. Kennedy spent as much as eighteen hours a day making appearances in locations that required only a short drive or a short hop in the *Caroline* between stops. We tried to avoid long cross-country flights in the *Caroline* because it was a prop plane, slow in comparison with today's jets, and subject to delays from head winds. Nixon, on the other hand, flew one day from a morning appearance at a labor union convention in St. Louis to a Republican women's meeting at Atlantic City and then to an outdoor night rally at Roanoke, Virginia. From Roanoke he flew to Omaha, only 350 miles from where he started that morning, wasting most of the day and night in the air and getting so exhausted he could hardly see straight.

Our schedule was geared geographically to the general strategy of our campaign, aiming our main effort at winning the nine big states that held between them 237 of the required 269 electoral votes — New York, New Jersey, Pennsylvania, Ohio, Michigan, Illinois, California, Texas and Massachusetts. When we started the campaign in Alaska, Dave reminded the Senator on the way to a Sunday mass at Anchorage that a Catholic can make three wishes when he enters a church for the first time. Kennedy said, "New York, Illinois and California." According to our original plan, which was agreed upon again when we reviewed it at our October first meeting, Kennedy himself would spend most of his time in the Midwest and the Northeast, particularly in the suburban areas around the big cities. He would leave Texas and the rest of the South, hopefully, to Lyndon Johnson. His time in California in the final month of the campaign would have to be limited to two days, in San Francisco and Los Angeles, during the last week before the election. Then he would appear on Friday in Chicago, Saturday in New York, Sunday in Connecticut, Long Island and New Jersey, finishing the campaign Monday with a tour of New England that would end in Boston.

All of us, except Kennedy himself, were basking in optimism when we gathered at the family compound on Cape Cod that first Saturday in October to go over the plans for the last month of the campaign. Kennedy figured correctly that the race would end up very close; he was apprehensive about how much help Nixon would get from President Eisenhower, who had not yet entered the campaign, and he was still worried about the religious issue. Unlike a lot of Republicans, Kennedy felt that Nixon was right in keeping Eisenhower out of the campaign as long as possible. If Nixon had brought Eisenhower into the campaign earlier, Kennedy would have charged him with hiding behind Ike's favorable image and being unable to stand up on his own record and merits. We agreed that when Eisenhower did come to Nixon's aid, as he did late in October, Kennedy would treat the President with courtesy and respect but hit hard at picturing Nixon as a losing candidate who was calling desperately for Eisenhower's help.

Kennedy did just that, very effectively, when Nixon toured New York on November 2 with Eisenhower, Lodge and Governor Nelson Rockefeller riding at his side. Kennedy had a fine time for days afterwards, joshing Nixon for hanging onto Ike's coattails and comparing the parade of Republican bigwigs to a parade of circus elephants. "You've seen those elephants in the circus," Jack said to the laughing crowds. "They have a long memory but no vision. When they move around the ring, they have to grab the tail of the elephant in front of them so they'll know where to go. Dick grabbed the tail of the elephant ahead of him in 1952 and 1956, but now, in 1960, he's the one who is supposed to be running, not President Eisenhower. I stand tonight where Woodrow Wilson stood, and Franklin Roosevelt and Harry Truman stood. Dick Nixon stands where McKinley stood, where Harding and Coolidge and Landon stood, where Dewey stood. Where do they get those candidates?"

But privately Kennedy knew that Eisenhower's late appearance in the campaign was doing Nixon plenty of good. He was shocked and disheartened at the same time by the news that the Catholic hierarchy in Puerto Rico had ordered Catholics on that island not to vote for Governor Muñoz-Marin's Popular Democratic candidates because that party favored birth-control instruction. Kennedy called Cardinal Cushing in Boston with a plea to the Cardinal to bring pressure to keep the Puerto Rican prelates from interfering in politics, but it was too late to prevent a wave of devastating statements from anti-Catholic groups all over the United States, who held up the incident as an example of the Catholic church's meddling in state affairs. "If enough voters realize that Puerto Rico is a part of the United States," Kennedy said bitterly, "this could cost us the election." The Ambassador, who was being charged in newspaper advertisements at the same time as an anti-Semite, said that he was thinking of joining the Jewish religion. "The Jews are giving us more help than we're getting from the Catholics," Joe Kennedy said.

Meanwhile the country was being flooded with jokes about Kennedy's Catholicism, some of them painfully cutting. There was a story about Kennedy planning to collect bowling balls in order to make a string of rosary beads for the Statue of Liberty, which would be renamed Our Lady of the Harbor. Somebody in Chicago came up with a slogan, "Join the church of your choice, while there's still time." Kennedy quarters were circulated, with the head of George Washington on the silver coin retouched with red nail polish so that it looked like a profile of Pope John XXIII. In Washington a Republican leader was quoted as predicting cheerfully, "I have a deep and abiding faith in the fundamental bigotry of the American people." Several advisers urged Kennedy to make another speech on religious tolerance over a television network on the Sunday night before the election, but he decided that such a plea would only give the issue more attention.

Going into the last hectic week of the campaign, Kennedy began to worry about losing California. After touring Los Angeles on Tuesday and covering the San Francisco Bay area on Wednesday, his first visit to that state since early in September, he sensed correctly that he was running no better than even with Nixon in California. He told me to change the schedule so that he could return to California and spend two more days there on the last weekend before the election instead giving that Saturday and Sunday to New York and Connecticut as we had planned.

"I'll be wasting my time in New York," he said. "I've got New York and I've got Connecticut. But I haven't got California. Give me those two days in California and I'll win there."

As usual, he was absolutely right. But I had to tell him, to his everlasting disgust and anger, that it was too late to make such a drastic change in the schedule. We had a firm commitment to appear on Friday night in Chicago at the gala parade of the Democratic ward clubs, a must engagement that could not be broken under any conditions. Considering the slowness of the *Caroline*, it seemed impossible to fly from Chicago back to California and arrive there early enough on Saturday to get anything done. Besides, we were locked into firm commitments in New York and Connecticut for that weekend. The one big trouble with a closely crowded schedule such as the one Kennedy and I had arranged for that week is that it becomes too inflexible. If you try to rearrange any small part of it at the last minute, there is chaos all the way along the line. But that did not concern Kennedy. He needed those two extra days in California, and he could not understand why I was not able to give them to him.

"You and your damned schedule," he said to me. "If we lose California, it will be your thick-headed fault."

He was miserable going to New York, and as my luck would have it, that Saturday turned out to be a miserable day, with a steady downpour of rain that ruined our tour of Manhattan, the Bronx and Queens and drove away the crowds. Kennedy gritted his teeth and kept muttering to me, "This is useless. I should have gone to California." When he was returning from the Long Island suburbs to Manhattan, with his clothing soaking wet from the rain, his police escort took him to the Biltmore, where Carmine DeSapio and Lyndon Johnson were waiting to appear with him in a parade, instead of to his rooms at the Carlyle, where Dave was waiting for him with a change of clothes. Kennedy went to a room at the Biltmore, stripped down to his undershorts, and then learned that he had no dry clothes to put on. Looking for Dave and his missing clothes, he ran to the door of the suite and opened it — and found himself, in his shorts, being stared at by a crowd of politicians, reporters and assorted spectators who had gathered in the corridor outside. Fortunately there were no photographers. I was in the corridor, too, being reluctant to approach him in this moment of wrath. I watched Lyndon Johnson open the door and go into the room. Lyndon came out as if he had been shot from a cannon, pale and shaken. "You better talk to him," Lyndon said to me. "That boy is very mad."

Dave finally appeared with the Senator's clothes and I edged into the room with him. I had been reminded by DeSapio that the scheduled parade through the streets of Manhattan was ready to start, and a crowd of people were waiting outside in the rain to get a glimpse of Kennedy and Johnson. While he was dressing, Kennedy berated me soundly for all of the day's mishaps. "Now go out there," he said, "and tell DeSapio that the parade is off. I'm not going to have seven thousand policemen tying up the entire city of New York in the pouring rain to have one stupid politician riding down the street. I don't care if they've got five million people out there. I'm not going to do it. If he doesn't call the parade off, call the police commissioner and tell him to do it. Either you tell him or I'll tell him myself."

I said, "I'll tell him, Senator."

When I told DeSapio what Kennedy had ordered, DeSapio became livid. "You can't do it," he cried. I said, "Either you cancel the parade, or I'll get the police commissioner to do it." The parade was canceled. I wished that I had changed the schedule and sent Kennedy to California. That night at the big rally in the Coliseum there was another hassle that rubbed him the wrong way. He asked Tammany Hall Democrats who were running the show to introduce Herbert Lehman, the distinguished New York liberal reformer who was their enemy, and to let Lehman say a few words to the audience. Mike Prendergast flatly refused the request.

Kennedy couldn't get out of New York City fast enough that night. Thankfully for all of us, Connecticut gave him a much warmer welcome, probably the most exciting demonstration of the whole campaign. We landed in the *Caroline* at Bridgeport after midnight and drove from there in a motorcade along Route 8 in the Naugatuck River Valley to Waterbury. All along the road, for more than twenty-seven miles, there were crowds of cheering people, waving torches and red lights, most of them wearing coats over their pajamas and nightgowns, and at the firehouses in every town the fire engines were lined up beside the road with their lights flashing, bells ringing, and sirens wailing. Although it was almost three o'clock in the morning when we reached Waterbury, there was a roaring crowd of more than forty thousand people in the city square outside of the Roger Smith Hotel where Kennedy was to spend the night.

He came out on the balcony of the hotel and made a speech, closing with a reminder that it was after three o'clock and time for everybody to get some sleep. The crowd refused to let him go. He introduced Governor Ribicoff, who said a few words. The crowd demanded Kennedy again and he had to talk to them once more. After he finally went inside the hotel and got into bed at four o'clock, the square remained filled with cheering people until daylight.

On Sunday the Senator appeared before big crowds in New Haven and Bridgeport, at the Long Island Arena in Commack, Long Island, and at Newark and Jersey City in New Jersey. Then he flew at night to Lewiston, Maine, arriving there at one-thirty. Lewiston was cold and the airport was dark and empty. The advance man and the few local party leaders who met us at the plane hurried Kennedy into a car and drove him into the city without saying anything about where he was going. The streets were quiet and empty. He glanced at me questioningly, wondering what he was doing in a freezing cold Maine factory town in the middle of the night when everybody seemed to be in bed. Then we drove into a park where a crowd of more than twenty thousand people were waiting, carrying torchlights. Coming from the cold darkness and stillness of the drive from the airport to the sudden glare of torchlighted arena, filled with warmth and excited people, Kennedy was stunned. "My God, isn't this unbelievable?" he said. When the crowd recognized him, there was a roar of cheering that could be heard for miles away.

Later that night we flew to Providence, where we started the next morning on the last day of campaigning through New England — Springfield, Hartford, Burlington in Vermont, Manchester in New Hampshire, and then the wild finale in Boston. At the North End of the city, where Kennedy's grandfather and mother were born, and where he started his campaign for Congress fourteen years earlier, the streets were so jammed with people that he could hardly get to the mass meeting at the Boston Garden. And then, inside the building, there was hardly enough room for him on the speakers' platform because it was so crowded with the same red-faced Boston Irish politicians who fought against Kennedy and Pat Lynch in their battle with Onions Burke for control of the state committee in 1956. There was another struggle through the noisy streets from the Garden to Faneuil Hall, scene of the protest meetings of the Revolution, where Kennedy appeared in the television show that closed his campaign. When we finally reached the peace and quiet of his suite at the Statler Hilton Hotel, and closed the door on the last of the enthusiastic well-wishers, Jack was almost completely exhausted. During the grind of the closing week of the campaign — Sunday and Monday in Philadelphia, Tuesday in Los Angeles, Wednesday in San Francisco, Thursday in Phoenix, Albuquerque, Amarillo, Wichita Falls and Oklahoma City, Friday in Virginia, Ohio and Chicago, Saturday in New York, Sunday in Connecticut, Long Island, New Jersey and Maine, and now Monday in New England and Boston — he had never gotten four hours of sleep on any night. Dave and I sat with him while he ate a chicken sandwich and drank a glass of milk.

"Well, it's all over," he said. "I wish I had spent forty-eight hours more in California."

He lost California by a mere 35,623 votes out of a total of more than six and a half million votes. Undoubtedly, if he had been able to spend two more days there before the election as he had wanted to do, he would have won California. As it turned out, he did well in the nine big states where he made his main drive, losing only two of them, California, which had been doubtful all along, and Ohio, a shocker because all of us thought it was a sure thing. There was no handy explanation for the loss of Ohio, beyond the assumption that its farmers and Southern-born laborers had voted against Kennedy on the religious issue. But he could put his finger on those two extra days that I refused to give him in California because such a last-minute change would have disrupted our schedule. For the next three years, whenever we had a political disagreement, he would remind me of that miserable Saturday I made him spend in New York when he should have been in California.

On the morning of Election Day, we woke him at seven-thirty so he would be ready to meet Jackie when she came from Cape Cod to vote with him at the polling place in Boston, near their legal home, the apartment at 122 Bowdoin Street on Beacon Hill. He was nervous leading Jackie through the cheering crowd that had gathered at the voting place, because she was then in her eighth month of pregnancy, and he held his arm in front of her to protect her from being jostled. After they voted, the Kennedys went to the airport in East Boston and flew to the Cape on the *Caroline*. Dave and I hurried home to vote and then hurried back to the airport to rejoin the rest of the Kennedy contingent for a flight to Hyannis, where we checked into rooms at The Yachtsman hotel and tried to get a little relaxation before moving on to Bobby's house for the long night of waiting for the election returns.

Bobby's large house in the Kennedys' waterfront compound, next to the Ambassador's mansion and across the back lawn from Jack's smaller cottage, had been converted into a communications and vote analysis center. Downstairs on the big enclosed porch there were telephones, staffed by fourteen girl operators, to be used for calling party leaders and poll watchers all over the country. In the dining room, there was a tabulating machine, more telephones connected to direct lines from various Democratic headquarters, and news service teletype machines. As the returns were received downstairs, they were sent upstairs to be analyzed by Lou Harris and compared with the votes of previous years. Harris and his helpers, working with slide rules, had taken over the children's large bedroom, where the cribs and playpens had been cleared away to make room for tables full of data sheets and past election records. Everywhere in the house there were television sets and trays of sandwiches and beer and soft drinks. In the nearby town of Hyannis, the local National Guard armory had been turned into a press head-quarters with another communications center.

The Senator made his first appearance in Bobby's house, where all of us were gathered around the television screens and the tele-phones, around seven-thirty in the evening, when the early returns from the East were full of good news. The three Kennedy sisters were jumping with glee, assuming that Jack had already been elected because he was carrying Connecticut by 100,000 votes and winning in Philadelphia. Morton Downey, the Ambassador's Irish tenor friend, was passing out sandwiches and crooning, "Did Your Mother Come from Ireland?" Everybody seemed to be trying to dig up a special bit of new and happy inside information that he could drop proudly on the candidate's lap, like a puppy bringing home a bone. Mayor Daley in Chicago complained to me later that before the polls in Illinois had closed, he received at least fifteen phone calls from various friends and relatives of the Kennedys whom he had never met. Jack surveyed the joyous scene without saying much, knowing that later in the night, when returns came in from the Midwest and the West, everybody would be in a quieter mood. He went back to his own house and had dinner with Jackie and their friend Bill Walton. When he returned to Bobby's house after ten o'clock, nobody was laughing. He was losing in Ohio, Wiscon-sin, Kentucky, Tennessee and in the farm belt west of the Mississippi, and he was not doing as well as he had expected in Michigan and Illinois.

Lyndon Johnson called from his ranch to say that Texas was very close, but safe. Kennedy hung up the telephone and told us with a smile that Lyndon had said to him, "I see we won in Pennsylvania, but what happened to you in Ohio?"

As the night went on, with the race getting steadily closer, Jack Kennedy was the most detached and composed person in the house. Now and then, but only briefly, he showed a flash of irritation with a return from a certain state or the expert predictions of a TV com-mentator. When the farm states that had been so bitterly opposed to the programs of Ezra Taft Benson, Eisenhower's agricultural secre-tary, began to go Republican, he said to me, "If that's what they want, I ought to give it to them — I ought to keep Benson in as Secretary of Agriculture for another four years." He became irked by John Chancellor, the NBC reporter in Chicago, who was predicting a Nixon sweep. Kennedy made a remark about Chancellor in very sailorish language. His mother, who was standing beside him at the time, did not turn a hair. He drew me aside and asked me if I had expected him to carry Ohio without any trouble. I told him that I had assumed all along that Ohio would be as safe as Massachusetts.

"That's what I thought, too," he said. "Now a lot of guys around here are telling me that they knew we were in trouble in Ohio. If they felt that way, how come they never mentioned it until an hour ago?"

At three o'clock in the morning, the outcome of the election depended on the seesawing returns from four still-undecided states, California, Illinois, Michigan and Minnesota. Mayor Daley telephoned me from Chicago and asked me to assure Kennedy that he would win in Illinois, even though the big lead he had taken in Chicago was being steadily whittled down by returns from the Republican areas downstate. "We're trying to hold back our returns," Daley said to me. "Every time we announce two hundred more votes for Kennedy in Chicago, they come up out of nowhere downstate with another three hundred votes for Nixon. One of their precincts, outside of Peoria, where there are only fifty voters, just announced five hundred votes for Nixon." In the many heavily black wards of Chicago, seven out of ten black people voted for Kennedy, giving him a plurality of more than 300,000 in the Chicago area, but he only managed to carry the state by 8,858 votes.

A few minutes after three, when Kennedy was still hanging at 261 electoral votes, eight short of what he needed for a victory, he watched Nixon make a sad appearance on television in the noise of the press room at the Ambassador Hotel in Los Angeles, with his tired wife, on the verge of tears, at his side. Pierre Salinger had been urging Kennedy to appear before the reporters and the television cameras at the armory in Hyannis. Munching on a sandwich calmly, Kennedy glanced at Salinger, pointed at the pathetic image of Nixon on the television screen, and said, "You want me to put on a performance like that at this hour of the night? Not me. I'm going to bed, and all of you had better do likewise."

Some of his friends complained angrily because Nixon went off the air without conceding. Kennedy turned on them as he was leaving the room and said, "Why should he concede now? If I were him,

I wouldn't." Dave walked with him across the back lawn to his house, neither of them saying a word to each other.

Bobby stayed up alone after everybody else went off to bed, making telephone calls to California, Texas, Chicago, Minnesota and Michigan and checking the late returns. When my wife and I were leaving, I noticed that he seemed perturbed, and I asked him what was worrying him.

"I'm worrying about Teddy," Bobby said. "We've lost every state that he worked in out West. Jack will kid him, and that may hurt Teddy's feelings."

While Kennedy was sleeping, he lost California but won Illinois, Michigan and Minnesota, and picked up another four electoral votes in New Mexico, giving him a total of 303 to Nixon's 219. It was so close, with a difference of only 118,550 in a popular vote of 68,832,818, that if Nixon had won the tight races in Texas and Illinois, he would have been elected. At seven o'clock that morning, two hours before Kennedy woke up, Burrell Petersen stationed a detail of Secret Service agents around his house. After breakfast with Jackie and Caroline and a walk on the beach, the President-elect watched Herb Klein, Nixon's press secretary, reading a message of concession and congratulations on television. Then he posed for a family group picture in his father's living room and insisted that the Ambassador must come out of his long self-imposed obscurity and make his first public appearance in more than a year with the rest of the Kennedys at the victory press conference in the National Guard armory at Hyannis.

I was standing with Helen, my wife, on the steps of the armory when we saw John F. Kennedy for the first time after his election as the President of the United States. He was already a different man from the Jack Kennedy we had talked with the night before. There was a change in his manner and bearing. He came to us, kissed Helen on her cheek, shook hands with me and thanked me for the work I had done for him over the past eight years. It was a very emotional moment.

NINE

Forming a Government

SHORTLY AFTER the President-elect acknowledged his victory on television at the armory in Hyannis ("Now my wife and I prepare for a new administration, and a new baby"), I received a visit from Burrell Petersen and Jim Rowley, the Secret Service agents in charge of his security detail. Petersen informed me, much to my surprise, that he had been told by President Kennedy, as all of us called him from that day on, that the Secret Service detail was under my direction and would be reporting to me for guidance and instructions. This was how I learned that I would become the President's special assistant charged with general administration of his White House staff, his daily schedule of work and appointments, his travel and security arrangements and any political problems that might be bothering him. All that Kennedy himself said to me, when I saw him later that day, was, "You and Dave are coming to Florida with me, aren't you?"

Bobby drew me aside and explained that the new President would be spending the next few weeks at his father's seaside house at Palm Beach, trying to get a little much-needed rest and recuperation from the campaign strain, and talking with various notable visitors about forming the new administration. During the following week, he would pay a visit to the LBJ Ranch in Texas. Later in the all-too-short period of seventy days remaining before the inauguration, he would be traveling to Washington and New York; interviewing prospective Cabinet members; conferring with Clark Clifford and Richard Neustadt, the political science professor at Columbia, who were advising him on transition procedure; visiting the White House to be briefed by President Eisenhower on current government affairs; working with Ted Sorensen on future programs and the inaugural address; and talking with hundreds of other people about the hundreds of pressing problems facing an incoming President, including the filling of some twelve hundred executive branch jobs. While Dave and I were at Palm Beach with the President-elect, Sarge Shriver, his brother-in-law, would be recruiting outstanding talent for the top posts in the government. Another group, Larry O'Brien, Ralph Dungan and Dick Donahue, were lining up people for the important secondary positions in the Cabinet departments and regulatory agencies. During those busy two months after the election, when I was trying to keep up with the mounting pile of appointments that Kennedy wanted me to make for him and trying to fend off the favor-seekers who wanted to talk to the next President, I found myself spending more than half of my time working with the FBI and the Secret Service on security clearances for the multitude of newcomers who were joining the Kennedy administration.

Fortunately for Kennedy, he owed nobody a big job. Unlike other recent Presidents, he had won the nomination and the election largely on his own with no help from big business and the so-called Eastern Establishment, and he was under no strong commitment to anybody in the Democratic party. He was anxious to reward a few longtime and unselfish supporters, such as Abe Ribicoff, who had backed him since 1956, but those were personal rather than political obligations. Most of his political creditors, like Bob McDonough in West Virginia, Dick Daley in Illinois, Jesse Unruh in California and Mike DiSalle in Ohio, were too involved in their own state politics to want any part of a job in the Federal government.

On the Friday after Election Day, Dave and I flew to Florida with the President, stopping at Washington to leave Jackie and Caroline there, and to drop off my wife and other staff members. At the airport, we happened to meet Lady Bird Johnson, who arrived there at the same time on a flight from Texas. She congratulated the President, reminding him that he would be visiting the Johnson ranch during the following week, and as she was walking away from us, she turned back and called to him, "I hope you get a deer."

Kennedy looked at me with a frown and said, "What was that all about?"

"Lyndon must be planning a hunting trip," I said.

"Not me," Kennedy said. "I've got enough on my mind right now without getting a guilt complex from shooting a poor dumb animal."

The next morning at Palm Beach when he came out on the patio in his swimming trunks to take a dip in the pool, he was annoyed to see four Secret Service agents, dressed in business suits, lurking behind the shrubs and palm trees. "For God's sake," he said to me, "if they have to hang around like that, tell them to take off their jackets and ties and put on sport shirts." He eyed the surf on the beach for a moment and then, to the horror of the Secret Service men, he took a running dive into the ocean and swam out beyond the breaking waves. One of the agents complained to me, "We can't have him swimming out there alone." From then on, for the rest of our stay at Palm Beach, a Coast Guard cutter patrolled the water in front of the Ambassador's house, partly to protect the swimming President and partly to guard him against intruders who might try to visit him by boat. The patrolling cutter irritated Kennedy. "Are they expecting Castro to invade Palm Beach?" he asked. The Secret Service agents had another scare at noon that day when Dave and I were sitting on the patio with the President, having a beer before lunch, and a small plane swooped low over our heads. It was carrying a photographer from *Life*, who snapped a clear picture of Dave with a bottle of Heineken's in his hand.

The President invited our wives to join us for a week at the Palm Beach Towers, where his staff people and secretaries were quartered. When Jo Powers, Dave's wife, arrived from Boston, she was invited to have dinner alone with the President and Dave at the Ambassador's house on Saturday night. As busy as he was that weekend, Kennedy wanted to spend an evening with Jo to make up for the three months that Dave had been away from his family during the campaign. "When he put his hand on my shoulder," Jo told us later, "and said to me, 'You know I couldn't have done it without Dave,' I was actually so happy and thrilled that I almost forgot about those three months I had gone through alone with a new baby on my hands."

The next day, Sunday, the President invited all of our wives to dinner. He arranged for a showing of *Sunrise at Campobello*, Dore Schary's movie about Franklin Roosevelt, on the patio during the evening. Soon after the movie started, all of us, except Kennedy himself, fell asleep. He stood up and asked the projectionist to stop the film. "I'm the only one watching it," he said, "and I should be working. All of you might as well do your sleeping someplace else."

On Monday, at the suggestion of Herbert Hoover and the Ambassador, Kennedy flew in a helicopter to Key Biscayne to pay a courtesy call on Richard Nixon. I asked him what he would say to Nixon. "I haven't the slightest idea," he said. "Maybe I'll ask him how he won in Ohio." I sat with him while he and Nixon talked, and I cannot remember either of them saying anything that was interesting or amusing. Nixon did most of the talking while Kennedy studied him quietly, as if he was saying to himself, how did I manage to beat a guy like this by only a hundred thousand votes? When we were climbing back into the helicopter to return to Palm Beach, Kennedy said to me, "It was just as well for all of us that he didn't quite make it."

Abe Ribicoff came to visit us on Tuesday. Kennedy played golf with him, talked with him for two hours, and offered him the Attorney General's post in the Cabinet. Ribicoff turned it down for a sensible reason. He pointed out that the Attorney General would be mainly involved in civil rights and that it would hardly set well in the Protestant South to have an Irish Catholic President and a Jewish Attorney General enforcing desegregation in the schools. He decided to join the Cabinet instead as Secretary of Health, Education and Welfare. But if Ribicoff had wanted the Attorney Generalship, Kennedy would have given him that important position in preference to Bobby or anybody else. Abe was the President's first choice; Bobby was an afterthought.

The next day we traveled to Texas for an overnight visit to Lyndon Johnson's ranch. Dave was excused from the trip, to his immense delight, so he could remain at Palm Beach to entertain our wives. I said to the President, "You don't really need me on this one, do you?"

"I certainly do need you," he said. "It's time that you and Lyndon became better acquainted."

For additional company, we brought with us Torbert Macdonald, the Massachusetts Congressman who was one of Kennedy's closest friends, and another Boston Irishman, Bill Hartigan, who had toiled in the vineyard during the campaign and had signed on as a member of the future White House staff. We were followed by a large contingent of newsmen.

At the airstrip on the LBJ Ranch, we were met by the Vice-President-elect, who was wearing a cream-colored leather jacket, cowboy boots and a ten-gallon cowboy hat. He took Kennedy on a tour of the ranch in one of his white Lincoln Continental convertibles with the top down, despite a drizzle of rain. While he drove, Johnson frequently interrupted his conversational flow to give orders on the car's radio-telephone to various foremen and ranch hands and to secretaries and housekeepers back at the ranch house. He pointed out such sights as the Perdenales River, the graveyard where his grandfather was buried, and the three flags flying on three flagpoles in front of the house, the flag of the United States, the flag of Texas and the LBJ flag, white letters on a blue background, which is flown when he is in residence.

That evening we gathered for a pleasant dinner, with Bobby Baker and Bill Moyers joining the party. At nine o'clock, Johnson looked at his watch and announced that it was time for all of us to go to bed because we had to get up in the morning at five o'clock to go on a deer hunt. A look of shock and anguish came over Kennedy's face. He asked if Johnson was joking.

"Of course I'm not joking," Lyndon said. "You just can't leave this ranch without shooting a deer."

Kennedy sat up for another hour after the Johnsons retired, discussing with Macdonald and me how little he liked the idea of the deer hunt. Before five the next morning, Johnson came into my room and wakened me, telling me to get Kennedy up. I looked at my watch and said to him, "Mr. Johnson, I'm a very courageous fellow, but I wouldn't have the guts to go into that room and wake up the next President of the United States at this hour. You do it." We argued about who was going to wake Kennedy, who was in the room next to mine, and finally Johnson agreed to do it. He went outside in the hall, hesitated for a moment and then went downstairs and sent a servant up to knock on Kennedy's door.

I visited Kennedy while he was dressing. "This is ridiculous," he said. "It's still dark outside."

"Just like that time in Wisconsin," I said, "when we got you up to shake hands at the meat-packing plant. Only this time the animals are alive."

We were joined at breakfast by the sleepy Torby Macdonald, who had tried to avoid being called by leaving his bed at four o'clock and hiding in his bathroom, curling up in the tub with a pillow and blanket. Johnson had found him and roused him up. Macdonald and I were both hopefully assuming that we might be able to return to bed after Johnson and Kennedy went off to hunt. But Kennedy was having none of that. "If I go hunting," he said to us, "you two guys go hunting, too. There's plenty of room for them in the car, isn't there, Lyndon?" Johnson said he had already arranged for Macdonald and me to have a car and guns of our own, so there was no getting out of it.

We drove around the lonely back roads on the ranch for more than an hour before we spotted a few deer in the distance, rather small and scraggly little creatures. The President got out of Johnson's car reluctantly, having no zest for shooting any kind of wildlife. But at the same time his Kennedy competitive spirit was aroused, and he had no intention of losing face with those Texans watching him critically. He got his deer on his second or third shot.

Johnson came back to the car where Macdonald and I were sitting. "Now it's your turn," he said. Macdonald said his glasses weren't right and protested that we would be glad to go on back to the ranch house because we did not want to hold the party out in the field all morning. But Johnson insisted. Macdonald joined Kennedy and Johnson in their car and I went off in the opposite direction with a burly Texan as a guide. We finally saw a deer about a hundred yards away from us, and a rifle was thrust into my hands. I had not shot a gun since I was in the Air Force in World War II, and I was never much of a marksman then, but somehow I managed to raise the rifle and fire it. The poor deer toppled over and collapsed on my first shot. We drove off to the home of Judge West, a neighbor of Johnson's who was with us, to have coffee, and as we were getting out of the car Kennedy and Johnson drove up with Macdonald, who had missed several shots and injured his shoulder when his rifle kicked back on him.

"Where do you think you're going?" Kennedy said to me.

"We're going in here to have some coffee," I said.

"Oh, no, you're not," he said. "You don't get any coffee until after you've shot your deer."

"I've already shot my deer," I said nonchalantly.

"You couldn't have done it that fast," Kennedy said. "We only left you fifteen minutes ago. You're lying."

"Ask these fellows who were with me," I said. "Right after you left me, I went out there and shot my deer. With one shot. What was I supposed to do? Hang around here all morning?"

Kennedy was furious with me, and he became even more furious when the guide and the Secret Service man who were with me told him that I had indeed knocked off my deer easily on my first shot. He and Johnson had been thrashing around in the underbrush trying to help Torby Macdonald get a deer and now he had been looking forward to seeing me go through the same comedy routine. He was so mad because I had deprived of him of his fun, and because I had shot my deer quicker than he had shot his deer, that he did not speak to me for the next two hours.

Although Lyndon and Lady Bird never mentioned it, Kennedy found out from somebody at the ranch that that day, November 17, was the Johnsons' twenty-sixth wedding anniversary. He sent off Bill Hartigan secretly to a nearby town to buy them a gift, a small silver box with an inscription on it, and presented it to Lady Bird that night at dinner with a nice speech. She was completely surprised and touched by his thoughtfulness, and so was Lyndon.

That was not the end of the deer hunt episode. A few months later, after the inauguration, Johnson came to the White House one morning carrying the head of the deer that Kennedy had shot, mounted as a trophy, and proudly presented it to the President. Kennedy eyed the antlers and the sad face of the animal with distaste, and shuddered when Johnson suggested that it could be displayed on the wall of the President's oval-shaped office, beside his paintings of naval battles, Commodore John Barry's sword and flag, and the two silver replicas of the lanterns hung in Boston's Old North Church on the night of Paul Revere's ride. After the Vice-President left, the President said to Dave and me, "Let's get rid of this thing. Put it down in the cellar where nobody can see it." But the next day Johnson called and wanted to know if the deer's head had been hung up yet. I gave him an evasive answer. He announced that my deer's head had been mounted, too, and he was having it delivered to my house. A week later, the President said to me, "Lyndon keeps asking me about that damned deer. If we don't hang it up somewhere around here, he'll have a fit." We dragged the deer's head up from the basement and hung it above the door of the Fish Room, the reception room beside the West Lobby where President Roosevelt kept tanks of tropical fish and where President Kennedy had already placed the nine-foot sailfish that he had caught on his honeymoon at Acapulco. That satisfied Johnson.

After the visit to the LBJ Ranch and a week of work at Palm Beach, Kennedy flew to Washington to spend Thanksgiving with Jackie and Caroline. The expected date of her confinement was then two weeks away. They had a pleasant Thanksgiving dinner at their home in Georgetown, where I met him that evening to fly back to Palm Beach with him on the *Caroline*. The press contingent followed us on a chartered DC-6 airliner. Not long after our takeoff from Washington, when Kennedy was in a relaxed and happy mood, talking about the kind of men he wanted in the Cabinet, we received word on the radio that Jackie had been rushed to the hospital. He became tense and very nervous and restless, stricken with remorse because he was not with his wife. "I'm never there when she needs me," he said. We debated about what to do. Howard Baird, the pilot, suggested that when we landed in Florida the President could go back to Washington immediately on the DC-6 press plane, which was much faster than the *Caroline*. While we were at the airport in Palm Beach, Kennedy talked on the telephone with John Walsh, Jackie's obstetrician, who told him that she was in the operating room, about to undergo Caesarean surgery.

When we boarded the DC-6, the President hurried forward into the pilot's cabin, clamped a pair of radio earphones on his head, and stood there anxiously, waiting for further reports. At one-seventeen in the morning he heard that John F. Kennedy, Jr., had been born safely and that Jackie was having no serious problems. The President took off the earphones and smiled for the first time in two hours. Pierre Salinger made an announcement on the plane's loudspeaker system: "We have been advised that Mrs. Kennedy has given birth to a baby boy. Both mother and son are doing well." The press correspondents in the plane, who had been silently sweating out the delivery along with the worried father, applauded and cheered. The President waved cheerfully and took a bow. He sat down, much relieved, and after a few minutes he began to talk again about selecting a Cabinet.

For the next two weeks, Kennedy stayed close to Jackie and John and Caroline, spending most of his time in Georgetown. He visited Jackie and John in the hospital three times a day, in the morning, after lunch, and again in the evening. He took Caroline for walks and brought her to the Virginia estate of his mother-in-law, Mrs. Hugh Auchincloss, for pony rides. During the same period, between and after calls to the hospital, he was busy discussing appointments to his Cabinet and other high positions in his administration, making such appointments and announcing them at daily press conferences. Because his house at 3307 N Street was too small to accommodate all of the many reporters who were covering his activities, he held press conferences outside on the front steps. The weather in early December that year was unusually cold. One freezing morning when Kennedy appeared on the steps to greet the journalists, he noticed Bill Lawrence, who was then covering JFK for the *New York Times*, bundled up in a heavy overcoat and wearing a Russian Cossack-style fur hat pulled down over his ears. "I see we have a man from Tass with us today," Kennedy said.

Kennedy told us that he had expected that appointing outstanding men to top posts in the government — and turning down the prominent second-raters who yearned for those same positions — would be one of the most enjoyable satisfactions of the Presidency, as pleasing as one of Walter Mitty's dreams. He found out that picking the right man was not that easy, because he himself and his friends and advisers within the Kennedy circle often did not know the right man, somebody with the special kind of experience, judgment and sophistication that he wanted in that particular job. One night on the patio at Palm Beach, Kennedy said to us, "For the last four years, I spent so much time getting to know people who could help me get elected President that I didn't have any time to get to know people who could help me, after I was elected, to be a good President."

Kennedy made that remark while he was saying that he wanted to become better acquainted with Robert A. Lovett, the New York Republican banker who had served in Roosevelt's wartime administration and in Truman's Cabinet as Secretary of Defense. He admired Lovett and planned to offer him a choice of any of the top posts in the Cabinet — State, Defense or Treasury. Kennedy's frame of experience had given him a wide knowledge of people in politics, journalism, Ivy League college faculties and the labor movement. He did not know many industrialists, scientists, military officers, diplomats and foundation executives, and he was sensitively conscious of his lack of personal contact with the old-school-tie leaders of the New York banking and legal establishment, such as Lovett and John J. McCloy. The Lovett-McCloy community is oriented to the Republican party, Wall Street and the Links Club, and has been deplored by liberals as the rock-ribbed heart of the staid Eastern Establishment, but Kennedy was willing to knock on its door to seek talent as able and solid as it had sent to previous Democratic administrations.

"Henry Stimson was one of those New York Republicans, and Roosevelt was glad to get him," Kennedy said while we were mildly arguing the point. "I'm going to talk with Lovett and see what he can do for me. If I string along exclusively with Galbraith, and Arthur Schlesinger and Seymour Harris and those other Harvard liberals, they'll fill Washington with wild-eyed ADA people. And if I listen to you and Powers and Bailey and Maguire, we'll have so many Irish Catholics that we'll have to organize a White House Knights of Columbus Council. I can use a few smart Republicans. Anyway, we need a Secretary of the Treasury who can call a few of those people on Wall Street by their first names."

Lovett declined Kennedy's offer of a place in the Cabinet because he was in poor health. Lovett called Kennedy's attention to McGeorge Bundy, then the dean of Harvard College, who had helped Henry L. Stimson in writing his memoirs. Kennedy had already been thinking of Bundy, whose intelligence he had admired for many years. After a long talk with Bundy one day at the Carlyle Hotel in New York, Kennedy was so impressed by his views and his style that he told me later he was seriously considering Bundy as Secretary of State. Kennedy finally decided, however, that Bundy, only forty-one years old, was too young for the job.

While he was still undecided about his Secretary of State, Kennedy sidetracked Adlai Stevenson from running for that post by calling him to Georgetown and offering him the Ambassadorship to the United Nations. If there was one thing that Kennedy was certain about in selecting a Cabinet, it was his refusal to give in to the constant pressure from the loud claque of Stevenson's liberal admirers who wanted Adlai to head the State Department. Kennedy has been disenchanted by Adlai's antics at the Los Angeles convention, regarded him as too hesitant in making decisions, and too unpopular with both the Democratic and Republican Congressmen to be given a major role in foreign policy shaping. But Adlai was quite sure that the Secretary's job belonged to him. The only way to get that notion out of his head was to put him in the United Nations.

Adlai protested that he could not accept the UN Ambassador assignment until he knew who was going to be his commanding officer in the Secretary's chair. He had heard that Mac Bundy was being considered for the State post in the Cabinet. He informed Kennedy indignantly that he could not work under a forty-one-year-old Republican who had voted against him in two Presidential elections. Later on, after Rusk was appointed Secretary of State, Stevenson readily accepted the United Nations Ambassadorship, and his persistent admirers got off Kennedy's back.

Kennedy carefully considered giving Senator William Fulbright the appointment as Secretary of State because he liked Fulbright's views on foreign affairs and respected his work as chairman of the Senate Foreign Relations Committee. But Fulbright had to be ruled out because he had taken a segregationist stand in his Arkansas constituency on the civil rights issue. Chester Bowles and Mennen Williams, two other contenders, did not measure up to the top job in Kennedy's opinion; Bowles was appointed as Under Secretary of State and Williams was made Assistant Secretary of State for Africa. That narrowed the field down to Rusk, Lovett's candidate, and David Bruce, the experienced career diplomat and an Under Secretary in Truman's administration, who was high in Kennedy's book. But Rusk was younger than Bruce, had more background experience in Asian affairs and, as president of the prestigious Rockefeller Foundation, had a wider knowledge of health, education and technical problems in underdeveloped nations. He was also a new face in Washington, a Democrat, a Rhodes Scholar, which always won extra points with Kennedy, and, most of all, he was highly recommended by Lovett.

Kennedy had little or no knowledge of Bob McNamara, then the newly appointed president of the Ford Motor Company. Lovett had been highly impressed by McNamara's work as a cost and budget expert in the Air Force during the war. When Kennedy first heard about McNamara from Lovett, he frowned at the mention of McNamara's Irish name and wanted to know if he was a Catholic. If McNamara had been both Irish and Catholic, he would have been stricken from Kennedy's list then and there, but he turned out to be a Protestant and a Republican who had voted for Kennedy, as well as an admirer of *Profiles in Courage*. At their first meeting, after Kennedy asked McNamara several probing and rather personal questions, McNamara startled Kennedy by asking him if he had written *Profiles in Courage* without the help of a ghost.

Before he saw McNamara, Kennedy sent Sarge Shriver to his office at the Ford Company in Dearborn, Michigan, to sound him out about accepting the Treasury secretariat. McNamara said he had no desire to leave his position at Ford and to sell his company stock to take a job in Washington setting interest rates. He was not much interested in Defense, either, but he agreed as a matter of courtesy to talk with the President-elect in Washington the next day. Meanwhile Kennedy asked me to check on McNamara with Jack Conway of the United Automobile Workers. Apart from McNamara's executive ability, which was well proven, Kennedy wanted an opinion from the UAW people on whether he had the broad liberal outlook that was urgently needed at the Pentagon. Conway gave me an unqualified yes to that question. He had served with McNamara on the Citizens for Michigan, a group studying the state's tax legislation problems, and the union man and the industrial executive had shared almost exactly the same point of view on every topic under discussion. Although McNamara was not a Rhodes Scholar, Kennedy raised an approving eyebrow when he heard that instead of living among the other wealthy automobile manufacturers at Grosse Pointe or Bloomfield Hills, McNamara made his home in the distant university community of Ann Arbor, where he belonged to a study group that read books on existentialism, Communist China and fine arts.

McNamara met Kennedy at the house on N Street one evening in December, slipping in through the back door to escape the reporters and photographers who were camped on the front steps. As reluctant as he was to leave Ford, McNamara was completely taken in by Kennedy's charming persuasion. "That's a very impressive brother-in-law you have," he said later to Sarge Shriver. After thinking it over for a few days, he returned to the Georgetown house, this time through the front door, to appear with the President at the sidewalk press conference where his appointment would be announced. I remember that McNamara was fascinated when he saw Kennedy himself writing in longhand on a yellow legal pad the statement that he would read to the reporters outside on the front steps.

"When the president at Ford makes a statement to the press," McNamara observed, "it has to be prepared and edited by the public relations department and approved by the vice-president in charge of public relations. It's nicer when you can just pick up a ball-point pen and write it yourself."

As one of the conditions under which he agreed to become Secretary of Defense, McNamara had the final say on selecting his sub-Cabinet assistants. He had no regard for the political niceties. Kennedy was anxious, for example, to reward Franklin D. Roosevelt, Jr., for his yeoman contribution in the West Virginia primary by appointing him Secretary of the Navy. McNamara decided that Frank was not right for the job, and that was that. He preferred John Connally, an appointment, incidentally, that Lyndon Johnson had nothing to do with, contrary to everybody's assumption at the time. Speaker Rayburn had recommended John Connally in my presence, and President Kennedy readily agreed, as did McNamara. But McNamara flatly refused to accept Joseph D. Keenan, George Meany's candidate and a devoted Kennedy campaigner, as his Assistant Secretary for Manpower. This is hardly the conventional reaction to a nomination supported by both the president of the AFL-CIO and the President-elect of the United States. McNamara wanted to give the position instead to Jack Conway, Walter Reuther's assistant at the UAW, which would have driven the already overwrought Meany into a stroke of apoplexy. With some difficulty, McNamara was cajoled into accepting a faculty member from the University of Wisconsin, and a feud between Meany and Reuther was averted. Such are the problems of forming a new administration.

McNamara's acceptance of the Defense post left the Treasury secretary's seat open for Douglas Dillon, whom Kennedy had been considering for that position all along. Dillon was frowned upon by the Harvard economists because he was a Republican and had served as Eisenhower's Under Secretary of State, and was a son of a prominent Wall Street banking family. But Kennedy wanted a Secretary of the Treasury who would give Wall Street some assurance that the New Frontier's fiscal policy would stay reasonably close to the middle of the road. Kennedy also valued the experience in foreign economic problems that Dillon had gained in the State Department. A prime mover behind Dillon's appointment was Philip Graham, the publisher of the *Washington Post* and *Newsweek*, who was close to Kennedy and often exchanged confidences and inside political gossip with him. Before Kennedy announced his appointment of Dean Rusk as Secretary of State, the story appeared in headlines on the front page of the *Washington Post*. Kennedy summoned Pierre Salinger and ordered him to find out immediately which of us was responsible for the leak. Two hours later Salinger called Kennedy and said that he had discovered the identity of the leaker.

"Who was it?" Kennedy asked.

"Didn't you tell Phil Graham last night that you were appointing Rusk?"

"Yes, I did," Kennedy said.

"Did you tell him not to use the story?" Salinger asked.

There was a silence. "No," Kennedy said, "I guess I didn't."

Picking the Cabinet and other·high officials in the executive branch of the government sometimes had its lighter moments. When it came to Agriculture, a field that perplexed him, Kennedy was in a quandary. One of the prospects who had been highly recommended for Secretary of Agriculture was a farm organization leader from Missouri. Kennedy invited him to Georgetown for a talk that turned out to be so dull and aimless that Kennedy, as he told us later, almost fell asleep in the middle of the conversation. He excused himself, went out of the room, and called Bobby. "Will you go in and talk to him?" he said to Bobby. "I must be wrong, but he doesn't seem up to the job." Bobby came out of the room a half hour later and said, "I know more about agriculture than he does." The next day Kennedy called Orville Freeman, who had been a liberal governor in the farming state of Minnesota, and Freeman quickly accepted. When somebody asked Freeman later how he happened to be selected, he said, "I think it had something to do with the fact that Harvard does not have a school of agriculture."

The Cabinet member who put up the strongest fight against being pulled into the boat was Bobby. When we left Hyannis Port after the election, Bobby went off to Acapulco for a well-earned vacation with Ethel, Joan and Teddy. We did not see him again until the Sunday after the birth of young John, when he visited Jackie at the hospital and came to the President's house for dinner. We brought him up to date on the people who were being considered for the Cabinet, the White House staff and various other appointments in the departments and agencies. His brother asked him what he wanted to do for the next four years. The President explained that he had been trying to persuade Robert Lovett to accept the Secretary of Defense position for one year with Bobby as his Under Secretary, with the understanding that when Lovett retired Bobby might succeed him. But Lovett felt unable physically to take a Cabinet position for even a short period. The President also pointed out that Abe Ribicoff's refusal to serve as Attorney General had left that job open, and he urged Bobby to take it.

Bobby listened quietly and then said that he felt unable to accept any high position in the government because the appointment would cause too much public controversy and embarrassment. Four days earlier, before Bobby had even spoken to his brother about his future, the *New York Times* had already published an editorial warning the Kennedys against the repercussions that would come from placing him in a major appointment. We all agreed that it would be impossible to put him on the White House staff. I talked to him about taking the vacated Kennedy seat in the Senate, which would be filled for the duration of its term by an appointment by the governor of Massachusetts, but Bobby flatly rejected that idea. He said he would never serve in Congress unless he was elected.

As reluctant as he was to expose the President to criticism, Bobby was just as reluctant to make a complete withdrawal from the Washington scene. He could not picture himself missing the excitement of the new administration. I suggested the possibility of a sub-Cabinet position that involved foreign affairs, such as the liaison assistantship between the Defense and State Departments that was later\filled by Paul Nitze. But he could not make up his mind. On one of the President's busiest days in that early December period, the same day that he asked Adlai Stevenson to be the Ambassador to the United Nations instead of Secretary of State, the same day that he had his first unpublicized meeting with Rusk and a few hours before he carried John to the Georgetown University chapel to be baptized, he said to me,

"What is Bobby going to do?" The Bobby problem began to worry all of us for a selfish reason. Since 1952, when he came to Boston to straighten out Jack's disorganized Senatorial campaign, Bobby had been our only reliable intermediary in our dealings with his brother. When we wanted to let Jack know about a problem too sensitive for one of us to mention to him, Bobby could tell him about it and bring back an answer. When Jack was in one of his inaccessible moods, Bobby could always reach him and make him listen to reason. Now Jack was Mr. President, and we were about to begin working with him in the White House. Without Bobby?

On Friday, December 9, the President-to-be was in a gay mood when we flew to Palm Beach with Jackie, Caroline and the baby to leave his family at his father's house until after Christmas. He sat in the back of the plane, talking at a merry clip, and blowing cigar smoke around the baby's bassinet until Jackie demanded that he take himself and the cigar up forward. That weekend he talked seriously with Dave about how much he needed Bobby in the Cabinet. "What if he does happen to be my brother?" he said. "I want the best men I can get, and they don't come any better than Bobby." It was said later that his father forced him to appoint Bobby as the Attorney General, but I never heard that from any of the Kennedys. The Ambassador had plenty to say in favor of Bobby's appointment, but nobody forced it upon the President. He weighed the liabilities, found them lighter than Bobby's merits and his own need for Bobby, and after he made his decision it was only a question of how much time it would take him to make Bobby give in to it.

On the Wednesday morning after that weekend at Palm Beach, Bobby gave in while having breakfast with his brother at the Georgetown house. The following Friday, December 16, the appointment of Bobby as Attorney General, along with that of Douglas Dillon as Secretary of the Treasury, was announced on the front steps at N Street. Bobby brought Arthur Goldberg with him to the house for moral support. Goldberg had been appointed Secretary of Labor the day before. When the President saw him with Bobby, he said, "Back so soon, Arthur? Have you already decided to resign?" The Kennedy wisecracks flew thick and fast that morning and were repeated all over the country afterwards. ("I'll stick my head out that front door, and look up and down the street, and if nobody's around, I'll whisper the announcement.") When they were ready to face the reporters, the President said, "Bobby, before we go out there to tell the press that you are to be the next Attorney General of the United States, would you mind combing your hair?"

After Bobby's appointment, we learned from the Secret Service that the President-elect might have been assassinated in Palm Beach on the previous Sunday morning if he had not decided to bring Jackie and his children to Florida with him that weekend. A demented Kennedy hater from New Hampshire named Richard P. Pavlick had been waiting outside the Ambassador's home in his automobile with seven sticks of dynamite, planning to ram his car into Kennedy's car when Kennedy got into it to drive to mass at Saint Edward's Church, and to set off an explosion.

Fortunately, when Kennedy was leaving to go to the church, Jackie and Caroline came to the door with him and waited outside to watch him drive away. Pavlick felt that he could not attempt the killing, and his own suicide, before the eyes of Kennedy's wife and child, and decided to postpone it until the following Sunday. A few days later the Secret Service received a tip from Pavlick's hometown in New Hampshire that he was in Palm Beach, searched for him, and picked him up. When we told Kennedy about the plot, he was completely fascinated by it, wanted to know all about Pavlick and the details of his confession, and even asked to see a copy of the letter he was carrying, which charged that "the Kennedys bought the Presidency and the Whitehouse." But Kennedy was not a bit upset or worried by the ugly incident. It merely intrigued him.

Kennedy spent the Christmas holidays with his family at Palm Beach, playing a lot of golf, working on his inaugural address, and planning the details of the inauguration. He wanted the men to wear top hats instead of black homburgs, the approved headwear at Eisenhower's inaugurations. He asked Robert Frost to write and recite a poem, and invited Marian Anderson to sing "The Star-Spangled Banner." I sent two Secret Service men to Boston to find Grandfather Fitzgerald's family Bible for the oath-taking. Tom Fitzgerald, Rose Kennedy's brother, located the Bible in his attic and wrapped it in a shopping bag before handing it over to the agents.

On January 9, Kennedy made a trip to Boston himself to speak to the Massachusetts legislature, attend a meeting of the Board of Overseers at Harvard, and to meet at Arthur Schlesinger's house in

Cambridge with Mac Bundy and Jerome Wiesner, the M.I.T. scientist, who were joining the White House staff as his special assistants. After deciding against appointing Bundy as Secretary of State, Kennedy had wanted him to be the Under Secretary, but Rusk, for reasons of his own, preferred to have Chester Bowles in that position. Bundy agreed to come to the White House as the President's foreign affairs and national security assistant, where he did an excellent job. Kennedy also signed up Arthur Schlesinger that day for duty in the White House as a special assistant without a special portfolio, to be a liaison man in charge of keeping Adlai Stevenson happy, to receive complaints from the liberals, and to act as a sort of household devil's advocate who would complain about anything in the administration that bothered him. Kennedy said to Arthur, "We'll keep your appointment quiet until after the Senate confirms Chester Bowles. I don't want the Senate to think I'm bringing the whole ADA down to Washington."

I asked Kennedy later if he was taking Schlesinger into the White House to make notes for the official history of the Kennedy administration. "I'll write my own official history of the Kennedy administration," he said. "But Arthur will probably write one of his own, and it will be better for us if he's in the White House, seeing what goes on, instead of reading about us in the *New York Times* and *Time* magazine up in his office at the Widener Library at Harvard."

During that visit to Boston, Kennedy enjoyed the nostalgic experience of sleeping overnight for the last time in the small and rather drab little third-floor apartment at 122 Bowdoin Street on Beacon Hill that had been his living quarters during his Congressional and Senatorial campaigns. Joe Murphy, the janitor of the building, cooked his breakfast of boiled eggs and broiled bacon downstairs in his own apartment and brought it up to the President on a tray, as he had done every morning in earlier years. It was Kennedy's last visit with Joe, who died not long afterward. The apartment on Bowdoin Street is still rented by the Kennedy family. Teddy used it as an office in his Senatorial campaigns. In recent years it has been the intown office of the John F. Kennedy Library staff.

In Palm Beach Kennedy took care of one last matter of unfinished local business; he arranged with his old adversary, Massachusetts Governor Foster Furcolo, to have an old friend, Ben Smith, a Harvard roommate and the mayor of Gloucester, Massachusetts, appointed to his seat in the United States Senate to serve the remaining two years of his uncompleted term.

Thursday, January 19, 1960, the day before the inauguration, was one of Kennedy's most hectic but happiest days. Jackie threw him out of the house on N Street because she was going to be moving their things to the White House and having a series of fittings for the gowns that she would be wearing that night and the next night to the various inaugural events and the gala balls. He moved into Bill Walton's nearby home with his secretary, Evelyn Lincoln, and used it for various appointments and meetings. In the morning he went to the White House with Rusk, McNamara and Dillon for a final briefing on current government problems with President Eisenhower and the outgoing State, Defense and Treasury secretaries, Christian Herter, Thomas S Gates and Robert Anderson.

First Eisenhower took Kennedy into the oval Presidential office, showed him around, talked to him about his daily duties, and taught him how to use the panic button that would bring a helicopter to the back lawn of the White House in a hurry. Eisenhower pushed the button and Kennedy watched the fluttering helicopter coming down outside the windows within a few minutes.

Then they joined their secretaries in the Cabinet Room to talk about various important items of unfinished business — Cuba, Berlin, Africa, the balance of payments, and Laos. Kennedy had been told for the first time back in November by Allen Dulles, the day after we came back from the LBJ Ranch, about the rebel force that was being trained by the CIA in Guatemala to invade Cuba. Eisenhower urged him to keep on supporting this plan to overthrow Castro. But Eisenhower talked mostly about Laos, which he then regarded as the most dangerous trouble spot in Southeast Asia. He mentioned South Vietnam only as one of the nations that would fall into the hands of the Communists if the United States failed to maintain the anti-Communist regime in Laos. Kennedy was astonished to hear Eisenhower telling him that American combat troops might have to fight alone in Laos if we could not persuade our allies to help us defend that government. Kennedy told us later, "There he sat, telling me to get ready to put ground forces into Asia, the thing he himself had been carefully avoiding for the last eight years. And he was very calm about it. I was finding out that things were really just as bad as I had said they were during the campaign."

When I think of Kennedy and Laos, I remember the day much later at the White House when General Phoumi Nosavan, the so-called right-wing military strong man of that country, came to visit the President. I am not tall, but Phoumi's head seemed to be about as high from the floor as my waistline. The President stared down at the tiny general, unable to believe that any soldier could be so small. After Phoumi left the office, the President frowned thoughtfully for a moment, looked at me and said, "Are you thinking the same thing I'm thinking?"

I said, "I don't know, Mr. President. I was thinking if that's our strong man in Laos, we're in trouble over there."

The President asked Major General Chester V. Clifton, his military aide who was with us, if Phoumi was the average-sized Laotian soldier. Clifton said that most Southeast Asians were not much bigger. The President mentioned our intelligence reports from Laos, which constantly complained of the unwillingness of the anti-Communists to fight in combat operations. "I was thinking of the rifles we're sending over there," Kennedy said. "If I were that small, I couldn't fight after carrying one of our M-14s for ten miles. I'd be too tired to fire it. Our rifles are bigger than he is. He couldn't reach the trigger unless he held most of the butt under his armpit."

He went into a dissertation on how silly it was for the Pentagon to expect Asians, so different from us physically, to use our kind of weapons. He asked Clifton to draft a recommendation to the Joint Chiefs of Staff asking for smaller and lighter rifles to be sent to Southeast Asia.

On that eve of Inauguration Day there was one of the heaviest snowstorms we had ever seen in Washington, creating the worst traffic tie-ups in the history of the city. On every street there were cars stalled in the drifts. At eight o'clock that night, when the President-elect left his house with Jackie and Bill Walton to go to the preinaugural concert at Constitution Hall and then to the gala entertainment arranged by Frank Sinatra and Peter Lawford at the Armory, the whole capitol seemed to be at a standstill. As if by some miraculous omen, Kennedy's car and the Secret Service car traveling with it somehow managed to be two of the few vehicles in Washington that were able to move. They went to a reception for

Eleanor Roosevelt at Herbert Lehman's and to a party at Phil Graham's house, and then to Constitution Hall, where most of the seats were empty because of the storm. Bill Walton remembers Kennedy reading Thomas Jefferson's inaugural address, which was in the concert program brochure, and saying, "It's better than mine." When their car was crawling through the snow to the show at the Armory, people walking beside them in the snowdrifts recognized them, knocked on the windows of the car, and waved to them. Kennedy said to the driver, "Turn on the light inside here so they can see Jackie."

Frank Sinatra's entertainment program at the Armory had been delayed and disorganized by the storm and ran much later than it had been planned. Jackie left the Armory and went home after midnight to rest for the next long day of ceremonies, but her husband had to see all of the show, and stayed on with his father, smoking a long cigar and applauding such performers as Harry Belafonte, Ethel Merman, Ella Fitzgerald, Sir Laurence Olivier, Helen Traubel, Bette Davis and Leonard Bernstein. Then he went to the party that the Ambassador gave downtown at Paul Young's restaurant, where Dave and Jo Powers shared a table with Helen and me. He had a glass of champagne with us, and said, "You two are living like Presidents tonight. I suppose you'll be laughing it up here for another three hours after I go home and get into bed with my inaugural address."

He hated to leave the party. I watched him go out of the room, stopping and looking back at us rather wistfully, as if he was reminding himself that this was the end of his last carefree night on the town, the last time that he would be able to enjoy himself in a public restaurant for years to come.

The next morning he was up early and went to mass alone at a church in Georgetown, delighting his mother, who had walked through the snow to go to the same mass and was sitting by herself in another part of the church when she saw him coming in. "I had not urged him to go," she said later. "The fact that he did go on his own, and did think it was important to start his administration with mass in the morning gave me a wonderfully happy feeling." After mass, he walked across N Street to the home of Charles Montgomery, opposite his own house, where he presented to Mr. Montgomery and his daughter, Helen Montgomery, a bronze commemorative plaque, a gift from the newsmen who had been given shelter and coffee by the Montgomerys, along with the use of their telephone, during the previous two months of covering press conferences on Kennedy's front steps.

At ten-forty that morning Sam Rayburn and Senator John Sparkman, chairman of the Congressional Inauguration Committee, arrived at N Street in the Presidential bubble-top Lincoln limousine to escort the Kennedys to the Capitol. They stopped at the White House to pick up the outgoing President, and stayed there for a pleasant half hour, having coffee with the Eisenhowers. This was a noticeable change from the procedure at Eisenhower's own first inauguration in 1953. On that morning, when Eisenhower stopped at the White House to pick up President Truman so that they would ride together in the parade to the Capitol, Truman had invited him to come inside but Eisenhower refused to get out of the automobile. He was still mad about some of the things Truman had said about him during the campaign.

The relationship between Eisenhower and Kennedy during the transition period was always friendly. Kennedy found Eisenhower to be a warm and interesting personality, and thought highly of his farewell address, which warned against the growing power of the military–defense-industry complex. When Kennedy was in the White House, he frowned upon comical or critical remarks about Eisenhower from any of us on his staff, pointing out sharply on more than a few occasions that even in private conversations a past President was entitled to be treated with the respect due to his office. For a few months after Kennedy moved into the White House, there were stories told in Washington about how he enjoyed showing visitors the spike marks on the floor around his desk left by Eisenhower's golf shoes. The spike marks were there, but I doubt that Kennedy ever pointed them out to anybody except, maybe, Jackie or Bobby. There were many visitors, however, who made a big joke about pointing them out to President Kennedy, much to the President's distaste. The only time I ever heard him mention the spike marks was after the departure of one such visitor. The President observed to me that most of the people who were now joking about Eisenhower's spike marks were people who would have been only too willing to get down on their knees to shine Eisenhower's golf shoes a few months earlier.

When Eisenhower and Kennedy were sitting together on the reviewing stand during the inauguration, waiting for the ceremonies to begin, they became engaged in an earnest and lively conversation. Along with millions of people who were watching the scene on television, I wondered what pressing problem of the government they were discussing. I asked Kennedy about it later. He laughed, and said that they were talking about a book that both of them had recently read, Cornelius Ryan's *The Longest Day*, an account of the invasion of Normandy in World War II.

"He had some interesting things to say about our meteorologists," Kennedy said. "It seems they did a better job of predicting the weather than the German meteorologists."

Kennedy was well pleased with his inaugural address, as he should have been, and enjoyed the long parade, except for one moment when the cadets of the Coast Guard Academy marched past the reviewing stand and he noticed that there was not one black face in their ranks. One of his first official acts as President was to issue an order to correct that situation. Despite the bitter cold, he stayed on the reviewing stand for the entire three and a half hours of the parade.

That night the President and Mrs. Kennedy appeared with the Vice-President and Mrs. Johnson at each of the five inauguration balls in Washington. At the second ball they attended, at the Statler Hotel, the President disappeared for a half hour, leaving Jackie sitting with Lady Bird in the Presidential box, and dashed upstairs alone to take a quick look at the private party Frank Sinatra was throwing for the stars of stage, screen and television who had entertained him the previous night. He was too curious, as always, to resist sneaking off to such a gathering of celebrities. When he finally returned to Jackie and the Johnsons, looking rather sheepish and carrying a *Washington Post* under his arm, as if he had just gone outside to pick up the newspaper, his knowing wife gave him a rather chilly look.

Later that night, when the President was leaving the ball at the Armory, he noticed in the crowd standing outside in the snow an old familiar face from his first political campaign back in 1946 — Joe Leahy from Somerville, who traveled with him that year to rallies in such places as the Ward Room on Bunker Hill Street, Newcombe Hall in Somerville and the Michelangelo School in the

North End of Boston. One of Joe's functions was to sing Kennedy campaign songs, or such Irish tunes as "Danny Boy" and "Galway Bay." Seeing Leahy in the crowd outside the Armory, the new President of the United States rolled down the window of his limousine and beckoned to him.

"Joe," the President said, "How about giving us a few bars of 'Danny Boy'?"

Joe obliged in his clear and loud Irish tenor voice. The President thanked him, and drove away smiling to spend his first night in the White House, sleeping soundly in the Lincoln bedroom.

TEN

The White House

THE KENNEDY INAUGURATION took place on a Friday. Any other new President of the United States might have waited until Monday before starting his work, but Kennedy was so eager to get into his official duties that he ordered all of us on the White House staff to be at our desks on Saturday morning at nine o'clock. He was there himself at ten minutes before nine, testing the buzzers on his desk and frowning at the bare walls of the oval Presidential office, which had been stripped of President Eisenhower's belongings and freshly painted in a rather nauseous shade of green. Kennedy immediately asked to have the office repainted in a cheerful off-white. He hurried back to the executive mansion's living quarters and returned with pictures of his wife, Caroline and John, and a watercolor painting by Jackie.

In the next week such personal mementoes as his pieces of scrimshaw — bits of whale teeth etched with sailing ship designs — and his Navy identity card encased in a glass ashtray and the famous coconut shell from Nauro Island in the Solomons began to appear on his desk. The coconut shell was carved with the SOS message that he sent from Nauro by a native messenger after the survivors from the wrecked PT-109 were stranded on that island in 1943. (NATIVE KNOWS POSIT HE CAN PILOT 11 ALIVE NEED SMALL BOAT KENNEDY.) The President later decorated his office with naval paintings, ship models, flags, and a plaque given to him by Admiral Hyman

Rickover inscribed with a Breton fishermen's prayer, "O, God, Thy sea is so great, and my boat is so small." While she was rummaging in the White House basement, Jackie found a magnificent desk, made from the timbers of the British warship H.M.S. *Resolute*, that Queen Victoria had presented to President Rutherford B. Hayes in 1878. President Franklin D. Roosevelt had used it for his Fireside Chat radio broadcasts. She had it sanded and refinished and moved it into her husband's office early in February, much to his delight.

The desk had a hinged panel in its side that opened like a door. When John became old enough to walk and talk, the President would often bring him to the office in the morning after Caroline had gone to school. John would hide under the desk while the President was talking to me and other staff members about the day's appointments. We would hear a scratching noise behind the panel of the desk, and the President would exclaim, "Is there a rabbit in there?" The panel would swing open and John would pop out of the desk, growling and then rolling on the carpet screaming with laughter.

Kennedy's first visitor in the White House that Saturday morning was Harry Truman, paying his first call to the executive mansion since he had left it eight years before. Truman assured the news photographers in the West Wing's lobby that Kennedy would be a President who would allow them the one more picture that they were always asking for. "I heard the other fellow wouldn't stand for it," he said. Truman was followed by Dick Daley, with his wife and six children, who posed for a picture with the President, the only favor asked for by the mayor of Chicago in return for delivering Illinois.

Later in the morning, the members of the White House staff were sworn in as a group. Mac Bundy, the special assistant in national security and foreign affairs, was the only staff member who had not worked for Kennedy during the election campaign; most of the rest of us had been with him for many years. Ted Reardon, who took over as the assistant in charge of Cabinet affairs and Cabinet meetings, had been Kennedy's administrative assistant in Washington since 1947. Ted Sorensen became the special counsel of the staff and Larry O'Brien along with Dick Donahue assumed the liaison work between the White House and Congress. Donahue was a veteran of the battles against Henry Cabot Lodge and Onions Burke.

Ralph Dungan, a key member of the White House staff who handled many diverse and important assignments — problems with the labor unions, Latin American affairs, speech writing, talent scouting and political troubleshooting — had been on Kennedy's staff as a legislative assistant since 1956. Pierre Salinger, our press secretary, was a comparative newcomer who did not join us until 1959, although he had worked before then with Bobby and me on the McClellan committee.

Dave Powers, the President's all-around right-hand man, also served as my assistant during our White House years, in charge of receiving visiting notables and trying to keep the President's crowded appointment schedule moving smoothly. Dave would greet a visitor in the West Lobby and hold him in the Cabinet Room or the Fish Room until he could be escorted through my outer reception office into the President's office. One day in the Cabinet Room Powers found himself making small talk with the Deputy Premier of the Soviet Union, Anastas Mikoyan, while Mikoyan was waiting to be received by the President. "Tell me," Powers said to the Russian, "Are you the real Mikoyan?" When the Shah of Iran came to the White House, Dave tried to put him at ease by saying to him cheerfully, "You're my kind of Shah."

Dave also served as President Kennedy's resident statistician and walking memory bank. He has a total recall of election votes in various states and cities and can recite them in a flash, not in round figures, but in precise numbers down to the last digit. One day when we were in Minneapolis, Kennedy decided to entertain the two Minnesota Senators who were with us, Hubert Humphrey and Eugene McCarthy, by putting on a display of Dave's memory power. "Dave, what was my vote against Lodge in Massachusetts in 1952?" the President asked.

"One million, two hundred and eleven thousand and nine hundred and eighty-four," Powers said.

"And what was Lodge's vote?" the President asked.

"One million, one hundred and forty-one thousand and two hundred and forty-seven."

Dave had his back turned toward the President and the two Senators. He did not know that the President was writing down the two total vote figures and was subtracting Lodge's vote total from his own vote.

"And now, Dave," the President said, "what was my plurality?"

"Gosh, Mr. President, you ought to know that," Powers said. "It was seventy thousand seven hundred and thirty-seven."

Kennedy looked at the subtraction on the card in his hand, saw that it checked exactly with the plurality figure that Dave had just rattled off from memory, and became flustered with amazement.

"Dave, you're right!" the President said. "All these years I didn't think you really knew those plurality figures. I thought you were just making them up and throwing them at me."

I acted as the administrator of the White House staff, among my other varied duties, so I had problems during the first few months of the new administration trying to find space in the overcrowded West Wing for the staff members who felt that the government might collapse if their office was not located within twelve feet of the President's office. Kennedy had made it clear that he wanted no assistant to have the executive powers of Sherman Adams, who had screened all of the matters of government business brought to President Eisenhower and ruled on many of them himself without passing them on to the President. With the exception of John Foster Dulles, who always had access to Eisenhower, many of the government officials who wanted to talk to Eisenhower usually ended up talking to Adams. Kennedy wanted as much advice and assistance as he could get from his staff and Cabinet members, but he wanted to make all of his own decisions and he wanted nobody to speak for him.

When we were assigning office space to the staff, I suggested to the President that we could establish the idea that there was no Sherman Adams in his White House by leaving the large office formerly occupied by Adams conspicuously empty. He agreed to this suggestion. Later we divided the Adams office into two smaller offices. One staff member whom I placed in a second floor office complained to the President until I had to move him and his assistant downstairs to the same floor as the President's office. But actually there was very little jockeying for position and power among the staff members. Each of us had our own clearly defined areas of work and authority, and the President saw to it that we stayed within those boundaries.

My desk in the reception office next to the President's office had to be closer to him than anybody else's desk, because of my duties as his appointments regulator. There were three doors leading into the President's office, one from my office, one from the office of his personal secretary, Evelyn Lincoln, and one from the main corridor outside. There were also doors behind his desk leading outdoors to the Rose Garden, but it was understood that nobody except the Vice-President and Bobby could enter the office through those garden doors, unseen from inside the White House, and neither of them abused that special privilege. The main door of the office, connected with the corridor, was always closed when the President was at his desk or sitting in the rocking chair before the fireplace, talking with a visitor. When it was open, staff members knew that the President's office was vacant. The only time that visitors used the main door was when they came to the office in a large group, the White House press corps attending a special news conference around the President's desk, or a reception for a delegation of Congressmen, student leaders, or foreign dignitaries or Boy Scouts or clubwomen. All other visitors, whether or not they had an appointment, or if they were staff members or government officials summoned on the spur of the moment, or even if they were members of the Kennedy family dropping in to say hello, were supposed to enter through my office, with my knowledge and consent. We had to limit the access to the President's office to this one door in order to protect him from unwelcome intruders, time-wasting well-wishers and small-talkers and other appointment-schedule wreckers.

Very soon, in the first month of the administration, we found that the open door between the President and Evelyn Lincoln's secretarial office was a threat to his privacy. Mrs. Lincoln was too kind-hearted and too cordial to bar a friend from an unnecessary visit to the President, and she was incapable of screening him from an unimportant phone call. One day during the crisis of the civil rights battle over James Meredith's admission to the University of Mississippi, when President Kennedy was trying desperately to reach Governor Ross Barnett on the telephone in an effort to stop bloodshed on the campus, Mrs. Lincoln was sitting beside his desk while he paced the floor, waiting for his call to be returned. The telephone rang. Mrs. Lincoln picked it up, chatted and giggled for a few moments with the person at the other end of the line while the President stared at her. She handed the phone to him, smiling, and said, "It's Red Fay. He just wants to say hello." I thought that the

President was going to grab the telephone out of her hand and throw it through the window.

Staff members, military aides, old college friends and a few relatives who wanted a word or two with the President, and knew that my door would be barred against them, began to hang around in Mrs. Lincoln's office, watching the President from her doorway. When he was alone, or seemed to be unoccupied, they would stick their heads into his office and ask if he had a moment to spare. The President was too polite to turn them away. It never occurred to Mrs. Lincoln that she could ask them to get lost. "If I called her in here and told her that I had just cut off Jackie's head," the President said, "and then said to her, 'Mrs. Lincoln, would you bring me a nice large box so I can put Jackie's head in it?' she would say to me, 'Oh, that's lovely, Mr. President, I'll get the box right away.'"

The traffic from Mrs. Lincoln's office became so heavy that the President issued an order that its door had to be kept shut at all times when he was in his office. Two days later, after he arrived for work in the morning, he rang for me and pointed at Mrs. Lincoln's door. It had a newly bored peephole in it. "We can't win," he said.

I did my best to shield President Kennedy from unnecessary or time-wasting visitors, but never without his knowledge that I was doing so. My problem was not keeping people away from him, but trying to find time on the schedule for all of the people that he always wanted to see. He was the most accessible President of our time. Too much of the valuable time of any President of the United States is taken up by ceremonial duties required by his function as head of the state rather than by his work as chief executive officer of the government — seeing callers who would be received in England by the Queen instead of by the busy Prime Minister. But Kennedy enjoyed such duties. He was particularly pleased to meet young people, high school or college students, and asked them all kinds of questions. After reading the newspapers for a half hour in the morning, he would want to see enough people in and out of the government to fill his appointment schedule for the next two days. "Did you see that story in the *Times* about Formosa?" he would say. "Get Averell Harriman over here this afternoon — I want to ask him a few things about it." Much of our work in the White House, not only appointments but staff assignments in general, and a great deal of work in the entire executive branch of the government for that matter, came out of Kennedy's intensive scanning of the morning newspapers.

I remember one morning when he called me at home so early, around seven o'clock, that I was not yet awake. "Did you see this story in the *Detroit Times*, about the closing of that government installation out there in Michigan?" he said. I did not bother explaining that I seldom saw the *Detroit Times* at any time, and certainly not at that hour of the morning. The details of the story escape me now, but it had to do with a local protest against the shutdown of a Government Services Administration procurement operation in a small Michigan town that threatened to cause some unemployment. It sounded like a minor matter to me, but the President said, "Call Bernie Boutin right now and tell him that I want a written report about the whole thing on my desk no later than nine o'clock this morning."

The report was on the President's desk when he arrived at his office. He went over it carefully, called Boutin, the head of GSA, and asked him several questions. That afternoon when Kennedy appeared on a nationally televised press conference, a reporter from Detroit asked him if he could say anything about the closing of the GSA installation. I was astonished by the reporter's question, and the reporter no doubt expected the President to be puzzled by it because nothing about the shutdown had been published outside of Michigan. Kennedy quickly ticked off four logical reasons why the installation was being closed, discussed in detail the needless duplication in procurement procedure that had been involved, and recited several specific figures to show how much money the government would save and how little unemployment would actually be caused by the closing of the operation. The reporter sat down stunned, apparently realizing that the President knew more about the whole matter than he did. Call it luck that Kennedy had happened to see the story in the *Detroit Times* that morning, or score a point for his insatiable curiosity about a news item that most of us would have overlooked.

This was the way it went during all of his years in the White House; very few small details about the running of the government escaped him, and if he had been able to see all of the Cabinet members and agency heads that he wanted to question about something that he heard about or read about in their departments, he would have had no time to sleep or eat. Because he wanted to see so many people, he had to lean more and more on my judgment in selecting the people who wanted to see him. Knowing that he was not a President, like Eisenhower or Nixon, who wanted to be shielded from appointments, I never crossed anybody off the list without his consent, unless, as often happens in the White House, the would-be visitor's reason for seeing the President seemed so idiotic that I could not bother him about it. Usually if a staff member wanted him to see a Congressman or if Pierre Salinger was seeking a private interview for a reporter, they would mention it to him first and he would say, "See if Kenny can fit him in." Then they would come to me for an appointment. If I thought such an appointment was a needless waste of time or a bad idea, we would go back into the President's office and argue about it with him. About half of these arguments were decided in favor of the staff or Salinger, and in the other 50 percent of such requests the President agreed with me. Now and then he would say to me, "John Smith wants to drop in to say hello. Can you put him down?" I would point out to him that John Smith happened to be in the transportation business and that he had a strong vested interest in a transportation bill that was coming up in the House of Representatives next week. "Oh, is that so?" the President would say. "I thought he just wanted a social visit. Tell him I'm too busy."

Sometimes President Kennedy made so many closely crowded appointments that Dave and I found ourselves piling up so many waiting visitors that we ran out of waiting room space. The Cabinet Room and the Fish Room would be filled with callers, and we would be sticking others into the Rose Garden, my office, Ralph Dungan's office, Evelyn Lincoln's office, and any other place in the West Wing where a few square feet of empty space happened to be available. Invariably on such crowded days, a few important unscheduled visitors would also show up at the last minute unexpectedly, seeking an audience that could not be denied, and Dean Rusk or another State Department officer would want thirty minutes of the President's time for an urgent discussion involving top-priority national security matters.

Such a day, Tuesday, September 25, 1962, must have been the longest and busiest working day of any President of the United

States in modern times. President Kennedy had eleven appointments before lunch, four more in the afternoon and evening and then made appearances at night at the theater and at a supper dance at the British Embassy. His day started at eight-forty-five with a breakfast meeting of the Senate and House legislative leaders that the Vice-President, O'Brien, Salinger and I also attended. After the breakfast, the leaders walked outside to the Rose Garden to meet the press. When the press conference was breaking up, a photographer snapped a very funny unposed picture of the Senators and the Congressmen that President Kennedy prized as one of his favorite White House photographs. He had a print of the picture blown up to a huge size, four feet by six feet, and presented it to Mike Mansfield. It hangs today in Mansfield's office.

The picture caught the legislators in various stages of suspended motion. It shows Lyndon Johnson staring glumly at the loudspeaker microphone that had been used during the press conference, while Hubert Humphrey peeks over his shoulder. John McCormack is gazing vaguely at Johnson, Hale Boggs is looking at Humphrey and Carl Albert is staring down at his own shoes. George Smathers is smiling at the camera. Mike Mansfield has turned his back on the rest of the befuddled group and is seen walking quickly out of the picture.

On the inscribed blowup of the photograph that he presented to Mansfield, President Kennedy wrote, "To Mike, who knows when to stay and when to go."

After breakfast with the legislators, the President met in his office with two hundred members of the Burros Club, an organization of administrative assistants to Democratic members of Congress. Then he had an important fifty-two-minute meeting with Nguyen Dinh Thuan, Secretary of State for Security in the South Vietnam government. He warned Thuan once again, as he had warned Diem and Nhu continually, that the Diem regime would get no more military or economic support from the United States unless it gave more political freedom to its opponents and stopped its persecution of the Buddhist monks. The discussion with the South Vietnamese security secretary was to be followed by an eleven o'clock meeting with Robert G. Menzies, the Prime Minister of Australia. But while the President was talking with Thuan, I received word from Bobby's office that on that morning of all mornings Barney Ross, who had served with Kennedy on PT-109, was on his way to the White House with Ben Kevu, the Solomon Islands native who had saved the lives of the surviving members of Kennedy's crew by carrying the message to Kennedy on Nauro Island from the Australian coast watcher at Gomu. Kevu, I was told, would be arriving at the President's office within a few minutes.

We kept the Prime Minister of Australia waiting in the Cabinet Room while we brought to the President this other celebrated visitor from the same part of the world. Kennedy had not seen his rescuer since 1943. They embraced, and the President and Barney Ross sat down and talked happily with Kevu, who was now fifty-four years old and had been brought to the United States by Jack Paar for a special television show. Kevu explained to the President that he had had to paddle "many miles" in his canoe to reach the island where he boarded a plane for the trip to America. The President went to his desk, picked up the coconut with the SOS message scratched on it, and showed it to Kevu. "Do you remember this, Ben?" he asked. Kevu studied the coconut and nodded. "Rendova," he said. Then the President took down from the wall of his office the framed message from the Australian coast watcher, Lt. Arthur Reginald Evans, that Kevu had carried back to Kennedy and Ross on Nauro:

To Senior Officer, Naru Is.
Friday 11 pm. Have just learnt of your presence on Naru Is. and also that two natives have taken news to Rendova. I strongly advise you return immediately to here in this canoe and by the time you arrive here I will be in radio communication with authorities at Rendova and we can finalise plans to collect balance your party.

A. R. EVANS, LT.
R.A.N.V.R.

Will warn aviation of your crossing Ferguson passage.

Kennedy then picked up a handful of PT-109 tie clasps and asked Kevu how many children he had. "Six," Ben said.

"Give these to your children," the President said. "And give some of them to those other fellows who were with you in the canoe that day."

The President asked Dave to bring in the Prime Minister of Australia, who was waiting patiently in the Cabinet Room, and introduced Menzies to Kevu. The President walked outside with Kevu when Ross and Ben were leaving, and watched him going into the West Lobby where he was besieged by reporters and photographers. "Just think of it, Dave," the President said to Powers, "if it wasn't for Ben Kevu, you wouldn't be here in the White House today."

"You mean *you* wouldn't be here," Dave said.

"I meant just what I said," Kennedy said, laughing. "If it wasn't for Ben, you wouldn't be here."

While President Kennedy was having an hour meeting in his office with Prime Minister Menzies, we were arranging for the President to swear in W. Willard Wirtz as his new Secretary of Labor at a ceremony in the Cabinet Room, which would take place, hopefully, fifteen minutes after the Prime Minister's departure. Between the meeting with Menzies and the swearing-in of Secretary Wirtz, we were planning to sandwich in another ceremony at noon, a presentation to the President of an oil painting of the Battle of Bunker Hill, entitled "The Whites of Their Eyes." The painting, by Ken Riley, was to be presented by Major General D. W. McGowan, chief of the National Guard Bureau. Meanwhile, I received a hurried call from a distinguished Democratic Congressman, James E. Burke, who needed a favor from the President. Jim was anxious to have a photograph made of himself and Kennedy shaking hands for use in his coming campaign for reelection in Massachusetts. He came to the White House and we placed him in a small empty room, which Dave and I referred to as the "Confessional Booth," where he was to wait for the opportune moment. At the same time that Burke appeared, we received a call from the White House social office, informing us that the Ballet Folklórico, a dancing group from Mexico, was visiting the mansion and wanted to do a dance for the President. Dave led the Mexican dancers into the Rose Garden and asked them to wait there for a few minutes.

So while the President was concluding his talk with Prime Minister Menzies at a few minutes before noon, we had the National Guard general with a painting of the Battle of Bunker Hill waiting in the Fish Room, the newly appointed Secretary of Labor Wirtz with his family and many friends, including Arthur Goldberg, Adam Clayton Powell, Walter Reuther, George Meany, Paul Douglas and Walter Heller, waiting in the Cabinet Room, Jim Burke waiting in the Confessional Booth, and the Mexican dancers waiting in the Rose Garden. Then came a call from the State Department: George Ball and George McGhee wanted to have an urgent off-the-record meeting about the growing Cuban crisis with the President before he went to lunch.

That meant that the President's lunch would have to be postponed for at least a half hour, because after the Wirtz ceremony, he was scheduled to attend a meeting with a group of directors of the United Negro College Fund.

Somehow or other all of the appointments managed to go off smoothly, and somewhere in between them, Jim Burke got his picture. "How is everything back in Milton, Jim?" President Kennedy said to the Massachusetts Congressman as they posed for the photographer. "I hope it's quieter there than it is around here." When the President was hurrying from the presentation of the Bunker Hill battle painting to the Wirtz swearing-in ceremony, he said to Dave, "Who are all those people standing around out in the Rose Garden?" Dave explained that they were a troupe of Mexican ballet dancers. "Well, that's interesting," the President said. After his fifteen-minute meeting with the directors of the United Negro College Fund, which lasted until quarter to one, he joined the Ambassador from Mexico in the garden and watched the dancers do a few fast numbers. By the time he finished his talk with the State Department officials and went to the White House pool with Dave to take his daily swim before lunch, it was close to two o'clock.

"It's been a long morning," the President said to Dave while they were undressing. "I had to get up at seven-thirty to read some bills that I wanted to talk about with Mansfield and McCormack at that breakfast meeting."

The President and Dave reminisced, while they were swimming, about the 1946 Congressional campaign and people in Charlestown whom Kennedy remembered from that year when he was breaking into politics. "How is Matty Loftus?" he asked Dave. "Have you seen him lately?" Matty Loftus, the proprietor of the Horseshoe Tavern in Charlestown, was a devoted admirer of Kennedy's and a staunch supporter in his Congressional and Senatorial campaigns. Dave told the President that Matty Loftus had not been feeling well.

"I'm sorry to hear that," the President said. "Let's see if we can

[261]

get him on the phone right now. I'll talk to him and maybe I can cheer him up."

The marvelous White House switchboard operators, who always seemed to be able to reach anybody anywhere in the world within a few minutes, had no trouble reaching Matty Loftus at his home in Charlestown. The President climbed out of the pool, slipped into a robe, and talked to Matty for several minutes. Then he dressed and went to lunch in the executive mansion. Years before when he was a young Congressman, Kennedy was talking one day outside the Federal Building in Boston with a girl from the nearby West End of the city who worked in a government office. He asked her how she liked her Federal job. "Oh, it's a great job because I can go home for lunch every day," she said. Kennedy often repeated the line and used it frequently in the White House when somebody asked him how he liked being President of the United States.

Lunch for the President that day was a light meal served on trays to him and his wife as they sat talking in the living room of their second floor apartment in the mansion — soup, a sandwich, tea and milk. As usual, after lunch the President went to his bedroom, undressed and stretched out in bed, wearing the horn-rimmed reading glasses that he never wore in public, and looked at some intelligence reports on the building of missile sites in Cuba that he had brought from the meeting with Ball and McGhee. George Thomas, the President's valet, came in to hang up his discarded clothing, and asked what time he wanted to be awakened from his nap. "Bobby will be coming here at four o'clock," the President said, "so you better wake me around three-thirty." A few minutes later he dozed off to sleep.

That day he did not have much time to rest in the afternoon. In less than three-quarters of an hour, George Thomas was in his bedroom, telling him that it was three-thirty and he was picking up the telephone beside his bed to tell the White House switchboard that he was awake. Bobby came to the apartment in the mansion at four o'clock, with John McCone, the chief of the CIA, and Carl Kaysen, Mac Bundy's assistant in national security affairs on the White House staff, who was filling in for the absent Bundy that day. They discussed the continuing construction of missile bases by Soviet technicians in Cuba, which had been photographed by U-2 reconnaissance planes in the previous week. The President authorized another U-2 flight over Cuba for the following day. At that point, the photos still showed no offensive missiles capable of attacking the United States, only defensive, short-range surface-to-aircraft, or SAM, missiles. Khrushchev had assured the President that the only Soviet weapons being sent to Cuba were defensive missiles, requested by Castro for protection of the island. That Tuesday afternoon late in September in the President's sitting room, McCone doubted that Khrushchev would keep his word. The CIA chief was the only one of the President's advisers who felt then that the Soviets might go to the brink of nuclear war by putting long-range missiles into Cuba.

After McCone and Kaysen left the apartment, Bobby stayed behind and talked alone with the President for twenty minutes. Then the President went downstairs and walked over to his office, where he talked with me for a few minutes about the next day's schedule and gave me a brief report on his meeting with McCone and Bobby. At five o'clock he had a meeting on the Cuba situation in the Cabinet Room with Secretary of Defense McNamara, General Lyman Lemnitzer and a few people from the State Department, including George Ball, Averell Harriman, William Bundy and Mike Forrestall. The meeting lasted for an hour. At six, the President spent some time in his office, going over some paper work and discussing the day's activities with Dave and me. "I'm still wondering how I got mixed up with those Mexican dancers," he said. "Seeing Ben Kevu for the first time in nineteen years was enough of a surprise for one day without you guys hitting me with the Mexican dancers. What will you think of next?"

I reminded him that his day was not over yet. In a few minutes the Ambassador from Colombia, Carlos Sanz de Santamaria, and his wife, would be arriving at the White House.

"Gosh, that's right," the President said. "They're going to the theater with us, and then to a party at the British Embassy. But I still want to hit the pool and do my back exercises. Dave, can you stick around for a while?"

He explained his plan for the evening. He was scheduled to appear at the National Theater with Jackie and his mother for a special benefit performance of the new Irving Berlin musical comedy about life in the White House, *Mr. President*. "I hear that one of the songs in the show is called 'The Secret Service Makes Me Nervous,' " the real life Mr. President said, "so you can imagine how much like the White House it must be. I decided I wouldn't be missing much if I spent the first act swimming with Dave in the pool, and Jackie agrees." He had arranged to stay behind for a swim while Jackie and his mother appeared at the theater for the first-act curtain. Then, after his swim, he would join them in the Presidential Box around ten o'clock, in time for the second act. "If we're lucky, Dave," the President added, "maybe we can see some of the Patterson-Liston fight on TV before I have to go to the theater."

Dave was accustomed to being summoned for night duty at the White House when Jackie was absent. He called himself "John's Other Wife." The President hated to be alone in the evening. It was understood that Dave would be available to keep him company in the mansion even on nights like this one, when Jackie would be out of the house for only a short time. During the summer months, when Jackie and the children were at Hyannis Port and the President faced solitary confinement in Washington in the evenings from Monday until Thursday, Dave stayed with him until he went to bed. Their nightly routine was always the same. The White House kitchen staff would prepare a dinner of broiled chicken or lamb chops that would be left in the second floor apartment on a hotplate appliance so that they could eat it late in the evening alone, without keeping any of the staff waiting to serve them. Then they would watch television, or sit outside on the Truman Balcony, or the President would read a book and smoke a cigar while Dave drank several bottles of his Heineken's beer. "All this Heineken's of mine that you're drinking costs me a lot of money, Dave," the President would say. "I'm going to send you a bill for it one of these days." Around eleven o'clock, the President would get undressed and slip into the short-length Brooks Brothers sleeping jacket that he wore in preference to pajamas. Dave would watch him kneel beside his bed and say his prayers. Then he would get into the bed, and say to Dave, "Good night, pal, will you please put out the light?" Dave would put out the light, leave the apartment, say good night again to the Secret Service agent on duty in the downstairs hall, and drive home to his own house in McLean, Virginia.

The President also disliked swimming alone in the White House pool, which he did twice a day, even on his busiest days, before lunch and again in the evening. If Dave was not available to join him, he would bring another friend to the pool. The water in the pool was heated to a temperature of ninety degrees, too warm for most people's taste, but Kennedy found that swimming in such heated water relaxed and eased the stiffness and pain in his disabled back muscles. Before swimming he performed a series of prescribed calisthenics under the direction of the Navy chief petty officers assigned to the White House as physical therapists. The exercises brought a marked improvement to his back ailment during his last year in the Presidency.

That Tuesday night George Thomas brought the evening clothes that the President would wear to the theater downstairs to the dressing room beside the swimming pool. While he and Dave were getting dressed, they watched the televised heavyweight bout between Floyd Patterson and Sonny Liston, which did not delay the President's departure for the theater. Liston knocked out Patterson in the first round. At ten-twenty, in time for the second act of *Mr. President*, the President slipped into his seat beside Jackie and his mother at the Presidential Box in the National Theater. After the show, he went backstage to meet Robert Ryan, the actor who played the title role. He remembered Ryan's performance as the villain in the old Spencer Tracy movie *Bad Day at Black Rock*, one of Kennedy's favorite pictures, and told him how much he admired that performance. Ryan later talked to a friend of mine about the President's backstage visit that night.

"I did some traveling and talking for Stevenson in the 1952 campaign," Ryan said. "I was in Boston that fall with Adlai on a night when the Massachusetts Democrats were giving him a dinner at the Statler, and I was wandering around in the hotel lobby, trying to find the ballroom where the dinner was taking place, when this young fellow came up to me and said, 'You must be looking for the Stevenson dinner. Come with me, and I'll show you where it is.' Well, I was considerably surprised later that night when I saw the same fellow being introduced at the head table as the Democratic candidate for the Senate. He seemed too young for the job. Now ten years pass by, and he's in my dressing room at the National Theater, the President of the United States. I said I had met him once before but it was long ago and he wouldn't remember it. He said to me, 'I saw you in the lobby of the Statler Hotel in Boston in 1952 when you were trying to find the Stevenson dinner. I showed you where it was.' Some memory."

From the theater, the President went with Jackie and his mother and Ambassador and Mrs. Santamaria to the supper party at the British Embassy. He always enjoyed visiting that embassy because the British Ambassador, David Ormsby-Gore, now Lord Harlech, was one of his closest friends. They had met in London when Kennedy's father had been the American Ambassador there, and had been companions ever since. The President saw Ormsby-Gore frequently, and turned to him for advice in such situations as the Berlin crisis and the Cuban missile crisis. The French Ambassador in Washington, Herve Alphand, and his superiors in the French foreign office in Paris were naturally well aware of the close personal connection between Kennedy and Ormsby-Gore. It made them uncomfortable.

One day in 1961 I received a telephone call from Joe Alsop, Alphand's good friend, inviting me to have lunch with him and the French Ambassador at Le Bistro. Alphand lost no time getting to the point over the first martini. He understood that the British Ambassador enjoyed the enviable privilege of being able to visit President Kennedy at any time in his office, without going through the usual channels at the State Department. He wondered if it would be possible for him to have the same privilege.

"Certainly," I told him. "Any time you want to see the President, just call me."

Alphand was delighted. During the rest of the Kennedy administration, he called me on the telephone about ten times a year to ask if he could see the President about some problem. I would tell him to come right over. He did not realize that I cleared each of his visits with Mac Bundy, our foreign affairs assistant, and the State Department. Shortly after President Kennedy's death, when I was handling President Johnson's appointment schedule, Alphand called me anxiously one day and said, "Is our deal still on?"

I assured him that he could still feel free to visit the President whenever the spirit moved him. He came to see Johnson quite frequently — so frequently, in fact, that Bundy came to the President and complained that Johnson was seeing the French Ambassador too often. Bundy pointed out that Johnson had seen the French Ambassador three times in the past month and during the same period of time the British Ambassador had been to the White House only once. Johnson heard him out in silence and then pointed his finger at Bundy:

"I'm getting tired of both of those fellows running in here to bother me every time they got something on their mind. Seeing the French Ambassador and the British Ambassador is your job, not mine, and I'm sick of doing your job for you. From now on, you see them or send them to somebody in the State Department. Keep them out of here. I've got too many other things to do."

That night after the theater, President Kennedy found the company at the British Embassy so enjoyable that he stayed there until two-thirty-five and did not return to the White House with Jackie until quarter to three. Dave figured out later that between the time he had gotten up in the morning and when he went to bed at night, the President had been working at his desk, attending meetings and ceremonies and social events, or on his feet, for nineteen hours and fourteen minutes. That day was somewhat longer than most of his typical working days in the White House, but otherwise it was about the same as usual, busy, interrupted often by unexpected visitors, and never dull.

When we look back today at the Presidency in the 1960s, most of us think of that decade as a time when the chief executives in the White House were mainly concerned with the war in Vietnam. During most of Kennedy's three years as President the situation in Vietnam was a minor problem, overshadowed in Southeast Asia by the Communist attempt to take Laos and obscured by the more immediate threat of a nuclear war with the Soviets over the showdowns in Berlin and Cuba. When Kennedy came into office in 1961, his first big worries, along with the economic recession at home, were the two legacies of trouble overseas that he inherited from the Eisenhower administration — the civil warfare in Laos, and the long-planned and ill-advised CIA proposal to overthrow Castro by landing a force of Cuban rebels, already armed and trained by U.S. officers, on the coast of the Bay of Pigs. As it turned out, the failure of the Bay of Pigs expedition made Kennedy so mistrustful toward his military advisers that he turned down their repeated requests for a large-scale commitment of American combat troops in Laos. "If it hadn't been for the Bay of Pigs," he said later, "we might have gotten up to our necks in a fight with the Communists in Laos."

President Kennedy took a firm stand against the Soviet-supported Communist Pathet Lao's attempt to take control of the neutral Laotian government in 1961, backing up his warnings to Khrushchev by moving the aircraft carriers of the Seventh Fleet into the South China Sea and landing a detachment of U.S. Marines by helicopter in Thailand, near the Laotian capital city of Vientiane. But he was determined to protect the neutrality of Laos by making a political settlement with Khrushchev rather than by making war on Khrushchev's allies in Southeast Asia. At their meeting in Vienna that June, Kennedy found that Khrushchev was quite willing to make such a deal on Laos. As tough as he was on the Berlin issue and the nuclear test ban proposal at that summit meeting, the Soviet leader shared Kennedy's distaste for getting involved in a conventional land war in Asia. Later on, much to the disgust of the hawks in the State Department and the Pentagon, Kennedy and Averell Harriman brought economic pressure on Phoumi Nosavan, the violently right-wing general in Laos who had been supported by Eisenhower, and forced him to agree to a cease-fire truce with the Pathet Lao. Then, with the help of the Soviets, Kennedy established a neutral government in Laos, with the native Communists sharing authority with the moderate neutralists. This solution was no victory for the United States, but it cooled off a trouble spot with no loss of American soldiers — and that was enough to satisfy President Kennedy.

A year later, at the time of his death, President Kennedy was hoping to work out a similar solution in South Vietnam. Just as he had twisted Phoumi's arm in Laos, he was cutting financial and military aid to Diem in an effort to pressure the Saigon regime into taking a more liberal and tolerant attitude toward its political and religious enemies, the first step toward a reasonably compatible neutral government that would be neither strongly pro-American nor violently pro-Communist, and not anti-Buddhist, either. Kennedy often remarked to us that a settlement might have been made with the Viet Cong, like the compromise pact with the Pathet Lao in Laos, if Khrushchev had been as powerfully influential in Asia in 1963 as he had been in 1962. But in 1963 Red China had broken away from Khrushchev. And that final parting of the ways came about as a result of Kennedy's successful put-down of Khrushchev in the 1962 Cuban missile crisis.

President Kennedy's recent critics, who now claim that he was "out of his depth" in the Presidency, might reflect on the fact that he guided the United States government through three tense years when it was being challenged by a belligerent Khrushchev in Berlin, Cuba and Asia, without sending a single U.S. military combat unit into action. Up until the time of his death, he was determined to limit American military assistance to Vietnam to technicians, helicopter pilots and Green Beret advisers — no combat troop units and no bombers. He came closest to being forced to break his resolution against putting American troops into combat, not at the Bay of Pigs or in Vietnam, but in Laos, when he was determined to keep the capital city of Vientiane from falling into the hands of the advancing Pathet Lao Communist forces. It was then, in April, 1961, that he reluctantly sent five hundred Marines into the nearby friendly territory of Thailand, where they could stand ready to support the Royal Laotian soldiers in Vientiane. At the same time, Kennedy turned to other nations in the free world for help in defending the independent government of Laos. Britain's Prime Minister Harold Macmillan met Kennedy at Key West in Florida and agreed, after some reluctance, to send troops to Laos if it became necessary. I remember Macmillan saying to the President, "After the cheering stops, you and I will probably be left out there alone." Charles de Gaulle sent word that we could expect no military help from France under any circumstances. He explained to Kennedy later in Paris that he would support the United States in a total war against Russia, but after his own bitter experience of fighting in Southeast Asia during the early 1950s, he wanted no part of warfare in that area of the world. "You should stay out of there, too," he added emphatically.

President Kennedy managed finally to stop the Communist advance on Vientiane with political, rather than military, pressure, but he remembered afterward that along with Britain the only nations that offered him help when the going in Laos was rough were Thailand, the Philippines and Pakistan. The tough president of Pakistan, Ayub Khan, won Kennedy's lasting gratitude and admiration when he offered to send into Laos no small token force but five thousand of his best-trained soldiers. "Anything Ayub wants from me from now on," the President told us, "he can have." A few months later when Ayub visited Washington, he was given the fanciest and most glamorous reception that Jackie Kennedy could dream up — an outdoor dinner served on a summer evening on George Washington's front lawn at Mount Vernon. The guests, led by the President and Ayub, boarded the two Presidential yachts, the *Honey Fitz* and the *Patrick J.*, and Navy Secretary John Connally's cruiser, the *Sequoia*, for a memorable sail down the Potomac River from Anacostia to Mount Vernon. The procession of yachts was escorted by the last remaining World War II PT boat in the Navy's service, the *Guardian*. Mount Vernon's grounds were lighted for the dinner party by spotlights, the first electrical lighting equipment ever installed at the estate. After the dinner, the guests listened to a concert by the National Symphony Orchestra on the lawn beside the river.

Those of us who were with President Kennedy during the sad night in the White House when he heard the news of the defeat and capture of the Cuban rebels at the Bay of Pigs remember it as one of his most courageous moments. Any other President of the United States, especially one who had been in office for only three months, might have tried to save himself from such a humiliation by sending Marines and Navy jet fighters to beat back Fidel Castro's defending forces and to rescue the outnumbered invaders. Kennedy had made up his mind not to involve any American combat troops or planes in this fight between two Cuban political factions, even though the rebels had his approval and the support and direction of his government's Central Intelligence Agency. When the reports of failure came from the beachhead, he refused to give in to his military advisers, who had accepted his earlier order against any American participation in the invasion, but now argued that we had to change the plan and send in American reinforcements to beat Castro and save the prestige of the United States. Kennedy firmly disagreed. As sorry as he felt for the stranded rebels on the beaches, he preferred the embarrassment of defeat to the use of American military force against a small and independent nation.

"I'll take the defeat," he said that night to the generals and admirals, "and I'll take all of the blame for it."

The Bay of Pigs operation, during its planning stages, was the most closely held secret of the Eisenhower and Kennedy administrations, and most of us who usually shared the President's confidential problems were not included in the Bay of Pigs discussion meetings. The planning had been done over the previous year by CIA people under the direction of Allen W. Dulles, the highly respected head of that agency, and his deputy, Richard Bissell, with the knowledge and approval of the Joint Chiefs of Staff. The President agreed, for security reasons, that the fewer new faces in the government brought into the discussions, the better kept the secret would be. He did not mention the project to me until he had given it his final approval, only a few days before the air strike and the landings.

The President said then that the plan was so advanced when he came into office in January that it seemed almost impossible to cancel it. The brigade of fourteen hundred anti-Castro Cubans had been in training under CIA officers on a plantation in Guatemala for several months; they were fully armed and eager and ready to go into action. "If we decided now to call the whole thing off," the President said, "I don't know if we could go down there and take the guns away from them." The President was also under pressure not to postpone the takeoff date of the invasion force any longer. The government of Guatemala was worried about the presence of one thousand four hundred armed foreigners in its country. The President of Guatemala had asked President Kennedy to get the Cubans out of his republic before the end of April, which was then less than two weeks away. Intelligence reports said that Castro was about to receive MIG jets from the Soviet Union, along with Cuban pilots trained in Czechoslovakia to fly those fighter planes. The rebels had to stage their attack before the Russian planes were available for duty in Cuba. The President said he had finally agreed with some reluctance to approve the plan and the date of the landings, Monday, April 17, after the CIA and the Joint Chiefs of Staff accepted his strict stipulation that no American forces could take part in the invasion. He mentioned that Dean Rusk had showed a lack of enthusiasm for the project but was willing to go along with it, provided that the President's insistence on no American military participation was scrupulously observed.

I asked the President if any top official in the government had spoken against his support of the Cuban rebels in this planned revolt. "Not one," he said, "unless you count Bill Fulbright among our top officials." Senator Fulbright, in his capacity as chairman of the Senate Foreign Relations Committee, had been told of the plan, and voiced strong opposition to it as a bad move in foreign relations that would bring discredit on the United States. The President asked Fulbright to repeat his disapproving argument at a meeting attended by Rusk, McNamara and two of the State Department's officers in charge of Latin-American affairs, Thomas C. Mann and Adolf Berle. None of the others at the table agreed with Fulbright.

On the other hand, all of the Joint Chiefs of Staff and Allen Dulles were in favor of the expedition. Dulles was a legendary figure in the government, never known to have made a mistake. Kennedy's first move on the day after he was elected was to announce that he would reappoint Dulles as director of the CIA. On the Friday before D-Day, when he first talked to me about the Bay of Pigs invasion, the President showed me a message that he had received that morning from a Marine Corps colonel who had just made an inspection of the Cuban Brigade at its camp in Guatemala. The message glowed with approval. The colonel reported that he was confident that the Cubans in the task force were highly capable of carrying out their combat mission and going on from there to overthrow Castro. It was this impressive message from the colonel, Kennedy told me, that finally prompted him to give the go-ahead.

On the following Tuesday night, when the confirmed news of the complete failure of the invasion and the capture of the greatly outnumbered rebels reached the White House, President Kennedy had little to say to anybody. Pierre Salinger and I watched him walk out of his office into the Rose Garden. We waited while he stayed in the garden alone for almost an hour. I remember saying to Pierre, "He must be the loneliest man in the world tonight."

During the next few days he made it plain to all of us that he wanted no blame for the failure placed on anybody except himself. One member of the White House staff planted a story in the newspapers charging President Eisenhower with responsibility for the Bay of Pigs fiasco because the plan had been originally approved and supported by Eisenhower. Stewart Udall, the Secretary of the Interior, made the mistake of echoing the charge in a television interview. The President was incensed. Knowing which staff member had started the original Blame Eisenhower campaign, the President called him and said, "Tell Stu Udall I don't want to hear any more about Eisenhower."

Arthur Schlesinger, who had acted as an intermediary between the President and the leaders of the exiled Cuban Liberal Revolutionary Council in the United States, also had written a memorandum to Kennedy, endorsing Fulbright's opposition to the invasion on political and diplomatic grounds. In his book on the Kennedy years in the

White House, *A Thousand Days*, Schlesinger recalls a discussion that he attended before Kennedy's first postmortem Bay of Pigs press conference at which the President stressed that all of his senior advisers had backed the expedition but he alone was finally responsible for it. The President said to the group, "There is only one person in the clear — that's Bill Fulbright. And he probably would have been converted if he had attended more of the meetings." Mac Bundy, who was present, reminded the President that Schlesinger was also on the record as having been opposed to the invasion. "Oh, sure," Kennedy said with a smile. "Arthur wrote me a memorandum that will look pretty good when he gets around to writing his book on my administration. Only he better not publish that memorandum while I'm still alive. And I have a title for his book — *Kennedy: The Only Years*."

At the press conference that followed, the President made his widely quoted remark about the second-guessing on the Bay of Pigs disaster, "There's an old saying that victory had a hundred fathers and defeat is an orphan." Schlesinger asked him later where he had gotten the highly appropriate line. "Oh, I don't know," he said. "It's just an old saying." But subsequent research showed no evidence that the supposed old saying had ever been said or written by anybody before Kennedy.

As much as he insisted on taking all of the blame and responsibility for the Bay of Pigs defeat in public statements, President Kennedy felt free in private talks with a few of us to point out the big flaw in the military plan of the operation. He wondered why the Joint Chiefs of Staff and the CIA had expected the small landing force of one thousand four hundred rebels to survive in Cuba without help and reinforcements from one of the only two possible sources — either from inside the island, from internal uprisings, sabotage and armed attacks on the Castro forces by underground revolutionists timed to coordinate with the landings, or from outside military support by American troops and air cover. When the Joint Chiefs and the CIA agreed to the President's strict ruling against American military participation in the assault, he assumed that plans had been set for a widespread uprising against the Castro government inside Cuba.

Soon after the collapse of the invasion attempt, when he began to find out the details, the President was shocked to discover that there had been no plans for a coordinated revolt in Cuba. The leaders of the organized anti-Castro underground movement in Havana did not even know the date of the landings. "Everybody in Miami knew exactly when those poor fellows were going to hit the beaches," President Kennedy said to us, "but the only people in Cuba who knew about it were the ones who were working in Castro's office." The exiled Cuban leaders in New York and Miami, who were supposed to take over the government in Havana if the invasion succeeded, said that the CIA had discouraged them from alerting their followers in Cuba on the grounds that spreading such information would endanger the secrecy of the expedition.

At the same time, the CIA officers who were working in Guatemala with the leaders of the invasion force assured them that they would be getting strong American military support. The Cubans were told that the Navy's aircraft carrier *Essex* would be standing offshore near the Bay of Pigs, as indeed it was, and that U.S. Marines and Navy jets would be available when needed.

The absence of any preparations for an organized uprising in Cuba, and the assurances of military support given to the rebels in the landing force, led President Kennedy to a bitter conclusion: the Joint Chiefs of Staff and the CIA must have been assuming all along that the President would become so worried at the last minute about the loss of his own prestige that he would drop his restriction against the use of U.S. forces and send the Marines and the Navy jets into the action.

How else, the President asked us, could the Joint Chiefs approve such a plan? "They were sure I'd give in to them and send the go-ahead order to the *Essex*," he said one day to Dave Powers. "They couldn't believe that a new President like me wouldn't panic and try to save his own face. Well, they had me figured all wrong."

Outwardly President Kennedy seemed to accept the defeat at the Bay of Pigs with his customary calmness and resignation, but within the privacy of his office he made no effort to hide the distress and guilt that he felt when he thought of the one thousand one hundred Cuban patriots who had been captured by Castro — and during the months after the invasion he thought of those prisoners constantly. One morning when he came to his desk he remarked to me that he had had no sleep the night before. "I was thinking about those poor guys in prison down in Cuba," he said. "I'm willing to make any kind of a deal with Castro to get them out of there." The President's determination to get the prisoners released, at any cost to his own pride, led him into one of the most ill-advised moves in his career. In May, 1961, he quickly accepted an offer from Castro to release the survivors of the Cuban rebel brigade in return for five hundred tractors, or bulldozers, or $28,000,000.

President Kennedy talked Milton Eisenhower, Eleanor Roosevelt, Walter Reuther and Cardinal Cushing, among others, into organizing a Tractors for Freedom committee. The obviously vulnerable project was soon demolished by political controversy. The Republicans denounced the idea of bartering with Castro for human lives. Milton Eisenhower became embarrassed and begged off the committee. "Ike must have told Milton to be more careful about answering his phone," President Kennedy observed, "especially when the White House is calling."

Bobby Kennedy, trying to relieve his brother's concern for the prisoners, pushed ahead with another prolonged attempt to ransom them out of Cuba during the following year. Bobby arranged for James B. Donovan, the New York lawyer who had negotiated the exchange of the Soviet spy Rudolf Abel for Gary Powers, the U-2 pilot, to go to Havana and negotiate with Castro. The negotiations dragged on into the fall of 1962, into the tense period of the Cuban missile crisis, but Bobby and Donovan persisted, even in those dark months, in seeking to get the prisoners freed before Christmas. Finally, in December, Castro agreed to exchange the survivors for $53,000,000 worth of food and medicines. Then at the last minute, only a few days before the Christmas Eve deadline that Bobby was eager to meet, Castro demanded another $2,900,000 in cash, which he said was owed to him by the Cuban refugee organizations in the United States as a payment for sick and wounded Bay of Pigs veterans already released.

In desperation, Bobby raised $1,900,000 in a hurry with the help of General Lucius D. Clay and, at the suggestion of the President, asked Cardinal Cushing to get up the other million.

"Bobby called me on the telephone, and asked me if I could get a million dollars before the day was over," Cardinal Cushing recalled later. "He said they had to have the money right away in order to get the prisoners sent to the United States before Christmas, which was only a couple of days away. I remembered a talk I had with Jack about the Bay of Pigs prisoners. It was the first time I ever saw tears in his eyes. So I said I would call Bobby back in three hours. I called him that afternoon and told him I had gotten the million dollars and promised to have it delivered at the White House before six o'clock that night. I borrowed it from a few friends, a few Latin-American friends in particular, and I promised them it would be repaid within three months, and it was."

General Clay, a senior partner in a New York banking firm, found himself in the Attorney General's office the next morning signing a note for $2,900,000, and arranging a transfer of the money from a bank in Canada to a Canadian bank in Havana. The prisoners were released that afternoon and flown to Miami. Jim Donovan later regaled the President with an account of his trip to Havana that day with John E. Nolan, Jr., another New York lawyer who was helping him to arrange the transaction. The tension of the recent missile crisis was still fresh in Castro's mind. When Castro met Donovan at the airport in Havana, where the prisoners were waiting to be turned over to Americans, a flight of Cuban MIG fighter planes swooped low over the runway. Donovan, a witty Irishman, dug his elbow into Castro's ribs and yelled at him, "It's the invasion!" Castro seemed startled, but then laughed. The other Cubans, seeing Castro laughing, laughed, too.

The President spent the Christmas holidays that year, as usual, at Palm Beach. The leaders of the Cuban brigade visited him there and invited him to review their troops at a demonstration of Cuban rebels in the Orange Bowl in Miami on December 29. The President was eager to accept their invitation, but he realized that considering the present delicate relationship between him and Khrushchev and Castro such a gesture would be politically unwise. The President telephoned me and asked me what I thought of the invitation. "Don't go there," I told him. "After what you've been through with Castro, you can't make an appearance in the Orange Bowl and pay a tribute to those rebels. It will look as though you're planning to back them in another invasion of Cuba."

"You're absolutely right," the President said. "I shouldn't do it."

Dean Rusk and Mac Bundy also strongly advised him against appearing at the Orange Bowl ceremony. But Bobby told him to go ahead and accept the invitation. Bobby knew the President so well that he often realized, better than the President himself, what was the right and best thing for him to do. Bobby knew how heavily the disaster of the Bay of Pigs had been weighing on JFK's conscience, and Bobby decided correctly that if a public appearance with the rebel brigade would ease the President's sense of guilt, it would be well worth the political risk involved. Bobby was right, and the rest of us were wrong. The President went to the Orange Bowl with Jackie, who made a speech in Spanish hailing the bravery of the members of the brigade. Kennedy was so overwhelmed with emotion when he was presented with the rebel flag from the Bay of Pigs that he declared in his address that "this flag will be returned to this brigade in a free Havana." Diplomatically, it was the worst possible gesture that a President of the United States could have made at that time, but, as Bobby expected, it did John F. Kennedy a lot of internal good. He came back to the White House to start the new year in a much happier frame of mind.

As General Douglas MacArthur remarked privately to the President, he was lucky to have learned so much about the value of his military advice from an operation like the Bay of Pigs disaster, where the strategic cost was small. Kennedy learned another lesson when he delivered an ill-advised speech to the American Newspaper Publishers Association, strongly implying, in a somewhat petulant manner, that the press had revealed too much advance information about the invasion plans, and stressing a need for "far greater official secrecy." He was promptly lambasted in editorials all over the country. Coming on top of the failure in Cuba, such a criticism of the press seemed to be a childish attempt to shift the blame. Kennedy himself regretted the speech almost as soon as the words were out of his mouth. One of his great qualities was his readiness to admit a mistake, and he was quick to admit this one. "I should have realized," he told us later, "that there is no way of keeping a clandestine operation like this one a secret in a free democracy. And that's as it should be."

The Bay of Pigs experience brought several significant changes in the Kennedy administration. The operations and authority of the CIA, which had had a free hand under Eisenhower, were limited and tightened. Allen Dulles retired with Kennedy's sympathetic good wishes, and was replaced by John McCone, a former chairman of the Atomic Energy Commission. The White House staff became more involved in foreign and defense affairs. McGeorge Bundy's office was moved from the Executive Office Building across the street to the basement of the White House, close to the President's communications center, where he took on more responsibility in military intelligence. General Maxwell Taylor was called out of retirement to be Kennedy's military adviser, and later became chairman of the Joint Chiefs of Staff. And Bobby Kennedy took on a larger general role as his brother's personal troubleshooter.

When the President began to receive the first bad reports from the beach at the Bay of Pigs, he said to me, "I should have had Bobby in on this from the start." From then on, Bobby was brought in on so many of the President's urgent problems in the State and Defense departments and in the CIA that he had to delegate many of his Attorney General's duties to his deputies in the Justice Department. Bobby was the one man whom JFK trusted and depended on in a time of pressure more than anybody else. The closeness of the two brothers led many people in Washington to assume that Bobby was making Presidential decisions. The President himself remarked jokingly, and sometimes not so jokingly, that even members of the Kennedy family thought that there were two number one men in the Kennedy administration.

Bobby never had such a delusion. He remembered which Kennedy had been elected to the Presidency. If he had ever forgotten, he would have been straightened out fast by his older brother. The President drew a line between trusting Bobby's judgment, and depending on him to handle a problem, and the further step of allowing Bobby, or anybody else, to make a Presidential decision. Bobby would suggest or argue for a course of action, and very often the President would agree to it after considering the pros and cons. But *nobody* told President Kennedy what to do. Bobby knew with a brother's instinct just how far he could go in arguing against the President before running into a cold and final wall of disapproval. The President was much the toughest of the Kennedy brothers.

Far from being influenced easily by Bobby, the President was quick to pick out an error or weakness in one of Bobby's proposals. During the Berlin crisis, when the President was anxious to alert the nation to the danger of a nuclear war with Russia, Bobby suggested at a Cabinet meeting that one certain way of making the American people aware of the seriousness of the international situation would be to raise their income taxes. Abe Ribicoff and Arthur Goldberg quickly agreed with Bobby. To the President's surprise, none of the other Cabinet members disagreed. It was obvious to the President, always more of an astute politician than Bobby, that announcing a tax raise during that period of economic recession would be the worst possible political move, as well as a bad blow to the economy. It would only excite the people against the administration needlessly because Congress would never pass such a measure anyway.

"I couldn't believe that they were serious," the President said to me afterwards. "How could three supposedly experienced politicians like Bobby, Abe Ribicóff and Arthur Goldberg even think of raising income taxes at a time like this? I won't mention it now to Bobby, and don't you say anything to him. We'll let him find out for himself how wrong he is."

Wilbur Mills, the chairman of the House Ways and Means Committee, called me when he heard about Bobby's proposal, and told me to warn the President that such a tax bill would never get out of his committee. I assured Mills that the President had no intention of asking for a tax raise. Walter Heller, the President's economic adviser, told me that he wanted to argue against Bobby at a White House meeting on the question which was set for a few days later.

"What did you tell Walter?" the President asked when I reported Heller's opposition to him.

"I told him not to be afraid to raise his voice," I said. "I don't know anything about his economic views on the matter, but politically he's right."

"There's no need of having this meeting," the President said, "because I'm not going to ask a tax raise no matter what anybody says. But we'll let Bobby listen to Heller talk about it."

At the meeting, Heller spoke forcibly on the economic decline that could be caused by a tax raise. Then the President went through the motions of disapproving the idea which he had already decided against. (And Seymour Harris, the Harvard economist, later wrote an article describing how Heller had persuaded the President not to ask Congress for a raise in income taxes.) After the meeting, Bobby came to me and said, "I understand you were against this all along."

"That's an understatement," I said. "Bobby, that tax bill would have been stuck in the House of Representatives for the next twenty-five years."

"Gosh, you might have mentioned that to me a couple of days ago," Bobby said quietly.

Usually when I disagreed privately in a conversation with the President on something suggested by Bobby, the President would call me later into his office or to the living quarters in the mansion when Bobby was with him, and say to me, "Tell Bobby why you think that idea of his is terrible." Then the President would sit back and enjoy our argument. He would arrange similar confrontations between me and other members of the Kennedy family, and with Cabinet members and members of the White House staff. It did not make me popular with any of them. Often the President agreed with my side of the argument. As he frankly admitted, he found it comfortable to have me burdened with the task of saying no for him.

When Byron ("Whizzer") White, a close personal friend of the Kennedy brothers and Bobby's Deputy Attorney General, was nominated for the Supreme Court, I could not resist making a sarcastic comment to the President. I had no objections to White's nomination, but I reminded the President that he had been getting a hard time from Bobby and his friends in the Justice Department whenever we tried to reward a nice young man, who had helped us politically, with an appointment to a Federal judgeship. The Justice people always complained that our nominee was either too young, too inexperienced, had not served as a judge, or had not attended Harvard Law School.

"And now Bobby wants to put Whizzer White on the Supreme Court," I said to the President. "I'm sure Whizzer will be fine on the Court, but it seems to me he doesn't have any of that Oliver Wendell Holmes background that the Justice Department is always demanding when we try to give somebody a judge's job."

As I expected, that afternoon the President called me to the second floor apartment in the White House, where he was sitting with Bobby. He said, "Tell Bobby why you think we'll have a hard time getting Whizzer White on the Supreme Court."

Bobby bristled. I said to him with a straight face, "I don't see how we can get the Justice Department to approve the nomination. After all, Whizzer is only a lawyer from Denver who never served as a judge, and he didn't go to Harvard Law School."

Catching on to the ribbing, Bobby glared at both of us and we all laughed. But from then on, the President seemed to have less difficulty with the Justice Department in appointing Federal judges.

When the Bay of Pigs experience prompted the President to give Bobby a wider and more influential role in the administration, Bobby found himself gaining a wider circle of influential friends from the liberal intellectual set in Washington. Ethel and Bobby began to hold at their home a series of group discussion encounters with visiting sociologists, philosophers, historians and literature professors, which became known as the Hickory Hill Seminars. The President took an amused view of the seminars, but he was always eager on the morning after one of the meetings to get a full report on who was there, what was said, and who disagreed with whom. He especially relished the accounts of arguments at Hickory Hill on religion and moral issues between agnostic intellectuals and his convent-educated sisters and sisters-in-law. Many of the liberal activists who frequented Hickory Hill prodded Bobby to use his influence with the President to remove Dean Rusk from the State Department because Rusk was too stolid and too much of a conservative establishment man for their taste. Bobby was easily swayed against Rusk, whom he blamed for the State Department's traditional slowness in getting things done and making decisions. As Bobby's relationship with the Secretary of State became strained, he was often too quick to criticize Rusk on the slightest excuse. Bobby was appalled when Rusk stayed in Washington to attend a State Department ceremony instead of traveling to Nassau with the President for the Skybolt discussions with Harold Macmillan. Bobby did not know what the President and Rusk both knew about Macmillan, namely that the British Prime Minister preferred to talk alone with Kennedy over a drink, and did not care to have other officials sitting in on their conversations.

President Kennedy listened to Bobby's complaints about Rusk without much interest because he regarded Rusk as a Secretary of State well suited to his needs in that office. Neither Rusk nor McNamara had the authority in making policy under Kennedy that they later assumed in the Johnson administration. Unlike Johnson, and even more so than Franklin D. Roosevelt, Kennedy directed his own foreign policy decisions. Rusk carried out Kennedy's directives with no arguments and no second-guesses. He was always discreet, well respected by Congress, and not a flashy publicity-seeker, all of which qualities Kennedy valued highly. The President was also aware that the slow motion of the State Department's working mechanism, which irked Bobby, was not the Secretary's fault and, indeed, bothered Rusk as much as it annoyed the Kennedys. One day after a talk with Bobby, the President said to me, "Don't you think we ought to get somebody in the State Department with a little more pep?" I gave him the arguments in defense of Rusk that he often expressed himself, because I felt that Rusk was his kind of Secretary. "Do you want somebody like Dean Acheson over there?" I said to him. "Somebody who would be fighting everything you want to do, and antagonizing the Congressmen on the foreign policy and appropriations committees, and talking to the newspapers?"

"Thanks for reminding me," the President said. "I'd be foolish to get rid of Rusk."

The President was annoyed by the reports circulated in Washington shortly before his death that he had decided to replace Rusk in 1964, a rumor as baseless as the story of the same vintage that said he was planning to dump Lyndon Johnson. Arthur Schlesinger later included that speculation in his book on the Kennedy Presidency, and now JFK's alleged determination to remove Rusk keeps appearing in print as an established fact. I was with President Kennedy in his office one day when Schlesinger urged him to replace Rusk. Kennedy looked up from a paper on his desk that he was studying, glanced at Schlesinger, and said to him, "That's a great idea, Arthur." After Schlesinger left the office, no doubt certain that Rusk's days as Secretary of State were numbered, the President looked at me, shook his head, laughed, and said, "Arthur has a lot of good ideas."

The best description of Bobby Kennedy is one that says he was not a simple man but many different simple men. He could be at times incredibly naïve, too impressed by celebrities, too impulsive or too unrealistic. At most other times, especially when his older brother was depending on his firm support, he was wise, calm, restrained, full of courage and understanding, and very realistic in getting at the hard facts of the situation. Always he was the kindest man we ever knew. It is often said that the experience of the Bay of Pigs was a blessing because it gave President Kennedy an understanding of the military pressures that he had to resist in order to keep the world at peace during the later tensions of the Cuban missile crisis. The Bay of Pigs disaster also did all of us an invaluable service by serving as the frustration that turned President Kennedy to bringing Bobby into the high councils of the government, where Bobby strengthened and carried out his brother's resistance to a nuclear war as perhaps no other adjutant could have done.

The Kennedy brothers seldom mentioned or displayed openly their deep feeling for each other. Dave Powers, who was probably closer to the President than anybody outside of the Kennedy family, remembers him speaking warmly of Bobby only once, on the black Saturday of October 27, 1962, at the height of the Cuban missile crisis. Time was running out. The air strike against the Soviet bases in Cuba that the President had been striving to avoid all week could not be postponed much longer. While the President sat with Dave that night in the White House, sharing a dinner of warmed-over broiled chicken, he talked about Bobby's determined stand against such advocates of an air attack as John McCone, Dean Acheson, Douglas Dillon, Maxwell Taylor, Paul Nitze and Mac Bundy at meetings where the President was absent, about how Bobby later brought Dillon, Taylor and Bundy around to supporting the President's plan for a naval blockade of Cuba instead of a war-provoking bombing strike, about Bobby's repeated meetings with Soviet Ambassador Anatoly Dobrynin, and about Bobby drafting the President's conciliatory reply to Khrushchev's first tentative offer to remove the Soviet missiles from Cuba. Then the President paused thoughtfully for a moment, and said, "Thank God for Bobby." It is hard to believe that both of these brothers, who did so much to prevent an outbreak of violence between the world's two great nuclear powers, were later struck down in violent deaths themselves.

ELEVEN

The Showdown with
Khrushchev

A FULL ACCOUNT of President Kennedy's brief time in the White House would be crowded with important events, plans, problems, hopes and intentions that this book of scattered personal memories does not attempt to cover — his fights for civil rights and militant enforcement of desegregation in the South, and against inflation, poverty and urban decay and unrest, his launching of the space program that later landed the first men on the moon, his unfulfilled Latin-American programs, and his successful turnaround of the receding domestic economy that headed the United States into the most prolonged period of peacetime prosperity that the country has enjoyed since before World War II. All of his other accomplishments were overshadowed, of course, by his brave stand against Nikita Khrushchev that saved the world from a nuclear war during the prolonged Berlin crisis in 1961 and the more dangerously strained thirteen days of the Cuban missile crisis in 1962. As Harold Macmillan said later, when President Kennedy faced the risk of war to force the Soviet Union to remove its missiles from the Western Hemisphere, he did what the earlier leaders of England, France and the United States failed to do in the critical years before the two German world wars.

"If Kennedy never did another thing," Macmillan said, "he assured his place in history by that single act."

Facing up to Khrushchev's armed challenge in Cuba required a great courage in President Kennedy, because he had a deeper fear of nuclear war than most of his advisers realized. He could discuss the possibility of such warfare at the conference table with a calm composure, but later reflections on that possibility in private talks with one or two of us made him distressed. Whenever he talked to me about the danger of an atomic war, as he did on the plane when we were leaving Vienna after his meetings with Khrushchev, and often later during the crisis periods in Berlin and Cuba, he always said the same thing in the same words: "I keep thinking of the children, not my kids or yours, but the children all over the world." The thought of shaking the big stick at the Soviets by conducting nuclear tests, as he was forced to do during the Berlin crisis, appalled him. "We test, and then they test, and we have to test again," he said, "and then it becomes easier to use them on each other." One rainy afternoon, after one of our tests, he was talking in his office with Jerome Wiesner, the White House science adviser, about the contamination from such explosions. He asked Wiesner how the fallout returned to earth from the upper atmosphere.

"It comes down in rain," Wiesner said.

The President turned and looked out the windows at the falling rain in the Rose Garden. "You mean there might be radioactive contamination in that rain out there right now?" he asked.

"Possibly," Wiesner said.

After Wiesner left the office, the President sat in his chair looking at the rain in the garden for several minutes, without saying a word. I never saw him more depressed.

On the President's trip through the West in 1963, he was shown a huge crater in New Mexico that had been opened by an underground test blast. Two nuclear scientists who were with us explained to him enthusiastically that they were working on a much smaller bomb that would produce a bigger and more powerful explosion. He listened to them with a puzzled frown, and said to me later, "How can they be so damned cheerful talking about a thing like that? They keep telling me that if they could run more tests, they could come up with a cleaner bomb. If you're going to kill a hundred million people, what difference does it make whether it's clean or dirty?"

But despite his determination to avoid a nuclear war, President Kennedy was equally determined not to back away from a threat of such a war if there was no other means of stopping the Soviets from dominating the Western world. He came into office realizing that Khrushchev was certain that the United States would never take the risk of atomic war to defend its position of world leadership, and he decided that one of his first hard duties as President was to convince Khrushchev and the other Communists that their confident assumption was wrong. "I have to show him that we can be just as tough as he is," Kennedy said when he first discussed the possibility of a meeting with Khrushchev. "I can't do that sending messages to him through other people. I'll have to sit down with him, and let him see who he's dealing with."

Negotiations for a Kennedy-Khrushchev meeting in Europe began in March, less than two months after the 1961 inauguration, but the date and the place, the first weekend in June at Vienna, were not finally set until May, after the Bay of Pigs setback and after Kennedy's refusal to send U.S. military troops into Laos. The critics argued that this was the wrong time for the President to be talking to Khrushchev about a nuclear test ban agreement and the tense situation in Berlin, where the Soviets were renewing their demands for a removal of Allied occupation forces. Kennedy's reluctance to make a show of military force in Cuba and Laos, it was said, would put him at a disadvantage in contending with Khrushchev at Vienna. The President disagreed. "Getting involved in a fight between Communists and anti-Communists in Cuba and Laos was one thing," he said. "But this is the time to let him know that a showdown between the United States and Russia would be entirely something else again."

The European journey was arranged so that the President and his wife would meet with General de Gaulle in Paris on their way to Vienna and then stop over in London on their way back to Washington, ostensibly to attend the christening of Stash and Lee Radziwill's new baby, but actually to give Harold Macmillan a report on what was said in Paris and Vienna. This was my first experience in making advance arrangements for a Presidential trip to Europe, a highly interesting reconnaissance mission, in many respects more memorable than the subsequent main event itself. I found that our American Secret Service agents, checking the schedules, routes and security arrangements, got along fine with the French, Russian and Austrian secret policemen. In fact, most of them turned out to be old friends who had worked with our agents on previous summit meetings. On the higher level, planning the schedules of receptions, public appearances and appointments with our opposite numbers in the French and Russian governments, we had some minor difficulties that were soon ironed out. If the French had their way, Jackie Kennedy would have spent most of her time in Paris promoting the French dressmaking and wine industries. The Russians in Vienna were striving to subdue the fanfare of Kennedy's arrival for fear that he might attract a bigger and more enthusiastic crowd than Khrushchev. They were annoyed with our plan for an airport arrival and a motorcade from the airport to the American Embassy, in the traditional U.S. gala style, because Khrushchev was coming into Vienna on a train with no grand welcoming parade. The more they objected to our motorcade, the more we pushed for it and added more limousines and flags to it, while the Austrians enjoyed every minute of the debate.

The Austrians, Russians, and our State Department were insisting that President Kennedy lay a wreath on the Tomb of the Unknown Soldier in Vienna. When this became a real crisis, Bill Hartigan, our advance man, called me from Vienna for a final decision. My reply was: "The Unknown Soldier was probably a Nazi, but you tell them that while Khrushchev is laying a wreath on his grave, President Kennedy will be at Saint Stephan's Cathedral praying for his soul."

One of my duties on the advance trip was to select the American interpreter for Kennedy in his talks with De Gaulle. Our Army generals in Europe were pushing one of their high-ranking officers, who had been an interpreter for Eisenhower when he had been the NATO commander, which made me take three steps backward for a critical look at him. I had lunch in Paris with the Army's candidate and a few of our State Department officers, and decided that the military linguist was too much of an automobile-salesman type of orator for Kennedy's quiet taste. The State Department men maintained a discreet silence and made no effort to influence my judgment in the selection. When we left the Army officer and returned to our embassy, one of the State Department officers said to me, "Do you want him?" I said, "No, get somebody else. We've got General de Gaulle making a fresh start with a new President of the United States, so let's get a new face in the interpreter's chair, too." The State Department men heaved a collective sigh of relief, and expressed fervent thanks to God, or words to that effect. It seems that the Army's favorite interpreter had been doing all of the talking at Eisenhower's meetings with De Gaulle, while Ike and De Gaulle sat and listened to him. "Eisenhower would make a brief remark," one of the embassy officials said, "and then this fellow would turn to De Gaulle and talk to him in French for twenty minutes. Then De Gaulle would say something in French to the interpreter, and the interpreter would go into another long dissertation in French. The whole conversation would be between De Gaulle and the interpreter, with Eisenhower looking out the window." We heard later that De Gaulle was very amused when he saw that Kennedy had engaged a new interpreter.

The trip to Europe was a painful physical ordeal for the President. Shortly before he went to Paris, he paid a visit to Canada, where he dislocated the maimed muscles at the base of his spine while planting a ceremonial tree on the lawn of the capital at Ottawa. Once again, for the first time since his spinal fusion surgery in 1954, he needed crutches to walk, but, of course, he refused to appear in public on the European tour with crutches. The crowds of people who admired the erect and smiling young President in Paris and Vienna, and De Gaulle and Khrushchev, who found him always cheerful and relaxed at their long private meetings, never suspected that he was in constant excruciating pain.

When the President had a free few minutes in the busy round of meetings, lunches, receptions and dinners, he would hurriedly soak himself in a tub of steaming hot water to give his throbbing back some relief. On the morning when he and Jackie arrived in Paris, and more than a million people lined the streets to see them, he could hardly wait long enough to get his clothes off before climbing into the huge bathtub in the palatial apartment at the Quai d'Orsay where the French government puts up its visiting dignitaries. The bathtub was plated with gold and about as wide and long as a Ping-Pong table. "God, we ought to have a tub like this in the White House," the President said. Dave suggested that if he played his cards right with De Gaulle, he might take home the gold tub as a souvenir.

The apartment at the Quai d'Orsay where the President stayed was called "The King's Chamber." It had a large sitting room and a huge bedroom and then another bedroom, evidently for the King's knights-in-waiting, off the King's bedroom, where Dave and I slept. Jackie had another apartment about the same size across the hall, where the bathtub was silver instead of gold. The only trouble with the arrangement, as Dave and I quickly noted, was that we had to walk through the President's bedroom to get to our bedroom from the front hallway. But Dave soon discovered that there was a back door from our room to a flight of back stairs leading down to the service entrance of the building, which, he assured me, could be used after the President retired for the night.

That first day in Paris all of us in the President's party were invited to an official luncheon at the Elysée Palace, where General de Gaulle was so busy talking in French with Jackie about the history of France that he hardly touched the magnificent food. He turned to the President and said, "Your wife knows more French history than any Frenchwoman." Then he turned back to Jackie and did not take his eyes off her for the rest of the meal. The President was taking in Jackie's success with a satisfied smile, not missing the obvious chagrin of Madame Herve Alphand, the wife of the French Ambassador to the United States and supposedly the most chic and attractive lady in the government set, who was trying hard to win some attention and finishing a poor second. All of the Frenchmen in the room, like De Gaulle, were staring at Jackie and saying to each other, "Well, after all, she's French, isn't she?" That afternoon, when the President hurried from another private session with the General to plunge again into the golden tub, he said to us, "De Gaulle and I are hitting it off all right, probably because I have such a charming wife."

That night we went to a spectacular formal dinner for the Kennedys at the Elysée where Jackie was again the hit of the show. Each of us was announced by a majordomo in knee-length breeches before we passed along the receiving line and were escorted to a table. When Powers appeared at the head of the stairs, the announcer called out in his booming voice, "Monsieur Law-Poor!" Jackie was convulsed, and the President was startled. As Dave came to the Kennedys in the receiving line, the President said to him, "What was the big idea of telling that guy you were Peter Lawford? Everybody knows you don't look like Lawford."

"He didn't say Lawford," Dave explained. "You don't understand French. He said Le Peur, which means Powers in French. I figured it would sound better if you didn't have too many Irish names in your party."

After the dinner, Dave persuaded Pierre Salinger and me to compare a few of the cafés in Paris with the taverns in Boston and Charlestown. "Don't worry about coming back late to our little room at the Quai d'Orsay," he told me. "We can sneak up the back stairs." When he arrived at the back stairs around three o'clock, we found it guarded by two of the French secret service agents, who did not recognize us. To get to our bedroom, we had to go in through the front hall and crawl through the President's bedroom on our hands and knees. Such are the problems behind the scenes at a summit conference.

The President's widely quoted remark at a press conference, describing himself as "the man who accompanied Jacqueline Kennedy to Paris," was not meant lightly. Privately he gave Jackie credit for establishing an easy and intimate understanding between himself and De Gaulle, and it was obvious to everybody in Paris that week that her charm and style gave the French people as a whole a warmer feeling for America than they had shown during the previous postwar years. Kennedy had been warned that De Gaulle would be distant and difficult to reach. The General's strained wartime relationship with Roosevelt and Eisenhower made him suspicious of American Presidents, and, as Kennedy fully appreciated, he regarded the NATO alliance as a plot by the United States and Britain to undermine France's independence. But De Gaulle was captivated by Jackie's knowledge and interest in France, and by her fluency in the subtleties of his language. Acting as his interpreter, she drew him into long and entertaining conversations with her husband that probably made him more relaxed with Kennedy than he had ever been with another head of a foreign government.

De Gaulle, as a historical celebrity, naturally fascinated Kennedy. During the few days they spent together, Kennedy asked him a great many personal questions about his past experiences and his opinions of Adenauer, Khrushchev and Macmillan. De Gaulle answered with a frankness that astonished the French experts in our State Department. After a talk with De Gaulle — and later in Vienna after his talks with Khrushchev — Kennedy would rush into his bathtub to ease the pain in his back. While he soaked in the hot water, he would give Dave and me an instant replay of his latest conversation. Looking back on that European journey now, it seems as though I spent practically all of my time in Paris in the bathroom at the Quai d'Orsay's King's Chamber, and a great deal of our two days in Vienna in the bathroom at the American Embassy residence, listening to tub talk, as Dave and I called it, but despite the steam that I had to inhale with it, the talk was always interesting.

Kennedy lost no time asking De Gaulle if Churchill was a better statesman than Franklin Roosevelt. Both of them, De Gaulle said, were great wartime leaders, but they had been outfoxed by Stalin at Yalta. "Churchill was impossible at times, and I fought with him constantly, but I liked him," De Gaulle told Kennedy. "I had no disagreements with Roosevelt but I never liked him." The President of France, never an admirer of the British, went on to claim that Britain never had an outstanding Prime Minister in modern times who was a pure-blooded Englishman. "Disraeli was a Jew," he said. "Lloyd George was a Welshman. Churchill and Macmillan had American mothers."

De Gaulle regarded Khrushchev as a bluffer, and advised Kennedy not to be intimidated by his threat to seize West Berlin. "Khrushchev will tell you," De Gaulle said, "that he is going to sign a separate treaty with East Germany within the next six months, breaking our Potsdam agreement and driving us out of Berlin. He's been saying that for three years. When the six months are up, he postpones the treaty with East Germany for another six months, and then another six months. He'll never sign that treaty because Russia does not want a war."

De Gaulle and Kennedy agreed that the three Western powers and Russia had created an impossible situation for themselves at the Potsdam conference in 1945 when they divided Berlin, surrounded by Soviet territory, into Communist and anti-Communist zones with the understanding that the city would eventually become the capital again of a reunified Germany. It soon became obvious that the Soviets would never permit East Germany to reunite with West Germany. The Americans, British and French could not pull out of West Berlin without breaking the Potsdam agreement and betraying our West German allies. Such a sellout to the Russians, Kennedy and De Gaulle firmly agreed, was unthinkable, so our rights in West Berlin would have to be defended by military force. De Gaulle pointed out, and Kennedy reluctantly agreed with him, that we could never defend ourselves in Berlin, completely surrounded by Soviet troops, if we limited our use of force to nonnuclear conventional combat. A military move by the Russians in Berlin could only be stopped by a nuclear attack on the Soviet Union. Khrushchev realizes that only too well, De Gaulle told Kennedy, and you must not let him forget it.

"So we're stuck in a ridiculous situation," Kennedy said in the tub at the Quai d'Orsay. "It seems silly for us to be facing an atomic war over a treaty preserving Berlin as the future capital of a reunified Germany when all of us know that Germany will probably never be reunified. But we're committed to that agreement, and so are the Russians, so we can't let them back out of it."

The only area of disagreement in Kennedy's talks with De Gaulle was the General's insistence that France must have nuclear power of its own. "You can't blame him for wanting France to be as strong as the other world powers," Kennedy said to us later. "But I had to argue against him. Too many of us have nuclear power as it is." De Gaulle argued that France needed nuclear weapons because the United States would be reluctant to strike the first blow if Russia threatened war against Western Europe. Kennedy promised him that if the Soviets prepared an attack on France and its neighbors, the United States would not hesitate to hit the first blow in the war. If it came to such a crisis, Kennedy said, the United States would defend Western Europe as quickly as it would defend North America. "I know you mean that," De Gaulle said, but he added that he still wanted nuclear power of his own, just in case.

The talks in Paris ended with a firm handshake, much warmer and more mutually friendly than either our State Department or the French Foreign Office had expected. De Gaulle said good-bye to Kennedy calling him "Mon ami," and assuring him that "I now have more confidence in your country." Obviously De Gaulle looked on Kennedy with a respect that he could not quite feel for Eisenhower, whom he linked with the British and NATO. He backed Kennedy strongly during the later Cuban crisis, and talked about coming to the United States to visit the President and Jackie in the spring of 1964. Ambassador Alphand suggested that De Gaulle could get together with Kennedy at Palm Beach. "That would be showing him the worst side of American life," Kennedy said. "We'll bring him to Cape Cod."

Kennedy could not take his eyes off Khrushchev when they met for the first time. Watching the President study the stubby little

Soviet leader when they shook hands and posed for news photographers on the steps of the American Embassy at Vienna that Saturday afternoon, I wished that I had a movie camera to preserve the whole scene. Kennedy gave Khrushchev the same greeting that he gave to voters in Sheboygan and South Boston, "How are you? I'm glad to see you." Then Kennedy forgot about the cameramen who were crowding around the two men, pleading for one more handshake, and, instead of posing for pictures, he stepped back and looked Khrushchev over from head to feet, for what seemed like five minutes. Khrushchev began to get uncomfortable, glanced at Kennedy a couple of times, tried to smile for the cameras, and muttered something in Russian to Andrei Gromyko, who was standing beside him. The Soviet Ambassador to Washington, Mikhail Menshikov, stepped on Dean Rusk's foot and jumped back, apologizing to Rusk. Kennedy, with his hands in the pockets of his jacket, continued to stare at Khrushchev, not unpleasantly, but, with that deep curiosity of his, sizing him up.

Later I remarked to the President that he had given Khrushchev quite an eyeballing. "After all the studying and talking I've done on him in the last few weeks," he said, "you can't blame me for being interested in getting a look at him." Before Kennedy came to Vienna, he had read all of Khrushchev's writings and speeches and every available bit of material on him in Washington, including the minutes of his previous talks with Eisenhower, and he had talked with nearly every American official who had met the Soviet leader. I asked Kennedy if Khrushchev in the flesh was much different from what he had expected.

"Not at all," he said. "Maybe a little more unreasonable. From what I read and from what people told me, I expected him to be smart and tough. He would have to be smart and tough to work his way to the top in a government like that one."

When Kennedy led Khrushchev into the embassy for the first of their talks, he introduced the Premier to members of his party. All of the other Americans in our group gave Khrushchev a polite smile when they shook his hand, but I looked him straight in the eye with a cold stare and no smile, which amused Kennedy. "My God, you didn't have to act that tough with him," the President said to me afterwards. "He must have thought you were a spy from the IRA." Hugh Sidey, who was then covering the White House for *Time* and

Life, said that the President told him later that I had given Khrushchev the coldest look he had gotten in Vienna, and Kennedy had then added, "Maybe we'd get along better with the Russians if we didn't smile at them so damned much."

We had arrived that morning in Vienna in a downpour of rain, but a huge crowd of Austrians had turned out to give Jackie and the President a wild welcome when our motorcade made its way through the streets from the airport to the Alte Hofburg, the Austrian White House, where the Kennedys were received by President Adolf Scharf. The Austrians told us that the Kennedys drew a much bigger and warmer crowd in the rain than Khrushchev had attracted when he came into the city by train and in bright sunshine the day before. This contrast in the welcomes might have contributed to the tough show of belligerence that Khrushchev displayed in his private talks with Kennedy. I could imagine Khrushchev saying to himself, the crowds love him and his pretty wife because they are so young and handsome, but wait until I get him alone.

The first talk at the American Embassy started with some bantering between the President and the Premier. Khrushchev reminded the group that he had met Kennedy before, in 1959, at a meeting of the Senate Foreign Relations Committee in Washington. "I remember you said that I looked young to be a Senator," Kennedy remarked, "but I've aged a lot since then." Khrushchev said that he had seen to it that Nixon had lost the Presidential election in 1960 by refusing to release Gary Powers, the imprisoned U-2 pilot, before the election. If Khrushchev had released Powers before the election, he said, Kennedy would have lost the Presidency by at least 200,000 votes. "Don't spread that story around," Kennedy said to Khrushchev. "If you tell everybody that you like me better than Nixon, I'll be ruined at home." Later, Khrushchev asked Kennedy how he got along with Gromyko. "All right," Kennedy said. "My wife thinks he has a nice smile. Why do you ask?"

"Well," Khrushchev said, while Gromyko squirmed, "a lot of people think that Gromyko looks like Nixon."

But when the conversation moved into serious channels, Khrushchev began to get rough and blustery. "He is no slouch in an argument," Kennedy told us later. "When I complained about his support of Communist minorities fighting popular majorities, he came back at me with our support of Franco and Chiang Kai-shek."

But those of us who were with Kennedy during the Vienna talks — and that includes the principal American advisers, such as Rusk, Llewellyn Thompson, Charles Bohlen and Foy Kohler, who sat in on the conversations — have no recollection of the President being cowed or overpowered by Khrushchev's fist-waving as some of the recent Kennedy-downgraders now claim. In every exchange of hard shots, Kennedy gave as good, and often better, than he received. Khrushchev himself said later that he came away from Vienna with a respect for Kennedy's reasoning and firmness. "Unlike Eisenhower," Khrushchev said in his memoirs, "Kennedy had a precisely formulated opinion on every subject."

Khrushchev was often backed into a corner where he had no choice but to change the subject. Kennedy's intensive study of previous American-Russian discussions and his own debating skill made him well prepared to handle Khrushchev's thrusts. At one point Khrushchev complained because he had not been invited to sign the Japanese peace treaty. "You went over that at length with President Eisenhower in 1959," Kennedy said. "Why bring it up again? It's an old issue." Khrushchev drew back in surprise and switched to another question. When Khrushchev was demanding a withdrawal of Allied troops from Germany, he pointed out that Roosevelt had promised at Yalta to make such a withdrawal within two to four years after the end of World War II. "President Roosevelt said we would withdraw our troops if Germany was reunited under one government," Kennedy said. No further argument.

At another point in a heated debate, Kennedy said, "Do you ever admit a mistake?"

"Certainly," Khrushchev said. "In a speech before the Twentieth Party Congress, I admitted all of Stalin's mistakes."

"Those were Stalin's mistakes," Kennedy said. "Not your mistakes."

In the first day's talk, Kennedy made a reference to the danger of a miscalculation by Russia that might set off a war. "Khrushchev went berserk," Kennedy said later, while recalling the scene in the embassy's bathtub. "He started yelling, 'Miscalculation! Miscalculation! Miscalculation! All I ever hear from your people and your news correspondents and your friends in Europe and everyplace else is that damned word, miscalculation! You ought to take that word and bury it in cold storage and never use it again! I'm sick of it!'"

Kennedy paused thoughtfully for a moment, and then added, "So I'm trying to remind myself, the next time I'm talking to Khrushchev, don't mention 'miscalculation.'"

It was at lunch that day that Kennedy made his remark about the Lenin peace medal that Khrushchev was wearing: "I hope you get to keep it." After the luncheon, Kennedy and Khrushchev went outside for a walk in the garden, alone except for their two interpreters. Dave and I watched them from the window of our room on the second floor of the embassy, while we drank a couple of bottles of Austrian beer. Again I wished that I had a movie camera. Khrushchev was carrying on a heated argument, circling around Kennedy and snapping at him like a terrier and shaking his finger, while Kennedy strolled casually on the lawn, stopping now and then to say a few words, not at all upset or angry.

Later while the President was soaking his sore back in the tub, Dave told him that we had watched the scene in the garden and said, "You seemed pretty calm while he was giving you a hard time out there."

"What did you expect me to do?" Kennedy said. "Take off one of my shoes and hit him over the head with it?"

Khrushchev had been complaining in the garden about the Berlin situation and the American support of a reunified Germany. He had no sympathy for Germany, he said, because his son was killed in the war by the Germans. "I reminded him that my brother had died in the war, too," Kennedy told us, "and I also reminded him that we didn't come here to Vienna to talk about a war of twenty years ago. I told him that we can't turn our backs on the West Germans and pull out of Berlin, and that's that. But he keeps on yelling about signing a separate treaty with East Germany, just as De Gaulle said he would threaten to do."

When the formal talks resumed that Saturday afternoon, Khrushchev gave in quickly and easily on the Laos problem, agreeing to a cease-fire in the war there between the Communists and the government troops. "I thought he would use Laos to give himself more leverage against us in Berlin, as he could have done," Kennedy said later. But Khrushchev refused to budge on the Berlin issue and on Kennedy's request for a nuclear test ban. Urging the test ban, Kennedy used the Chinese proverb, "A journey of a thousand miles begins with one step."

"You seem to know the Chinese very well," Khrushchev said.

"We may both get to know them better," Kennedy said.

Khrushchev groaned, and said, "I know them well enough now."

That night at the Austrian President's state dinner at the Schonbrunn Palace, Khrushchev sat next to Jackie Kennedy and joked with her all evening. On Sunday morning the Kennedys went to a nine o'clock mass at Saint Stephan's Cathedral, where they listened to the Vienna Boys' Choir, and an hour later the President went to the Soviet Embassy for the last of his scheduled meetings with Khrushchev. Their talk was so unsatisfactory that Kennedy asked for one more session alone with Khrushchev after lunch. "I can't leave here without giving it one more try," he said.

That afternoon in their last private talk together Khrushchev flatly threatened Kennedy with war if the United States insisted on defending its rights in West Berlin after Russia signed a separate treaty with East Germany, which, he said, would take place in December of that year, six months away. All of Berlin would then become East German territory, and if the Western Allies did not withdraw their troops from the city before that deadline, "force would be met with force." The only concession that Khrushchev tentatively offered was one that he knew Kennedy could not accept: the Russians and East Germans might agree to let a small token force of American and Western European troops remain in West Berlin, not as occupation forces but as a part of a United Nations police force along with an equal number of Soviet military units. But, Khrushchev shouted, his decision to sign the treaty allowing East Germany to seize West Berlin in December was "firm" and "irrevocable" and "you can tell that to Macmillan, De Gaulle and Adenauer, and if that means war, the Soviet Union will accept the challenge."

Kennedy looked at Khrushchev calmly and said to him, "It's going to be a cold winter."

A few minutes later when Kennedy and Rusk were leaving the Soviet Embassy and the President and the Premier posed before the photographers with a final handshake, Khrushchev was his old merry self again, laughing and joking, but Kennedy was not smiling. I would describe the President's mood when he returned to the American Embassy that afternoon as cool and controlled, not at all rattled or discouraged by Khrushchev's attempt to bully him, the impression that he gave to Scotty Reston in an interview at the time which was picked up and exaggerated by other correspondents. When we were getting ready to go to the airport, I told him that Reston wanted to see him, and that we had enough time to sneak Scotty upstairs to his room if he was agreeable.

"That might be a good idea," Kennedy said. "I'd like to get across to the people at home the seriousness of the situation, and the *New York Times* would be the place to do it. I'll give Scotty a grim picture. But actually, as De Gaulle says, Khrushchev is bluffing and he'll never sign that treaty. Anybody who talks the way he did today, and really means it, would be crazy, and I'm sure he's not crazy."

The picture that Kennedy gave Reston must have been grim indeed. When Scotty came out of the room, he said to me, "He seems very gloomy."

I said, "Did you expect him to be dancing a jig?"

Reston's story in the *New York Times* described Kennedy as "shaken" and "angry." He was certainly angry with Khrushchev's attitude and with the situation that Khrushchev was creating, but if he felt any panic, he kept it well concealed. That night on the plane, while we were flying from Vienna to London, he called me into his cabin and talked with me alone for more than an hour about what he had been through with Khrushchev over the past two days, and about the danger of a possible war with Russia that he would be facing in the months to come. This was a most unusual thing for President Kennedy to do. He seldom revealed his deep feelings or talked about them at any length. In a serious conversation about an important decision or a course of action, he usually seemed to be thinking of many things that he never mentioned. On the flight from Vienna that Sunday night, however, he was in the mood to talk freely about the many questions and doubts concerning the Berlin crisis that were troubling him, as if talking about them would help him to weigh them and put them into order in his mind. Why he decided to talk to me alone, instead of to some of the State Department brass and experts on Soviet affairs who were on the plane, I don't know, except that perhaps he wanted to unburden himself without anything that he said going beyond the closed cabin door.

Uppermost in his mind that night, and during the months of

tension in our dealings with Khrushchev that followed over the next year, was the disproportion between cause and effect in allowing a dispute over questionable West German rights to Berlin to start a nuclear world war. "All wars start from stupidity," Kennedy said. "God knows I'm not an isolationist, but it seems particularly stupid to risk killing a million Americans over an argument about access rights on an Autobahn in the Soviet zone of Germany, or because the Germans want Germany reunified. If I'm going to threaten Russia with a nuclear war, it will have to be for much bigger and more important reasons than that. Before I back Khrushchev against the wall and put him to a final test, the freedom of all of Western Europe will have to be at stake."

The issue in Berlin was never as simple and clear-cut to Kennedy as it was to such extremely anti-Soviet hard-liners as Dean Acheson and John Foster Dulles, who had backed the West German government's claim to the old capital city as a move toward winning the East Germans away from Communism. Kennedy honored our commitment in West Berlin as a pledge that never could be broken, because he felt that pulling out of the city would turn West Germany against the United States and Britain, and lead to a breakup of the NATO alliance. At the same time he was realistic enough to see the hope of a reunited East and West Germany as an impossible dream, and he could understand Russia's dissatisfaction with the continued presence of Western occupation forces and a pocket of Western free enterprise economy in Berlin, deep in the heart of Communist German territory. The real reason why Khrushchev wanted to seize and seal off West Berlin, Kennedy said that night — and Khrushchev himself later frankly admitted in his memoirs — was an economic one. The Soviet leader wanted to shut down West Berlin's thriving capitalistic business system, which was luring thousands of job-hungry East Germans from the socialist side of the city and seriously draining East Germany's manpower. "You can't blame Khrushchev for being sore about that," Kennedy said.

There were also certain aspects of our relationship with Konrad Adenauer and his West German government that irked Kennedy. Adenauer was blocking American and British efforts to work out a peaceful settlement of the Berlin problem, and there were constant complaints from the Bonn government that the United States was not taking a firm enough military stand against Khrushchev.

"So there are many sides to this whole mess," Kennedy said. "We didn't cause the disunity in Germany. We aren't really responsible for the four-power occupation of West Berlin, a mistake that neither we nor the Russians should have agreed to in the first place. But now the West Germans would like us to drive the Russians out of East Germany. It's not enough for us to be spending a tremendous amount of money on the military defense of Western Europe, and particularly on the defense of West Germany, while West Germany becomes the fastest growing industrial power in the world. Well, if they think we are rushing into a war over Berlin, except as a last desperate move to save the NATO alliance, they've got another think coming."

Again Kennedy expressed strong doubt that Khrushchev, for all his shouting, would ever actually sign a separate treaty with East Germany. But we would have to be careful in the months to come, he added, not to make a sudden military move or a quick buildup of force that might alarm Khrushchev into making a rash countermove. I particularly remember Kennedy's closing remark when the plane was descending for its landing in London. "If we're going to have to start a nuclear war," he said, "we'll have to fix things so it will be started by the President of the United States, and nobody else. Not by a trigger-happy sergeant on a truck convoy at a checkpoint in East Germany."

Even though Kennedy's meeting with Khrushchev in Vienna ended in flat disagreement on the two big issues, Berlin and nuclear testing, both of them gained an understanding and a respect for each other during the talks that served the United States and Russia well in the later crisis periods. As annoyed as he was at times with Khrushchev over the next two years, Kennedy often found him more reasonable than some of our allies. It was obvious in their later correspondence that Khrushchev had a strong personal admiration for Kennedy. His first letter to the President after their rough farewell session in Vienna sounded as if he was anxious to assure Kennedy that his threats at the conference table should not be taken too seriously:

Dear Mr. President,

In Vienna, you told me that you are fond of collecting models of vessels. It is with pleasure that I am sending you a model of an

American whaler of which I told you during one of our conversations. This model made of walrus tusk and whalebone was carved from memory by a talented, self-taught Chuktchi craftsman. Such sail-steam vessels were in use in the end of the 19th century in the Chuktchi Sea for whale-fishing and they would visit Russian harbors. I will be glad if the model of this vessel becomes part of your collection.

It is also a pleasure for Nina Petrovna and myself to fulfill Mrs. Kennedy's wish and to send to you and your family little "Pushinka," a direct offspring of the well known cosmos-traveler "Strelka," which made a trip in a cosmic ship on August 19, 1960, and successfully returned to earth.

I would like to express my hope that the model of the vessel and "Pushinka" will be of pleasure to you and will serve as a good remembrance of our meetings and conversations in Vienna.

I avail myself of this opportunity to extend on behalf of Nina Petrovna and myself our best wishes to you, your wife and all your family.

Yours respectfully,
N. KHRUSHCHEV

Dave and I happened to be with the President and Jackie in their apartment in the White House on the day when the Soviet Ambassador and two of his staff men appeared with the ship model and Pushinka, a nervous and white fluffy puppy, and a daughter of the dog that traveled into outer space on the second Soviet Sputnik flight. The President stared at the dog and then stared at Jackie, who put her hand to her mouth and whispered, "I was only trying to make some conversation." It seems that at the state dinner in Vienna she had asked Khrushchev about the space-flying dog, and when he said that the dog recently had pups, she said, "Why don't you send me one?" In due time, Pushinka made herself at home in the White House and became a pampered member of the family.

The summer the growing crisis in Berlin and the urgent question of how to cope with Khrushchev took up almost all of the President's working hours, and in the evenings at the White House, when Jackie and the children were at Cape Cod, he continued to discuss and study the problem with advisers until a late hour. He was definitely committed to a firm stand against Khrushchev, but how firm and how threatening that stand should be depended on how dangerous Khrushchev's intentions really were, and that was a hotly debated question in the White House. Kennedy liked to sit back and listen to a strenuous argument between two opposing points of view before making up his own mind on which course to follow. To get a hard-line opinion on the Berlin situation, he brought Dean Acheson to Washington for temporary duty on the White House staff. For a more moderate view, the President leaned heavily on the advice of Llewellyn Thompson, who returned from his post as Ambassador in Moscow to sit in on the discussions. Kennedy felt that Thompson knew Khrushchev personally better than anybody in the government.

Acheson argued that Khrushchev was using Berlin as an excuse to draw the United States into a showdown test of its leadership as a world power. Instead of trying to negotiate a political arrangement with the Soviets, Acheson wanted the President to declare a national emergency, calling for an immediate buildup of armed forces and nuclear weapons, wage and price controls, a big increase in the defense budget and higher taxes. This was the only way to show Khrushchev that we were ready to go to war to protect the free world against Communism, he contended, and the only move that would make the Soviets back down.

Kissinger and Thompson both doubted that Khrushchev was challenging the United States to a battle for world power. They felt that the Soviet leader was making an issue over the Berlin situation and his threat to sign a treaty with East Germany only to bolster Soviet prestige in Eastern Europe. To rule out political negotiation, they argued, would be a serious mistake on our part. Thompson pointed out that Khrushchev's offer at Vienna to let Western powers maintain police forces in West Berlin under United Nations supervision showed that he was more concerned with local face-saving than with driving the United States into a nuclear confrontation. Kissinger and Thompson contended that a declaration of a national military emergency would make us seem hysterical, and might force Khrushchev into a rash countermove that he really did not want to make. We should build up our military forces, they agreed, but not too suddenly or sensationally.

The President favored the Kissinger-Thompson view that Khrushchev should not be pushed too hard. "But we've got to make some moves and still leave the door open for negotiations," he said. "That guy doesn't pay much attention to speeches. He has to see you make a move." On July 25, the President made a televised speech to the nation, declaring that we would never be driven out of Berlin but not mentioning any emergency. He asked for a 3.25 billion dollar increase in the defense budget, new weapons, a calling-up of some reserve and National Guard units and an enlarged civil defense program. At the same time, he invited consideration of any agreement in Germany consistent with maintaining peace and freedom, and warned both sides against a misjudgment that could bring about a nuclear devastation. It was while he was preparing his speech on the Berlin crisis that Kennedy quietly dismissed Bobby's Spartan belt-tightening proposal of an income tax raise.

Then, on August 13, the East Germans built the Berlin Wall. It was said and written at the time that the building of the wall shocked and depressed Kennedy. Actually, he saw the wall as the turning point that would lead to the end of the Berlin crisis. He said to me, "Why would Khrushchev put up a wall if he really intended to seize West Berlin? There wouldn't be any need of a wall if he occupied the whole city. This is his way out of his predicament. It's not a very nice solution, but a wall is a hell of a lot better than a war."

To reassure the excited West Berliners, Kennedy sent Lyndon Johnson to their city to wave the American flag and to make a fiery speech pledging our armed support to their freedom and independence. The Vice-President was not happy about making the trip, especially when he learned that the President had ordered a battle group of fifteen hundred American troops to move into West Berlin from Helmstedt in West Germany while he was there. "There'll be a lot of shooting, and I'll be in the middle of it," Lyndon said. "Why me?" It took some coaxing before he agreed, with a deep sigh, to undertake the mission.

But the convoy of American infantry soldiers moved along the Autobahn in East Germany into Berlin with no interference from the Soviet occupation troops. Johnson was waiting to greet them when they arrived, and his appearance in the city was a big success. He came back to Washington thrilled by the whole experience. When the Berlin Wall was built, Kennedy was attacked by some critics because he did not knock it down. I asked him later if anybody in the government had suggested such a move. "Not one person in the Defense Department or the State Department ever mentioned such an idea," he said. "What right did we have to touch that wall? It was in East German territory."

As Kennedy had predicted, the building of the wall brought the situation in Berlin down to a slow simmer, stemming the flow of refugees from East Germany, the immediate cause of Khrushchev's dissatisfaction. The Soviets tried to keep up the tension during the next few months by exploding a series of nuclear bombs, a move that made Kennedy furious, because Khrushchev had promised him in Vienna that he would make no further atomic tests unless the United States tested first, and because the Russian tests brought pressure to resume our testing, which the President had been trying to avoid. Kennedy and his advisers regarded the Soviet tests, however, as psychological threats rather than serious preparation for a nuclear war.

At the same time, Khrushchev tried to disrupt the United Nations organization by demanding after the death of Dag Hammarskjold that the Secretary General's office should be shared by a troika of three secretaries, one selected by the Western powers, one representing the Communists and one from the so-called neutral nations. Kennedy took a firm stand against the Russian proposal in a speech on September 25 to the United Nations General Assembly. He pointed out that a troika was the Russian term for a team of three horses pulling a wagon or sled. But the three horses in a Russian troika, he added, did not have three drivers, each wanting to drive the team in a different direction. "To install a triumvirate, or any panel or rotating authority, in the United Nations administrative offices," Kennedy said, "would replace order with anarchy, action with paralysis, confidence with confusion."

On a Friday evening in October Andrei Gromyko came to the White House for a long talk with the President on both the Berlin and United Nations problems. "This is really the first time since Vienna that they've wanted to talk," Kennedy said to us that afternoon. "It looks like a thaw." He brought Gromyko to the Oval Room in the second-floor living quarters of the mansion, which has a dazzling view from its Truman Balcony of the Washington Monument and the Jefferson Memorial. The President apologized because his wife was in Newport, visiting her mother. "Give her my best regards," Gromyko said.

The meeting lasted for more than two hours, first with a discussion of the well-known Berlin situation. Gromyko had nothing new to offer, but it seemed to Kennedy that the Russians were more resigned to accepting the status quo. Kennedy, smoking a cigar, did more listening than talking and made no concessions. When Gromyko brought up again Khrushchev's offer to let West Berlin become an international zone with a joint Western and Communist police force, Kennedy shook his head and said, "You're offering us an apple for an orchard."

Then Gromyko turned to the troika argument. Kennedy glanced at a book on the table beside his rocking chair, and picked it up as if it had just caught his eye. It was a book of Russian fables by Ivan Andreevich Krylov, the Russian Aesop, printed in the Russian language.

Earlier in the week Ted Reardon had brought a copy of the book to the President at the suggestion of Walter Besterman, a staff assistant to the House Judiciary Committee, who remembered Krylov's fables from his childhood in Poland. Besterman showed Ted a story in verse in the book which told of a comic troika, a swan, a crab and a fish, attempting to pull a wagon. In translation, the verse read:

> *When partners with each other don't agree*
> *Each project must a failure be,*
> *And out of it, no profit come but sheer vexation.*
> *A Swan, a Pike and Crab once took their station*
> *In harness, and would drag a loaded cart;*
> *But when the moment came for them to start,*
> *They sweat, they strain, and yet the cart stands still;*
> *What's lacking?*
> *The load must, as it seemed, have been but light;*
> *The Swan, though, to the clouds takes flight,*
> *The Pike into the water pulls, the Crab keeps backing.*
> *Now which of them was right, which wrong, concerns us not;*
> *The cart is still upon the selfsame spot.*

President Kennedy, of course, was overjoyed by the fable, and, after reading it, immediately called the Government Printing Office on the telephone himself and arranged to have several copies of the book reproduced and handsomely bound. He handed one of the deluxe editions to Gromyko, opened it to the fable of the swan, the pike and the crab, and watched Gromyko read it.

"It's a delightful little book," Kennedy said. "I want you and Mr. Khrushchev to share it as a gift. I have a special copy for you to bring to him and one for you, too."

Gromyko looked up from the book and began to laugh. He was still laughing when he stood up and shook hands with the President and walked out of the room with the two books under his arm. About ten days later, the Soviets announced that they were dropping their troika proposal and would offer no opposition to the selection of a single successor to Dag Hammarskjold, clearing the way for U Thant's election as Secretary General of the United Nations.

Around the same time, on October 21, Khrushchev told the Congress of the Soviet Communist party that he was not going to insist on signing a separate treaty with East Germany before the end of the year. Temporarily, at least, the Berlin crisis was over.

But after the tension subsided, our sensitive and vulnerable situation in Berlin remained constantly in President Kennedy's mind, especially when he was facing the Soviet missiles in Cuba a year later. If he made a strike against the missile bases in the Caribbean, it seemed almost certain that the Russians would retaliate in Germany, starting a nuclear world war. If he tried to avoid a confrontation with the Soviets in Cuba, Khrushchev would be likely to take this reluctance as a sign of American weakness or timidity, and feel free to seize West Berlin. After one of the Cuban crisis meetings, Sander Vanocur, who was then covering the White House for NBC, happened to walk through the empty Cabinet Room and noticed on the table in front of the President's chair a yellow legal pad on which he had been writing during the discussion, "Berlin . . . Berlin . . . Berlin . . . Berlin . . . Berlin . . ."

Yet despite the risk of nuclear world war from a repercussion in Berlin, President Kennedy challenged Khrushchev in Cuba with none of the nagging doubts and irritation that had worried him a year earlier after the talks in Vienna. Our outstanding memory of the two weeks of strained suspense in the White House during the Cuban missile crisis is the President's calmness and cool relaxation throughout that whole hectic period. The discovery of the Soviet offensive weapons in the Caribbean brought a kind of peace to his mind because now Khrushchev had crossed the Rubicon and the guessing game was over. There were no more questions about whether a risk of war was worth taking; the issue no longer concerned access rights to West Berlin or the defense of a non-Communist government in Laos. The Russians had placed in the Western Hemisphere nuclear medium- and intermediate-range missiles, capable of destroying Washington and New York; and the next move was up to the President of the United States. He was ready to make it with a clear and easy conscience. "If I don't do anything about removing those missiles from Cuba," he said to us at the time, "I ought to be impeached."

When the Soviet offensive missile installations in the San Cristobal area of Cuba were first photographed by two Air Force U-2 reconnaissance planes on Sunday, October 14, 1962, President Kennedy was on a campaign tour in the Midwest and upper New York state, speaking for Democratic candidates in that year's Congressional and state elections. There had been some disagreement among his advisers as to whether or not the President should take on a personal role in stumping for our candidates in that midterm campaign. Some of the White House staff people thought that he should remain aloof from party political fights while in office. The Irish partisan politicians in his circle, namely John Bailey, Dick Maguire and myself, felt that he was urgently needed in the off-year campaign because our party desperately needed to increase its slim majority in Congress. The President, who loved to campaign and mix with the crowds, required little or no urging from us when the time came to hit the trail. We were campaigning on the progress made on domestic problems during the Kennedy administration's first two years, the rise in employment and our need for more Democrats in Congress to push our social programs, particularly Medicare. The number one issue of the Republicans was the Soviet buildup of weapons and military aid in Cuba.

Senator Kenneth Keating, the New York Republican, and Senator Homer Capehart, who was running for reelection against the young Birch Bayh in Indiana, both claimed that the Soviets were turning Cuba into an offensive missile base. Keating contended that he had private proof that six intermediate-range ballistic-missile launching sites were under construction on the island under Russian supervision. But Keating refused to give the government his sources of information, or specific locations of the alleged installations, so the President assumed that the Republican Senator was using rumors or unsubstantiated or exaggerated reports from Cuban refugees in Florida to make political campaign propaganda.

Military intelligence officers in the Pentagon could find no basis for Keating's charges. It was well known to our observers that the Soviets had built at least eight defensive, or surface-to-air, antiaircraft missile bases in Cuba, but there was no evidence, before that mid-October Sunday, that any of the missiles on the island were offensive, surface-to-surface medium- or intermediate-range weapons, capable of reaching the United States. Our intelligence people strongly doubted that Khrushchev would ever take the risk of shipping offensive nuclear weapons to the Caribbean. Khrushchev had often boasted that if he wanted to launch a nuclear attack on the United States, he could do so from Poland or Hungary with long-range intercontinental missiles. Robert McNamara and the Joint Chiefs of Staff all assumed that the Soviets had such long-range missile capability, and that Khrushchev had no need to put medium- or intermediate-range missiles into Cuba, within shorter and easier striking distance of Washington and New York.

The big question that perplexed President Kennedy long after the Cuban missile crisis had been resolved was: Why did Khrushchev take the dangerous gamble of putting offensive nuclear weapons into Cuba? On the other hand, maybe the Defense Department's assumption that the Soviets had long-range intercontinental missile capability in 1962 was wrong. Colonel Oleg Penkovskiy, the Allied spy in Russia, reported at that time that Khrushchev's boasts of such capability was so much idle talk. According to Penkovskiy's information, which he claimed to have received from Soviet military sources, many of the big Russian missiles, designed to reach the United States from Eastern Europe, were still on the drawing board that year, or only in the prototype testing stage. If that report was accurate, Khrushchev was forced to take the risk of putting his workable shorter-range missiles into Cuba in order to be able to defend himself against the United States in the event of a nuclear war. Khrushchev's own later explanation of why he sent the missiles to Cuba, which appeared in his memoirs in 1970, would have amused Kennedy. Khrushchev claimed that he never had any intention of firing the missiles. He said that he installed the nuclear weapons in Cuba only to frighten the United States into an agreement not to invade Castro's island. "This goal we achieved," he said, while admitting frankly that his later capitulation and removal of the missiles discredited him in the estimation of the Chinese Communists and the Cubans. Actually, of course, President Kennedy never had any intention of invading Cuba, but the installation of Soviet missiles there almost forced him to do so against his will.

President Kennedy never felt that the installation of the missiles really changed the balance of military power. He knew we possessed overwhelming military superiority. He viewed the Russian insanity with fear because it made no sense; it was a direct thrust at the credibility of the American position in NATO and, I think, most of all, an attempt to undermine a program which he held so dear, the bringing together of Latin America with the United States. As one who sat with him through the discussions from which emerged the Alliance for Progress, I know that he was sensitive to the wrongs of the past and dedicated to redressing them. To bow to the Soviets' intrusion would have been a tremendous psychological blow.

Whatever Khrushchev had in mind, the possibility of Soviet offensive missiles being installed in Cuba seemed so unlikely in the early days of October, 1962, that President Kennedy assumed that the charges of Keating and Capehart were merely Republican campaign talk. We had warm discussions on how he should answer their attacks. I argued that the whole question of whether Cuba was a menace to America's security should be completely ignored by the Democrats. I insisted that the average voter could not care less about what was going on in Cuba, and that full employment and Medicare mattered more to the people in Chicago and Pittsburgh than the debate about whether the Soviet missiles in the Caribbean were defensive or offensive in range. "I hope you're right," Kennedy said, "but I doubt it."

On the Sunday when the two U-2 planes photographed the offensive-missile sites near San Cristobal, the morning newspapers carried reports of Kennedy's campaign speech in Indianapolis the day before, ridiculing Capehart's demand for an immediate invasion of Cuba. "These self-appointed generals and admirals who want to send somebody else's son to war," the President said, "ought to be kept at home by the voters and replaced by somebody, like Birch

Bayh, who has some understanding of what the twentieth century is all about." He said to me later, "How did you like that one?" I remarked that he was being more vociferous than usual, but, if he insisted on stooping to reply to the Cuban charges, that was certainly the way to do it. We went on to Buffalo where a crowd of three hundred thousand cheering people greeted him at the Pulaski Day parade and a Polish-American audience of one hundred thousand listened to his nine-minute speech at City Hall, going wild when he shouted, "*Jeszeze Polska nie zginela* — Poland is not yet lost!" He was demagoguing on that campaign trip in a style that James M. Curley would have admired.

From Buffalo, we flew to New York for a meeting with Adlai Stevenson, and did not get back to Washington until close to two o'clock on Monday morning. All of us were exhausted from the barnstorming tour so there was not much work done that day, except for a luncheon and reception at the White House for Prime Minister Ben Bella of Algeria. That Monday night, the President had a quiet dinner with his father, who was visiting him that week, and went to bed early. The next morning, Tuesday, October 16, I was standing at my desk, waiting for the working day to begin and looking at the newspapers, when the President came out of his office and said to me, "You still think that fuss about Cuba is unimportant?"

"Absolutely," I said. "The voters won't give a damn about Cuba. You're wasting your time talking about it."

"You really think it doesn't amount to much?" he said.

"Not as a campaign issue," I said.

He beckoned to me to follow him into his office. "I want to show you something," he said.

On his desk there were enlarged prints of U-2 photographs, showing a clearing in a wooded area, with a few tents, trucks, trailers and scratchy markings around construction sites. He held a magnifying glass over one of the prints and said to me, "You're an old Air Force bombardier. You ought to know what this is. It's the beginning of a launching site for a medium-range ballistic missile."

I felt myself getting pale. "I don't believe it," I said.

"You'd better believe it," the President said. "It was taken Sunday, and checked and rechecked yesterday. We've just elected Capehart in Indiana, and Ken Keating will probably be the next President of the United States. Rearrange the schedule so we can have a meeting on this in the Cabinet Room at eleven-forty-five, and not a word to anybody about what it's all about. Stick to all the other appointments for the day. We want it to look as though nothing unusual is going on around here."

His coolness amazed me. That morning at nine-thirty he had a previously arranged meeting with Walter Schirra, the astronaut who had made a space flight a few days earlier. He received Schirra and his wife and two children, presented the youngsters with PT-109 tie clasps and bracelets, and took them outside and showed them Caroline's pony, Macaroni, as if he did not have a care on his mind. Later he calmly sat through a meeting of his White House Panel on Mental Retardation. Then, shortly before noon, he met in the Cabinet Room with a carefully limited number of officials and advisers, the only people in the government, outside of a few military commanders and intelligence experts, who shared the secret of the discovery of the missiles in Cuba until the President delivered his public ultimatum to Khrushchev a week later.

This discussion group, later referred to as the "Ex Comm," or the Executive Committee of the National Security Council, included, along with the President and the Vice-President, Secretary Dean Rusk, Under Secretary George Ball, Deputy Under Secretary U. Alexis Johnson, Latin-American Assistant Secretary Edward Martin and Llewellyn Thompson from the State Department; Secretary Robert McNamara, Deputy Secretary Roswell Gilpatric, Assistant Secretary Paul Nitze and General Maxwell Taylor, chairman of the Joint Chiefs of Staff, from the Defense Department; Attorney General Robert Kennedy, Secretary of the Treasury Douglas Dillon, John McCone and General Marshall S. Carter of the CIA, McGeorge Bundy, Ted Sorensen and myself from the White House staff. Dean Acheson, Adlai Stevenson and Robert Lovett attended some of the later meetings at the President's invitation, as did Don Wilson, deputy director of the U. S. Information Agency, substituting for the ailing Ed Murrow. Chip Bohlen sat in on the first day's session but, for appearances' sake, had to leave the next day for his new assignment as Ambassador to France.

Most of these men met daily during the crisis period, first to thrash out and argue over recommendations for a course of action for the President to select and follow, and later to discuss ways and means of meeting Khrushchev's countermoves and his replies to the

President's demands. The President himself did not attend all of the Ex Comm meetings, partly because he had to keep his official appointments and campaign engagements during the first week of secrecy in order to put on a show of ignorance for the Soviets. The President decided that the discussions were freer, less inhibited and more useful when he was not present to dominate the table. Dean Rusk was also forced to miss several meetings because prolonged absence from his other official duties would have aroused suspicion and lowered the veil of security, but he was always in close touch with what was going on and took part, along with the President, in the important decision-making after the preliminary arguments were fought out and various alternatives were recommended. Later insinuations by Rusk's critics that he avoided some meetings to dodge a role of responsibility during the crisis are both unfair and ridiculous.

Although my name was on the closely restricted Ex Comm list, I took no part in any of the strategy discussions and attended only those meetings at which the President was present. My assignment from the President was to watch and listen to the proceedings so that he could talk with me later about what had been said and compare his impressions and conclusions with mine. He wanted an observer in the room who would follow the various arguments more or less objectively, without becoming involved or committed to any point of view. Sitting in on those historic meetings, watching a group of men with high intelligence and impressive administrative and diplomatic experience groping for the first time with an enemy's armed threat against the United States, I was taken aback by the uncertainty that many of them showed under pressure, the inability of some to make a thoughtful judgment and stick to it, without changing their minds impulsively the next day. As much as I had admired President Kennedy over the previous years, I saw him in an entirely new light during the two weeks of the Cuban missile crisis meetings. Compared to many of the other committee members, he stood out as a rock of solid good sense and unwavering strength and firmness. Bobby and I often speculated later on what might have happened if one of the other Ex Comm members had been the President at that grim time. Bobby contended that at least six of the group would have provoked Khrushchev into a disastrous nuclear world war. On the other hand, Bobby would add, if somebody other than Khrushchev had been the Soviet leader, the world might have been blown up. Along with a deeper admiration for John F. Kennedy, the crisis meetings gave me many dark thoughts about what could happen if the wrong kind of President happened to be occupying the White House at a sensitive time in history.

President Kennedy himself said later that if we had been forced to make a quick decision on how to remove the missiles from Cuba, the chances of our selecting a wrong and disastrous course of action would have been much greater. The main point brought out by the CIA's photo-reading experts at that first Ex Comm meeting on Tuesday was that the missile launching sites appeared to be at least ten days away from completion, so we had almost a week for deliberation before deciding what to do. This allowance of time to consider and weigh the various alternatives enabled the President and Bobby, with the support of McNamara and Gilpatric, to bring the committee around to favoring a naval blockade of Cuba instead of an immediate air strike, which most of the members, including General Taylor, Nitze, Dillon, and Acheson, wanted at the start of the discussions. The idea of a naval blockade, which turned out eventually to be the saving solution of the crisis, was not even mentioned as a possible alternative at the first meeting on Tuesday morning. It did not begin to be considered until the committee met again for later discussions that evening, and it did not win substantial backing until Thursday and Friday. As late as the following Sunday, the day before the President appeared on television to announce the blockade and demand the removal of the missiles, he was still fighting opposition from Air Force leaders who were still urging an air strike. Undoubtedly, if the President had had to make a firm decision within twenty-four hours after the discovery of the missiles, he would have been under severe pressure to order a surprise attack on Cuba from the air, which would have had to be followed by an invasion. But the grace of a few more days that was given to him to consider other tactics allowed him time to work out the blockade plan, a strong and dramatic action against Khrushchev, but still a delaying move that enabled the Soviet leader to back away from the brink before the shots were fired.

At the first meeting on Tuesday, the President stressed the necessity for utmost secrecy while we were considering and agreeing upon a course of action because he had to make a militant and well-planned move which would surprise Khrushchev before the missile sites became operational. This ruled out a diplomatic or political approach, such as an appeal to the United Nations or our NATO allies, because by the time that we had made our complaints through diplomatic channels the work on the sites would have been completed and the missiles would be ready to be fired. Since surprise had to be the essence of our threat against the Soviets, it was agreed that the President had to keep up an appearance of business as usual until he was ready to deliver his ultimatum, and this meant that for the rest of the week, while the Ex Comm advisers were debating for a blockade versus an air strike or an invasion, and the U-2 planes were stepping up their photographic flights over Cuba, the President would be making campaign speeches in Connecticut and Illinois. And on Thursday, October 18, at five P.M., he would be having a previously arranged meeting at the White House with Andrei Gromyko, of all people.

The decision to have the President meet his political campaign commitments for the remainder of that tense week, at least, came as an immense relief to me. We had given Mayor Richard Daley our firm promise that the President would appear on Friday in Chicago to speak for Congressman Sid Yates, the Mayor's Democratic candidate in the Illinois Senatorial race that year against Everett Dirksen, the Republican leader in the Senate. There was much speculation in the press and in political circles about whether Kennedy might refrain from giving Yates his sincere support because Dirksen was friendly with the President and a cooperative and valuable, if quiet, supporter of the administration's programs in the Senate. Lyndon Johnson, a close crony of the silver-tongued Republican leader, was anxious to keep Dirksen in the Senate. One evening after we had given the President's commitment to Mayor Daley, and a week or so before the Cuban missile crisis arose, I was in the upstairs Oval Room in the White House with Kennedy and Johnson, who became involved in a serious conversation while I was talking with somebody on the telephone. The President said to me when I hung up the telephone, "Come over and listen to this — Lyndon's got a pretty good point here." The Vice-President delivered an impassioned speech on what a disaster it would be for the administration if Dirksen was defeated in Illinois and we had to deal with Tom Kuchel of California, who would then become the Republican leader in the Senate.

The President said to me, "What do you think of that?"

I was wondering what Dick Daley would say if he could hear this conversation. I said, "I wouldn't mind dealing with Tommy Kuchel every day in the week if I could knock off the Republican minority leader in the Senate in this election. Don't you two realize that would be quite a feather in your hat? Everett Dirksen is Mister Republican."

Johnson glared at me. Kennedy shook his head, laughed, and said, "Well, Kenny, this is one time when Lyndon is right and you're wrong. But I've got a commitment to go to Chicago and help Yates, and I've got to stick to my commitment."

It was Kennedy's admiration for Dick Daley that brought him to Chicago. The rumors persisted that the President would find an excuse at the last minute to cancel his appearance. We heard that Yates himself was making bets that Kennedy would not show up. I was getting telephone calls from everybody in Illinois, asking me if the President was trying to duck Yates. It became plainly apparent that if Kennedy failed to go to Chicago, even for the most pressing legitimate reason, there might be an explosion within the Democratic party. Then the missiles were discovered in Cuba.

At the first Ex Comm meeting, when the question of whether the President should continue his campaigning came up, I held my breath. Kennedy turned to me with his quizzical smile, and said, "Did you call off that trip to Chicago yet?"

"I didn't call off anything," I said. "I don't want to be the one who has to tell Dick Daley that you're not going out there."

The President laughed, along with several others at the table, and quickly assured me that the Chicago appointment would have to be kept as a security cover.

Later that day, keeping to his business-as-usual routine, the President spoke to a group of editorial writers and radio and television commentators who were attending a foreign policy conference at the State Department. He talked with far deeper feelings than any of his listeners suspected of the dangers of nuclear war. "I don't think it is unfair to say that the United States, and the world, is now passing through one of its most critical periods," he said. "Our major problem, over all, is the survival of our country, the protection of its vital interests, without the beginning of the third and perhaps the last war." He ended his talk with the recital of a verse, reflecting his very sharp feeling of lone responsibility at that moment, which the unknowing editors and commentators found rather amusing:

> *Bullfight critics row on row*
> *Crowd the enormous plaza full,*
> *But only one is there who knows,*
> *And he is the one who fights the bull*

The next morning, Wednesday, Bundy and McCone showed the President new and more definite photographic evidence from Cuba, which revealed some visible missiles and the construction of at least twenty-eight launching sites for both medium- and intermediate-range ballistic missiles. The medium-range missiles could travel one thousand miles, or as far as Washington or Saint Louis, and the intermediates, with a range of more than two thousand miles, could hit New York or Chicago with nuclear warheads four times more powerful than our Hiroshima bomb. The President told me later that morning that our intelligence people figured that the Soviets were building enough launching sites in Cuba to fire a single volley of missiles capable of killing eighty million Americans.

With this terrible burden on his mind, the President went to the Cabinet Room at ten o'clock and patiently sat through a meeting with the West German foreign affairs secretary, Dr. Gerhard Schroeder, that lasted for an hour and a half. Before going to a luncheon at the Libyan Embassy, given in his honor by the Crown Prince of Libya, the President took his usual noontime swim in the pool with Dave, and asked Dave to ride to the embassy with him. On the way they stopped at Saint Matthew's Cathedral. "We're going in here to say a prayer," the President said. Knowing nothing yet about the missiles in Cuba, Dave was surprised by the visit to the almost empty cathedral and the President enjoyed his perplexity. "Have you forgotten," he said, "that I proclaimed today as a National Day of Prayer? Right now we need all the prayers we can get." Kennedy was a more deeply religious man than he appeared to be, or wanted to appear to be.

That afternoon the President flew to Connecticut to campaign for Abe Ribicoff, who had left the Cabinet to run for the Senate in his home state. When he landed at the airport in Bridgeport, a crowd of more than ten thousand cheering people was waiting for him. He said to Dave happily, "My God, doesn't anybody have to work on Wednesday afternoons around here?" He drove from Bridgeport to Waterbury, where another crowd of fifty thousand was jammed into the city's square, bringing back memories of his late-night visit there before the 1960 election. "Waterbury either is the easiest city in the United States to draw a crowd in," he said in his speech for Ribicoff, "or it has the best Democrats. I'm coming back here to finish my campaign in 1964, just as I did in 1960." In New Haven, where he had received an honorary degree from Yale a few months before, he was booed by a few students. "I have enjoyed the warm reception I have gotten from my fellow Elis," he said, "but they will learn, as this country has learned, that the Democratic Party is best for them, as it is for the country."

While the President was campaigning in Connecticut, the Ex Comm group was having a heated session in George Ball's office in the State Department. The President had seen to it that the discussions of the Cuban missile crisis would not be as agreeable as the meetings before the Bay of Pigs invasion, when not a word of dissent was heard from anybody in the councils. The Ex Comm meetings had no presiding officer, no rules of order. Everybody was encouraged to speak out freely, regardless of his rank. Military officers disagreed violently with the Secretary of Defense and Under Secretaries clashed with Secretaries and with each other. That Wednesday, we heard later, Bobby Kennedy had it out loudly with Dean Acheson. Arguing in favor of the blockade, Bobby insisted, with a vehemence that startled most of the men in the room, that a surprise air attack on Cuba would be a Pearl Harbor–type deception that would blacken the reputation of the United States. "We're not going to make my brother the Tojo of the 1960s," he said. Acheson, the author of the sternly anti-Communist Truman Doctrine, denounced Bobby's comparison with Pearl Harbor as so much poppycock. The Monroe Doctrine and President Kennedy's repeated previous warnings in September that the United States would be forced to remove offensive missiles installed by the Soviets in Cuba, Acheson declared, were enough justification for an air strike. Bobby continued to hammer on the moral question of a sneak attack by a big nation on a small independent country, and his persistent crusading finally turned several members of the group from favoring the air strike. Among these converts were General Taylor, Douglas Dillon, Paul Nitze and McGeorge Bundy. "I had wanted an air strike," Dillon said later. "What changed my mind was Bobby Kennedy's argument that we ought to be true to ourselves as Americans, that surprise attack was not in our tradition. Frankly, these considerations had not occurred to me until Bobby raised them so eloquently."

Aside from the moral question, the President himself had practical and realistic doubts about using an air attack as the first step in forcing a removal of the missiles. First of all, he knew that a strike from the air would not destroy all of the missile bases, and it would certainly kill some of the Russians who were manning the sites. As Tommy Thompson pointed out, Russian deaths in Cuba would force Khrushchev into attacking the United States from the surviving missile bases that were still operable. An air strike would have to be followed by a troop invasion of Cuba, which would take a considerable amount of time to launch. A naval blockade seemed preferable as a first move, not only because it would give Khrushchev a chance to back off before any shots were fired, but because it could always be followed by a military attack if it failed to bring any results. The Air Force's argument, which the President conceded as valid, was that by the time the naval blockade had been tried and failed, the Soviet missiles would be ready to operate.

On Thursday morning, at an Ex Comm meeting that the President attended, General Curtis Le May, the tough Air Force Chief of Staff, argued strongly for an air strike as soon as possible.

"How will the Russians respond?" the President asked him.

Le May said that Russians would do nothing.

"Is that what you really think?" Kennedy said. "Are you trying to tell me that they'll let us bomb their missiles, and kill a lot of Russians, and then do nothing? If they don't do anything in Cuba, they'll certainly do something in Berlin."

After the meeting, the President said to me, "Can you imagine Le May saying a thing like that? These brass hats have one great advantage in their favor. If we listen to them, and do what they want us to do, none of us will be alive later to tell them that they were wrong."

Later on that Thursday afternoon, when Andrei Gromyko came to the White House for his previously arranged talk with the President, the possibility of a surprise air attack on the Soviet missile bases had not yet been definitely ruled out. Thus the President was forced to sit in his rocking chair and listen politely while Gromyko assured him with a straight face that the Soviets had no intention of putting offensive weapons into Cuba, and that the arms sent to Castro from Russia were only for defensive purposes. "I was dying to confront him with our evidence," Kennedy said later, but to do so at that time would have spoiled our chance to make the first surprise move which could catch Khrushchev at a disadvantage and reveal him to the world doing something that he was pretending not to be doing. If Kennedy had tipped his hand to Gromyko that Thursday, before he was ready with a plan to make a public demand for the removal of the missiles, the Russians could have come out first with an announcement of threats and demands, putting us in a defensive position.

So the President listened to Gromyko talk about Berlin, and the possibility of Russia signing a treaty with East Germany — ostensibly the reason for their meeting—and then go into a talk about Cuba's desire for peaceful coexistence. Meanwhile the President was fighting back the temptation to show the Soviet diplomat our photographs. Kennedy read aloud to Gromyko his September fourth warning that the United States would take action against an introduction into Cuba of offensive missiles. "In effect, I told him that there had better not be any ballistic missiles in Cuba," the President said that night. "And he told me that such a thought had never entered Khrushchev's mind. It was incredible to sit there and watch the lies coming out of his mouth."

The next morning when the President left Washington to make his scheduled campaign trip to Cleveland and Chicago, he had definitely made up his mind to start his action against Khrushchev with a naval blockade of Cuba, which he would announce on television to the world on the following Monday night. The blockade, he said, seemed to be a strong opening move with the least immediate danger of starting a war. Even though he had made his decision, he still wanted a consensus of support from the Ex Comm members. Before we went to the airport that Friday morning he told Bobby, "If you have any trouble, call me and I'll call off the trip and come back and talk to them."

I said to him, "What if you can't get a consensus?"

"I'll make my own decision anyway," the President said. "I'm the one who has the responsibility, so we'll do what I want to do." He told the story about Abraham Lincoln at his Cabinet meeting, saying, "All in favor vote 'Aye.'" The whole Cabinet voted aye, Lincoln voted no, and then announced that the no's had it.

"You'll probably have to cut the trip short," Kennedy said to me. "I'll make that speech in Chicago for Sid Yates and Dick Daley that you're worrying about, but I don't know about Wisconsin and the Seattle Fair." We were scheduled to fly to Milwaukee and the Pacific Coast after the President's appearance in Chicago.

At our first stop, Cleveland, the President made a fiery speech on domestic issues to a huge crowd in front of the Cleveland Sheraton Hotel. Then we flew to Springfield, Illinois, where the President placed a wreath at Lincoln's tomb and addressed another big crowd at the Illinois Fairground Coliseum with Sid Yates and Governor Otto Kerner and Senator Douglas at his side. When we checked into the Sheraton-Blackstone Hotel in Chicago, Pierre Salinger came to our suite to tell the President that Robert S. Allen and Paul Scott were coming out with a story in their Washington column about an invasion of Cuba, and Carleton Kent of the *Chicago Sun-Times* was asking about a report that a parachute unit had been alerted for a jump on Cuba.

Up until then, the security cover on the missile crisis had been amazingly tight, partly because the press had been distracted by the political campaign. Even Scotty Reston of the *New York Times*, whose sources of information in the government were more numerous and higher placed than those of most correspondents, did not begin to hear anything of what was going on until Saturday, five days after the discovery of the missiles. We had managed to keep Salinger in the dark, but it became obvious in Chicago that night that we would not be able to keep him there much longer. When Pierre reported the invasion rumors, I could see that the President was silently cursing the Joint Chiefs of Staff.

"Call Kent and tell him that report is all wrong," the President said to Pierre. "We have no plan to invade Cuba." He asked me to call McNamara and to have him ask Allen and Scott not to print their column, which I did. The President downed a bowl of oyster stew before going off with Mayor Daley and John Bailey, our national chairman, to make his big pitch for Sid Yates at a hundred-dollar-a-plate

Democratic dinner at McCormick Place. He asked me to stay in the hotel suite and keep in touch with Washington. Dave agreed to keep me company. After the President went to the dinner, Pierre returned, looking perplexed, trying to persuade me to let him in on what was going on.

"All I can tell you now," I said, "is that the President may have to develop a cold tomorrow. If he does, we'll have to cancel the rest of the trip and go back to Washington."

We had agreed on a story about a cold as a cover, and I had made arrangements with Dick O'Hare in Washington to cancel the remainder of the campaign trip on five minutes' notice if necessary, with no questions asked. I talked with Bobby, Rusk and Bundy that night on the telephone while we were waiting for the President to return from the dinner. There was nothing to be gained from rushing him back to Washington that night, but he would have to return early in the morning. Security was beginning to fall apart, there was still considerable opposition among the military people to the blockade, and the President's speech to the nation and the world, demanding the removal of the missiles, had to be written and approved before Monday. It was also necessary to round up the Congressional leaders, scattered throughout the country on recess and on campaigns, and to give them a secret briefing before the President made his announcement on the air. When the President came back to our hotel suite around ten-thirty, he called Bobby and agreed to return in the morning. He asked me to get in touch with Rear Admiral George G. Burkley, his White House physician who was accompanying us on the trip, to have him on hand in the morning to diagnose a cold.

When the President awoke the next day, a Saturday, we staged a scene with Admiral Burkley standing beside his bed, and summoned Pierre. "I have a temperature and a cold," Kennedy announced seriously to Salinger. "Tell the press I am returning to Washington on the advice of Doctor Burkley." When Pierre started to leave, Kennedy called him back and said to him, "Take this with you. We better make sure that all of us are saying the same thing." He reached for a telephone message pad, and wrote on it, "Slight upper respiratory. 1½ degree temperature. Weather raw & rainy. Recommended return to Washington. Cancelled schedule."

For the benefit of the reporters, the President boarded Air Force One that morning wearing a hat, the first time he had appeared in public with a head covering since he had worn a tall silk top hat at his inauguration. Nobody except an alert editor on the *Washington Post* noticed that Lyndon Johnson, who was campaigning that day in Hawaii, also interrupted his schedule and made a hurried return to Washington because he, too, was suddenly afflicted by a cold. The editor called Salinger and asked if it was an epidemic or a coincidence. Pierre made no comment.

That Saturday afternoon we had a meeting of the Ex Comm in the Oval Room, upstairs in the White House, where the President announced and discussed his decision to put the blockade into effect during the following week. Rusk, who had been for the air strike earlier, supported the President, and so did McNamara, who had been for the blockade all along. Cool and composed, the President made it plain that his mind was made up and that he had decided to take the most uncompromising action short of military attack — which could come later if necessary — to force Khrushchev to remove the missiles. Then Adlai Stevenson spoke out with an impressive show of lonely courage to question the President's refusal to compromise. If the removal of the Soviet missiles from Cuba was worth any price, Stevenson asked, why not offer in exchange for their removal a withdrawal of our Jupiter missiles from Turkey and the closing of our Naval base at Guantanamo Bay? Any such diplomatic bargain was worth considering, he said, if it would save the world from a nuclear war.

Stevenson was sharply criticized by Dillon, Lovett and McCone, and no doubt he would have been roughly manhandled by Dean Acheson if Acheson had been present at the meeting. Annoyed because the President disapproved the air strike proposal, Acheson had departed in a huff from the Ex Comm the day before and was sulking on his farm in Maryland. The President explained to Stevenson that he did not feel that any concessions should be made to the Russians in view of the deception that they had shown in sneaking the offensive missiles into Cuba while protesting that they had no intention of doing so. Furthermore, Kennedy added, making a trade for the Jupiter missiles would have a disrupting effect on the NATO alliance. De Gaulle would be quick to charge that the United States was selling out its friends in Europe in a deal to protect America's security.

When the meeting broke up, the President walked out on the

Truman Balcony with Bobby and me to talk with us about what had been said, particularly to talk about what Adlai had said. Bobby was furious with Stevenson for suggesting a compromise with Khrushchev. "He's not strong enough or tough enough to be representing us at the UN at a time like this," Bobby said to the President. "Why not get him out of there, and put somebody like John McCloy in his place?"

"Now wait a minute," the President said. "I think Adlai showed plenty of strength and courage, presenting that viewpoint at the risk of being called an appeaser. It was an argument that needed to be stated, but nobody else had the guts to do it. Maybe he went too far when he suggested giving up Guantanamo, but remember we're in a situation here that may cost us millions of lives, and we should be considering every side of it and every way to get out of it. I admire him for saying what he said."

The President was deeply upset and angry when Stewart Alsop and Charles Bartlett later wrote an article on the missile crisis meetings for the *Saturday Evening Post* which depicted Stevenson as seeking a "Munich" settlement with Khrushchev. Because Bartlett was a close personal friend of the Kennedys, it was assumed that the article had the President's approval, but it actually had his strong disapproval. I had never been much of an admirer of Stevenson up to that time, but it seemed to me, as it did to President Kennedy, that Adlai's readiness to take a stand at the Oval Room meeting in favor of a compromise offer was the kind of unselfish political courage seldom seen in Washington.

While he was talking on the balcony after the meeting, the President remarked that Stevenson had made a good point in emphasizing that a lot of foreign observers would question our right to remove the Soviet missiles from Cuba when we were maintaining our own Jupiter missiles in Turkey, close to the border of Russia. The ironic and irritating side of this question was that the Jupiter missiles were more or less useless to us militarily; the role of such land-based weapons had been taken over long ago by the more maneuverable submarine Polaris missiles. President Kennedy had asked repeatedly over the past year to have the Jupiters removed from Turkey, but the Turkish government, anxious to keep the American missile-base payrolls in their country, had pleaded against the closing of the bases, and our State Department had given in to the Turks' request. Now as we were moving against the Soviet missiles in Cuba, the Jupiter missiles were still in Turkey, an embarrassment to us, and a valuable propaganda weapon for Khrushchev, who could save face by demanding their removal in return for his removal of the Soviet missiles in Cuba.

"I wouldn't mind so much if the damned things were serving any useful purpose," the President said. "They should have been taken out of there back in the Eisenhower administration."

That Saturday afternoon, as he prepared to deliver his ultimatum to Khrushchev, President Kennedy betrayed the only sign of nervousness that we saw him show during the entire thirteen day period of the missile crisis. He telephoned Jackie at Glen Ora, where she was spending the weekend with Caroline and John, and asked her to come back to the White House with the children that evening so that he and his family could be together if there was a sudden emergency. The intelligence officials had pointed out to us that if the Russians learned of President Kennedy's discovery of the missiles and his plan to demand their removal, Khrushchev might try to beat him to the punch by ordering a surprise nuclear attack on Washington.

The President had selected a group to be with him in the event of a crisis, and Commander Tazewell Shepard, the President's Naval aide, was in charge of logistics. Shepard told Dave and me about the plan for evacuating the White House and handed both of us pink identification cards, which meant that we were to be in the group that would accompany the President and Mrs. Kennedy to an underground shelter at an unspecified location outside of the city. Shepard showed me the complete list of people who were to be with the President after the White House was evacuated, and I remember seeing the names of Rusk and McNamara and Ted Sorenson, but the other names I have long since forgotten.

When Dave was handed his pink card, he came to me and said, "After you and I go off to this underground apartment with the President, what happens to our wives and kids?" Neither Shepard nor I knew what to tell him. Helen, my wife, raised the same question later that weekend. "While you're safe with the President under a rock somewhere," she said, "what am I supposed to do with your five children?" Ted Reardon called me with the same complaint from the wives of several Cabinet members. A plan of evacuation was then drawn up for the families of government officials but, as I recall it, it was not too reassuring. There would have been a warning period of only eighteen minutes, and they would have been forced to drive in their own cars to a location somewhere near Quantico, which was supposed to be outside the probable impact area. Their chances of escaping would have been slim. There was really no hope of survival for most of the population if Washington was hit by nuclear missiles. Later that week, when we were waiting for a Russian response to the blockade, the President asked Jackie to move out of Washington, so that she could be closer to their assigned underground shelter if a sudden attack came, but she refused to leave him alone in the White House.

After Jackie and the Kennedy children returned to the White House that Saturday from their weekend home in Virginia, the President took his usual evening swim in the pool with Dave. While they were swimming, the President talked about the crisis situation and about the danger of a nuclear world war with the same feeling and in almost the same words that he had spoken to me on the plane after the Vienna meetings with Khrushchev. "Dave, if we were only thinking of ourselves, it would be easy," he said, "but I keep thinking about the children whose lives would be wiped out." Later Dave went to the upstairs apartment in the mansion with a folder of reports that the President wanted to study that night. Coming into the dimly lit living room to give the President the papers, Dave heard his voice as he talked quietly and assumed that he was alone, speaking to somebody on the telephone. Then he saw the President sitting in a chair with Caroline on his lap, reading to her from a story book.

"I watched him sitting there with Caroline," Dave said to me later. "I thought of what he had been saying to me in the pool, about how worried he was about the children everywhere in the world, and, you know, I got the strangest feeling. I handed him the papers, and got out of there as fast as I could. I was all choked up."

Helen and I had been invited to a party that night at Jim Rowe's house, one of those big parties where almost everybody of importance in Washington would be seen and heard. It was said later that the President ordered me to go to the Rowe party because my absence would arouse suspicions, but the President had no interest whatsoever in where or how his assistants were spending their Saturday nights. I simply decided that I would be better off with a drink in my hand in congenial company that evening than sitting at home watching television. Adlai Stevenson was at the party. He came to Helen and me, and asked me what the President had thought of his performance at the Ex Comm meeting that afternoon. I assured him that the President admired his courage in bringing up an opposing view that needed to be discussed at the meeting, and appreciated his earnest effort to urge a peaceful solution to the crisis. Stevenson seemed to be very much relieved.

"I know that most of those fellows will probably consider me a coward for the rest of my life for what I said today," he said. "But perhaps we need a coward in the room when we are talking about a nuclear war."

Stevenson came to me again about a half hour later and told me that both Al Friendly of the *Washington Post* and Scotty Reston of the *New York Times* had heard about the missile crisis. "They haven't got the details," Adlai said, "but they're onto the story. Perhaps you ought to call the President."

I called the White House on the telephone in Jim Rowe's bedroom.

"I suppose everybody at the party is talking about it," the President said. "This White House is like a sieve."

"Sieve?" I said. "You did very well to keep a story like this one out of the papers for the last five days. Now you'd better get somebody to call the *Post* and the *Times*, and ask them to hold on it until Monday night."

"Get somebody to call the *Post* and the *Times*?" the President said. "Are you kidding? I'll call them myself, right now."

He called the newspapers, and both of them agreed in the interest of national security to withhold any mention of the discovery of the missiles until after the President confronted Khrushchev with the findings and his demands. On Sunday morning, after he attended mass at Saint Stephen's Church, Kennedy gave the Air Force generals one last chance to argue for an immediate bombing of the missile sites. He again ruled against an air strike when General Walter C. Sweeney, commander of the Tactical Air Force, admitted that it would be impossible to take out all of the missile sites in one blow. It had to be all or nothing, the President said, because we had no way of knowing which sites, if any, were operational and which ones weren't. We might miss or overlook a few operational sites, which could immediately open fire on the United States.

Meanwhile Larry O'Brien and Pierre Salinger were rounding up Congressional leaders all over the country and bringing them back to Washington so that the President could brief them on his plan Monday before announcing it on the air. Congress was not in session because of the election campaigns at home. Finding some of the leaders was difficult. Hale Boggs was fishing on the Gulf of Mexico. An Air Force helicopter picked him up from his boat and carried him to New Orleans, where an Air Force jet took him to Washington. When the Senators and Congressmen assembled in the President's office for the briefing, Kennedy grinned at Everett Dirksen and said, "Well, tonight you're going to get reelected." Dirksen laughed and said, "That was a nice speech you gave for Sid Yates in Chicago. Too bad you caught that cold making it." Tom Kuchel, running for reelection to the Senate in California, seemed more interested in getting a picture of himself taken with the President, to show the voters that he was solving the missile crisis, than he was interested in looking at the pictures of the missile sites.

The meeting itself was not pleasant. After McCone presented and explained the photographic evidence, and after Rusk and McNamara outlined the reasons for the blockade plan, Senator Richard B. Russell, the Democratic chairman of the Armed Services Committee, loudly denounced the President's course of action as too soft and half-hearted. Russell demanded a military attack on Cuba. Much to the President's astonishment, Senator J. William Fulbright, speaking as chairman of the Senate's Foreign Relations Committee, backed Russell's demand for an invasion. Fulbright had been the only high-ranking member of the government to speak out against the Bay of Pigs invasion in 1961. Supporting a military invasion of Cuba seemed to be totally out of his character. Fulbright appeared to have been influenced on the spur of the moment by Russell's angry outburst of disagreement with the President, and I almost had the feeling, sitting there and watching him with some amazement, that he regretted his words while he was saying them. The President questioned Fulbright, "You're for an invasion of Cuba, Bill? You and Senator Russell? Is that right?" Fulbright shuffled his feet, and squirmed in his chair, before he replied, "That's right."

In an article written for the *New Yorker* on the Truman Doctrine nine years later, published on January 8, 1972, Fulbright expresses some second thoughts on the Cuban missile crisis, wondering if it was "so enormous a crisis as it then seemed." He suspects now that perhaps we made a mistake in assuming that Khrushchev was making an aggressive move against the United States when he shipped the offensive missiles to Cuba. He speculates that Khrushchev was only trying to appease the hawkish militarists in Russia, and if so, he writes in his article, we should not have been so quick to take a firm stand against him and impose a defeat on him, helping to strengthen the military and conservative opposition to him within the Soviet Union that forced him out of the government two years later. The removal of the Soviet missiles from Cuba, Fulbright now says, "might have been accomplished by means less embarrassing to Khrushchev, such as a *quid pro quo* under which we would have removed our Jupiter missiles from Turkey." But back there in the President's office on October 22, 1962, when Fulbright was seconding Russell's demand for an invasion of Cuba, he did not appear to be concerned about the embarrassment that such an invasion might bring to Khrushchev, or about our Jupiter missiles. The Cuban missile crisis on that day apparently seemed to him, as it seemed to all of us at the time, very enormous indeed.

The President snapped back hard at Russell and Fulbright. "Last Tuesday, I was for an air strike or an invasion myself," he told them, "but after four more days of deliberations, we decided that was not the wisest first move, and you would, too, if you had more time to think about it." He pointed out that a military attack might be the second step, that the armed forces were not yet prepared to stage an invasion. Senator Dirksen supported the President's plan. Charlie Halleck, the Republican leader in the House, went along with Dirksen, but did not improve the President's mood when he announced that he wanted the record to note that Kennedy had informed the Congressional leaders of the blockade, but had not consulted them for advice on it. The President was trying to hide his rage when the Congressmen filed out of his office.

"Oh, sure, we support you, Mister President," Kennedy said to us when the door closed behind them. "But it's your decision, not ours, and if it goes wrong, we'll knock your block off."

An hour later, when President Kennedy was sitting at his desk, waiting for the signal to start the most important speech of his life, he looked up and saw his motherly private secretary, Evelyn Lincoln, advancing toward him with a hairbrush in her hand. He waved her aside impatiently, listened to the announcer's voice saying, "Ladies and gentlemen, the President of the United States," and began to talk as his image appeared on millions of television screens across the country:

"Good evening, my fellow citizens: This government, as promised, has maintained the closest surveillance of the Soviet military buildup on the island of Cuba. Within the past week, unmistakable evidence has established the fact that a series of offensive missile sites is now in preparation on that imprisoned island. The purpose of these bases can be none other than to provide a nuclear strike capability against the Western Hemisphere. . . ."

The President went on to demand the removal or elimination of the missiles, listing several steps that he was taking immediately, beginning with the naval blockade of Cuba, which he referred to as a "quarantine." Any ship bound for Cuba and carrying offensive weapons or missile-firing equipment would be stopped and turned back. He was careful to add that necessities of life would not be denied at that time to Cuba, as the Soviets had tried to do in their Berlin blockade of 1948. He said that he was also reinforcing the Navy's base at Guantanamo, calling for action by the Organization of American States, asking for the United Nations to force a dismantling and withdrawal of the weapons, and calling upon Khrushchev to halt "this clandestine, reckless and provocative threat to world peace."

"It shall be the policy of this nation," President Kennedy said, "to regard any nuclear missile launched from Cuba against any nation in the Western Hemisphere as an attack by the Soviet Union on the United States, requiring a full retaliatory response on the Soviet Union." And any hostile move by the Russians anywhere in the world against the safety and freedom of peoples to whom we are committed, he added, "including in particular the brave people of West Berlin," would be met with action.

Before the President went on the air, a copy of his address was delivered by Foy Kohler, our new Ambassador in Moscow, to Khrushchev's office at the Kremlin. With the President's demand for the removal of the missiles, Kohler carried a personal letter from

Kennedy to Khrushchev which got to the heart of their mutual problem — the Soviet Union's disbelief that the United States would stand up and fight against a Communist threat to its security. "The one thing that has most concerned me," the President wrote to Khrushchev, "has been the possibility that your government would not correctly understand the will and determination of the United States in any given situation, since I have not assumed that you or any other sane man would, in this nuclear age, deliberately plunge the world into war which it is crystal clear no country could win and which could only result in catastrophic consequences to the whole world, including the aggressor."

The next morning the President came to his office smiling. He had half expected that Khrushchev might make an immediate response to his demands for the removal of the missiles by closing down the access routes to West Berlin, or bombing our Jupiter missiles in Turkey. But Tuesday was bright and clear, without a sound from Khrushchev, and there was good news on the home front — the Latin-American nations in the OAS supported our use of force in the blockade, which was to go into effect on Wednesday morning at ten o'clock.

With the blockade legally authorized by the OAS nations, we had a meeting Tuesday evening to decide how the Navy should proceed in stopping a Soviet vessel that tried to run through the barrier. It was agreed that any ship refusing to halt and to be searched would have to be fired upon, but the President was anxious to avoid sinking a ship and losing lives. McNamara suggested crippling the vessel by shooting out its propellers and rudder, and then towing it to Charleston or Jacksonville. President Kennedy said, "And what happens after you shoot up the ship and tow it all the way to Florida, and then find out that it wasn't carrying anything except baby food?"

There were reports from the Navy that at least twenty-five Soviet ships of various descriptions and a few Russian submarines, possibly nuclear-armed, were heading toward Cuba. We agreed gloomily that there was likely to be some shooting as soon as the blockade went into effect the next day. After the meeting, Bobby, Ted Sorensen and I sat with the President in his office and talked about the rash and impulsive actions, rising from pride or misunderstandings, that can start wars. The President had recently read Barbara Tuchman's book *The Guns of August*, a study of the beginnings of World War I, and was greatly impressed by its accounts of blundering stupidity on both sides. He quoted a passage in which the German Chancellor is asked how the war started and says, "Ah, if we only knew."

"I wish we could send a copy of that book to every Navy officer on every Navy ship right now," the President said. "But they probably wouldn't read it."

Khrushchev's first angry reply to President Kennedy's blockade announcement reached the White House later that night. The Soviet leader flatly warned Kennedy that he had no intention of observing the blockade, that the captains of Russian vessels bound for Cuba had been instructed not to obey stop-orders from the U.S. Navy, and that any interference with Soviet ships would force him "to take measures which we deem necessary and adequate to protect our rights." The President and the members of the Ex Comm group studied and discussed Khrushchev's warning on Wednesday morning while we waited in the Cabinet Room to hear from the Navy what would happen when the blockade went into effect at ten o'clock and the first Russian ships approached the barrier line about a half hour later.

All of us in the room assumed from the firm and definite tone of Khrushchev's threat that the Soviet ships would refuse to stop, that our Navy ships and planes from the carrier *Essex*, which was standing near the line, would be forced to open fire, and the Russians would then respond with missiles from Cuba or long-range ICBMs from Eastern Europe, or perhaps by seizing West Berlin. Since Sunday our own nuclear missiles, on the Polaris submarines and at the Jupiter stations in Turkey, Italy and Britain had been on a ready alert, aimed at the Soviet Union. The Strategic Air Command's B-52 bombers were in the air, fully loaded with atomic weapons. The Navy had 180 ships deployed in the Caribbean area. The Army's First Armored Division and other combat units had been moved from Texas to Georgia and Florida, ready to invade Cuba. If shooting started at the blockade line, a nuclear war could quickly follow. It seemed to us as we waited in the Cabinet Room that everything depended on what Khrushchev would do within the next two hours.

A few minutes after ten, when the blockade had gone into effect, the Navy reported to McNamara that two Russian ships were within a few miles of the quarantine line, moving ahead steadily on a course toward Cuba. Then came another report that the two ships were being escorted by a Soviet submarine.

"What do we do now?" the President asked.

McNamara explained that a destroyer could have halted the ships, but the presence of the submarine now made an approach by a destroyer risky. The *Essex* would send a sonar signal to the submarine, ordering it to come to the surface and identify itself. If the submarine refused to surface and stop, a small explosive would be dropped on it by a helicopter from the *Essex*. I looked at the President. He seemed calm enough, but he was opening and closing his right hand into a tight fist. After a few minutes, he said, "Does the first ship we stop have to be a submarine? Couldn't we pick something else?"

McNamara said that the submarine could not be ignored.

We went back to waiting and wondering what was about to happen. Then a messenger came into the room and handed a note to John McCone, who read it quickly and said, "Mr. President, we have a preliminary report which indicates that some of the Russian ships are stopping." The preliminary report was then verified, and a Naval intelligence officer came to the meeting with a full report that twenty Russian ships had come to a stop before reaching the blockade line. Some of them were standing still in the water and others had turned around and were heading back toward Europe.

Dean Rusk, who was sitting beside the President, said quietly, "We're eyeball to eyeball, and I think the other fellow just blinked."

Coming from Rusk, who is not noted as an eloquent wit, it was a surprisingly good line, and one that well summed up the sudden feeling of relief that came over all of us. I felt then, and the President later agreed with me, that when those first Russian ships and submarines turned away from the blockade on that historic Wednesday morning, we had reached and successfully passed the real climax of the Cuban missile crisis. Kennedy had drawn a line across the Atlantic Ocean and had challenged Khrushchev to cross it. Khrushchev had backed away from the challenge. From then on it was downhill.

We heard later that several high-ranking Naval officers in the Pentagon were bitterly disappointed when the Soviet vessels failed to make a run through the blockade. They had been looking forward eagerly to sinking or capturing a few Russian submarines. One prominent officer of Irish-American ancestry was so disgusted when he heard that the Soviet ships were stopping and turning around that he shattered the quiet decorum of the Navy's plotting room by uttering a loud four-letter obscenity. Well aware that the Navy would have liked to rub it in, President Kennedy immediately sent strict orders to the *Essex* and to Admiral George W. Anderson, the Navy's gung-ho chief of operations, that none of the Soviet ships and submarines outside of the blockade interception zone were to be stopped, boarded or harassed in any way. The President assumed that Khrushchev was probably already taking enough criticism from his rivals in the Kremlin, and he wanted no incident that might cause a new flare-up.

That night McNamara, with his deputy secretary, Roswell Gilpatric, visited the Navy's Flag Plot, or command center in the Pentagon, where the blockade operation was being directed, to make sure that the President's orders were being observed. He found Admiral Anderson himself in the room, watching a single American vessel that was shown on the plotting board to be standing alone far outside of the interception zone. McNamara asked what the ship was doing out there. Anderson explained that it was watching a Soviet submarine.

The Secretary of Defense pointed out to the admiral that the President was anxious not to bother any Soviet ships needlessly, that the Russians must be allowed to retreat or to stand outside the blockade zone with no humiliation. Anderson informed the Secretary that the Navy needed no advice on how to manage a blockade, and suggested that the Secretary could leave the room. A few months later Anderson retired from the Navy, at President Kennedy's suggestion, to become our Ambassador to Portugal.

The tension at the blockade zone continued for the next three days. On Thursday, President Kennedy allowed a Russian oil tanker, the *Bucharest*, to pass through the blockade without being boarded or searched after the captain assured the Navy that he was only carrying petroleum and no military weapons or materials. Some of the Ex Comm members thought that the *Bucharest* should have been searched anyway to keep Khrushchev from getting the notion that our attitude toward him was softening. When the Soviet-chartered Liberty-ship freighter *Marucla* approached the blockade line on Friday, one of the destroyers that stopped it happened, by pure coincidence, to be the *Joseph P. Kennedy, Jr.*, the Navy ship named after the President's older brother who had died heroically in World War II, and on which Bobby had served as a seaman. "I suppose everybody will say that I sent the *Kennedy* in there deliberately," the President said, "to give our family some publicity."

Meanwhile, Adlai Stevenson gave the Soviet Ambassador to the United Nations, Valerian Zorin, a rough going-over in a debate on the missiles before the Security Council. Zorin tried to deny the photographic evidence of the missile sites, which was displayed at the council meeting, and Stevenson demolished him with a courtroom-style cross examination. "I am not in an American courtroom," Zorin said to Stevenson at one point, "and therefore I do not wish to answer a question that is put to me in the fashion in which a prosecutor puts questions." Stevenson said, "You are in the courtroom of world opinion right now and you can answer yes or no." Watching Stevenson in action on television, the President was impressed and surprised by his dramatic performance. "I never knew Adlai had it in him," Kennedy said. "Too bad he didn't show some of this steam in the 1956 campaign." Stevenson told us later that when he met Khrushchev at the signing of the nuclear test ban treaty in Moscow the following summer, the Soviet Premier growled at him, "Stevenson, we don't like to be interrogated like a prisoner in the dock."

On Friday we received a feeler for a settlement from the Russians outside of diplomatic channels. A member of the Soviet Embassy staff in Washington, Aleksandr S. Fomin, who was generally supposed to be their intelligence chief, approached John Scali, the ABC television reporter who covered the State Department, and asked Scali to sound out Rusk on the possibility of exchanging a promise of removing the missiles and a pledge of no more offensive weapons in Cuba in return for a United States pledge not to invade Cuba. Scali carried the proposal to Rusk, who brought him to the White House. While Scali and Rusk were waiting in the corridor outside my office for a chance to see the President, Pierre Salinger came upon them unexpectedly and assumed that Scali was trying to get an exclusive interview with the President behind Pierre's back, and with my conniving.

"What the hell are you doing here?" Pierre shouted at Scali.

I ran out of my office to quiet down the commotion and Rusk said to Salinger, "It's all right, Pierre. I brought him here."

I led Scali and Rusk into the President's office, where the President listened to Fomin's proposal and told Scali to take back a reply that it was completely acceptable as a basis for a settlement. "But don't use my name," Kennedy added. "That's against the rules. Give them the impression that you talked to me, but don't say so. Tell them you've gotten a favorable response from the highest authority in the government."

Later that Friday evening the President received a long private letter from Khrushchev which contained the same proposal that Fomin had given to Scali — a removal of the missiles and a promise of no more offensive weapons in Cuba in return for a guarantee of no American invasion of that island. Since their meetings in Vienna, Khrushchev and Kennedy had been carrying on an informal and off-the-record correspondence outside of official channels. It was obvious that Khrushchev had written this letter himself, probably without consulting anybody in the Kremlin, and that he intended it to be received, like his previous personal letters to Kennedy, as a man-to-man expression of his feelings rather than as an official communication. The letter was never made public in the Soviet Union and, out of respect for Khrushchev, Kennedy did not allow it to be published in the United States, although some brief excerpts and paraphrases of certain passages did appear in print after the President's death. When the President showed me the letter that Friday night after he read it for the first of many times, I was deeply moved by Khrushchev's anguished fear that he had provoked Kennedy into a fighting mood and a readiness for war. He pleaded with Kennedy not to lose his "self-control" and begged him not to let "the two of us pull on the ends of the rope in which you have tied the knot of war because the more the two of us pull, the tighter the knot will be tied. . . . Let us not only relax the forces pulling on the ends of the rope, let us take measures to untie that knot. We are ready for this."

The President and all of us who saw the letter from Khrushchev — so long that it was transmitted by teletype in four separate installments — went to bed that Friday night to enjoy the first relaxed sleep we had all week. The suspense in Washington during the days and nights after the President delivered his demands on Monday had been tense and nerve-racking. Every night that week Dave's next door neighbors in McLean, Virginia, stayed up and waited until they saw him come home from the White House before they went to bed. When they saw the lights in Dave's house turned off, they felt that it was safe for them to sleep, too. The President remarked on several occasions that week that the lack of panic during the danger of a nuclear attack showed either a remarkable courage in the American people or an even more remarkable feeling of confidence in their government's stand against the Soviets. The White House, during the days when the outcome of the crisis was in grave doubt, was flooded with messages, letters and telegrams from people in all walks of life strongly supporting the President.

When the President was meeting with the Ex Comm group on Saturday morning to draft a favorable reply to Khrushchev's plea for a settlement, Radio Moscow announced the text of another letter from Khrushchev to Kennedy, completely different in tone and content from the private and unpublicized message that the President had received on Friday night. This second letter was stern and demanding, and it raised the price of the ransom, stipulating that the Soviets would remove their missiles from Cuba only if the United States agreed to take its Jupiter missiles out of Turkey, which, of course, amounted to a blackmailing trade instead of the reasonable exchange of peaceful guarantees that Khrushchev had asked for in his first letter.

The second letter was so unlike the first one that it raised alarming questions. Had Khrushchev been overthrown during the night by hawkish militarists in the Kremlin who were incensed by his willingness to cooperate with Kennedy? Were we now dealing with another leadership in Russia? Llewellyn Thompson, who had recently returned from the Ambassador's post in Moscow, took the more moderate and correct view that Khrushchev's advisers had convinced him that he was letting Kennedy off too cheaply, and talked him into making a try for a trade of our Jupiter missiles. To make matters worse, we received a report that Major Rudolf Anderson, Jr., one of the U-2 pilots who had originally photographed the missile sites, had been shot down over Cuba on a similar reconnaissance flight. Apparently Major Anderson's plane had been hit by a Soviet surface-to-air missile, which meant that those defensive weapons in Cuba were now operational. That made an air strike dangerous.

Angry at this sudden turn in the situation, the President left his office and went outdoors to walk in the Rose Garden in an effort to restrain his irritation. I followed him into the garden and paced the lawn with him. I found him not so much upset by Khrushchev's change in attitude as exasperated because the Jupiter missiles were still in Turkey, where the Russians could use them in a face-saving barter, several months after their removal had been ordered by the President. "Just to set the record straight," the President said to me, "will you find out when was the last time I asked to have those damned missiles taken out of Turkey? Not the first five times I asked for their removal, just the date of the last time." I went to my office and called Bromley Smith in Bundy's office and asked him to check the file. Sure enough, the President had ordered the removal of the Jupiter missiles in August, two months before the Soviet ballistic missile sites were discovered in Cuba.

The President sat down again with the Ex Comm members and began to review the new alternatives. They weighed the arguments for and against removing the Jupiter missiles from Turkey, and discussed a timetable for an air strike and an invasion, which now seemed unavoidable as the only means of stopping the construction of the Soviet ballistic missile sites. I was struck by the difference in the roles taken by the Secretary of Defense and by the Secretary of State in these crucial strategy discussions. McNamara seemed not to be questioning the values or the intrinsic merits of one course of action as it compared to another course, and he was making no effort to influence the President's final decision. A few days earlier, when the President was opposed to an air strike and an invasion, McNamara fully supported him. Now when an air strike and an invasion were being considered, McNamara came up with a wealth of factual information on how soon the Air Force could strike and how long it would take the Army to mount an invasion force. When the President raised the question of taking the Jupiter missiles out of Turkey and Italy to accommodate the Soviets, McNamara was ready to provide a program for getting the missiles removed as fast as possible, with no expression of opinion on whether the removal was the wise move to make. As Secretary of Defense, McNamara regarded himself not as an initiator of defense policy but as an engineer and expediter of whatever defense policy the President elected.

On the other hand, Rusk and his deputies from the State Department were offering the President opinions rather than hard factual information. When it came to speculation on the reaction of NATO countries to the removal of the Jupiter missiles, the men from the State Department could only venture educated and experienced guesses. "If we attack Cuba," the President asked at one point, "will the Chinese Communists attack Taiwan?" Rusk expressed doubt that the Chinese would become involved, but added that there was no way of predicting what the Peking government would do; nobody in the State Department had expected the Chinese Reds to support the North Koreans in the Korean War. By the nature of his position in the government, Rusk was concerned with evaluating the effect of each possible course of action on the interests of the United States in its foreign relations. Consequently, his role in the meetings seemed much more vital and important than that of McNamara, who was only concerned with how each course, if adopted, could be carried out. But Rusk, too, was not recommending or supporting any one particular choice. He was pointing out the advantages and disadvantages of the alternate routes, and leaving it for the President to decide which route the United States would follow.

Fortunately, the President of the United States who was left with the burden of making the decisions on that dark Saturday of October 27, 1962, was several steps ahead of the rest of us in his thinking and judgments. When we were about to recess the gloomy morning meeting for a lunch break, the President asked McNamara to sound out the NATO governments on what their reaction would be if we traded our Jupiter missiles for a settlement. Without questioning the wisdom of such a move, McNamara immediately agreed to make the inquiries. I looked at Bobby, and Bobby frowned at me.

"Let's get out of here for a little while," I said to Bobby when the meeting was adjourned. "We'll go to the Sans Souci for a drink and a sandwich."

On our way to the restaurant, we said nothing about the morning's meeting. After we had ordered our sandwiches, I said to Bobby, "Your brother will be making a terrible mistake if he pulls those missiles out of Turkey right now. Everybody in Western Europe will turn against us. And there's no need of it. He's got Khrushchev hanging on the ropes. As Thompson says, the Russians are only trying to salvage a little something extra to save their face."

"You're right," Bobby said. "Let's eat up quickly, and get back there and talk to him."

We found the President eating a quick lunch in the mansion after his usual noontime swim with Dave in the pool. When Bobby spoke to him about our discussion in the restaurant, he glanced at the two of us as if we were behaving like a couple of kindergarten children.

"Relax," he said. "You fellows ought to know me better than that. I have no intention of taking those missiles out of Turkey. The only reason I asked McNamara to talk to the NATO people about it was because I was wondering what they would say."

The President at that particular moment was more disturbed by the death of Major Anderson in Cuba than he was worried about Khrushchev. He had asked the Defense Department to find out if the U-2 pilot had a wife and family. While he was swimming in the pool before lunch, McNamara telephoned him there to tell him that Anderson was married and had two sons, five and three years old. The President hung up the telephone, and turned to Dave with a stricken look on his face. "He had a boy about the same age as John," he said.

That afternoon when the Ex Comm group met again in the Oval Room there was another report of a U-2 incident. One of our high-altitude reconnaissance planes, on an air sampling mission in the Arctic region, had strayed over Soviet territory, where a group of Russian fighter planes had intercepted it. American fighter jets from Alaska had picked up the wandering U-2 and were escorting it safely back to its base. The President had expressly banned such testing flights during the crisis period, but as he remarked when reading the report, "There's always somebody who doesn't get the message."

Then the Ex Comm group settled down to the main problem of the moment, how to reply to Khrushchev's latest demands. The State Department had prepared a draft of a message, refusing to remove the missiles from Turkey, but the President found it unsatisfactory. Bobby suggested ignoring the second Khrushchev letter and its missile trade demand, and writing instead a reply to Khrushchev's first private letter which the President had received on

Friday night. The President immediately agreed to that idea, and sent Bobby and Ted Sorensen into another room to work on such a reply.

In less than an hour, Bobby came back with a handwritten draft of a letter that accepted Khrushchev's Friday suggestion for a removal of the Soviet missiles from Cuba and no further shipments of offensive weapons to that island in exchange for a lifting of the blockade and a guarantee of no invasion by U.S. forces in the future. The letter made no mention of the Jupiter missiles in Turkey. The President reworked the text of the letter, changing words and sentences, and then had it typed, and signed it. He asked to have the letter released to the press at the same time that it was transmitted to Moscow, and asked Bobby to bring a copy of it to Ambassador Dobrynin at the Soviet Embassy in Washington.

"Tell him that if we don't get a reply by Monday," the President said, "we'll start a military action against Cuba."

The Ex Comm was told to meet again at nine o'clock that night. The President had sent Jackie and their children to Glen Ora for the weekend, so he asked Dave to stay in the mansion and have dinner with him that evening. "Dave, are you sure your wife doesn't mind being alone at home at a time like this?" he asked. "Of course she minds," Dave said, "but she's used to it." The President mixed himself a daiquiri and opened a bottle of white wine to share with Dave while they dined alone on the broiled chicken that the kitchen staff had left for them on a hot plate in the upstairs living room. While they were eating, Bobby returned from his visit with the Soviet Ambassador and asked if there was an extra chicken leg. "How did it go at the Embassy?" the President asked him.

Bobby said that Dobrynin had preferred to meet with him at the Department of Justice instead of the Soviet Embassy. Dobrynin had brought up the question of removing our missiles from Turkey. Bobby had told him that such a decision would need NATO approval, and could not be discussed under pressure or threats from the Soviets. He told the Ambassador that we would remove the missile base from Cuba if we did not hear by the following day that the Russians were willing to remove them.

The President turned and looked at Dave, who was busy eating and drinking while taking in Bobby's report on his conversation with Dobrynin.

"God, Dave," the President said, "the way you're eating up all that chicken and drinking up all my wine, anybody would think it was your last meal."

"The way Bobby's been talking," Dave said, "I thought it *was* my last meal."

The meeting that night was pessimistic, the most depressing hour that any of us spent in the White House during the President's time there. We agreed that our chance of receiving any reply from Khrushchev the next day was a long shot at best. The President asked McNamara to arrange a meeting the next morning with General Sweeney to discuss plans for an air strike, and signed an order calling to active duty twenty-four troop carrier squadrons from the Air Force Reserve, which would be needed for an invasion of Cuba. When the meeting was adjourned, the President stayed behind at his desk, writing on a pad of yellow paper. I asked him what he was writing.

"A letter to Mrs. Anderson," he said.

But he was still calm and collected. After the rest of us left the White House, he and Dave went to the projection room where they watched a showing of one of his favorite old movies, starring one of his favorite actresses, Audrey Hepburn, in *Roman Holiday*. Before turning off the light and getting into bed, he said to Dave, "We'll be going to the ten o'clock mass at Saint Stephen's, Dave, and we'll have plenty of hard praying to do, so don't be late."

Before he went to Sunday mass the next morning, the President heard the big news, reported first on the radio in Moscow, that Khrushchev had sent a reply to the Kennedy letter of Saturday, agreeing to a removal of Soviet missiles from Cuba and offering to meet "every condition for eliminating the present conflict." As he went off to church, the President said to Dave, "I feel like a new man. Do you realize that we had an air strike all arranged for Tuesday? Thank God it's all over." We learned later that one of our military leaders said, when hearing about Khrushchev's willingness to remove the missiles, "Does this mean our air strike has to be called off? Why can't we attack on Tuesday anyway?"

When he returned from mass and attended a meeting of the Ex Comm group to discuss the steps to be taken in the changed situation, President Kennedy showed us his greatness. Somebody excitedly suggested that he should appear on television to announce the victory over the Soviet aggressors. "There will be none of that," he said sharply. "I want no crowing and not a word of gloating from anybody in this government." We had avoided a war by allowing Khrushchev to back out of the crisis without complete humiliation, he said, and we must be careful not to cause him any further humiliation. The President issued only a brief statement praising Khrushchev's "statesmanlike decision" to stop building bases in Cuba and agreeing to dismantle offensive weapons as an "important and constructive contribution to peace."

When the full text of Khrushchev's letter of capitulation arrived at the White House, we saw that it included a few mild words of complaint about our U-2 plane that had strayed over Soviet territory on its way back from an air sampling mission near the North Pole on Saturday. Khrushchev said that the plane might have been mistaken for a bomber. I said to the President, when we were looking at the letter, "I'll bet that when they picked up that U-2 on their radar, they were sure that it was a nuclear bomber from our Strategic Air Force. It frightened the hell out of Khrushchev, and that was probably the thing that hurried him into asking you for a settlement."

"You could be right," the President said. "But if you think I'm going to give a medal to that U-2 pilot for getting himself lost over Russian territory, you're all wrong." In the reply that he wrote to Khrushchev, the President explained that the plane had been flying, without arms or photographic equipment, seeking samples of nuclear fallout, when it made an error in navigation, and that every precaution would be taken to prevent a recurrence of the incident.

Then the President hurried off to Glen Ora to spend the rest of that happy Sunday with Jackie and the children. A few weeks later he personally designed and ordered from Tiffany's thirty-four small silver calendars of the month of October, 1962, mounted on walnut, with the thirteen days of the Cuban missile crisis embossed more deeply than the other days on the calendar. He handed these mementoes privately, and with no ceremony, to members of the Ex Comm and others on his staff and to a few private citizens who had been helpful to him during that period. The initials of the recipient were etched in the upper left corner of the plaque and the President's own initials were inscribed on the upper right corner. Among the thirty-four recipients were two women, Jacqueline Kennedy and Evelyn Lincoln.

Dave and I keep our small silver calendars as reminders of the most momentous days in President Kennedy's public lifetime, the two weeks when the history of the next twenty years was changed and rewritten because the world's two great nuclear powers looked at each other and realized that neither of them wanted a nuclear war. Out of that realization and the diminishing of the fear of nuclear destruction in smaller nations came a weakening of both NATO and the Warsaw Pact, a loosening of Soviet domination in the Communist world, a surge of independence in the Western European democracies and the new African countries, and a break in the Russian-Chinese alliance that led to tension in India and Pakistan and American involvement in Vietnam. "The lessening of the threat of a world war after we stopped Khrushchev's attempt to shift the balance of power in Berlin and Cuba created a whole lot of new problems everywhere," President Kennedy said later. "But I'd much rather have those new problems than the ones we had before."

The problems that President Kennedy faced after the Cuban missile crisis, as he began his third and last year in the White House, were indeed preferable to the troubles of the Cold War and Khrushchev's blustering drive for world power that he inherited when he went into office. The critics who claim that John F. Kennedy was out of his depth in the Presidency might consider the historical fact that on November 19, 1962, a month after Kennedy confronted and defeated Khrushchev in the Caribbean, Khrushchev was announcing to the central committee of the Soviet Communist party that he had decided to concentrate on domestic economic problems in Russia instead of pursuing the world offensive any further. Kennedy often said about his Presidency, "All I want them to say about me is what they said about John Adams, 'He kept the peace.'" He certainly did that.

TWELVE

"Johnny, I Hardly Knew Ye"

Two MONTHS after the Cuban missile crisis, when President Kennedy sat in his office to be interviewed by the White House correspondents of the three television networks, Sander Vanocur, Bill Lawrence and George Herman, he had many good things to talk about. "I must say after being here for two years," he said, "that I have a good deal of hope for the United States. This country, which criticizes itself and is criticized around the world, has been the great means of defending first the world against the Nazi threat, and since then against the Communist threat, and if it were not for us, the Communists would be dominant in the world today. Now I think that is a pretty good record for a country with six percent of the world's population, which is rather reluctant to take on these burdens. I think we ought to be rather pleased with ourselves this Christmas."

The President could well afford to be rather pleased with himself during that merry Christmas season of 1962. Much to his delight, the November midterm Congressional and state elections, which traditionally go against the incumbent administration and which we had given up as hopeless when the Soviet missiles were discovered in Cuba, turned out much better than any of the Democrats had expected. Even Homer Capehart was beaten by the young Birch Bayh in Indiana. We gained four seats in the Senate and the Republicans only gained two in the House. Richard Nixon added to the President's satisfaction by losing the governorship to Pat Brown in California, and then telling the press that it wouldn't have Dick Nixon to kick around anymore. ("Why is he running?" Kennedy had said to us earlier. "He hasn't got a chance, and the risk of getting beaten by Brown far outweighs any advantages he could win from being elected.") In December, the President had done Harold Macmillan a big political favor by bailing his Conservative government out of the Skybolt embarrassment, probably the nicest Christmas gift that Macmillan ever received. Kennedy was also feeling free and easy enough about Nikita Khrushchev to concoct a comical parody on the Cuban missile crisis, which he delivered at the Gridiron Club dinner a few months later. Khrushchev's son-in-law, Aleksei Adzhubei, then the editor of *Izvestia*, had paid a visit to the Pope at the Vatican at the time. Kennedy compared this Soviet infiltration of the Holy See to the sneaking of the missiles into Cuba.

"I have a very grave announcement," the President said to the Gridiron members. "The Soviet Union has once again recklessly embarked upon a provocative and extraordinary change in the status quo in an area which they know full well I regard as having a special and historic relationship. I refer to the sudden and deliberate deployment of Mr. Adzhubei to the Vatican. I am told that this plot was worked out by a group of Khrushchev's advisers who have all been excommunicated from the church. It's known as Ex Comm. Reliable refugee reports have informed us that hundreds of Marxist Bibles have been unloaded and are being hidden in caves throughout the Vatican. We will now pursue the contingency plan for protecting the Vatican City that was previously prepared by the National Security Council. The plan is known as Vat 69. We are, in short, eyeball to eyeball over the Holy See, and the other fellow is cross-eyed. Speaking of the religious issue, I asked the Chief Justice tonight whether he thought our new educational bill was constitutional. He said, 'It's clearly constitutional. It hasn't got a prayer.'"

Later in the same speech, the President mentioned the criticism he had been getting from Arthur Krock. "The Vice-President complained to me that Doris Fleeson was still criticizing him," Kennedy said. "I told him I'd rather be Fleesonized than Krocked."

When I think of John Fitzgerald Kennedy, the practical-minded politician, I remember him worrying about the political disaster that faced Harold Macmillan when Robert McNamara decided to scrap the highly publicized Skybolt missile project. The Skybolt was a nuclear weapon designed to be fired from a bomber plane. It was a U.S. Air Force effort to give the manned bomber a new function and a longer usefulness, and to compete in the nuclear arms rivalry against the Navy's Polaris missile. At a meeting at Camp David in 1960, when the Skybolt was only an expensive idea on the drawing board, President Eisenhower made an agreement with Macmillan to provide the British with the missile for use on their Vulcan II bombers after the United States paid the whole cost of the research and development of the nuclear weapon. In return, Britain would allow the U.S. Navy the use of Holy Loch in Scotland as a base for its Polaris submarines. Macmillan dropped Britain's other missile projects and pinned the future security of his nation entirely on the assumption that the American-made, and American-paid, Skybolt would serve as Britain's one and only nuclear deterrent weapon. There seem to have been misunderstandings on both sides when the Eisenhower-Macmillan agreement was made; the Americans assumed that the British would be allowed to buy the Skybolt missiles if the development and testing worked out efficiently and successfully, while the British assumed that they had been definitely promised the weapon with no question about the possibility that it might not work when it was tested.

Pages now flutter from the calendar and new faces come into the Defense Department. McNamara decided in the fall of 1962, much to the dismay of the Air Force and the Douglas Aircraft Company, the contractor, that the Skybolt was both unreliable and unnecessary, and too expensive. Not only had the Skybolt failed several tests, but the President agreed with the Secretary of Defense that it was silly to spend 2.5 billion dollars on a questionable airborne missile when our nuclear deterrent needs were already well filled by the Polaris submarine weapons and the land-based Minuteman. McNamara was sent to London to break the news to the British government.

McNamara, no politician himself, failed to realize the political implications in the British government's loss of the Skybolt, and made the big mistake of telling reporters at the airport in London that the airborne missile project was being wiped out after five straight unsuccessful tests. Moreover, he made no mention of any American proposal for a replacement. The headlines in the next day's British newspapers were full of angry charges that Macmillan, who had been boasting for two years about the Skybolt agreement, had been double-crossed and sold a pig in a poke by the Americans. Thanks to his trust in the United States, the press and his Labor party rivals asserted, Macmillan's government now had no nuclear weapon and he should be voted out of office. It was even said that the Skybolt was not really a failure but that Kennedy was merely putting up a deception to threaten the British into increasing their military forces in NATO. McNamara's subsequent meeting with his opposite number in the British government, Defense Minister Peter Thorneycroft, was a disaster. McNamara expected Thorneycroft to come up with a suggestion for an alternative to the Skybolt, perhaps a plan for sharing the Polaris under American control, which could be modified by negotiation. Thorneycroft was demanding the Skybolt or nothing, as if the British were hoping that maybe, with the help of our Air Force and the Douglas contractors, they could pressure Kennedy into continuing the work program.

McNamara was mystified by the uproar he had created in London, because he still regarded the failure of the Skybolt as an unfortunate technical error rather than as a political nightmare for Harold Macmillan and his Tory government. Kennedy was irritated and perplexed by the British government's apparent lack of knowledge of the Skybolt's deficiencies over several previous months, when the missile's failures were common knowledge in military and scientific circles, and when Macmillan could have been preparing to cope with the political storm before it broke over his head in the newspapers and in the House of Commons.

"Why didn't he know about it in advance?" The President asked. "Why didn't he get ready for it? And why didn't *we* know that he didn't know about it?" The President was so puzzled by the breakdown in communications between the two supposedly closely allied governments that he asked for a comprehensive study of the whole Skybolt misunderstanding.

But we now had no time, the President said, to worry about why Harold Macmillan had been left out on the end of the limb. "We've got to help him out of this mess that we've put him in," Kennedy said. "He's been given the shaft, and we've got to remove it." Kennedy, the politician, was thinking about the political troubles of a fellow politician, and one of his favorite politicians at that.

A reporter once asked Dave Powers why Kennedy and Macmillan were so friendly with each other. "Maybe it's because they both speak English," Dave said.

We had already scheduled a meeting between Kennedy and Macmillan at Nassau in the Bahamas on other problems that were disturbing the Western allies. Macmillan was having trouble trying to get De Gaulle's approval for Britain's entry into the European Common Market because De Gaulle felt Macmillan was too close to Kennedy and not close enough to the continental nations. France and West Germany, both feeling their oats since Khrushchev had been put down in the Cuban missile crisis, were talking about developing their own nuclear weapons. But now the Skybolt controversy and the threat that it was aiming at Macmillan's shaky Conservative government became the number one topic on the agenda at the Nassau meeting.

When the President was boarding Air Force One for the flight to the Bahamas, he said to me, "We can't let him go home to London empty handed. I've got to come up with something to take the place of that damned Skybolt."

Kennedy told us later that evening, after he talked alone with Macmillan over a drink, that he suggested as an escape from the Prime Minister's predicament the proposal of continuing the Skybolt development, with Britain sharing the costs, fifty-fifty. Then, after a few months, Macmillan could gracefully back out of the arrangement and ask to have it called off by discovering that the agreement was too expensive. But Macmillan wanted no further association with the Skybolt project now that it had been so widely discredited. He was fishing for a Polaris missile exchange. But a straight bilateral nuclear deal between the United States and Britain, such as the one that Eisenhower made with Macmillan in 1960, was now impossible. Kennedy had refused earlier to provide weapons for a French nuclear force. The West Germans would be miffed if they were excluded from a handout of American missiles to another NATO nation, and if we gave nuclear weapons to West Germany, Khrushchev would be forced to provide missiles to the East Germans. The only way to share our Polaris missiles with Britain would be under a multilateral arrangement, on a vessel under NATO command with a crew of mixed allied nationalities, but with U.S. Navy personnel actually controlling the nuclear trigger.

Much to Kennedy's surprise, Macmillan accepted such a multi-lateral nuclear force proposal as a substitute for the Skybolt after the President agreed to a rather vague clause saying that a British submarine carrying a Polaris missile under NATO command might revert to British command in an unusual emergency where "supreme national interests are at stake." That, of course, could mean almost anything, but as the President himself remarked later, the beauty of the Nassau Pact of December, 1962, which saved Macmillan's Prime Ministership, was that it could be read by the British to mean one thing and also read by the State Department or by our Joint Chiefs of Staff to mean something quite different. The main thing about the pact, Kennedy said, was that it made Macmillan happy and gave him something to take home to Parliament.

That night, after the pact was agreed to, the President described it in some detail to Dave and me while we were having a drink with him before dinner, and asked us what we thought of it.

"A multinational ship?" I said. "We have trouble enough in our own Navy running a ship where everybody in the crew speaks English. You're going to have a NATO crew with people talking French, Italian, German, Greek and Flemish?"

"Who cares?" the President said. "It may take them a few years to straighten out the language problem, and longer than that to straighten out the other problems. But in the meantime Macmillan is as happy as a clam. He's going home to England with a nuclear missile ship. Maybe there'll never be such a ship and maybe nothing really happened here today, but that's beside the point. The point is that we got Macmillan off the hook."

Even after Kennedy and Macmillan officially flushed the Skybolt project down the drain, our Air Force tried desperately to keep it alive. An earnest promoter of the airborne missile in the White House was Brigadier General Godfrey McHugh, the President's Air Force aide, who severely tried Kennedy's patience by persistently plugging the interests of his branch of the service. McHugh talked so much about the intercontinental Atlas missile that when the President went to Vandenberg Air Force Base in California to watch its launching, he said to the general, "If this thing doesn't go off, McHugh, you'll be managing a PX on Monday." A few days after the Nassau conference, when the President went to Palm Beach for the Christmas holidays, an Air Force spokesman in Washington announced that the Skybolt had just been tested with great success. The enraged President made a quick phone call and learned that there had been no test. McHugh picked that unfortunate moment to rush into the room, waving a copy of the phony announcement and shouting, "Mr. President, did you hear the great news about the Skybolt?"

The multinational nuclear missile ship idea that saved Macmillan at Nassau never materialized in the Atlantic Alliance, to Kennedy's complete lack of surprise. The only members of NATO, other than the British, who showed any enthusiasm for the plan were the West Germans, delighted by any remote promise of a piece of nuclear action. When the proposal was offered to De Gaulle, he uttered a French phrase roughly equivalent to "Are you people out of your minds?" In January, De Gaulle held a press conference and shook the NATO alliance by announcing that France would take care of its own national defense and that he was barring Britain from the Common Market to protect the Western European community from American domination. The barring of Britain from the Common Market was blamed on the Nassau Pact, but Kennedy and Macmillan were not too disturbed by that charge. They felt that De Gaulle never had any intention of letting the British into the market anyway.

Shortly after De Gaulle turned down the Nassau multilateral nuclear force proposal, the President and his wife attended with André Malraux, the French minister of cultural affairs, a showing of the *Mona Lisa*, which had been lent by France to the National Gallery of Art. Kennedy could not resist a playful comparison to recent events when he made his remarks at the gallery. "I must note," he said, "that this painting has been kept under careful French control, and that France has even sent along its own commander in chief, Monsieur Malraux, and I want to make it clear that grateful as we are for this painting, we will continue to press ahead with an effort to develop an independent artistic force and power of our own."

President Kennedy's last winter in the White House, as he expressed it at the time, was not a winter of discontent. After he delivered his State of the Union message to Congress on January 14, he said to Dave while they were swimming in the White House pool, "Things are not as bad as they might be. As I told them on the Hill, I only have to worry about Berlin, Cuba, Vietnam, Laos and

NATO. This is still the best White House I ever worked in."

To stir up a diversion from the routine White House news, the President started a rumpus for the benefit of the press correspondents about ordering Pierre Salinger and other members of his staff to make a fifty-mile hike to prove their physical fitness. The hike story was released as a suggestion from General David M. Shoup, the Marine Corps commandant, but it was originally the President's own idea. He came across a letter written in 1908 by President Theodore Roosevelt to the commandant of the Marines, recommending an occasional fifty-mile hike for Marine officers. President Roosevelt added that he would ask members of his own staff to pass a similar fitness test. Kennedy sent the Roosevelt letter to General Shoup with a memo attached to it:

"Why don't you send this back to me as your discovery? You might want to add a comment that today's Marine Corps officers are just as fit as those of 1908, and are willing to prove it. I, in turn, will ask Mr. Salinger for a report on the fitness of the White House staff."

There was quite a to-do in the newspapers about Pierre training for a scheduled fifty-mile hike in the company of forty-seven news correspondents along the Chesapeake and Ohio Canal's towpath, but the hike was finally called off. "I may be plucky," Pierre was quoted as saying, "but I'm not stupid." But Bobby Kennedy walked a full fifty miles from Washington to Camp David and, before the tempest subsided, the President's Polish brother-in-law, Prince Stash Radziwill, and his close friend Chuck Spalding, marched fifty miles in Florida with Jackie, Lee and the President cheering them on.

A few weeks later when King Hassan II of Morocco was visiting the White House, President Kennedy decided to walk with him from the executive mansion to Blair House, on the opposite side of Pennsylvania Avenue, where the King was staying. The President's spur-of-the-moment urge to leave the White House and to take a stroll across the street caught his Secret Service guards and passersby by surprise. Engrossed in conversation with King Hassan, he paid no attention to the traffic, and when they were in the middle of the avenue, a speeding hospital ambulance had to make a zigzag turn to avoid hitting them. When the President and the King reached the opposite curb, a boy in a high school sweat shirt stared at them and said, "Hey, President Kennedy, are you starting a fifty-mile hike?"

President Kennedy spent a considerable amount of time personally answering letters picked at random from the enormous mail received at the White House addressed to him from private citizens. Letters to the President averaged around five thousand a day. Every fiftieth letter was pulled from the pile and sent to his office. Frequently he wandered into the mail room and took a few letters from the sacks, carried them to his desk, and read them. If the writer was seeking help on a personal problem concerning a government agency, the President would send the letter to that office or to a staff member, requesting an inquiry into the matter and an immediate reply. More often, he wrote an answer himself, had it typed by Evelyn Lincoln, and then added a handwritten postscript before having it mailed.

Early in March that year the President showed us a letter that he had received from a youngster in Fremont, California, who had evidently been giving some thought to the approaching Saint Patrick's Day, and apparently was aware of Kennedy's Irish ancestry:

Dear President Kennedy:

I like you very much. I am in special class in Fremont, California. I am 10 years old. Where do the little people live? Do they live under bushes? Do they have horses? Can only the Irish see them? Can you see them?

MARK AARON PERDUE

The President wrote the following reply:

Dear Mark:

I want to thank you for your nice letter. I enjoyed hearing from you and hearing about your school.

Your questions are quite pertinent, coming as they do just before St. Patrick's Day. There are many legends about the "little people," but what they all add up to is this: If you really believe, you will see them.

My "little people" are very small, wear tall black stovepipe hats, green coats and pants, and have long, white beards. They do not have horses. I have never been able to determine where they live. They are most friendly, and their message is that all the peoples of the world should live in peace and friendship.

Since you are interested in the Irish, I want to wish you a happy St. Patrick's Day.

Sincerely,
JOHN F. KENNEDY

Saint Patrick's Day was always a special occasion for all of the Kennedys. The President spent his last Saint Patrick's Day in 1963 with his father at Palm Beach. Jackie was not with him because he was leaving from there the next day on a trip to Costa Rica, for a meeting with the presidents of the Central American nations, and she was unable to travel because of her pregnancy. The Ambassador, still paralyzed from the stroke that he had suffered in 1961, was unable to speak, but enjoyed being entertained by the President, Bobby, and Dave at a small party in his home during the evening. When the President and Dave sang "The Wearin' of the Green," the Ambassador was smiling happily, but when they came to the last line of the stirring old patriotic song — "They're hanging men and women for the wearin' of the green!" — his eyes were filled with tears.

The President loved Irish songs and translations of Gaelic poetry. Not long after his inauguration, Thomas P. Kiernan, the Irish Ambassador in Washington, came to the White House to present him with a silver antique christening tankard, sent to the President by the people of Wexford in honor of the birth of his infant son. At the ceremony, the Ambassador explained that he had no words prepared for the occasion, and asked the President's permission to recite, from memory, some verses written by an Irish poet friend thirty years earlier to celebrate the birth of his own son, Colm Patrick. "Go ahead," the President said. After pausing for a moment to recall the lines, the Ambassador began to recite:

> *We wish to the new child*
> *A heart that can be beguiled by a flower*
> *That the wind lifts as it passes*
> *Over the grasses after a summer shower,*
> *A heart that can recognize*
> *Without aid of the eyes*
> *The gifts that life holds for the wise.*
> *When the storms break for him,*

May the trees shake for him their blossoms down.
In the night that he is troubled
May a friend wake for him
So that his time be doubled,
And at the end of all loving and love,
May the Man Above
Give him a crown.

When Kiernan finished speaking the verses, the President was not able to talk for a few moments. As he accepted the silver cup, he said to the Ambassador quietly, "I wish that poem had been written for me." Then, restraining his emotion, the President glanced at the pretty Irish Airlines stewardess who had brought the cup from Ireland, and delivered the only out-and-out commercial plug ever heard at a White House ceremony. "I want it known," he said, "that this cup was brought from Ireland through the courtesy of Irish International Airlines."

During that last springtime of his life, President Kennedy was busily concerned with his battles over racial segregation in Birmingham and at the University of Alabama, his struggles with Congress on civil rights legislation, and his negotiations with Khrushchev that led to the later atmospheric nuclear test ban treaty, which the President regarded as his greatest accomplishment. Our memories of those months are filled with happenings and scenes that never made headlines. There was the day when we brought into the President's office four blind students who had won scholastic achievement awards, one of them a son of Italian immigrant parents, a history major at Harvard in the top 5 percent of his class with a record of straight A's in every course. "Which one is the boy at Harvard?" President Kennedy asked. When he was introduced to the blind student, Patrick Peppe, the President asked, "Is your father here?" Joseph Peppe, a man with one arm, stepped forward nervously to meet the President. "What kind of work do you do, Mr. Peppe?" the President asked. The student's father said that he had a newsstand on the Grand Concourse in the Bronx. "I used to live in the Bronx when I was a boy, at 222nd Street and Independence Avenue in Riverdale," President Kennedy said. "I'll bet I used to buy newspapers at your stand. Which papers in New York are selling best these days? Dave, ask a photographer to come in here so that Mr.

Peppe can have a picture of us to put up on his stand." He described his office and its displays of historical objects to the students, and arranged for them to have a descriptive guided tour of the White House.

There was the surprise party arranged by the President in the Cabinet Room for Dave on his fiftieth birthday. The President gave Dave a sweatshirt with "Vigah" stenciled on its front, a fifty-mile hike certificate "for hiking to my icebox to drink up all my beer," and a silver beer mug inscribed with a quotation from an Indian philosopher, "There are three things which are real, God, human folly and laughter. The first two are beyond our comprehension, so we must do what we can with the third." Then there was the surprise party for President Kennedy on his forty-sixth birthday in the White House basement's mess hall. We roped him downstairs to the party by pretending that there was an urgent call for him on the special scramble telephone in the communications room. One of his gifts, from Jackie, was a basket of grass from his Rose Garden, an in-joke about his squabbles with the White House gardeners over his efforts to improve the quality of the lawn outside his office. At one time he had threatened to bring one of the Kennedy landscape gardeners from Hyannis Port to make the garden's grass greener.

There was also the memorable outdoor reception for 234 winners of the Congressional Medal of Honor, young ones from the Korean War and older ones from the two world wars and a few elderly men who were cited for heroism in the Spanish-American War. It was the first time that a President had invited so many Medal of Honor veterans to the White House. We noticed one uninvited visitor, standing alone on the edge of the crowd, saying nothing, watching the guests with fascination in his eyes — Bobby Kennedy, the admirer of heroic courage, had heard that his brother was entertaining the medal winners, and he was unable to resist sneaking into the party to get a look at them. A few days later, after attending Memorial Day services at Arlington National Cemetery, the President quietly began the practice of sending a memorial certificate to the nearest surviving relative after the death of a war veteran. It was his own idea. He arranged with the Veterans Administration to be notified when that agency received word of the death of anybody who had served in any war, and he ordered and approved the design of the certificate which was to be mailed with his signature in a White

House envelope to the veteran's next of kin. This unexpected re-membrance, coming from the President of the United States to fami-lies who assumed that their man's service in the armed forces had been long forgotten, brought many moving letter of thanks from all over the country. The President showed us a letter from a widow in Colorado who wrote, "I want to thank you for the certificate honor-ing my husband. It brought tears from the realization that the head of a nation so big could put importance on details so seemingly small. It fills me with an overwhelming love for my country."

That spring the Kennedys gave up their rented weekend estate at Glen Ora and began to build a house of their own, to be called Atoka, in the Virginia hunting country near Middleburg. They spent the spring weekends at Camp David, the Presidential retreat in the Catoctin Mountains of Maryland. The President fell in love with Camp David. It had everything that he wanted, beautiful scenery, comfortable living quarters with military intelligence communication facilities, a heated swimming pool, a stable of horses for Jackie and Caroline, a three-hole golf course, and, best of all, because it was a government reservation with security regula-tions, complete privacy for himself and his family. There was even a Sunday mass in the military mess hall, so he did not need to cope with photographers at a local church. "Gosh, Jackie," he said to his wife one day at Camp David, "Why are we building Atoka when we have a wonderful place like this, for free?"

In June, however, the President did not have much time to enjoy Camp David, because that was a month of traveling, first a five-day trip to Hawaii with stops along the way at the Air Force Academy in Colorado, the White Sands missile range, a meeting with Texas Democrats at El Paso, an inspection of Naval bases and weapons in California and a thousand-dollar-a-couple dinner of the President's Club in Los Angeles. Then the President enjoyed one of the greatest experiences of his life, his memorable journey to Germany, Ireland, England and Italy. I remember that June visit to El Paso with no pleasure because it was there that the Vice-President and Governor John Connally arranged the President's political trip to Texas for the following November. Before we went to California, the Presi-dent received a letter from a group of students at the John Bur-roughs High School in Los Angeles, complaining to him because their school prom had been evicted from a ballroom at the Beverly

Hilton to make space for the thousand-dollar-a-couple dinner being given in his honor by the local Democrats. Kennedy contacted the dinner committee and asked them to give the room back to the high school prom. That evening he left the dinner to visit the students at their dance, bringing Jack Benny with him. Introducing Benny to the roaring youngsters, he said, "I want you to meet my kid brother, Teddy." Benny was too stunned to make a comeback.

From Honolulu, where he addressed the United States Conference of Mayors, the President flew overnight directly back to Washington, arriving at Andrews Air Force Base shortly before nine o'clock the next morning. He hurried to the White House, changed his shirt, and drove to the commencement exercises at the American University, where, at ten-thirty, as tired as he was from the long flight from Hawaii, he delivered the most important foreign policy speech of his career, and probably one of the best speaking performances of his lifetime. Jackie told us recently that she considered the American University speech, which failed to get the attention it deserved in the next day's newspapers, to be one of the President's three best speeches, along with his inaugural address and the spirited talk that he gave in West Berlin two weeks later. We are inclined to add his talk to the ministers in Houston during the 1960 campaign to the top of that list. As Dave says, if Kennedy had not given the speech in Houston, he might not have been able to deliver the other three.

Kennedy referred to the American University address as "the peace speech," because it was an appeal for a lasting peace between the United States and the Soviet Union, directed at Khrushchev, who had hinted that such a new message from the President might help to bring a favorable reaction to Kennedy's proposal for a nuclear atmospheric test ban treaty.

"It is an ironic but accurate fact," President Kennedy said in his appeal to the Russians, "that the two strongest powers are the two in most danger of devastation. All we have built, all we have worked for, would be destroyed in the first twenty-four hours. For we are both devoting to weapons massive sums of money that could be better devoted to combating ignorance, poverty and disease. We are both caught up in a vicious and dangerous cycle in which suspicion on one side breeds suspicion on the other, and new weapons beget counterweapons. . . . If we cannot now end our differences, we can at least make the world safe for diversity. For in the final analysis, our most basic common link is that we all inhabit this small planet. We all breathe the same air. We all cherish our children's future. And we are all mortal."

The American University speech brought an immediate thaw in our relationship with the Soviets. Khrushchev told Averell Harriman later that it was the best speech delivered by any American President since Franklin D. Roosevelt. It was the first important speech by a United States government official in many years that was allowed to be heard in its entirety in a Voice of America radio broadcast to Russia and other Eastern European countries without being interrupted or jammed by Soviet monitors. Russian newspapers published the full text. And a few weeks later Khrushchev made a speech in East Berlin, endorsing Kennedy's atmospheric test ban proposal.

The President's trip to Europe that June was planned originally as a visit to West Germany to strengthen that country's allegiance to the NATO alliance. Then the Italians complained that their strong loyalty to the United States and NATO deserved recognition, so Italy was added to the itinerary. The State Department, always concerned about preserving "our special relationship with Britain," urged the President to include a short visit to Macmillan. One day when I was discussing with the President our plans and dates for the journey to Germany, Italy and England, he said, "I've decided that I want to go to Ireland, too."

"Ireland?" I said. "Mr. President, may I say something? There's no reason for you to go to Ireland. It would be a waste of time. It wouldn't do you much good politically. You've got all the Irish votes in this country that you'll ever get. If you go to Ireland, people will say it's just a pleasure trip."

"That's exactly what I want, a pleasure trip to Ireland," he said.

I didn't take him too seriously. I talked to Mac Bundy, our resident expert on foreign affairs, and Bundy agreed with me that a visit to Ireland would only prolong the President's trip unnecessarily because there were no political or diplomatic advantages to be gained by such a sentimental excursion. The next day I went back to the President and told him what Bundy had said. He looked up at me from the newspaper that he was reading with an air of exasperated impatience.

"Kenny, let me remind you of something," he said. "I am the President of the United States, not you. When I say I want to go to Ireland, it means that I'm going to Ireland. Make the arrangements." So I quickly made arrangements for him to go to Ireland, where, as he often said later, his visit was one of his greatest emotional experiences.

Before we left for Europe, the President read Irish histories, traced the lineage of the Kennedys and the Fitzgeralds, studied the writings of John Boyle O'Reilly and the exploits of the Irish Brigade in the American Civil War, and arranged with the successors of that brigade, the New York "Fighting 69th" Irish National Guard regiment, to present one of its flags from the battles of Fredericksburg, Chancellorsville and Gettysburg to the Republic of Ireland. "He's getting so Irish," Dave said, "the next thing we know he'll be speaking with a brogue." Dave showed the President a Kennedy family tree from the Library of Congress which traced his descent from a member of the royal Brian Boru family named Cinneide, which can be translated from the Gaelic as "Helmet Head." "Let's keep that quiet," the President said. He learned that most of the outstanding Kennedys were forced to flee "like wild geese" after the Cromwellian invasion of Ireland to become exiled soldiers in foreign countries. He was fascinated by a line of verse describing their plight and quoted it often, "War battered dogs are we, gnawing a naked bone, fighting in every land and clime, for every cause but our own."

Our first stop on the European tour was in West Germany, where the President attended mass with Konrad Adenauer at the ancient Cologne Cathedral. The cathedral was surrounded by a massed crowd of nearly four hundred thousand people, including thousands of children waving tiny American flags. Kennedy eyed the flags, and said to Adenauer, "Where did the flags come from? Don't tell me these families just happened to have American flags in their homes. An advance man must have done some work here." Adenauer smiled and said, "Oh, we arrange things like you do in your election campaigns. But we didn't arrange this huge crowd. The Cardinal is wishing right now that he could attract this many people to the Cathedral for one of his masses." There were bigger and wildly enthusiastic crowds at Bonn, Frankfurt and Hanau during the next two days, and then in West Berlin on June 26 when he made a forty-mile tour of the city, President Kennedy was thrilled by the sight of the biggest crowds he had ever seen anywhere. It was said that more than half of West Berlin's two and a third million people were in the streets that day, lined up four deep along his route and crowding every window and rooftop. The square outside of the Schoneberg City Hall, when he delivered his famous speech of challenge to the Communist world, was jammed solidly as far as he could see in every direction by a tightly crowded mass of people, chanting steadily "Ken-ah-dee!" and shouting a roar of approval when he repeatedly punctuated his thrusts at compromising appeasers ("There are those who say that Communism is the wave of the future . . . even a few who say Communism is an evil system, but it permits us to make economic progress . . .") with the resounding refrain, *"Let — them — come — to — Berlin!"* The crowd was swept by a surge of pride and warmth, and deeply stirred as few such massive audiences in history have ever been moved, by Kennedy's opening and closing words, "Today, in the world of freedom, the proudest boast is 'Ich bin ein Berliner' . . . All free men, wherever they may live, are citizens of Berlin, and therefore as a free man, I take pride in the words, 'Ich bin ein Berliner.' " A German government official told us later that Adolf Hitler, at the peak of his popularity and power, had never attracted a crowd as large and as warmly emotional as the crowd that listened to Kennedy that day in Berlin. That afternoon when he boarded Air Force One to leave Germany, the President said to us, "We'll never have another day like this one."

Kennedy's fighting speech in Berlin, as magnificent as it was, actually was a grave political risk, and he knew it. Such a heated tribute to West Berlin's resistance to Communism could have undone all of the success of his appeal for peace and understanding with the Soviets in his American University speech two weeks earlier. But Kennedy could not prevent himself from saying what his heart wanted him to say. He was carried away by the courage of the West Berliners, and shocked by the sight of the Berlin Wall that he had seen that morning, and he had to tell the people how he felt about them. When he stopped to look at the Brandenburg Gate, a guard handed him a bouquet of flowers that had been thrown over the wall with a note asking that it be given to him. Later, when we stopped at Checkpoint Charlie, the American-controlled gate to

East Germany, a small group of East Berliners beyond the gate waved and cheered him. When he reached City Hall, and saw the huge mob of people waiting for a few words of hope and encouragement, he had to speak out to them passionately to give them the reassurance that they desperately wanted to hear, even if it meant the ruin of his cherished ambition to make a nuclear test ban treaty.

In fact, most of his emotional talk in Berlin was spontaneous and unprepared, put together from a few thoughts that came to him that morning. When we were arriving in Berlin, he said to me, "What was the proud boast of the Romans — Civis Romanus sum? Send Bundy up here. He'll know how to say it in German." When Bundy translated the phrase into "Ich bin ein Berliner," the President said, as he wrote it down, "Now tell me how to say in German, 'Let them come to Berlin.' " From City Hall, Kennedy went to deliver another speech at the Free University of Berlin, where he tried to repair some of the damage that he might have done earlier in the day by returning to the peace theme of his American University address. "As I said this morning," he ad-libbed into the prepared text of his Free University talk, "I am not impressed by the opportunities open to popular fronts throughout the world. I do not believe that any democrat can successfully ride that tiger. But I do believe in the necessity of great powers working together to preserve the human race." Fortunately, Nikita Khrushchev, who undoubtedly remembered a few ill-timed emotional outbursts of his own, decided to ignore the City Hall speech and to accept the Free University speech, and went ahead with his endorsement of the atmospheric test ban treaty.

That afternoon, with the important diplomatic and political work of his mission done with and behind him, the President flew to Ireland to enjoy himself. On the plane he recalled to us his previous visit to Ireland in 1947, when he stayed with his sister Kathleen at Lismore Castle in County Wexford, the palatial home of her noble British in-laws, the Duke and Duchess of Devonshire, who were related to Harold Macmillan's wife and David Ormsby-Gore. One day he borrowed one of the castle's station wagons and drove to Dunganstown, near New Ross, looking for the home that his great-grandfather, Patrick Kennedy, had left during the potato famine in 1848 to emigrate to Boston. He took with him, for company, an English lady who was also staying at the castle. They found the

Kennedy farm, and visited his father's second cousins in their whitewashed thatched cottage, drinking a cup of tea in the dirt-floored kitchen with chickens and a pig wandering around them. When they were driving back to Lismore, the English lady said, "That was like Tobacco Road." The President said to us, recalling the scene on the plane to Dublin sixteen years later, "I felt like kicking her out of the car. For me, the visit to that cottage was filled with magic sentiment. That night at the castle Kathleen and I had dinner with the other guests, Anthony Eden, Randolph Churchill and the Earl of Roselyn. I looked around the table and thought about the cottage where my cousins lived, and I said to myself, 'What a contrast!' Kenny, how soon will we be going back to see my cousins in Dunganstown?"

"Tomorrow," I said to him. "They'll be all there waiting for you with a big spread of salmon and tea." When Pierre Salinger and I went to Ireland a month earlier to advance the President's visit, we found ourselves in the middle of a family argument at Dunganstown about which relatives should be invited to the party. Mary Ryan, the matriarch of the cottage, pointed her finger at one man, and shouted at him, "You haven't shown your face at this door in twenty years, and now you're horning in here because President Kennedy is coming!" I turned to the abused fellow and asked his name. "John Kennedy," he said.

I said to the President, "This time in Ireland you won't be mixed up with any members of the British nobility."

"Good," he said.

The mood of tense anxiety that we had just left in Berlin made the completely happy crowd of people along O'Connell Street in Dublin seem all the more joyous and carefree. The whole noisy city was bursting with Gaelic pride. Men were holding small children above their heads to get a look at the President, women were screaming, "Bless you!" and everybody seemed to have tears in their eyes. When we reached the elegant American Embassy in Phoenix Park, where we were to spend the next three nights, the President said to Dave, "What did you think of it?" Dave said, "If you ran over here, you'd beat De Valera in his own precinct." Kennedy was up early the next morning, eager to get going to Wexford and Dunganstown. He looked out the window at the green lawns of the park, one of the biggest and most beautiful city parks in the world, and said, "This would be a great house to live in." Matt McCloskey, the Philadelphia contractor who had been rewarded with the Ambassadorship for his champion fund-raising efforts, was waiting for us when we came downstairs. "Matt, this is a much better place than the White House," the President said. "The party is running into debt, and we need you back there." Matt said, "No, no, leave me alone. If you need money, send Dick Maguire over here and I'll tell him who to see." Kennedy announced that in 1968 he would support the Democratic candidate who would promise to appoint him Ambassador to Ireland.

After the President had a talk with Sean Lemass, the Irish Prime Minister, we boarded the helicopters outside of the Embassy and flew to New Ross, the pretty port town on the tidal River Barrow, near Dunganstown. Schoolchildren, wearing white sweaters, were stretched out on the green grass of the park below the descending helicopters, spelling out FAILTE, the Gaelic word for welcome. Another group of youngsters sang to the President one of his favorite Irish songs, "The Boys of Wexford." ("We are the boys of Wexford, who fought with heart and hand to burst in twain the galling chain and free our native land.") The nun in charge of the singers asked if he would like to hear something else. "Another verse of 'The Boys of Wexford' would be just fine," he said. The nun handed him a card with the lyrics of the song, and he sang with the children. Then he asked the nun if he could keep the card, and slipped it into his pocket.

There was a civic welcoming ceremony at the New Ross riverside docks, where the President's great-grandfather boarded the ship that took him to America. "When my great-grandfather left here to become a cooper in East Boston," Kennedy said, "he carried nothing with him except two things, a strong religious faith and a strong desire for liberty. I am glad to say that all of his great-grandchildren have valued that inheritance." He pointed across the river at the Albatross fertilizer plant, and said, "If my great-grandfather had not left New Ross, I would be working today over there at the Albatross Company." The crowd roared with laughter.

Then we were on our way to Mary Kennedy Ryan's cottage on the old Kennedy farm at Dunganstown. The President remembered that when he was making his way to his ancestral home in 1947 he had asked a man named Robert Burrell for directions. "Ask somebody on a road in Ireland for directions," he said, "and you get a more entertaining performance than you'll get at a Broadway show. When we get there, see if you can find that Burrell fellow." A Secret Service man located Burrell in the crowd at Dunganstown, and said to him, "Would you like to meet President Kennedy?" Burrell glanced at the agent, unimpressed, and said, "I met him sixteen years ago." The President greeted Mary Ryan and several other third and fourth cousins, and followed them into the cottage where a bright turf fire was burning in the fireplace and a platter of cold salmon and a silver pot of tea and a tray of brown wheat bread were spread on the white linen tablecloth. "The fire feels good," he said to Mrs. Ryan. "I picked up a newspaper in New Ross and it said that you were having a cattle auction here this coming weekend. How is everything going with the farm?" A cousin named Jim Kennedy poured him a large Irish whisky, which he quietly handed, behind his back, to Dave when nobody was looking. Dave knocked off the whisky obediently and handed the empty glass back to the President. The family doctor, Martin Quigley, presented a sheepskin floor mat, and said to the President, "This is to be put beside Mrs. Kennedy's bed for the arrival of the twins in August." Jim Kennedy gave the President a blackthorn stick for himself, porcelain for Jackie, a handkerchief for Caroline and a hand-carved boat for John. The President lifted his cup and said, "We want to drink a cup of tea to all the Kennedys who went and those who stayed."

Frank Aiken, the Irish Minister of External Affairs, reminded the President that we had to be moving on to Wexford, where a crowd was waiting to watch him place a wreath on the monument of Commodore John Barry, the Irish-born founder of the American Navy in the Revolutionary War and one of Kennedy's favorite heroes. Mary Ryan turned on Aiken and said to him, "You won't be hurrying him out of here until he plants a juniper tree in our garden so we'll have something to remind us of this day in the years to come." Dave and I looked at each other, remembering what had happened to the President's back the last time he had planted a tree, in Ottawa in 1961. But the tree was planted with a round of cheers. As the President was leaving, he kissed Mary Ryan warmly on her cheek while his sisters, Eunice and Jean, who were traveling with us, stared at him in wide-eyed astonishment. He seldom displayed such affection.

The next morning the President enjoyed every minute of our visit to Cork, the hotbed of the Irish Revolution. He pointed with glee to one hand-lettered sign held up in the crowd, linking him as a Yank with Eamon de Valera, who was born in New York. The sign said, "JFK and Dev, for Boston and New York — but the boys who beat the Black and Tans were the boys from County Cork." Another sign said, "Don't worry, Jack. The Iron Curtain will rust in peace." The huge crowd in the streets around Cork's City Hall, where the Lord Mayor, Alderman Sean Casey, conferred the freedom of the city on the President, had more than one hundred thousand people. "Everybody in Kerry, Tipperary, Kilkenny and Wexford is here today," the Lord Mayor said to us. "And a few spies from Belfast, too." Kennedy was in top form, as the Irish say, when he spoke to the crowd. He pointed out various people in our entourage who had Cork ancestors, among them Dave Powers, who was sitting with seven local first cousins. "Dave looks more Irish than his cousins," the President said. "I also want to introduce Monsignor Michael O'Mahoney, the pastor at the church I go to, who comes from Cork. He is the pastor of a poor, humble flock in Palm Beach, Florida." The crowd roared with laughter.

We flew back to Dublin for a luncheon that the President gave for President de Valera and Prime Minister Lemass at the American Embassy, with songs by the Irish girls who entertain at the nightly medieval-style dinners at Bunratty Castle near Shannon Airport. The Bunratty singers, in their fifteenth century costumes, sang such ancient folk tunes as "A Jug of Punch," "The West's Awake," "Roisin Dubh" and "Pucae Boille." The President listened patiently, and then beckoned to Dave. "Ask them to sing 'Danny Boy,'" he said. The girls sang "Danny Boy," and the President joined them in an encore.

From the luncheon, Kennedy and Lemass went to memorial services at Arbour Hill in Dublin, where the executed leaders of the 1916 Easter Week Rebellion are buried. Standing at solemn attention, the President watched with fascination a crisp drill ceremony performed by cadets from Ireland's Military College at The Curragh. Later when we were discussing the various memories of our trip to Ireland, the Kennedy sisters, Eunice and Jean, and Lee Radziwill, Jackie's sister, who was also with us, agreed that the President's stirring speech to the Irish parliament later that Friday afternoon was the outstanding highlight of his visit. The President shook his head. "For me, the highlight was the ceremony at Arbour Hill," he said. "Those cadets were terrific. I wish we had a film of that drill so that we could do something like it at the Tomb of the Unknown Soldier." He described the Arbour Hill memorial services to Jackie so impressively that she made arrangements on the flight from Dallas to have the same group of Irish cadets at the President's grave during his burial.

Kennedy's speech to the combined houses of parliament, the first ceremony in the Dail's legislative chamber ever seen on national television, was just the kind of talk that Ireland wanted to hear from him, flashes of easy wit, graceful literary quotations, moving praise of Ireland's courageous history, its contributions to culture and to America. "Franklin sent leaflets to Irish Freedom Fighters," he said. "O'Connell was influenced by Washington, and Emmet influenced Lincoln. Irish volunteers played so predominant a role in the American Army that Lord Mountjoy commented in the British Parliament, 'We have lost America through the Irish.' " Speaking of the Irish immigrants who contributed to the building of the United States, he mentioned James Joyce's description of the Atlantic as "a bowl of bitter tears." A writer for the *Irish Times* commented the next day that this was the first time that the name of the great Irish modern novelist had been mentioned in the hall of Dublin's parliament, except in legislative arguments about censorship. It was in this speech that President Kennedy first used the now well-worn quotation from George Bernard Shaw later taken up by Bobby, and repeated so often by him that it is now often credited to Bobby instead of to Shaw. "This is an extraordinary country," the President said, while pointing out that Ireland had produced more literary and artistic genius than most larger nations. "George Bernard Shaw, speaking as an Irishman, summed up an approach to life: 'Other people see things, and say why. But I dream things that never were, and I say, why not?' "

After the President's speech, while he was struggling through the crowd of well-wishers in Leinster House, an Irish woman pointed out to me two legislators in the hall who were excitedly talking to each other about the day's event. "Those two are political enemies," she said. "This is the first time they've spoken together in twenty years. All of us love your President Kennedy, and that's the only thing that all of the people in Ireland have completely agreed upon since the British passed the Conscription Bill in 1918."

When we left the Dail, President Kennedy said to me, "Kenny, of those you've met, who do you think are the best politicians in America?" I said, "Daley and Mansfield." The President nodded. "I agree with you. The Irish do seem to have an art for government." He paused a moment, then smiled: "Perhaps we are both prejudiced."

The President then hurried to Dublin Castle, where he was invested as a freeman of the city and received honorary degrees from both the Catholic National University of Ireland, where President de Valera and James Joyce both studied as youths, and the Protestant Dublin University, better known as Trinity College. Before he was awarded the National University doctor of laws degree, he was dressed by De Valera in the purple, green and scarlet robe and the floppy, wide black velvet academic hat of that school. He removed the hat as quickly as possible after the awarding of the degree. Then the President marched out of the castle's Saint Patrick's Hall where the ceremony had taken place, and the officials and dons of the university filed out of their plush seats on the spectators' benches. The seats were then filled by the officers and dons of the Trinity faculty, and President Kennedy reappeared, wearing the scarlet and rose Trinity robe, to receive his second doctoral degree from Trinity's Vice-Chancellor, the Earl of Rosse. When he passed us in the outside corridor in the Protestant academic gown, Dave said to him, "Is this the *real* John F. Kennedy?" The President gave us that quick disapproving look, which meant, "Knock it off." In his speech of acceptance, Kennedy delivered a remark that broke up the academic ritual with a roar of laughter.

"I want to say how pleased I am to have this association with these two great universities," he said. "I now feel equally a part of both, and if they ever have a game of Gaelic football or hurling, I shall cheer for Trinity and pray for National."

That evening, his last night in Ireland, the President and his party were the guests of President de Valera at a rather small and informal dinner, where the conversation was sparkling and the laughs plentiful. While he was talking with admiration about the memorial ceremony at Arbour Hill, the ever-curious Kennedy could not resist asking the dignified and reserved De Valera a rather pointed question: why was he the only leader of the 1916 Easter Week Rebellion who was not shot by a British firing squad? De Valera explained that he had lived in Ireland since his early childhood, but he was born in New York City, and because of his American citizenship, the British were reluctant to kill him. "But there were many times when the key in my jail cell door was turned," he said, "and I thought that my turn had come." While Kennedy listened, spellbound, De Valera went on to talk about Ireland's war for independence and his troubles with David Lloyd George and Winston Churchill, who was the Home Secretary in the British government suppressing the revolt in Ireland in 1920 and 1921 until King George V intervened to seek a peace treaty. "If you are weak in your dealings with the British, they will pressure you," he said. "If you are subject to flattery, they will cajole you. Only if you are reasonable, will they reason with you, and being reasonable with the British means letting them know that you are willing to throw an occasional bomb into one of their lorries."

We became involved in a warm discussion with Brendan Corish, leader of the Irish Labor party, Deputy John A. Costello and Tom Kiernan, the Irish Ambassador to the United States, about the merits of various Irish fighting songs. Kiernan contended that "A Nation Once Again" could arouse the fighting spirit in the meekest of men, while Costello favored the inspirational qualities of "O'Donnell Abu." "Ah, you're wrong," Corish exclaimed. " 'O'Donnell Abu' will make you want to fight, but it won't stir you one bit." The President called upon Dave to tell the gathering a few Boston Irish jokes, a difficult task before a Dublin Irish audience. Dave obliged with a tale about two Irishmen who were reading headstone inscriptions in an old cemetery where British soldiers killed at the Battle of Bunker Hill were buried. The stone above one narrow grave had an epitaph which said, "Here lies an Englishman and a good man." One of the Irishmen said to the other, "Now, Mike, sure that grave doesn't look as if it had room enough for two people, does it?" The Dubliners approved of that one.

The President was sitting between Mrs. de Valera and Mrs. Sean T. O'Kelly, the wife of a former Irish President. He was entranced by Bean de Valera, a woman of great beauty and charm whose memory of obscure Irish poetry amazed the President. When he mentioned that he would be leaving Ireland from Shannon Airport the next day, Mrs. de Valera recited to him an old poem about the

Shannon River. He copied the verse's lines on his place card and on the place card of Mrs. O'Kelly, memorized the words the next morning while he was eating his breakfast, and recited the poem when he was saying good-bye to the crowd at the airport that afternoon.

On the way to Shannon, we made two stops on the west coast of Ireland, at Galway and Limerick. An honor guard of twenty-four members of the local American Legion post was waiting to greet the President when he stepped out of the helicopter at Galway. He looked at me and shook his head. "You can't get away from the American Legion no matter where you go," he said. "I'll bet they have a post at the South Pole." He had a difficult time trying to keep a straight face when one of the Irishmen in the legion stepped up to him, handed him a letter in an envelope, and said, "It's about my pension. Would you use your influence and see if you can get me an increase?" The President assured the legionnaire that his request would get every consideration, and handed the letter to Dave. A few weeks later, back in the White House, the President said to Dave, "Did you take care of that fellow in Galway?" Fortunately for Dave, he had contacted the Veterans Administration the day before, and the pension increase had been put through. The city square in Galway was crowded with more than eighty thousand people, all of them cheering so loudly that the bells of Saint Nicholas Church, ringing "The Star-Spangled Banner," could hardly be heard above the din. "How many of you have relatives in America whom you'd admit to?" Kennedy said to the laughing crowd. "Nearly everybody in Boston comes from Galway and they're not shy about it, at all. If you ever come to America, come to Washington and tell them at the gate that you come from Galway." A large number of people from Galway later turned up at the White House, one of them a young nun who sat down in the Cabinet Room and quietly refused to leave until she had shaken hands with the President himself. "If I go back there and tell the Mother Superior I didn't see him," she said, "she'll throw me out of the convent." We explained her situation to the President. He not only saw her, but summoned Cecil Stoughton, the White House photographer, to take a picture of their meeting so she could bring tangible evidence back to Galway. "Oh, Good God!" she exclaimed. "I'll never forget this day!"

At Limerick, the President left the helicopter, shaking hands with the people from the waiting crowd who surged around him, and turned back to us and yelled, "Kenny and Dave, come here!" We struggled to get to him, wondering what had happened, only to find him pointing happily at an elderly man who was standing beside him. "Isn't he the image of Honey Fitz?" the President said. "And his name is Fitzgerald." The lady mayor of Limerick, Frances Clondell, and a Protestant at that, introduced the President with an oration that was lengthy but glowing. He whispered to me while she was talking, "These introductions would seem awfully long if they weren't such good speakers. This is the best speech I've heard since I've been in Europe." When he began his own speech, the President got his biggest laugh in Ireland. He started to say that Limerick was his last stop before going to England and Italy. Instead he caught himself, and said, "From here I go to — another country — and then to Italy and back home to the United States." The crowd roared.

A deep quiet came over the crowd when he went on to say, "I carry with me, as I go, the orchestrated sentiments of appreciation to all of you. Last night somebody sang a song, the words of which I am sure you know, 'Come back to Erin, Mavourneen Mavourneen, come back arue to the land of thy birth, come with the shamrock in the springtime, Mavourneen.' This is not the land of my birth, but it is the land for which I hold the greatest affection, and I will certainly come back in the springtime."

When the helicopter took off from the racecourse park in Limerick for the short hop to Shannon Airport, Kennedy looked down at the green fields and said, "I wish I could stay here for another week, or another month." At Shannon, where Air Force One was waiting, he recited to the crowd the poem that Mrs. de Valera had given to him. "Last night," he said, "I sat next to one of the most extraordinary women, the wife of your President, who knows more about Ireland and Irish history than any of us. I told her I was coming to Shannon and she quoted this poem, and I wrote down the words because I thought they were beautiful:

" 'Tis the Shannon's brightly glancing stream,
"Brightly gleaming, silent in the morning beam, oh! the sight entrancing.
"Thus return from travels long, years of exile, years of pain
"To see Old Shannon's face again,
"O'er the waters glancing.

"Well, I am going to come back and see Old Shannon's face again, and I am taking, as I go back to America, all of you with me."

We drove across the field to Air Force One, where the girls from Bunratty Castle in their medieval dresses gave him one last chorus of "Danny Boy" before he waved and went inside the plane. While the girls were singing, I saw somebody in the crowd holding up a sign, scrawled with the title of another old song popular in Ireland, a sad ballad about a young man who left his girl to go off to fight and die in a war against the British. Four months later, when we were bringing President Kennedy's body back from Dallas, I thought of that sign at Shannon Airport and I think of it often now. It said, "Johnny, I Hardly Knew Ye."

After the President's plane left Ireland, it made an unscheduled and unpublicized stop at Waddington Royal Air Force Base in England. There he was met by the Duke and Duchess of Devonshire, who flew with him, and his sister Jean and Lee Radziwill, in a helicopter to their estate at Chatsworth to visit the grave of his sister Kathleen, who was married to the Duke's older brother, the Marquess of Hartington, for four months before he died in action in Normandy during World War II. Kathleen, or "Kick," as the President called her, remained in England after her husband's death, and was buried at Chatsworth after she was killed in a plane crash in France in 1948. This was the President's first and only visit to Kathleen's grave. He knelt and prayed, and watched Jean place a bouquet of red and white roses, picked in Ireland that morning, beside the headstone, which was inscribed with the words, "Joy she gave — Joy she has found."

From Chatsworth, Kennedy flew back to Waddington, and from there he went to Birch Grove, Harold Macmillan's country home, to spend the night with Macmillan and Dean Rusk, who had gone to England from Germany to discuss the nuclear atmospheric test ban treaty and the NATO situation. Dave and I were supposed to stay overnight with the President at Birch Grove, but a few minutes after we arrived there, while he was dressing for dinner, we sneaked out of the house and hurried off to Brighton, the English seaside resort, where we had arranged to enjoy a Saturday evening of relaxation with the crew of Air Force One and members of the press. I had hardly checked into my hotel room at Brighton when the telephone rang. It was the President, furious with both of us, not so much because he needed us at Macmillan's house, but mainly because we were having some fun that he was missing. "Thanks for leaving me stranded," he said. "I suppose you've been cooking up this little party for a week or more. Who's there? What's going on? I suppose you've got a big drink in your hand." Later in the night he telephoned Dave and said to him, "Tomorrow is Sunday. I want you here at seven o'clock in the morning to go to mass with me."

"Sorry, Mr. President," Dave said. "You'll have to go to mass by yourself. Remember not to drop any hundred-dollar bills in the collection basket."

Kennedy laughed, and hung up. This was a reminder of a news story about him going to mass in a church in California and putting a one-hundred-dollar bill in the collection box. He never carried money, and when he went to church Dave would hand him a ten-dollar bill for the collection. The President was horrified when he read about his alleged hundred-dollar donation, and said to Dave, "Was that a hundred-dollar bill you gave me?"

Dave replied, "Any time you can put ten dollars in the box and get credit for a hundred, you're ninety dollars ahead of the game."

The President persisted. "Are you sure it was a ten?"

"I'm positive," Dave said. "I handed you a ten. I never saw a hundred-dollar bill in my whole life."

That Sunday afternoon we flew to Italy. Shortly before we left Washington to start the European trip, Pope John XXIII died, and we offered to cancel our visit to Italy, assuming that the President's appearance there during the election and coronation of the new Pope might be an unwelcome distraction. The Italian government insisted that the President must come anyway. Kennedy telephoned Cardinal Cushing for a word of advice. "Stay away from Rome until after the coronation," the Cardinal said. "It's the biggest day of the man's life, and you don't want to take the play away from him." To avoid the coronation, which was taking place on the same Sunday that the President was arriving in Italy, we arranged for him to land at Milan and to spend the rest of the day at Lake Como, killing some time and getting a bit of relaxation before going on to Rome on Monday. We stayed overnight at the Villa Serbelloni at the shore of the lake. It was a beautiful, warm summer evening. The

President decided to take a drive, in his shirt-sleeves, through the village. The surprised townspeople who saw him called to their friends and neighbors, and the streets were quickly filled with people pouring out of houses and shops, cheering and running beside the President's car, trying to touch his hand.

Rome the next day seemed rather quiet, compared to the wild excitement and huge crowds that we had seen in Berlin and Dublin. The city was simmering in ninety-degree heat, and the Romans were emotionally drained after the ceremonies of the funeral of Pope John and the coronation of Pope Paul VI. But the square outside the Presidential Palace was thronged with cheering people when the President came out from his two-hour talk with Italy's President Antonio Segni, and security guards had to form a flying wedge to save him from admirers. When we were driving from the palace along the Via Sistina to Rome's Tomb of its Unknown Soldier, a group of women ran into the street from a beautician's parlor, with the hairdresser's towels still draped around their shoulders, trying to reach the President's car.

On Tuesday when Kennedy went to the Vatican for an audience with the Pope, there was a buzz of speculation among the reporters about whether the President would kneel before the Pontiff to kiss his ring, as most Catholics do. "Norman Vincent Peale would love that," the President said. "And it would get me a lot of votes in South Carolina." He had never considered kissing the Pope's ring, of course, because he was visiting Paul as a head of state, not as a Catholic. The President and the new Pope talked alone in the second floor library at Clementine Hall, with no interpreter present because the Pope speaks English fluently. Then Dean Rusk joined the meeting for fifteen minutes, and then the Pope received the rest of us in the President's party — Angier Biddle Duke, the chief of protocol, Jean Smith, McGeorge Bundy, Ted Sorenson, Pierre Salinger, Dave Powers and myself. Pope Paul recalled that he had met the President and other members of the Kennedy family almost twenty-five years earlier, during the coronation of Pope Pius XII, when Teddy was confirmed by that newly crowned Pope.

From the Vatican we drove to the North American College, where Cardinal Cushing was waiting on the front steps to give the President a bear hug, followed by a friendly left jab and a right hook to the ribs. After gruffly reminding us that he was the only

American cardinal remaining in Rome after the coronation to greet the President because he was the only true Democrat in the delegation, Cardinal Cushing said, "Jack, too bad you couldn't get here before Pope John died. You two would have hit it off fine." The Cardinal told the President that Pope John, looking forward eagerly to meeting John Kennedy, had planned to present to him an autographed copy of his famed "Pacem in Terris" encyclical, which Kennedy deeply admired. "And here it is," the Cardinal said, handing over the encyclical, "one of the only three signed copies in existence." The President studied the autographed document with stars in his eyes, and told the Cardinal that Pope Paul had just given to him a replica of Michelangelo's *Pieta*. "I know he did," Cardinal Cushing said. "I was the one who told him to give it to you."

Although Rome had been comparatively quiet, the President's visit to NATO headquarters in Naples before his departure to the United States touched off the noisiest demonstration of his European tour, with bigger crowds than we had seen in Berlin showing a more overwhelming explosion of hero worship than even the hero-loving Germans displayed. The streets in Naples and the balconies and windows were crammed with shouting people when Kennedy drove through the city on his way to the airport. At one point his car was engulfed by a cheering and flag-waving mob and separated from the motorcycle police escort and from the Secret Service backup car behind him, giving all of us, except the President himself, a bad fright. He remarked later that the crowd was too friendly to cause him any harm. One man tried to climb on the President's limousine to shake his hand, holding between his teeth a small American flag. A Secret Service guard on the running board gave him a quick backhanded brush-off, and the man fell backward into the roadside, lying there still smiling and waving both hands happily at the President, with the American flag sticking out of his mouth.

From Naples we flew directly to Washington. The President was at his desk the next morning at nine o'clock, starting a full day of work. The following day, the Fourth of July, was a Thursday, and he had planned to leave the White House early on that holiday to fly to Cape Cod for a long weekend with Jackie and the children, packing a bag of pictures and movie films of his visit to Ireland that he was eager to show to them. But he had to spend the morning of the holiday in an urgent meeting on the Vietnam situation, and then there was a long session with Secretary of Labor Willard Wirtz on the problems of a threatened nationwide railroad strike. He was unable to take off for Cape Cod until late in the afternoon.

The President returned on Monday, tanned and smiling, and announcing that he had just enjoyed his greatest Hyannis Port weekend in many years. He reported that Jackie, in her seventh month of pregnancy, was healthy and happy, that John had grown up to develop a colorful personality, that their choice of a rented summer home at Squaw Island, not far from the other Kennedy houses but more secluded than his cottage in the family compound, was a huge success, that he had had a pleasant three days of cruising on Nantucket Sound on the *Honey Fitz* with Jackie and his father, and, best of all, he had been able to play five holes of golf for the first time in two years.

During the month of July, Dave spent almost every night with the President after he worked late and took an evening swim in the pool. They ate broiled chicken or lamb chops from the hot plates in the upstairs living room, and sat on the Truman Balcony, enjoying the view of the Jefferson Memorial and the Washington Monument and listening to recordings on the stereo. His favorite tunes were dance numbers from his bachelor days in the thirties and forties — "Beyond the Blue Horizon," "The Very Thought of You," "Stardust," "Stormy Weather," "Body and Soul." He was having problems trying to get tax reduction and civil rights legislation through Congress, and he was irritated by the terrorism and steadily deteriorating prestige of the Diem government in South Vietnam under the fanatical influence of Diem's brother and sister-in-law. But he seemed to us to be more forceful and sure of himself, and more relaxed and happier than we had ever seen him to be.

Then on August 7, while the President was in a meeting with members of the Citizens Committee for a Nuclear Test Ban, I received word from Hyannis Port that Jackie was undergoing emergency surgery at the Otis Air Base hospital for a delivery, five weeks premature, of a baby boy. She had been stricken by pains that morning after taking Caroline to Osterville for riding lessons. Her obstetrician from Washington, Dr. John Walsh, happened to be vacationing at Hyannis Port, and he rushed her to the air base hospital. We had some trouble trying to find a plane to fly the President, Pierre Salinger and myself to Otis Air Base. One of his

Air Force jets was in Moscow with a group of test ban treaty nego-
tiators, another was being repaired and a third one was on a flight a
half-hour away from Washington. We finally found him an eight-
passenger Lockheed Jetstar that landed us at Otis at one-thirty in
the afternoon. By that time, Jackie had delivered by Caeserean
section a four pound and ten and a half ounce son, who was immediately baptized by the base chaplain with the name of Patrick
Bouvier Kennedy. The President found both Jackie and the baby
doing well.

But the baby soon developed a breathing difficulty, not serious
enough to keep the President from wheeling him proudly into
Jackie's room later in the afternoon and placing him in his mother's
arms for a few minutes. Dr. Walsh and Dr. James E. Drorbaugh, a
pediatrician from Boston, decided, however, to move the baby by
ambulance to the better-equipped Children's Medical Center in
Boston. The President went to Squaw Island to see Caroline and
John, visited Jackie again, and then flew to Boston to check on the
baby. He stayed there that night at the Ritz Carlton, and I went to
join him, bringing him a number of test ban papers that he wanted
to study.

We had breakfast together the next morning. The news from the
hospital was encouraging, but the President was worried. Patrick
had developed an affliction of the lungs, common in premature in-
fants, that coats the air sacs with a membrane and hinders their
ability to pass oxygen into the bloodstream. There is nothing that
can be done for such a condition except to hope that body functions
will dissolve the membrane. The baby was moved to Harvard's
School of Public Health and placed in a high-pressure chamber,
where oxygen was forcibly fed to him. The President visited the
hospital four times that day. Worrying about Jackie while he was
concerned about the baby, he also flew back to Cape Cod to see her
at the air base in the middle of the day, returning directly to the
Harvard medical center by making a landing in his Air Force helicopter on a nearby school's playground in that Jamaica Plain section of the city. He decided to spend the night near Patrick in a
vacant bed on the fourth floor of the hospital, with Dave, who had
flown up from Washington with Bobby that afternoon, sleeping beside him on a cot. Around two o'clock in the morning, Gerry Behn,
one of the Secret Service agents, roused Dave and told him that

Patrick's condition was taking a bad turn. Dave awakened the President.

While they waited for an elevator to take them downstairs to the room where the oxygen chamber was operating, the President paced the hospital corridor restlessly, and noticed in one of the rooms a small child who had been severely burned. He called the night nurse on duty and asked her how the accident had happened, and how often the child's mother visited the hospital. "Every day," the nurse said. "Could you tell me the mother's name?" the President asked. He borrowed a pen and a slip of paper from Dave, and wrote a note of sympathy and encouragement to the mother of the burned child. "There he was, with his own baby dying downstairs," Dave said to us later, "but he had to take the time to write a note to that poor woman, asking her to keep her courage up."

Two hours later the strain on the Kennedy baby's heart became unbearable, and he died. "He put up quite a fight," the President said quietly. "He was a beautiful baby." He went upstairs to the room where he had been sleeping, sat on the bed, and wept. "He didn't want anybody to see him crying," Dave said, "so he asked me to go outside and telephone Teddy."

The President went from the hospital to the helicopter in the school playground and flew to Otis Air Base, where he spent an hour alone with Jackie. Then he and Dave spent most of the day at Squaw Island with Caroline and John, playing with the children and taking them to the beach for a swim. Late in the afternoon, he said to Dave, "Would you go to Otis with me while I see Jackie again?" He looked at the rumpled and wrinkled summer suit that Dave had slept in on the hospital cot the night before. "You can't let Jackie see you in that horrible suit," he said. "Pick out one of mine and put it on." Dave selected from the President's closet an expensive suit that fitted him perfectly and, when they were at the hospital, the President led him into Jackie's room to model it for her. She clapped her hands and laughed while Dave went through a fashion showing routine, pirouetting and standing with his hands on his hips. "This is like the day I wore my first pair of long pants," he said.

Patrick's funeral mass, celebrated by Cardinal Cushing in the small chapel at the Cardinal's residence, was attended only by members of the family — the Kennedy brothers and sisters and their wives and husbands, Jackie's mother and stepfather, her sister Lee, and her step-sister and step-brother, Janet and James Auchincloss. The President telephoned his mother, who was in Paris on a vacation trip, and persuaded her not to return for the burial, which took place in a new plot at Holyhood Cemetery in nearby Brookline, not far from the house where the President was born. The President placed inside the small white casket a gold Saint Christopher's Medal that he had worn since Jackie gave it to him at the time of their wedding. After the President's death, Patrick and the unnamed stillborn Kennedy infant buried at Newport in 1956 were both reburied beside their father's grave at Arlington National Cemetery.

The President and Dave stayed with the children at Squaw Island until Jackie came home from the hospital four days later, except for one quick trip to a Cabinet meeting and a few other appointments at the White House. They brought back from Washington a surprise for the family, an eight-week-old blue roan cocker spaniel puppy, later named Shannon, a gift from the descendants of Commodore John Barry in County Wexford, Ireland. Shannon's arrival brought the dog count in the Kennedy household up to eight — along with the older residents, Clipper and Charlie, and Pushinka, the daughter of the Soviet space-traveling Strelka, Charlie and Pushinka had become the parents of four puppies, Streaker, Blackie, White Tips and Butterfly. On the day of her homecoming, Jackie sat on the lawn at Squaw Island watching her children playing with their assortment of American, Russian, Russian-American and Irish dogs.

The loss of Patrick affected the President and Jackie more deeply than anybody except their closest friends realized. Two months later when the President was spending an October weekend in Boston to attend a Democratic fund-raising dinner, we went with him to a Harvard-Columbia football game. Toward the end of the first half, Dave and I noticed that he was unusually silent, as if his mind was far away from the game. He turned to me and said, "I want to go to Patrick's grave, and I want to go there alone, with nobody from the newspapers following me." We made our way out of the stadium to his car, with Pierre Salinger and his entourage of reporters hurrying to their cars behind us. I said a few words to a Secret Service agent, who spoke to the Boston Irish police officer in charge of the parking lot. The policeman saw to it that Salinger and the reporters did not move until the President's car was safely out of sight. At the cemetery in Brookline, the President looked at the simple headstone with only one word, "Kennedy," inscribed on it, and said to Dave and me, "He seems so alone here."

When Jackie had recuperated, her husband sent her with her sister on a Mediterranean cruise. At the same time, during the last week of September, he made a trip through the Western states that was billed as a "conservation tour," but he was really more interested in building up his political image in areas where he did badly in 1960 than in promoting conservation of natural resources. Eight of the eleven states that he visited on the tour were ones that he lost to Nixon in 1960. On the day that he left Washington to start the tour, September 24, the Senate approved his atmospheric nuclear test ban treaty with the Russians, over strong opposition from Barry Goldwater and the military leaders, with only a few Southern Democrats and conservative Republicans voting against it. The President found that his audiences in the West were more enthusiastic about the test ban treaty than his plans for protecting natural resources, so, as the tour went on, he happily talked less about conservation and more about his efforts to keep the peace and to lighten domestic problems. We remember him going out of his way in Great Falls, Montana, to visit Mike Mansfield's elderly father, much to the astonishment and delight of Mike, and how impressed he was to learn that Mike's brother was a member of the local fire department. "I wonder how many majority leaders in the United States Senate have had a brother still working in the hometown fire department," the President said to me later. "And that fellow wouldn't take a job in Washington for any amount of money." We also remember the President feeding bread to a pair of deer outside the cottage where we stayed at Lassen Volcanic National Park. The next day at breakfast he said to George Thomas, his valet, "Where's the toast, George?" George said, "You fed it to the deers last night."

The tour was a big political success, and it ended with a pleasant weekend of sunny relaxation at one of the President's favorite places, Bing Crosby's estate at Palm Springs. We had stayed at Crosby's house on an earlier trip to the West. The President enjoyed the pool and the sun there so much that he asked Bing if he could visit there again. Our previous stay at the Crosby place had stirred up considerable chatter in Hollywood and caused a rift between

Frank Sinatra and the Kennedy family because, as we learned later, Sinatra had been planning to entertain the President at his Palm Springs home that weekend, and had even constructed a cement landing pad on his grounds for the President's helicopter. The President regretted Sinatra's hurt feelings because he liked Frank and enjoyed his company. The Sinatra misunderstanding was my fault, not the President's. When we decided to make a weekend stop at Palm Springs, I asked the Secret Service to select a place with the necessary seclusion and security advantages that they wanted. They reported that Crosby's home was ideal for their purposes and that Bing's family was not using it and Bing would be delighted to let the President stay there. Then I received a telephone call from Evelyn Lincoln. "Peter Lawford is hysterical," she said. "He promised Frank Sinatra that the President would stay with him at Palm Springs." Lawford called me and said, "Don't you realize Bing Crosby is a Republican?" I said, "I don't care if he's a Red Chinaman — the Secret Service likes his place better than Sinatra's place and that's it." I told the President about the uproar, but he was unconcerned. "We'll go where the Secret Service wants us to go," he said. "It's their problem, not mine." Later it was reported erroneously that the Attorney General had advised against staying at Sinatra's house because of Sinatra's associations with known criminals, but, as a matter of fact, after Peter Lawford and then Pat Lawford had pleaded with me to no avail, Bobby called me to put in a pitch for Sinatra, too. "Bobby, the Justice Department isn't arranging this trip," I told him. Bobby said, "Oh, all right. Have it your way." Later we heard that Sinatra was so incensed that he took a sledge hammer and smashed up the landing pad that he had built for the President's helicopter. Anyway, although Sinatra later became a Republican, the President spent his last September weekend enjoying the sun at Bing Crosby's pool in Palm Springs.

A week later, on October 7, 1963, President Kennedy performed a ceremony that gave him the deepest personal satisfaction of his three years at the White House — signing the formal ratification of the treaty between the three nuclear powers banning atomic testing "in the atmosphere, in outer space and under water." The treaty had been agreed upon and approved by Averell Harriman, Lord Hailsham and Andrei Gromyko in Moscow in July, and it was later signed in Washington by 102 nations. The history-minded President staged the ratification ceremony in the Treaty Room, on the third floor of the White House, where the Peace Protocol ending the Spanish-American War had been signed in 1898. More recently in the same room he had signed documents invoking Federal powers to obtain the admission of James H. Meredith, the black student, to the University of Mississippi. He used sixteen pens in signing his name to the test ban treaty ratification, handing them out as souvenirs to Dean Rusk, Harriman, John McCloy and members of the Senate who had supported approval of the treaty. Then he picked up a seventeenth pen, dipped it in ink, and drew a firm line under his signature. "This one is mine," he said with a smile, putting the pen in his pocket.

At the same time that the test ban was approved, the President heard that the Soviet Union was anxious to buy American wheat. A combination of a drought and an inefficient agricultural program had produced a severe grain shortage in Russia. It was obvious to the President, and to all of us on his political staff, that lending such a helpful hand to Khrushchev would bring strong political repercussions against the administration, particularly from the anti-Communist Americans of German and Polish descent, as well as from Irish Catholics, but Kennedy decided that selling wheat to Russia would be one more step forward on the road to a lasting world peace, even if it did hurt his popularity at home. Thinking of the Polish-American vote in 1964, I was against the wheat sale, and said so in our first meeting on the question. I knew that Lyndon Johnson would be on my side, and I passed the President a note, asking him to call upon the Vice-President for an opinion. Johnson shrewdly refused to take a stand in opposition to the President while certain members of the White House staff were listening. He had done so at staff meetings in the past, and his remarks had been quoted verbatim in the next day's newspapers. He said to the President, "Kenny and I will talk it over later, and he'll let you know how I feel about it." After the meeting he came to me and said, "Selling this wheat to Russia would be the worst political mistake he ever made."

But Kennedy felt that the benefits of the wheat sale as a gesture of peaceful help and cooperation, as well as the considerable income it would bring to the American farmers and shippers, were worth more than its political risks. The agreement was consummated when Air Force One was aloft between Milwaukee and Minneapolis. The President, Senator Mansfield and Senator Humphrey were enroute to speak for Senator McCarthy. The President informed me of the agreement, and told me to ask for a meeting between the Senate committees involved.

I went to Senator Mansfield, the majority leader, and received probably my greatest education in government when this close friend said to me, "The Congress handles its own problems; there is a separation of government, you know." The wheat arrangement the President sought was concluded and a member of the White House staff was educated.

As usually happened when Kennedy followed his instincts instead of playing it cautiously, the sale of wheat to the Soviets did him no political harm. A few Polish-American newspapers even supported his decision, which was widely praised as a sound peace move. A Gallup Poll taken that fall showed that people regarded the Democratic party as the party most concerned with keeping the country out of war.

With the easing of tension in his relationship with Khrushchev, the biggest and most pressing problem during most of his time in the White House, Kennedy was able to give more of his attention in the last three months of his life to the discouraging situation in Vietnam. As we noted earlier in this book, he ordered in October a withdrawal of one thousand U.S. military personnel from South Vietnam before the end of 1963 — an order that was quietly rescinded after his death — and he planned further reductions during the next two years so that there would be no Green Beret advisers, technicians or even helicopter pilots remaining in South Vietnam by the end of 1965. The President had viewed Vietnam as a political problem, rather than a military crisis, and he had hoped that the fighting between Diem's Saigon government and the Communist Viet Cong could be stopped by political compromising on both sides to work out a truce and a settlement such as he and Averell Harriman had effected in Laos in 1961 with Khrushchev's help. Such a solution became impossible because Diem's fanatical brother and sister-in-law, the Nhus, persecuting and terrorizing non-Communist political enemies and carrying on religious warfare against nonpolitical Buddhists, had turned the Saigon regime into a police state with no popular support. There was no hope of getting any kind of a peaceful settlement, or even a temporary cease-fire agreement, between the Diem government and the Viet Cong as long as the Nhus were in power, and all attempts to persuade Diem to get rid of his brother had gotten nowhere. Finally, in October, the President was resorting to cutting off economic aid and withdrawing military assistance, a move that was getting strong opposition in the Pentagon and from General Paul Harkins, then our military commander in South Vietnam and a strong supporter of Diem.

"They keep telling me to send combat units over there," the President said to us one day in October. "That means sending draftees, along with volunteer regular Army advisers, into Vietnam. I'll never send draftees over there to fight."

It is forgotten now that President Kennedy said the same thing in public interviews that he said privately. In a television interview with Walter Cronkite on September 2, 1963, he strongly emphasized the views that he held at the time of his death. "It is their war," the President said to Cronkite. "They are the ones who have to win it or lose it. We can help them, we can send them equipment, we can send our men out there as advisers . . . but in the final analysis it is their people and their government who have to win or lose this struggle. All we can do is help."

All of us who listened to President Kennedy's repeated expressions of his determination to avoid further involvement in Vietnam are sure that if he had lived to serve a second term, the numbers of American military advisers and technicians in that country would have steadily decreased. He never would have committed U.S. Army combat units and draftees to action against the Viet Cong. Lyndon Johnson's charge in his 1971 memoirs that the Kennedy administration's support of the coup that finally overthrew the Diem-Nhu regime in Saigon was "a serious blunder which caused deep political confusion" would have astonished Kennedy. Diem would have been overthrown anyway, and trying to prevent the coup against him would have been a far worse American mistake than allowing it to happen; the political confusion already caused by Diem and the Nhus was more damaging to the anti-Communist cause in South Vietnam than any trouble that could be then seen in the future. The killing of Diem and his brother during the coup, and after their safe removal from the country had been guaranteed by the military leaders of the revolt, came as a shock to President

Kennedy and made him all the more resolved to withdraw from further entanglement in the Vietnam war.

In his last three major public speeches during the month of October, with Vietnam on his mind, President Kennedy talked to audiences at the University of Maine, Amherst College and at a Democratic dinner in Philadelphia about keeping America and the world at peace. At Maine, when he received an honorary law doctoral degree, he promised to stand up and sing whenever he heard the university's Stein Song. That afternoon he paid his last visit to Boston. After slipping away from the reporters at the Harvard-Columbia football game to pay a visit to Patrick's grave, he headed downtown with Dave to get a butterscotch sundae at Schrafft's, where he stopped for nightly ice cream during his Congressional and Senatorial campaigns. While he was eating his butterscotch sundae at the soda fountain counter, he said to Dave, "Get me a chocolate frappe with vanilla ice cream to take out, so I can have it later at the hotel." Then he strolled along Boylston Street to the Sheraton Plaza Hotel in Copley Square, with Dave beside him carrying the chocolate frappe-to-go in a brown paper bag. "The automobiles on Boylston Street were bumping into each other, because the drivers were staring at the President," Dave says, "and everybody I knew in Boston wanted to know later what I was carrying in the paper bag." That night the President and Teddy appeared informally before a crowd of 7,700 local Democrats at a fund-raising dinner for the 1964 campaign at the Commonwealth Armory that brought the party $750,000. The President regaled the huge gathering with the wheeze about Teddy complaining that people were accusing him of trading on his family's name and asking to change it to Roosevelt. The President also commented on Barry Goldwater's appearance as a speaker at a Republican dinner in Boston earlier that week, noting that Leverett Saltonstall had introduced Goldwater with the words, "He and I have differed on many problems, but we like and respect each other." Kennedy said, "When I was in the Senate, I used to get better introductions than that from Senator Saltonstall."

Goldwater was already running hard for the 1964 Republican nomination, and Kennedy was hoping that he would get it. Apart from the huge popular-vote mandate that he was confident of getting in a contest with Goldwater, he was looking forward to the fun of dealing with Goldwater's archaic conservatism and gung-ho militarism in his campaign talks. At a press conference on October 31, the President was asked to comment on a recent charge by Goldwater that the Kennedy administration was falsifying the news to keep itself in office. "I am confident that he will be making many charges more serious than this one in the months to come," Kennedy said with a smile. "He has had a busy week, selling TVA and suggesting that military commanders overseas be permitted to use nuclear weapons, and attacking the President of Bolivia while he was here in the United States, and involving himself in the Greek elections. I don't think it would really be fair for me to reply to him this week."

Another reporter at the same meeting asked the President why he liked his job well enough to stay in it for another four years.

"Well, I find the work rewarding," he said. "I have given before to this group the Greek definition of happiness. It is the full use of your powers along lines of excellence. I find, therefore, that the Presidency provides some happiness."

We remember the President one day in November showing us a letter from a retired Marine Corps colonel, W. T. Bigger of McLean, Virginia. Kennedy was obviously moved and pleased to receive the letter, although he tried to be casual about it. "This is a little incident in my Navy career that wasn't written up in the *Reader's Digest*," he said. After his survival from the PT-109 sinking, Kennedy was ordered to return to the States for medical treatment but, to the astonishment of his fellow officers at the Rendova torpedo boat base, he asked to return to combat duty with another boat and a new crew. He was assigned to PT-59, which was converted from a torpedo boat to a makeshift and overloaded gun boat with extra 50-caliber machine guns and 40-millimeter Bofors automatics. The extra weight of the added weapons and the added men to operate them made the light motor boat slow and hard to manage, but Kennedy, according to his squadron commander, Al Cluster, took many wild chances using the PT-59 to attack Japanese supply barges and shore positions. Colonel Bigger's letter, dated November 2, 1963, reminded the President that twenty years earlier, on the same date in 1943, Kennedy had taken his boat under heavy enemy fire to a beach on the Choiseul River where Bigger's Marine riflemen were surrounded by the Japanese with their backs to the water. "When all seemed lost," the Marine officer wrote to the President, "you can well appreciate my relief to see the landing craft return-ing, escorted by PT boats, one commanded by you." The landing craft lost its power, but Kennedy rescued the Marines in his boat and brought them safely back to their base. "As I recall, we both had our hands full and there was little time for amenities. Please accept again my heartfelt thanks," the colonel wrote in his letter of twenty years later.

"Wasn't it nice of him to go to the trouble of writing that letter to me?" the President said to us.

At the White House on November 13 we had a three-hour meet-ing to discuss plans for the 1964 campaign — the President and the old hands from 1960, the Attorney General, John Bailey, Dick Ma-guire, Steve Smith, Larry O'Brien, Ted Sorensen and myself, plus one new face, Richard Scammon, director of the Census Bureau and an expert on population trends with many interesting ideas about where to find the most Democratic votes. At this first discussion of the coming election year, no great earthshaking decisions were made. It was decided, since Bobby obviously could not manage the campaign, that John Bailey and Steve Smith would organize it, that Richard Maguire would be the treasurer and that, obviously, every-one else would work for the reelection. As President Kennedy said, "As usual, the campaign will be run right from here."

The President talked with us about his plans to open the cam-paign with political tours later in the month to Florida and Texas, the two Southern states where he was aiming to make an all-out effort to beat the Republicans. He remarked with some irritation that he would be seeking campaign money as well as votes in Texas. "Massachusetts has given us about two and a half million, and New York has been good to us, too," he said, "but when are we going to get some money out of those rich people in Texas?" Actually, the trip to Texas that November had materialized out of the President's needling of Governor John Connally and Lyndon Johnson about campaign contributions during our visit to El Paso the previous June. Kennedy's first words to the two Texans when they met with him that night were, "Do you two think we're *ever* going to have a fund-raising affair in Texas?" Johnson passed the buck to Connally, and after Connally agreed to stage a hundred-dollar-a-plate dinner at Austin a week before Thanksgiving, the President agreed to travel to it with stops along the way at San Antonio, Houston, Fort Worth and Dallas.

At the campaign planning meeting in the Cabinet Room, the President also talked about how we could make the coming 1964 Democratic National Convention a little more entertaining and less boring than most political conventions. "For once in my life, I'd like to hear a good keynote speech," he said. But as I recall the conversation at that first and only staff meeting on the planning for John F. Kennedy's reelection campaign, most of it was devoted to a discussion between the President and Dick Scammon on such topics as: at what point in the upward climb on the economic and social ladder does a Democratic family become Republican, and how many Democrats remained Democrats after moving to the Republican suburbs. The President found such speculation fascinating, and only the lateness of the hour and a previous dinner engagement forced him to bring it to a halt. "We ought to have another one of these meetings in two or three weeks," he said to me, but of course we never had another meeting, or a campaign, either.

The next day the President landed in a helicopter on the Mason-Dixon line, between Delaware and Maryland, to cut a blue and gray ribbon opening a new stretch of the Federally financed Interstate Highway Route 95. From there he flew to New York to spend the night at the Carlyle before appearing at an AFL-CIO meeting the following day. His disregard for security precautions annoyed the New York Police Department and the Secret Service. He decided to travel the twelve miles from LaGuardia Airport to the hotel without the customary police escort clearing the highways, because he did not want to cause a delay in the evening rush-hour commuter traffic. Then, while the police escort waited outside the front door of the Carlyle, ready to accompany him to any place in the city where he wanted to go during the evening, he sneaked out a side door to Madison Avenue and walked with Dave and a few nervous Secret Service agents along Seventy-sixth Street to Jean and Steve Smith's apartment on Fifth Avenue. When the police guards waiting at the Carlyle learned later that the President had left the hotel without them, they were somewhat put out.

His last weekend before the trip to Texas was spent in Florida, relaxing in the sun and politicking. On Saturday morning he watched the firing of a Polaris missile at Cape Canaveral, and then on the patio beside the pool at his father's house at Palm Beach he watched the Navy-Duke football game on TV with Dave and Torby Macdonald. He took Navy, giving Dave and Torby ten points, and when Roger Staubach passed Navy to a 38-25 victory, he demanded an immediate payoff. Dave and Torby, in their swimming trunks, had to go upstairs to get their wallets. That night, after dinner, the President sang one of his favorite songs, "September Song," and sang it better than usual. The next day, Sunday, was spent in the pool and on the patio, with the President picking the Chicago Bears over the Green Bay Packers and winning another bet. That night there was a showing of a movie, *Tom Jones*.

On Monday, it was back to politics, with speeches at Tampa and Miami and an inspection of MacDill Air Force Base and an appearance before a meeting of the Steelworkers' Union. He stopped to talk with a group of women in the crowd at Miami who were wearing Uncle Sam–type hats with WIN WITH KENNEDY banners on the brims, and waved to a crowd of children who wore large cardboard badges lettered with MY MOM AND DAD ARE FOR YOU, PRESIDENT KENNEDY. We flew back to Washington late that Monday night, after the President delivered a speech to the Inter-American Press Association at Miami Beach.

Tuesday, two days before we left for Texas, was a busy day of work in the President's office. The White House correspondents were giving Pierre Salinger a hard time because I refused to let him release the specific street routes that the President's motorcade would follow on his visits to cities on the Texas tour. The Secret Service advised me not to give out such detailed information in advance of the trip, because the rough treatment of Adlai Stevenson by the crowd in Dallas when he visited there for a United Nations Day Ceremony on October 24 made it advisable to take precautions against planned disturbances.

The President met on Tuesday with Dean Rusk, who was leaving the next day for a trip to Hawaii and Japan. In Hawaii, he would meet with Henry Cabot Lodge, our Ambassador to Saigon, who was returning to Washington for talks on the Vietnam situation with the President. Then Rusk and several other Cabinet members would go to Tokyo for a joint meeting with the Japanese cabinet on economic problems. The President talked with Rusk about paving the way for his own planned visit to Japan during the tour of the Far East that he was to make with Jackie early in 1964.

After he talked with Rusk, the President told me that he and Jackie had been considering moving their departure on their trip to Japan, the Philippines, India and Pakistan forward to a date shortly after New Year's Day. "Right after we get back from Texas," he said, "you go out there to advance the trip. You could do it in about a month. You'll be gone during December, not a bad time for you to be away because it's quiet here during Christmas time. You could time it so that you could get back home on the day before Christmas."

I stared at him for a moment, wondering if he was joking.

"If I came home on the day before Christmas," I said, "after being away for the whole month of December, I would come home to an empty house."

The President looked at me in surprise.

"What do you mean?" he said.

"My wife is a patient woman," I said. "But if I was missing before Christmas, she'd pack up the kids and leave. Mr. President, my family situation is different from yours. You don't have to do any Christmas shopping, and you don't have to go out and buy the Christmas tree and put it up and string the lights on it and decorate it. If I wasn't home during the week before Christmas, Helen would divorce me."

Dave, who was listening, chimed in on my behalf.

"That's right, Mr. President," he said. "If the word got around in Boston and Worcester that you kept Kenny away from home before Christmas, not a woman in Massachusetts would vote for you in 1964."

The President laughed and said, "Oh, all right, put off the advance trip until sometime in January. But listen, are you sure I'll be leaving Texas in time to have lunch here with Cabot Lodge on Sunday? He's coming all the way from Vietnam to see me, and I don't want to keep him waiting."

"Don't worry about it," I said. "It's all set."

But on Sunday we were watching his casket being carried to the rotunda of the Capitol.

THIRTEEN

Our Short Stay with LBJ

PRESIDENT KENNEDY'S WAKE went on for several weeks after his death. His close friends visited Jackie at the Averell Harriman House in Georgetown, where she stayed with her children after moving out of the White House, and did what they could to ease her loneliness. She asked Dave Powers to come in every day to have lunch with John and to play games with the little boy. Bobby and I spent some time with Jackie almost every afternoon, both of us so troubled and uncertain about the future that she probably was more consoling to us than we were helpful to her.

During that gloomy Christmas season, those of us who had been closely associated with President Kennedy wondered if we could stay on in the government for the remaining year of his unfinished term. It was not that we had any resentment against President Johnson taking his place in the White House, but rather that we had little appetite for working under any President other than John Kennedy. It took me more than a month to make up my mind to go back to my job in the President's office. Meanwhile Johnson was patient and considerate with me. Bill Moyers, who became his chief aide, called me often at my home to ask how I was doing and to remind me that the President wanted me to come back to work. Dave returned to his job shortly after the funeral. One day he was talking in the President's reception office with Moyers and Walter Jenkins when Johnson came into the room and pointed at my empty desk. "That's

Kenny O'Donnell's desk," he said. "I don't want anybody else sitting at it, or using it. Hear?"

I went to Florida during the Christmas holidays and had several talks there about my problem of going back to work at the White House with Jackie and with other members of the Kennedy family who were spending Christmas at Palm Beach. Jackie had no strong feelings on the matter. Whatever I decided to do would be all right with her, she said. Some of the others were against Kennedy staff people working for Johnson. I had a long talk with Bobby. He and I agreed that if Kennedy's key people left the White House, their departure might cause a split in the Democratic ranks during the coming Presidential election campaign. At least, we thought, we owed it to President Kennedy to do our best to keep Barry Goldwater out of his office. I also felt that a walkout of Kennedy aides and Cabinet members might give the totally wrong impression that we were blaming Johnson for President Kennedy's death in Texas. So I decided to stick with Lyndon Johnson for the rest of the year, until after the election in November.

The first time I talked alone with President Johnson after the Kennedy funeral was on December 11, 1963, when he invited Helen, my wife, and me to travel with him and Mrs. Johnson to Philadelphia to attend the funeral of Congressman William J. Green, Jr., one of my best friends. Along with everybody else who talked with Johnson at that time, I was bewildered by his later assertion in his memoirs that he had no intention of running for the Presidency in 1964 until Lady Bird persuaded him to seek the nomination on the day after the opening of the Democratic convention, August 25, at Atlantic City. On the day that we traveled to Billy Green's funeral, two weeks before the previous Christmas, Johnson talked constantly about his plan to run for President in the coming year, and he continued to talk about it daily during the winter, spring and summer of 1964 while I was working with him in the White House. When we were flying to Philadelphia, he told me that he did not want Bobby Kennedy as his Vice-Presidential candidate.

"I don't want history to say I was elected to this office because I had Bobby on the ticket with me," he said. "But I'll take him if I need him."

In other words, if the Republicans nominated a more liberal candidate than Goldwater, Johnson would be forced to take Bobby as his Vice-President to win support from labor and from Kennedy Democrats. Many politicians felt that if the second Mrs. Nelson Rockefeller had not happened to give birth to Nelson A. Rockefeller, Jr., only a few days before the California primary in 1964, the Democratic party might have had a Johnson–Bobby Kennedy ticket that fall. Polls taken in the spring showed that Governor Rockefeller, after winning the Republican primary in Oregon, was running well ahead of Goldwater in the California primary campaign until pictures of Happy Rockefeller and her new baby appeared in the newspapers just before the voting day. If this sudden reminder of Rockefeller's divorce and remarriage had not saved Goldwater from losing to him in California, the Republicans might have nominated a more moderate compromise candidate that year, perhaps George Romney or Pennsylvania's Governor William W. Scranton. Then LBJ might have offered the Vice-Presidency to Bobby.

Whether Bobby would have accepted the offer is another highly doubtful question. During the six months after his brother's death, he was confused and uncertain about his future plans. He remarked to me one day that his brother Teddy felt that the Vice-Presidency was not worth Bobby's consideration. "It's not worth considering?" I said to him. "Have you forgotten that your older brother left no stone unturned in Chicago trying to get the Vice-Presidential nomination in 1956?"

With Bobby feeling understandably skeptical about his ability to get along with Johnson, and with Johnson delaying his choice of a running mate until he felt safe enough to bypass Bobby, I decided, with strong encouragement from the Kennedy staff people and my friends in the labor movement, to promote Hubert Humphrey for the second place on the 1964 party ticket. All of us in the Kennedy camp — Bobby, John Bailey, Larry O'Brien, Dick Daley, Jesse Unruh — admired Humphrey as a hard-line liberal fighter for civil rights. Johnson did not want Humphrey on his ticket for the same reason that he did not want Bobby if he could possibly avoid him — Johnson did not want to share the credit for his election with a Vice-Presidential nominee, like Humphrey, who had strong personal support from labor, the Negroes, the Jewish liberals and the Midwest farmers. Johnson was figuring that if Goldwater was his opponent, he could win the Presidency entirely on his own with a nonentity on his ticket. Then he would be able to claim all of the credit for his big victory. In fact, Johnson would have been happiest that year if he could have campaigned alone, with no Vice-Presidential candidate.

I felt that we had enough leverage to force Johnson to accept a Vice-Presidential candidate of our choice, namely Humphrey, if Bobby did not want the nomination. Johnson badly needed me and other Kennedy campaign veterans to promote his candidacy with Democratic leaders in the various states and big cities around the country. His own contacts with the party leaders at the state and city levels were slight and weak. His political experience was limited to the Senate and Texas, and he had a small knowledge of the party bosses elsewhere. Secondly, Johnson was anxious to avoid any unnecessary fight with Bobby Kennedy and Bobby's friends. He was obsessed that spring with a fear that Bobby might force himself into the Vice-Presidency, or maybe even make a bid for the Presidency, by suddenly appearing at the convention to start a floor fight. Johnson asked me almost every day at the White House if I knew what Bobby was planning. "Why doesn't he withdraw and save all of us a lot of worry and trouble?" Johnson would ask me. I would tell him that I was getting many telephone calls from party leaders across the country who were saying that Bobby could win a floor fight.

At this point in the cat-and-mouse game that we were playing with the President, I was in a unique position: Johnson had made me the executive director of his campaign, and at the same time I was his only communication contact with Bobby. Although Bobby was still in the Cabinet as the Attorney General, he and the President seldom spoke to each other. When either man wanted the other to know something, I was asked to pass the message. Johnson knew that I was being honest and straightforward in my dealings with him. He also knew that Bobby was one of my closest and oldest friends, and I had made it plain to Johnson that if Bobby decided to run for the Vice-Presidency, I would resign from the White House staff to work for him.

In his efforts to diminish Bobby's image, Johnson sought out another member of the Kennedy family, Sargent Shriver, Bobby's brother-in-law, and offered Shriver the Vice-Presidency with a suggestion that two terms in such a position of prominence might make him a likely Presidential prospect in 1972. I was sitting alone with Johnson in his office one day in March when the voice of Bill Moyers came on his interoffice talk box. Apparently not knowing that I was listening, Moyers told the President that he had sounded out Shriver about accepting the Vice-Presidential nomination, and that Shriver was agreeable and the Kennedy family had no objections. Moyers added that Shriver had said that Bobby would have no complaint if Shriver was on the ticket. Johnson, grinning, looked at me questioningly. I leaned toward the talk box and said, loud enough for Moyers to hear me, "The hell he wouldn't."

Afterwards I told Johnson that any move to nominate Shriver would be fought by the Kennedy faction because we felt that if any member of the late President's family was to be on the ticket it should be Bobby. Johnson accepted that argument gracefully, and the Shriver proposal was dropped. Then he said to me, "I think I need a Catholic running with me. How do you people feel about Gene McCarthy?

I said to him, "How can you pick the number two Senator in Minnesota over the number one Senator from the same state, Hubert Humphrey, who is better qualified and more strongly backed? It would be obvious that you were picking the number two man only because he is a Catholic, and the Catholics would resent that."

Johnson agreed, but in his inscrutable way, he sent Eugene Mc-Carthy to see Mayor Daley in Chicago and Jesse Unruh in Los Angeles to sound out those leaders about getting delegate support at the convention. "They both knew, while I was talking to them, that Lyndon had no serious intention of backing me for the nomination," McCarthy complained to me later. "Why did he put me to that embarrassment?"

Still trying to steer Humphrey away from the ticket, Johnson kept insisting that he needed a Catholic as a running mate. In the middle of April he called a meeting of his political advisers, Larry O'Brien, Dick Maguire, John Bailey, Jim Rowe, Jack Valenti, Walter Jenkins, Bill Moyers and myself. He asked Jenkins to read the findings of a poll that presumed to show the need for a Catholic on the ticket. He expressed amazement and anger when the Kennedy people present, all Catholics, disputed the findings of the poll and supported Humphrey. After the meeting broke up, he called me alone into another office, argued with me at length about our preference for Humphrey, and finally threw up his hands and said, "Well, if you want Humphrey that much, you can have him. You can leak it to the press right now that he's going to be my Vice-President. I won't deny it."

I couldn't believe that Lyndon Johnson would give in that suddenly and easily; there had to be a catch somewhere. I did not mention his offer to Humphrey or anybody else, because I figured that if I leaked such a message to the press, Johnson might claim that the Kennedy people were forcing Humphrey on him against his will, and that could be an excuse for him to drop Humphrey. Besides, if the President was serious about accepting Humphrey, he could spread the news himself instead of asking me to do it for him. We decided to keep him guessing about Bobby's plans. Bobby's recent trips to Poland and Berlin, where he was wildly acclaimed, added to Johnson's anxieties and deepened his suspicions of Bobby's intentions.

One night in May Bobby invited Teddy, Steve Smith, Larry O'Brien, Fred Dutton and myself to his home at Hickory Hill to discuss his situation and his plans. He told us that he had concluded that Barry Goldwater would win the Republican nomination, which meant that Johnson would never invite him to share the Democratic ticket, and besides he was certain that he could not work with Johnson. So he had definitely decided to forget the Vice-Presidency. He was planning to resign from the Cabinet and to go to New York immediately to begin a campaign there for the Senate against Kenneth Keating.

Ted and Steve urged Bobby to declare his candidacy for the Senate in New York as soon as possible. I asked him not to announce his plans until we could build up a solid base of support that would force Johnson to accept Humphrey. If Bobby pulled himself out of the running for the Vice-Presidency right now, I argued, we would lose our leverage on Johnson, and Johnson would feel free to pick a nonentity as his running mate.

A vigorous argument developed. Looking at it from Bobby's point of view, it was to his advantage to take himself out of the Vice-Presidential picture as soon as possible. Otherwise it would appear later as if he had decided to run for the Senate only as a last resort, after failing to get Johnson's invitation to be on the national ticket. He was already on shaky ground, seeking a Senatorial seat from New York, a state where he had no roots of residence, but by delaying his announcement of his candidacy for the Senate until after we had gotten Humphrey the Vice-Presidential nomination, Bobby would be laying himself open to severe criticism and political harm. Under the circumstances, no realistic and shrewd politician would have listened to the plea I made to him on a personal basis — that he owed to his brother's friends an obligation to do what he could to put a man with President Kennedy's liberal beliefs in the Vice-Presidency. "Hubert is the best man available who represents those views," I told him. Finally, Bobby agreed to put his own best interests aside and to go along with my plan for a delaying action because he felt that he had a personal responsibility to the party to help Humphrey.

To me it was one of the finest and most unselfish decisions of Bobby's controversial career. Nobody realized the risk he took by agreeing to delay his announcement of his candidacy in New York. When I was leaving his house that night, he followed me out to the driveway and called after me, "When they start that 'ruthless brat' stuff, O'Donnell, you'd better be there to bleed along with me."

So with Bobby keeping quiet about his plans, we were able to build up a solid support for Humphrey among the Democratic state leaders and in the labor unions during the month of June. When the Republicans nominated Goldwater in July, leaving Johnson free to cut loose from Bobby, Humphrey was well fixed with influential backing. Johnson's performance when he broke the news to Bobby caused some amusement in our circle. I arranged their meeting in the President's office, warning Bobby beforehand to select his words carefully, because Johnson usually recorded such conversations.

Their meeting was short and sweet. The President came to the point quickly, announcing that he did not want Bobby as his Vice-President, but offering him other jobs in the government. He also invited Bobby to be his campaign manager, an offer that Bobby promptly turned down, explaining that he had other plans. Bobby wished Johnson well and pledged him full support.

Leaving the White House, Bobby headed for the nearby Sans Souci restaurant, where Larry O'Brien and I were finishing our lunch. Bobby sat down with us, and gave us a full account of his conversation with Johnson. While he was talking, a telephone was handed to me. The President was on the line.

"I just had a talk with your friend," he said to me.

"Mr. President, I want to be honest with you," I said. "The Attorney General of the United States is sitting here with me right now."

"That's all right," Johnson said. "Can you come back over here? We've got to put out an announcement."

I returned to the White House, where Johnson gave me a version of his conversation with Bobby quite different from Bobby's version. Among other things, he said that Bobby had offered to manage his campaign.

"Mr. President," I said, "the Attorney General told me just the opposite."

Johnson bristled. "He did, did he?" he said. "Well, I'll bring Walter Jenkins in here and let him read to you exactly what he did say."

When the President asked Jenkins to read to us Bobby's conversation, he did not realize, as Walter and I did, that he was revealing to me that their talk had been recorded, as I had warned Bobby it would be. Jenkins tried to shake off the President with No signals, but it took a while before Johnson caught on and tried to correct himself.

"What I meant to say, Walter," he said, "was that I want you to read to us the notes that I made on what *I* said." Turning to me, Johnson said, "You see, I had a feeling this meeting might have historical significance, so before Bobby came in here, I wrote down exactly what I was going to say to him."

When it came to framing an announcement of why he had dropped Bobby as a Vice-Presidential running mate, Johnson was squeamish about admitting the simple truth, namely that he did not want Bobby on the ticket for personal reasons. He tried to get Bobby to put out a statement that he had withdrawn voluntarily from the Vice-Presidential field. Bobby refused, and said that the statement must come from the President, and that it must emphasize the fact that Bobby's withdrawal was not Bobby's idea.

Johnson then decided on a Johnsonian dodge that caused smiles all over Washington. He announced that he had made a ruling against selecting any member of the present Cabinet, including the Attorney General, of course, as his Vice-Presidential nominee. That required us to get all of the other Cabinet members, including Adlai Stevenson and Dean Rusk, to go through the sham rigmarole of putting out statements saying that they did not mind being disqualified for the Vice-Presidency. Bobby remarked wryly, "I'm sorry I had to take so many nice fellows over the side with me." We liked Johnson's scheme of knocking out the whole Cabinet in order to knock out Bobby, because it left a clear field for Hubert Humphrey. Watching Johnson go through this elaborate fuss to keep himself from looking like a villain while dumping Bobby, I wondered how loudly he would have exploded if he had discovered that Bobby himself, a few months earlier, had already decided against accepting the Vice-Presidency under any conditions.

That same night, after Johnson dropped Bobby, my wife called me at the White House to tell me that Humphrey wanted to see me at the Mayflower Hotel. I went there and told him what had happened. "Bobby just got the ax," I said to Hubert, "and you're next unless you put up a fight to get the nomination." He asked me if the Kennedy people would support him in a floor fight at the convention if that was necessary. I assured him that we would, positively.

The next day Humphrey and I had a drink with Jack Conway, Walter Reuther's political aide, who assured us that he would work to get an endorsement of Humphrey from the labor union leaders. The day after that, when Johnson released the announcement of the dropping of Bobby and the other Cabinet members, Bobby went to Humphrey's office in the Senate Office Building to put his arm around Hubert and to announce to the press that Humphrey was his choice for the Vice-Presidency. That startled Johnson, and he was more startled later when he was hit by a barrage of Humphrey endorsements from several state governors — Hughes of Iowa, Brown of California and Reynolds of Wisconsin, among others — and from such labor leaders as Reuther, George Meany and David Dubinsky.

As the pressure for Humphrey mounted, Johnson became resentful and peevish. He treated Humphrey roughly at White House legislative meetings and Washington social affairs, often asking him in front of a group of people what he thought of Shriver or Eugene McCarthy or Tom Dodd as a Vice-Presidential possibility. Humphrey held his tongue and his temper, and asked his supporters not to press Johnson too hard. Although a selection of Humphrey was more or less unavoidable, the President kept him in doubt right up until the last possible moment on the day when the delegates at the convention were to vote on the nomination, insisting to reporters that his mind was not yet made up.

During the week before the convention, Johnson made one last stab at dropping Humphrey and picking somebody else whom even Humphrey's supporters would have hesitated to oppose — Mike Mansfield, the Senate's majority leader. None of us who were working in the White House suspected that Johnson was considering Mansfield until the Senator from Montana was mentioned as a likely Vice-Presidential candidate in a column by William S. White, the newspaper commentator who was one of Johnson's closest Texan friends. White often sailed a kite for Johnson in his column so that the President could see which way the wind was blowing it. White's proposal of Mansfield was a clear indication that Johnson was still trying to ditch Humphrey. A few days later, on the Friday before the convention opened, when I was at home packing my bag for the trip to Atlantic City, I received a telephone call from the President.

"I still think we've got to have a Catholic on that ticket," he said.

With White's column fresh in my mind, I knew what was coming next.

"Mr. President," I said, "I thought we agreed that Senator Humphrey was going to be the Vice-President."

"Well, agreements come and go," he said. "The most important thing is that we get the Presidency. I've decided on Mike Mansfield."

I couldn't say anything.

"Kenny, you can't be against Mansfield," he said. "You nor any of the Kennedy people. He's one of you. You admire him and respect him. If you're thinking of Bobby running in 1972, he's no problem. He'll be too old to run then."

He had me there. Rather weakly, I replied, "Mr. President, I don't think Mike Mansfield will take the nomination."

"Let me tell you something," the President said. "That's what they said about old Lyndon Johnson in 1960. But when they lead you up on that mountain, and show you those green fields down below and that beautiful White House standing there — you know what you do? You take it. They all take it."

Then, without saying anything more, he hung up.

I went to Atlantic City, but I heard nothing there about the possibility of Mike Mansfield being nominated as Vice-President. I never mentioned my telephone conversation with Johnson to anybody until two years ago, when I went to Washington to talk with Mansfield about something else. When we finished our business conversation, I was unable to contain my curiosity any longer, and I asked Mike what had happened between him and Johnson in 1964. He took the pipe out of his mouth, and smiled.

"I, too, saw White's column," Mansfield said, "and like everybody else in Washington I knew what it meant. I waited a while, and then I decided to beat Lyndon to the punch. I went to the White House and said to him, 'Mr. President, I saw Mr. White's article about me in the newspaper, and I want you to know that under no circumstances will I ever accept the nomination as Vice-President.' That ended that."

Maybe Johnson was trying to play the same game with Mansfield that John Kennedy had played with him in 1960, offering him the Vice-Presidency to remove him from the leadership in the Senate. After dealing with the tough Irishman from Montana, Johnson had learned that he was not easy to manipulate. Or maybe Johnson was willing to put anybody in the Vice-Presidency except Humphrey, just to show Humphrey's many influential backers that nobody was going to tell Lyndon Johnson what to do.

Rather childishly, or sadistically, Johnson kept Humphrey in suspense even when Humphrey was invited to fly to the White House from Atlantic City on the Wednesday of the convention week, supposedly to be given the Vice-Presidential nomination. Johnson asked Tom Dodd, another possible selection, to come to Washington on the same plane with Humphrey, as if he might be switching to Dodd at the last minute. A group of Humphrey's supporters were so sure that the President was going to put up Dodd for the nomination that they began to raise money and round up speakers for an all-night floor fight against Dodd. When Humphrey and Dodd arrived together at the White House, the President talked first alone with Dodd, keeping Humphrey waiting in another room.

Even after he finally called Hubert into his office, Johnson talked a long time about the Vice-President's duties and his obligations to the President before he got around to mentioning that Humphrey would get the nomination. Then he said to Humphrey, "If you didn't know that I had you picked a month ago, maybe you haven't got brains enough to be the Vice-President."

After the convention, Johnson sounded me out about taking

John Bailey's position as national chairman of the Democratic party, which I refused because Bailey is a good friend of mine. Instead I moved into the national committee headquarters in Washington and handled the same job that I held in the 1960 campaign, arranging the schedule of the candidates, or deciding where they would go and making sure that they saw the people who would do them the most good after they got there. Campaigning against Barry Goldwater was so simple that Bailey and I had little to do after the schedule was set. We talked to each other on the telephone to kill time. Our only interesting diversion was an occasional bit of undercover work to keep Johnson and his people from sabotaging Bobby Kennedy's campaign for the Senate in New York.

Johnson was not particularly anxious to have Bobby in the Senate. His friends in New York were quietly active in organizing the Democrats for Kenneth Keating, Bobby's Republican opponent. Until Bailey and I stopped them, they tried to open a Johnson headquarters in New York City instead of a Johnson-Kennedy headquarters. One day a Johnson man in New York called me frantically from a hotel room, where two of Bobby's workers imported from Massachusetts, Matty Ryan and my brother Warren, were threatening to throw him out a window unless he agreed to schedule the President for an appearance in Brooklyn with Bobby during the last month of the campaign.

"Maybe the wise thing for you to do," I said to him, "would be to schedule the President for Brooklyn. After all, Matty and Warren are a couple of strong and husky boys."

A half hour later the President called me from Denver and said, "I'm not going to Brooklyn to take care of Bobby Kennedy."

"There's really no need for you to go there, Mr. President," I told him. "Forget it. If you go to Brooklyn with Bobby, everybody in the crowd will be looking at you and cheering for you instead of for him, so it won't do him any good."

Immediately Johnson decided to change the schedule of his planned tour of New York and went to Brooklyn with Bobby. They were both enthusiastically welcomed there by a huge crowd, even though there was a World Series game on TV that afternoon, and their joint appearance did them both a lot of good.

As a Presidential campaigner, Johnson pulled several boners that the politically astute John F. Kennedy never would have committed, but the 1964 fight against Goldwater was such a pushover that his mistakes did him no real harm. One night in Washington, when we were discussing the next week's schedule, I was appalled to hear him saying that he wanted to go to Delaware to attack that state's Republican Senator John Williams, who had exposed the influence-peddling of Bobby Baker, Johnson's protégé, when Baker was managing Johnson's Senate majority leader's office. Goldwater was doing his best to make Bobby Baker's exposure an issue in the campaign. By attacking Williams, Johnson would stir up damaging headlines about the Baker scandal.

"Mr. President, don't go to Delaware," I said to him. "The reporters there will be asking you questions about Senator Williams and the Baker case. Why put yourself into a situation like that?"

"I *want* to get Williams for what he did to poor Bobby Baker," Johnson said. "I don't care if it loses me the election. Put me into Delaware next week."

I kept him out of Delaware by arranging the schedule so that the only possible time when he would be free to go there would be on Sunday. Johnson had laid down two firm rules on his campaign scheduling: he said that he would not campaign on Sundays, and that he would not campaign in his opponent's home state, as a matter of courtesy. I could understand his reluctance to appear in Goldwater's state of Arizona, a waste of time anyway, but his refusal to campaign on Sundays, apparently because religious Southerners frowned on it, left me baffled. Sunday was Kennedy's big day on the campaign trail.

So on the Sunday that I deliberately scheduled Johnson for Delaware, he was home at the LBJ Ranch in Texas. The weather was clear and mild, so he decided to go to church — in Phoenix, Arizona, Goldwater's hometown. After flying from his ranch to Phoenix, Johnson drove from the airport to a downtown church, stopping at several places along the way to make speeches to street crowds with a bullhorn amplifier. The reporters who were with him said that he made at least twelve speeches and shook hands with hundreds of people. At the last stop he roared to the crowd through the bullhorn, "I'm sorry, folks, I got to go now. The minister's been delaying the services for two hours, and I don't want to keep the congregation waiting any longer."

The next morning when I read with surprise the newspaper reports on Johnson's visit to the church in Phoenix, I phoned Bill Moyers and said to him, "He never campaigns on Sundays and he doesn't go into his opponent's home state?"

It was a relief to see Lyndon Johnson safely elected on his own to the White House and taking over the Presidency with a solid feeling of security after the unhappy months of trying to fill out the remainder of John Kennedy's unfinished term and working uncomfortably with Kennedy's Cabinet and Kennedy's White House staff. He had wanted to be a good President when he was serving in the office as a stand-in for his dead predecessor, but he was always uncomfortably aware that most of the Kennedy-appointed people around him, particularly the Eastern Ivy Leaguers from the New Frontier administration, were cool toward him and regarded his presence in the White House as an unhappy accident. He was striving to do his best under unpleasant circumstances, and his situation was a hard one.

I particularly remember one evening that spring when all of us at the White House were invited to a cocktail party for Jacqueline Kennedy at the F Street Club. The President asked Larry O'Brien and me rather anxiously if we would go to the party with him. When we arrived at the club, we found that the three of us were the only men there in business suits. Everyone else was dressed in formal evening clothes. They were all going later to an embassy dinner that the President did not plan to attend. All of the guests were swarming around Jackie Kennedy, who was radiant and happy to be making her first social appearance since her husband's funeral, and nobody was paying much attention to Johnson. I stood in a corner with the President, having a drink with him while he quietly watched the scene. After a few moments he said to me, "I guess all of them are going someplace special for dinner. Are you going with them?" I said I had nothing planned. He said, "Would you mind coming back to the White House and having another drink with me there?" While we were driving to the White House, he was silent for a time and then he said, "Despite what they think, I am still the President of the United States. But I didn't want it this way."

President Johnson and I always had a pleasant relationship during the four years that I worked in the White House. When we argued over a difference in opinions, we never exchanged a harsh word. I reminded him often during the 1964 campaign that I was planning to resign from his staff and to move back to Boston after his election, but he did not take me seriously. Along with Dave Powers and Larry O'Brien, the other remaining Kennedy Irishmen on the White House staff, I submitted to Johnson a letter of resignation to be effective at the end of that year. He ignored our letters, and after the election he gave me several chores to keep me working for him, one of them the assignment of helping him to recruit a new Attorney General to replace Nicholas Katzenbach, Bobby's former deputy and close friend, who had been heading the Department of Justice since Bobby resigned from the Cabinet in August.

"Nick's a nice fellow," Johnson said, getting in a dig at Bobby. "But he's Bobby's friend, and we can't expect Bobby to keep on running the Justice Department now that he's in the Senate. Two jobs will be too much for Bobby."

I began to realize that I would never get away from Lyndon Johnson until I made the move on my own. I knew that might irritate him. He disliked having anybody leave his staff voluntarily. "Nobody leaves Lyndon unless Lyndon wants him to go," he often said.

One day in January, 1965, shortly before Johnson's inauguration, I told his assistants, Bill Moyers and Jack Valenti, to pass along the word that I was leaving whether my resignation was accepted or not. Moyers called me back and told me that the President would see me in his office in an hour. I found him standing at his desk with my letter of resignation in his hand. He was in a bad mood. "So you're really going to leave?" he said.

I explained to him that I wanted to go back to Boston. He did not ask me what I was planning to do there, and he did not wish me good luck, or even say good-bye. He said only, "Well, it's all right with me, and when you leave, take Powers with you. He's never worked for anybody around here except you and the Kennedys anyway."

Those were the last words I ever heard from Lyndon Johnson. He never spoke to me again.

FOURTEEN

Reminiscences

THE MEMORIES will always keep coming back. Dave and I were talking the other day about our exciting trip to Mexico with President Kennedy and Jackie in 1962 and its thrilling moment in the Basilica of the Virgin of Guadalupe when Jackie approached the altar carrying red roses as an offering. We were watching the President as he watched Jackie, deeply moved by reverent emotion. When she handed the flowers to the Archbishop, the President blessed himself with the sign of the cross, and all of the thousands of people crowded into the huge church applauded.

It was a rare show of his feelings with a gesture made impulsively, and meant to be private, and the sudden outburst of applause, which none of us had heard in a church before, embarrassed him. The thought that he might be suspected of making a display of his religious faith before an admiring audience made him squirm. Nobody hated crowd-pleasing ploys or show-off antics more than John Kennedy. There was never another political celebrity who was as sincerely unpretentious or who took himself less seriously. One night during the 1960 campaign he was speaking to a crowd of farmers in Sioux City, Iowa, where his clipped Cape Cod accent, with its broad and flat *a* sounds and no rolling *r*'s, seemed comically out of place. He reached a climax in his oration on agricultural depression with a shouted question, "What's wrong with the American fah-mah today?" He stopped for a momentary dramatic pause, and down from the balcony loud and clear came a reply from a comical listener in a perfect imitation of the New England accent, "He's *stah*-ving!"

The hall rocked with laughter, but nobody in the crowd was laughing harder than Jack Kennedy himself. He was doubled up and stamping around on the platform. There was not much seriousness in the rest of his speech.

The big crowds that he attracted on his tours as a candidate and as a President impressed and delighted him, but he would try to conceal his satisfaction and calm our elation with a crack of humor when we raved about the size of the audience in our way to the airport. One day in the University of California's football stadium he found himself speaking to ninety thousand people. "When I saw all those people in the stands," he said afterwards, "I didn't know whether to make the speech or to make a run down the field for a touchdown."

He was always asking all of us for a joke that he could use in his next speech. One of Dave's Boston racetrack gag lines would be switched to a complaint about the sad state of the farmer. ("I hope I break even this year — I need the money.") But his best-remembered and most widely quoted witticisms were his own originals, such as his remark when he entertained a group of Western Hemisphere Nobel Prize–winners, "This is the most extraordinary collection of talent, of human knowledge, that has ever been gathered together at the White House, with the possible exception of when Thomas Jefferson dined here alone." He despised clichés, and was probably the only President of the United States who flatly refused to make any mention of General Lafayette in a speech on good relations between this country and France.

When it came to poking fun at himself, Kennedy had no sensitive sore spots, no unhappy experiences that could not be laughed at later. He was often annoyed, irritated, upset and impatient, but we remember him being hotly angry only twice, the confused and disorganized Saturday before Election Day in 1960 when he was campaigning in New York instead of California, and the evening in 1962 when Roger Blough of U.S. Steel broke a Kennedy-arranged noninflationary agreement between steel labor and management by announcing a rise in steel prices. The Blough double deal pushed the President into the most painfully embarrassing predicament of his career, but a few days later, after he had pressured the steel companies into dropping the price rise, Kennedy was able to look back on his own embarrassment with a smile. Praising the entertainers at a White House Correspondents and Photographers dinner, he said, "I've arranged for them to appear next week on the *United States Steel Hour*. Actually, I didn't do it. Bobby did it." A year later, appearing at a Democratic fund-raising dinner, he learned with glee that in another room at the same hotel, the Waldorf Astoria, the steel industry was presenting Dwight D. Eisenhower with its annual public-service award. "I was their man of the year last year," he said to the audience. "They wanted to come down to the White House to give me their award, but the Secret Service wouldn't let them do it."

As casual as he seemed, President Kennedy was always striving for perfection in everything that he did. A few days before he was scheduled to throw out the first ball at the opening day game of the baseball season, a girl secretary on the White House staff found him alone in the Rose Garden, practicing throws with a baseball to get his arm in shape. During the 1960 campaign, when he was concerned about the strain of speaking so often on his daily tours, he quietly engaged a voice therapist, David Blair McClosky, to travel with him and to make recordings of his talks and criticisms of his inflection and delivery. He conscientiously followed McClosky's prescribed vocal exercises, one of which called for him to bark like a dog for thirty minutes every morning to strengthen his diaphragm. Trying to keep the vocal exercises unknown to the press and his fellow politicians, Kennedy did most of his barking in the bathtub. The first time that we heard the strange animal sounds coming from the bathroom, Dave opened the door to see what was happening. Kennedy looked at him from the tub, embarrassed. "I heard a funny noise," Dave said, "and I thought there was a seal in the tub." For the next few weeks we had to make up excuses when an early morning visitor at our hotel room asked what was going on in the bathroom.

He was the world's worst loser. Even in small things, a race against a traffic light or a bet on a golf match, he hated to be beaten. Dave remembers one summer day in 1946 at Fenway Park in Boston when he and Jack were watching Ted Williams come up to bat for the Red Sox. Jack asked what the odds were against Williams hitting a homer. "Fifteen to one," said Powers, the peerless statistician. Jack offered ten dollars to one that Williams would not hit a home run and Dave took the bet. On his first swing, Williams drove the ball into the right field stands. Dave leaped to his feet cheering wildly, along with everybody else in the park except Jack Kennedy. Kennedy sat in his seat with his head bowed in grief, so downhearted that he did not speak for the next two innings.

He would grouse and complain bitterly when he thought that a columnist or an editorial writer was treating him or his administration unjustly. President Nixon says that he seldom looks at a newspaper and gets his news from a summary of the day's events selected and condensed to the bare essentials by a staff member. President Kennedy devoured every newspaper and newsmagazine that he could get his hands on. During most of his time in the Presidency, he was convinced that the editors of *Time* were picking on him. He liked and admired *Time*'s White House correspondent, Hugh Sidey, but, as Sidey explained to the President, *Time*'s correspondence was rewritten and often changed by the editors in New York. The President was deeply irked one day by a story in *Time* which described him as being greeted in Cleveland by a crowd of twenty-five thousand people. "The police estimated that crowd as around one hundred thousand," Kennedy said to Sidey. "You were there. You know there were at least seventy-five thousand people, surely sixty thousand, but certainly not twenty-five thousand." Hugh said that somebody in New York had lowered his figure. That afternoon Henry Luce, the founder and editor of *Time* and *Life* and an old friend of the Kennedys, paid a visit to the White House. After talking alone in the President's office, Kennedy and Luce came outside to my office, where Sidey was waiting to escort his boss downtown.

"Who's the fellow up there in New York who changes the figures, Henry?" the President said to Luce in front of Sidey. "When Hugh tells them I drew a hundred thousand people in Cleveland last week, it comes out in the magazine as twenty-five thousand. You ought to look into it."

Luce looked hard at Sidey for a moment, and Sidey looked down at the floor. The President walked back to his desk with a smile of satisfaction on his face.

The President loved sports, football especially, and enjoyed meeting star athletes. We spent several hours in New York one day trying to locate Ernie Davis, because the President heard that he was in town and wanted to talk with him. Kennedy was a good athlete himself. He could throw a long and accurate pass with a football and he could hit a softball sharply to the opposite field. His appearance in swimming trunks was surprising. Weighing around 172 pounds, with muscular shoulders and arms and solid legs, he had the build of a light-heavyweight boxer and seemed much bigger and more powerful than he looked when dressed in one of his well-tailored suits. He loved the ocean and enjoyed swimming in it and sailing on it. When we spent a night on a Navy ship, he would pace the deck in the darkness, saying, "I want to feel the salt on my face."

One Sunday on a trip to California, he spent the afternoon at the beach home of Pat and Peter Lawford at Santa Monica, sitting in his swimming trunks beside the pool, reading a book, but glancing from time to time at the ocean surf. "Dave, look at that surf out there," he said to Powers, who was stretched out beside him. Dave was silently hoping that the President would be able to resist the urge to plunge into the surf, because the beach was open to the public and crowded with Sunday visitors who would rush upon Kennedy if they spied him heading toward the water.

But after an hour or so the dark glasses came off, the book was put down, and he was walking across the public beach toward the waves. Dave jumped up and hurried after him, wondering if he should summon the Secret Service guards from the front of the Lawford house for protection. He heard one sunbather saying, "He looks like President Kennedy, but President Kennedy isn't that big and powerful looking." The President plunged into the heavy surf and swam out beyond it while a crowd gathered, shouting and staring at his bobbing head. One woman dropped to her knees and prayed. "He's out so far!" she cried. "Please, God, don't let him drown!" Another woman, fully dressed, followed him into the surf before she turned back.

He swam in the ocean, about a hundred yards offshore, for ten minutes while a crowd of almost a thousand people gathered on the beach. When he was coming out of the water, a photographer in street clothes waded out to his waist to take pictures. Kennedy glanced at the photographer and said, "Oh, no, I can't believe it." The ten Secret Service men who were guarding him splashed into the water in their business suits, forming a protecting wedge around him with Dave and Peter Lawford to hold back the crowd that struggled to touch him and shake his hand while he made his way back across the sand to the house. The President returned to the lounge chair beside the pool, picked up his sunglasses and his book, and said contentedly, "That was the best swim I've had in months."

He took immense pride in the space program which he launched almost single-handedly in 1961 with the intention of putting American astronauts on the moon within ten years. In a speech at Houston, when NASA's Manned Spacecraft Center was being established there, he said, "Why, some say, the moon? Why choose this as our goal? Why climb the highest mountain? Why, thirty-five years ago, fly the Atlantic? Why does Rice play Texas?" But along with the desire to see Americans reach the moon and to benefit from the technological advances that such research would bring, President Kennedy pushed the space program because the money spent on it would boost the national economy. I listened to Senator Fulbright telling the President one day that the billions of dollars that his administration was asking Congress to give to space exploration would be better spent on education. "Bill, I completely agree with you," the President said. "But you and I know that Congress would never pass that much money for education. They'll spend it on a space program, and we need those billions of dollars in the economy to create jobs."

Everybody who worked with President Kennedy agrees with George Meany's estimation of him. "The outstanding impression I got of him," Meany says, "was that he wanted to know everything there was to know about a subject." This was particularly true of his diligent mastering of the difficult subject of economics. One of the economists on the White House staff remarked that during Kennedy's short time in the Presidency he taught himself more political economics than a graduate student can learn at Princeton or Harvard. His great accomplishment on the domestic front was to halt the rising unemployment that was up to 7 percent of the work force when he came into office and to cut down the balance-of-payments deficit and the outflow of gold to other countries. He did this by following the guidance of Walter Heller and breaking away from the long-established economic and fiscal prejudices of the previous administration and Congress to go for a planned budget deficit and a tax cut, which was passed after his death. The combination of a budget debt and a reduction of the government's income seemed to be an economic heresy, but Kennedy and the liberal economists saw it as a sophisticated move to increase the productive power of our industrial society, which it did successfully, giving the United States in the 1960s the longest stretch of peacetime prosperity that the country had enjoyed since the boom days of the 1920s.

Kennedy would tell us, with a smile, that in order to make the distinction between fiscal matters, concerning taxes and spending, and monetary problems, he had to remember that the name of the Federal Reserve Board's chairman, William McChesney Martin, began with an "M." "If Martin ever quits his job," he said, "I'll have to get somebody else with the same last initial." But no other President had a wider or more detailed knowledge of the government's spending and expenses and the international money market. We remember him on a plane flight to New Haven with a yellow legal pad on his lap, writing the notable speech on economic myths and clichés that he delivered at Yale's commencement exercises in 1962 with no help or advice from anybody. Getting on the plane in Washington that morning he noticed a a story in the *Wall Street Journal* which said that a budget deficit would cause inflation and an outflow of gold. He decided to rewrite the prepared text of his speech using the *Wall Street Journal* story as an example of the unrealistic prejudice that he was trying to avoid in setting a course toward prosperity. From memory, he cited years of budget debt when there had been no inflation or no gold flow, and then went on to write a discussion of a report that he had seen in a London newspaper the week before, in which conservative European bankers strongly disagreed with the traditional American financial establishment's preference for a balanced budget and easy interest rates.

Kennedy's speech on economic myths won him few converts among the old grads at Yale, who laughed heartily when he remarked after being awarded an honorary doctorate that he now had the best of two worlds, "a Harvard education and a Yale degree." But Walter Heller and many other experts declared that the President's discussion of the prefabricated ideologies and platitudes blocking the government's efforts to stimulate business, written when he was alone on the plane with no advisers looking over his shoulder, was one of the most eloquent and discerning talks on current economic problems ever delivered by a layman.

For a President who could consider an eleven-billion-dollar budget deficit without consternation, John Kennedy watched his own money with a careful scrutiny that amused us. He seldom carried cash in his pocket, and when he borrowed a ten-dollar bill from one of us for a haircut, he would often keep the change. "This can help to pay for some of my beer that you've been drinking up," he would say. He examined the White House expenses critically. Although he was not as frugal as Calvin Coolidge, who checked the contents of the refrigerator to make sure that the cook was not buying too much food, Kennedy complained about the six gardeners on the payroll. "I've got one man up at Hyannis Port who could take care of this whole place," he said. "And he would have it looking better, too." When Princess Grace of Monaco visited the Kennedys, she was surprised when he recognized her dress as a Givenchy. "I ought to know a Givenchy when I see one," he said. "I've paid for enough of them." He donated his hundred-thousand-dollar President's salary to charities, dividing it between Protestant, Jewish and Catholic causes and such organizations as the Boy Scouts and the Girl Scouts, stipulating that his gifts must be received with no publicity.

Above all, we remember John Fitzgerald Kennedy as the most skillful politician of his generation. The give and take of political intrigue, the winning of a reluctant leader's supporters, the whole business of getting votes always fascinated and excited him. When he ran for the Senate in 1952, the Democratic candidate for his vacated seat in the House of Representatives was Thomas P. O'Neill, Jr., better known as "Tip," who still serves that Eleventh District in Congress and now holds the party's position as whip in the House. Sharing the ticket in 1952, Kennedy got four more votes than O'Neill in a precinct in North Cambridge, Tip's own neighborhood. Jack Kennedy had to find out where those four votes came from, so he consulted O'Neill and went over the list of voters in the precinct with him. They decided that the extra votes for Kennedy probably came from a certain French-Canadian family who were cool toward O'Neill. In 1958, when they both ran again for reelection, Kennedy checked the returns from that precinct and noted with satisfaction that he had topped his running mate by the same four-vote margin once again.

"Now he's been elected President of the United States," O'Neill said recently, "and he's standing in his President's box in white tie and tails at one of the inauguration balls in Washington when he sees me on the floor dancing with my wife. He yells at me, 'Hey, Tip, how many votes did you get this time in that precinct in North Cambridge?' I gave him my total. He yells, 'How many did I get?' I told him his figure. A big smile comes on his face, and he says, 'That Lefebvre family is still voting against you.' "

Unlike some of the other young war veterans who went into politics out of a sense of duty to make a peaceful world, he never had a moment of regret. Getting out of bed in the darkness on a freezing morning to shake hands at a factory gate, or dealing with unsavory district leaders in a smoke-filled hotel room, he never gave a thought to how much easier his life might have been as a writer or a university teacher with a comfortable family income. Early in the game, after winning his first hard primary fight, he became impatient with his Ivy League friends and professors who regarded his calling as a distasteful and rather roughneck way of life. When he was invited a few months later to come back to Choate School as one of the speakers at its Fiftieth Anniversary Dinner, the young candidate for the House of Representatives took the invitation as an opportunity to say a kind word for politicians.

"In America, politicians are looked down upon because of their free and easy compromises," he said. "However, I do think it is well for us to understand that politicians are dealing with human beings, with all their varied ambitions, desires and backgrounds, and many of these compromises are unavoidable. We must recognize that if we do not take an interest in our political life we can easily lose at home what so many young men have so bloodily won abroad."

That early conviction that a career in politics would be his best way of helping to keep the world and the nation at peace was never weakened. To John Kennedy, politics was keeping peace. After standing up to Khrushchev and making the treaty that banned nuclear explosions in the atmosphere, he was determined to pull out of Vietnam and even more determined never to send an American draftee into combat there or anywhere else overseas. He was far too sensitive to the prevailing public opinion to commit himself any deeper to a war within Southeast Asia that was already dividing his own political party and turning the young people against the government. He died when he was looking forward to bright years, first a visit to Asia and a tour of Russia, then a lively campaign for reelection and a second term crowded with historic accomplishments.

James Reston said it well when he wrote, "What was killed in Dallas was not only the President but the promise. The heart of the Kennedy legend is what might have been. All this is apparent in the faces of the people who come daily to his grave on the Arlington Hill."

As the hand-lettered farewell message at Shannon Airport suggested, we hardly knew him.

Index

[415]

Barnett, Ross, 254
Barry, Commodore John, 364, 378
Bartlett, Charles, 323
Bayh, Birch, 307, 309–310, 344
Bay of Pigs, 14, 267, 269–278, 282, 286, 317, 327
Beck, Dave, 132, 134, 135
Behn, Gerry, 376
Belafonte, Harry, 246
Bellevue Hotel, Boston, 49, 51, 53, 56, 58, 73
Bellino, Carmine, 135, 136
Ben Bella, Ahmed, 310
Benitez, José, 131
Benny, Jack, 357
Benson, Ezra Taft, 223
Benton, Thomas Hart, 101
Berger, Andy, 34
Berle, Adolf, 272
Berlin, 14, 244, 268–269, 299–307 *passim*, 343, 350; crisis (1961), 9, 266, 267, 278, 284, 285, 301–306; in JFK–De Gaulle talks, 291–292; in JFK–Khrushchev talks, 291–292, 295–300; White House strategy for, 301–302; JFK–Gromyko discussion on, 304–306; crisis subsides, 306; and Cuban missile crisis, 318, 319, 329–331; blockade (1948), 329; RFK visits, 395. *See also* East Berlin; West Berlin
Berlin, Irving, his *Mr. President*, 263–265
Berlin Wall, 303–304, 360–361
Bernstein, Leonard, 246
Besterman, Walter, 305
Bethesda Naval Hospital, 33, 40, 41
Bevilacqua, Frank, 141
Bigger, Colonel W. T. (Ret.), 385–386
Billings, LeMoyne, 56, 94
Birch, John, 20, 23
Birmingham, Alabama, 354
Bishop, Jim, 41
Bissell, Richard, 270
Blough, Roger, 406–407
Boggs, Hale, 258, 327
Bohlen, Charles, 99, 295, 311
Bonn, Germany, 359
Boston Herald, 57, 90; endorsement of JFK (1958), 139
Boston Post, 108
Boutin, Bernie, 256
Bouvier, Jacqueline, *see* Kennedy, Jacqueline
Bowen, Lester, 71
Bowles, Chester, 178, 236, 243
Boyle, James Patrick, 123

Bradford, Robert, 71
Bradlee, Ben, 171
Bradlee, Tony, 171
Brandenburg Gate, 360. *See also* Berlin
Brewster, Owen, 99
Brighton, Massachusetts, 48, 63
Brinkley, Ann, 18
Brinkley, David, 18
Britain, 358; and Skybolt, 345–350; and Common Market, 348, 350; and multilateral nuclear force, 348–350. *See also* England.
Broderick, Tom, 64
Brooks Air Force Base, San Antonio, 21
Brown, Pat, 103, 148, 177–178, 185, 345; supports Humphrey (1964), 398
Bruce, David, 236
Bruno, Jerry, 164, 203–204, 211–212
Buchan, John, his *Pilgrim's Way*, 45
Bucharest, Russian oil tanker, 333
Buckley, Charlie (Charles A.), 61, 152, 173, 180, 215
Bundy, McGeorge, 235, 236, 243, 251, 262, 266–267, 276; and Bay of Pigs, 273; added responsibilities after Bay of Pigs, 277–278; and Cuban missile crisis, 283, 311, 316, 318, 321; and removal of Jupiter missiles from Turkey, 337; and JFK's trip to Ireland, 358; and JFK's trip to Berlin, 361; and JFK's Vatican visit, 373
Bundy, William, 263
Bunker Hill, 48, 260; Monument, 54
Burke, Grace, 80
Burke, James E., 260, 261
Burke, Onions (William H.), 104–110, 112–115, 123, 125, 167, 221, 251; JFK's power struggle with, 109–110; rumors of JFK vote-buying, 114; showdown with, 115–116; and JFK's Senate seat, 116; and 1958 Massachusetts primary vote, 141
Burkley, Rear Admiral (Dr.) George G., 29, 32, 34, 37, 103, 321
Burrell, Robert, 363–364
Burros Club, 258
Burroughs (John) High School, Los Angeles, 356
Byrd, Robert, 162, 168, 171

California, 24, 148, 153, 177–178; JFK fears losing of (1960), 218–219, 221–222; election returns, 224–225; $1,000-a-couple President's Club Dinner, 356–357

Cambridge, 48, 54, 55, 56, 63
Camp David, 346, 356
Cape Canaveral, 12, 387
Cape Cod, 39. *See also* Hyannis Port
Capehart, Homer, 307, 309, 310, 344
Caroline, Kennedy family plane, 150, 160,
163, 171, 172, 176, 178, 206, 215, 218,
220, 222, 233
Carpenter, Lester, 178
Carpenter, Liz, 178
Carr, John, 105
Carswell Air Force Base, Fort Worth, 25,
32
Carter, Cliff, 38
Carter, General Marshall S., 311
Casey, Joseph E., 50–51
Casey, Sean, 365
Castro, Fidel, 244, 263, 267; and Bay of
Pigs, 270–275 *passim*; and release of
prisoners, 275–276; and Cuban mis-
sile crisis, 319
Cecil, David, his biography of Lord Mel-
bourne, 45
Celeste, Vincent J., 77, 139, 144–146
Central Intelligence Agency (CIA): and
Bay of Pigs, 270–274 *passim*; limit-
ing of operations and authority of,
277
Chancellor, John, 223–224
Charlestown, Massachusetts, 41, 48, 51–
54, 63, 261; Powers as JFK man in
(1946), 55; typical Kennedy cam-
paign day in, 63–64; climax of JFK
(1946) campaign in, 70–71
Charlestown Navy Yard, 48, 52, 54, 63, 64
Chelsea Naval Hospital, 43
Chiang Kai-shek, 294
Chicago, *see* Democratic National Con-
vention (1956)
Chicago *Sun-Times*, 119
Chicopee, Massachusetts, 24
Children's Medical Center, Boston, 376
China, 15, 76, 338; and Sino-Soviet rift,
268, 343
Chinatown, Boston, 48
Choate School, 413
Churchill, Randolph, 362
Churchill, Winston, 291, 368
Citizens Committee for a Nuclear Test
Ban, 375
Clark, Jim, 177
Clark, Dr. Kemp, 30–31
Clay, General Lucius D., 275, 276
Clement, Frank, 120, 124
Clifford, Clark, 227

Clifton, Major General Ted (Chester V.),
33, 245
Cloherty, Peter, 122–123
Clondell, Frances, 370
Cluster, Al, 385
Cohn, Roy, 97–98
Collins, LeRoy, 187, 197–198
Colorado, 184
Columbia Trust Company, Boston, 48
Commager, Henry Steele, 213
Common Market, *see* European Common
Market
Commonwealth Armory, Boston, 384
Communist Party, U.S., 23
Conant, James B., 99
Connally, John, 11, 270, 356, 386; rift
with Yarborough, 3, 4, 12, 20–21, 23,
25–26; in Dallas motorcade, 27, 28;
at 1960 convention, 195; Cabinet ap-
pointment (Navy Secretary), 238
Connally, Mrs. John, 26; in Dallas mo-
torcade, 27, 28
Connecticut, 220, 222
Connell, Maurice, 151
Constitution, frigate, 48, 54
Conway, Jack, 137, 161, 194, 197, 237,
238; and 1964 campaign, 398
Coolidge, Calvin, 217, 412
Corbin, Paul, 157–158
Corish, Brendan, 368
Costa Rica, 353
Costello, John A., 368
Cotter, John, 48–49, 51, 52, 53, 55, 62,
63, 73; loses to JFK in 1946 primary,
71
Cronkite, Walter, 45, 383
Crosby, Bing, 379–380
Crotty, Peter, 61, 173
Cuba, 14, 244, 261, 262, 267, 269, 350;
Bay of Pigs, 14, 267, 269–278, 282,
286, 317, 327; missile crisis, 14–15,
266, 268, 275, 276, 282, 284, 306–343,
344, 348; U-2 reconnaissance in, 262–
263, 307, 309, 310, 314, 316, 336–337,
339, 342; and De Gaulle, 292; as issue in 1962 midterm elections, 307–
310 *passim*; and Ex Comm, 311–315,
317–319, 322; U.S. naval blockade of,
313, 314, 317–318, 319, 322, 325, 329,
330–334; and security concerning
missile crisis, 320, 326; Kennedy-
Khrushchev correspondence *re* missile crisis, 330–331, 335–336, 339–342;
U-2 pilot Anderson shot down over,
336–337, 339; mementoes of missile

Free University of Berlin, 361
Friendly, Al, 326
Frost, Robert, 242
Fulbright, William, 236, 410; his opposition to Bay of Pigs, 271–273; and Cuban missile crisis, 327–328
Furcolo, Foster, 85–86, 97, 102, 243; in 1958 elections, 139–142 *passim*

Galbraith, J. Kenneth, 235
Gallagher, Mary, 32
Galvin, Bill, 60
Galvin, John, 57, 68, 78
G and G Delicatessen, Dorchester, 42, 144
Gargan, Ann, 186, 190
Gargan, William, 182, 186, 187–188
Garner, John Nance, 8, 24–25
Garrity, Arthur, 140
Garvey, Dr. Skip, 30
Gates, Thomas S., 244
Gawler's Funeral Home, 41
George V, of England, 368
Georgia, 13
Germany, 295, 356. *See also* East Germany; West Germany
Gilpatric, Roswell, 311, 313, 333
Glen Ora, 356
Goldberg, Arthur, 193–194, 241, 260, 278–279
Gold Star Mothers, 53–55
Goldwater, Barry, 13, 135, 136, 138, 159; JFK's respect for, 213; and nuclear test ban treaty, 379; and 1964 Republican nomination, 384–385, 391, 392, 395, 396; in 1964 campaign, 401, 402
Gonzalez, Henry, 20
Gore, Albert, 122, 123, 124
Government Operations Committee, 99
Grace, Princess, of Monaco, 412
Graham, Philip, 189–190, 195, 196, 246; and appointment of Douglas Dillon, 239
Greater Houston Ministerial Association, 204–210, 357
Green, William J., Jr., (Bill), 152, 173, 176, 177, 180, 188, 215; death of, 391
Green Berets, 17, 269, 382
Greer, Bill, 40
Gridiron Club, 345
Griffith Stadium, Washington, 19
Gromyko, Andrei, 293, 294, 304–306, 314, 318–319; and nuclear test ban treaty, 380
Guantanamo Bay, 322, 323, 329

Guardian, Navy PT boat, 270
Guatemala, 244; Cuban Brigade trained in, 271, 272, 274

Hailsham, Lord, 380
Haley, Flo, 182, 186
Haley, Jack, 182, 185
Hall, Gus, 23
Halleck, Charlie, 328
Hammarskjold, Dag, 304, 306
Hammersmith Farm, Newport, 95
Hanau, Germany, 359
Harding, Warren, 217
Harkins, General Paul, 17, 383
Harlech, Lord, *see* Ormsby-Gore, David
Harriman, Averell, 106, 116, 117, 188, 255, 263, 358, 390; and Laos, 268, 382; and nuclear test ban treaty, 380, 381
Harris, Lou, 160, 161, 170, 222
Harris, Seymour, 235, 279
Hartigan, Bill, 230, 232, 287
Hartington, Marquess, 371
Harvard University, 45, 81; Board of Overseers, 129, 172, 242; School of Public Health, 376
Hassan II, king of Morocco, 351
Hawaii, 184–185, 356
Hayes, Rutherford B., 251
Healey, Joe, 55
Hearst, William Randolph, 184
Hearst newspapers, 44
Heller, Walter, 260, 279, 410, 411
Hemingway, Ernest, 164
Herman, George, 344
Hersey, John, 46, 66
Herter, Christian A., 88, 92, 93, 244
Hickory Hill, 96, 130, 133; RFK group seminars at, 281
Higgins, John P., 48
Hill, Clint, 28, 29, 32, 34, 37
Hiss, Alger, 109–110
Hoffa, Jimmy, 132, 133, 134, 135
Hollow Horn Bear, Chief, 210–211
Holyhood Cemetery, Brookline, Massachusetts, 378, 379
Honey Fitz, Presidential yacht, 270, 375
Honolulu, 357
Hoover, Herbert, 155, 159, 229
Horseshoe Tavern, Charlestown, Massachusetts, 96–97, 261
Hospital for Special Surgery, New York, 98–100
Hotel Commander, Cambridge, 65
House of Representatives, U.S.: JFK takes his seat in, 75–76; Labor Com-

Kennedy, John Fitzgerald (*continued*)
workers, 79–82, 130; O'Donnell's involvement in, 81–85; campaign organization, 79–80, 82–85, 87, 90–91; announces his candidacy, 82; O'Brien's involvement in, 85; and Foster Furcolo, 85–86, 97, 102, 140, 141; areas of Democratic joint effort, 87–88; political style, 87, 91–92; the primary elections, 88; nomination papers, 90–91; debate with Lodge, 91; extent of grass-roots organization, 92; victory, 92–93; political popularity in Massachusetts, 96–97, 101; reelection (1958), 132, 138–140
CONVENTION OF 1956, 104–127; and Massachusetts Democratic Committee, 105–117; and Onions Burke, 105–110, 114–115; pro-Stevenson views, 106, 113; and Pat Lynch, 110–112; and political patronage for Massachusetts, 113; takes command of party in Massachusetts, 114–117; and Margaret O'Riordon, 117; rise to nationwide prominence, 117, 124, 145; boommed as Vice-Presidential choice, 117–124; nominator of Stevenson, 118, 120, 121; changes in his view of his political role, 125; efforts on behalf of Stevenson campaign, 126–127; and Reuther, 134
DOMESTIC ISSUES, 267, 278–279, 284, 307; civil rights, 6, 7, 13; the space program, 8, 12, 21–22, 284, 410; low-cost housing, 73–75; the Saint Lawrence Seaway, 96–97; censure of Senator McCarthy, 97–99, 103, 108–109, 120; McClellan committee, 132–138; "conservation tour" of Western states, 379–380; economics, 410–412
FOREIGN POLICY, 267–269, 281, 284–343; Vietnam, 13–18, 382–384, 413–414; Cuban missile crisis, 14–15, 262–263, 306–343, 344; Laotian neutrality, 244–245, 267–269, 286, 296, 307, 350; Bay of Pigs, 270–278, 281, 282; Berlin crisis, 278, 299–306; nuclear testing, 285, 296, 300, 304; and Khrushchev, 286, 292–298, 300–302; in Paris with De Gaulle, 286–292; and Berlin Wall, 303; and Soviet suggestion for troika for U.N., 304–306; correspondence with Khrushchev *re* missile crisis, 330–331, 335–336, 339–342; and nuclear test ban treaty,

334, 354, 357, 375–376, 379, 380–381, 413; and Skybolt, 345–350; and Macmillan at Nassau, 348, 350; and multilateral nuclear force, 348–350; American University speech (1963), 357–358; and sale of wheat to Soviets, 381–382
AND JOHNSON: "dump Johnson" rumor before 1964 campaign, 5, 282; selection of as 1960 running mate, 7, 189–200, 400; attempts to assuage unhappiness of as Vice-President, 7–9; relationship with, 179–181; discusses choice of with O'Donnell, 192–193, 198; opposition to as Vice-Presidential choice, 192–197; factors involved in choice of, 198; and JFK campaign organization, 204–207, 216, 219; visits with at LBJ Ranch, 229–233; his access to Oval Office, 254; mission to West Berlin, 303
PERSONAL CHARACTERISTICS: back ailment, 4, 43, 72–73, 79, 86, 96, 97, 98, 102–103, 265, 288, 296; insatiable curiosity, 18, 248, 293, 367, 410; as journalist, 44, 46; aversion to hats, 54, 321–322, 367; his father's money, 55; stamina, 63–64, 103, 140; as competitor, 69–70, 407–408; unpretentiousness, 80–81, 404; courtship and marriage, 94–96; personal relationships, 94; spinal fusion operation, 98–102; adrenal insufficiency, 99, 103; authors *Profiles in Courage*, 100–101, 103; rumors of Addison's disease, 103; post-illness change in, 103–104; and Harvard Board of Overseers, 129, 172, 242; birth of John, Jr., 233–234; and decoration of Oval Office, 250–251; newspaper-reading habits, 256; dislike of being alone in White House, 264–265; and physical fitness, 351; correspondence with private citizens, 352–353; surprise forty-sixth birthday party, 355; and Camp David retreat, 356; birth and death of Patrick Bouvier Kennedy, 375–378, 384; White House pets, 378; love of crowds, 406; witticisms, 406–407; striving for perfection, 407; and the press, 408; love of sports, 408–409; physical description, 409; love of the sea, 409; and his own money, 412; love of politics, 413

New York, campaign activities in, 218–220

New York Daily News, 65, 138

New Yorker, 46, 328

New York Times, 176, 234, 240, 298; and Cuban missile crisis, 326

Nhu, Madame, 375, 382–383

Nhu, Ngo Dinh, 15, 16, 17, 258, 375, 382–383

Nitze, Paul, 240, 283, 311, 313, 318

Nixon, Pat, 224

Nixon, Richard M., 4, 16, 22, 168, 169, 180, 209; debate with JFK, 91, 170, 211–214; and 1956 campaign, 121; and JFK's choice of running mate (1960), 192–193; and Rayburn, 195; as Republican Presidential nominee (1960), 201; and 1960 campaign activities, 203, 205, 215, 216, 218; "kitchen debate" with Khrushchev, 212; and Eisenhower support in 1960 campaign, 216–217; and election day (1960), 224–225; JFK pays courtesy call upon, 229; inaccessibility of, 257; and Khrushchev, 294; in 1962 midterm elections, 344–345; and the press, 408

Nolan, John E., Jr., 276

Norris, George W., 101

North End, Boston, 47, 48, 54; and 1958 election, 141; 1960 campaign activities in, 221

Norton, Clem, 60–61

Nosavan, General Phoumi, 245, 268

Nuclear test ban treaty, 4, 285, 296, 300, 304; and JFK, 334, 354, 357, 375–376, 379–381, 413; and Khrushchev, 334, 354, 357–358, 361, 380–381; and Goldwater, 379; and Gromyko, 380; and Harriman, 380–381; and McCloy, 381; and Rusk, 381

O'Brien, Dan, 49

O'Brien, Lawrence (Larry), 6, 23, 24, 25, 94, 403; at Parkland Hospital, 30, 32, 33; accompanies JFK's body back to Washington, 37, 38, 40–42; selects JFK's casket, 41; joins 1952 Senatorial campaign organization, 85; and JFK's grass-roots organization, 92, 97; and Democratic party power struggle (1956), 105; and 1958 Senate reelection campaign, 140, 142; and 1960 campaign, 149, 160, 163,

170; at Los Angeles, 182; and recruitment for new administration, 227; as Congressional liaison, 251, 258; and Cuban missile crisis, 327; and JFK's 1964 reelection campaign, 386; and LBJ's 1964 campaign, 394; and RFK's 1964 campaign, 395–396; resigns from LBJ staff, 404

O'Connor, Edwin, his *The Last Hurrah*, 60

O'Connor, Frank, 21

O'Donnell, Helen (Mrs. Kenneth), 225, 227, 228, 246, 389, 391, 398; during Cuban missile crisis, 324, 325, 326

O'Donnell, Warren, 401

O'Hare, Dick, 215, 321

Ohio, 148–153, 221–224

O'Kelly, Mrs. Sean T., 368–369

O'Leary, "Muggsey," 41

Olivier, Sir Laurence, 246

O'Mahoney, Monsignor Michael, 365

O'Neill, Thomas P., Jr. (Tip), 93, 412–413

Oregon, 160, 171, 172, 178

O'Reilly, John Boyle, 359

Organization of American States, 329, 330

O'Riordan, Margaret, 117

Ormsby-Gore, David (Lord Harlech), 94, 266, 361

O'Shea, George, 113

Otis Air Force Base, 39, 114, 375–376, 377

Paar, Jack, 259

Pakistan, 8, 269

Palm Beach, 15, 75–76, 241; JFK recovers from spinal surgery in, 100–102; JFK forms his administration at, 226–227, 233, 234; abortive assassination attempt at, 242; JFK's last St. Patrick's Day at, 353; JFK's final visit to, 387–388

Paris, 13; JFK–De Gaulle talks in, 286–292; Quai d'Orsay apartment used by Kennedys, 288–290, 292

Parker House, Boston, 95

Parkland Hospital, Dallas, 28–31, 41–42

Pathet Lao, 268, 269

Patrick J., Presidential yacht, 270

Patterson, Floyd, 264, 265

Patterson, John M., 180

Paul VI, Pope, 372–374

Pavlick, Richard P., 242

Peace Corps, 20

Peale, Dr. Norman Vincent, 206, 373
Peck, Max, 22
Penkovskiy, Colonel Oleg, 308
Pennsylvania, 175–178, 223; religious issue in, 176–177
Pentagon, 14; and Cuban missile crisis, 308. *See also* McNamara, Robert S.
Peppe, Joseph, 354–355
Peppe, Patrick, 354
Petersen, Burrell, 225, 226
Petrovna, Nina, *see* Khrushchev, Mrs. Nikita
Philippines, 269
Pius XII, Pope, 373
Poland, 395
Polaris missile, 345–349
Poling, Dr. Daniel, 206
Potsdam Conference, 44, 46, 291
Powell, Adam Clayton, 260
Powers, Diane, 203
Powers, Gary, 275, 294
Powers, Jo (Mrs. Dave), 95, 131, 228, 246, 340
Powers, John E., 87, 111, 112; and JFK's 1958 Senate reelection campaign, 143–144
Prendergast, Mike, 173, 220
Profiles in Courage (John Kennedy), 100–101, 103, 156, 237; wins Pulitzer Prize, 129
PT-59, 385, 386
PT-109, 66–67, 165, 250, 258–259, 385

Quai d'Orsay, 288–290
Quigley, Martin, 364
Quincy, Massachusetts, 84

Radio Moscow, 336
Radziwill, Lee, 286, 351, 378; with JFK party in Ireland, 365, 371; accompanies Jackie on Mediterranean cruise, 379
Radziwill, Stash (Stanislas), 286, 351
Rankin, John, 74
Rauh, Joe, 197
Rayburn, Sam, 9–11, 76, 93, 104, 201, 205; and Stevenson, 106; and 1956 Democratic convention, 123; and Johnson's 1960 campaign, 149, 178, 183, 193; nominates LBJ for President at Los Angeles, 186; his view of LBJ as JFK's running mate, 195–196; and post-convention campaigning, 207–210; and John Connally's Cabinet appointment, 238; on Inauguration Day, 247

Reader's Digest, 46, 65–66
Reardon, Ted, 56, 64, 75, 76, 251, 305, 324; in West Virginia, 164
Reese, Matt, 164
Reston, Scotty (James), 298, 320, 326, 414
Reuther, Walter, 122, 189, 238, 260, 275, 398; and McClellan committee investigations, 133–138; and Humphrey, 148, 161, 398; and JFK's choice of running mate, 193–194, 197
Reynolds, John, 131, 398
Ribicoff, Abraham, 121, 122, 187, 188, 192, 195, 278–279; arranges peace conference between JFK and Truman, 202; and JFK campaign in Connecticut, 220; reward for his help in the election, 227; Cabinet post, 229, 240; and 1962 midterm election campaign, 316–317
Rice Hotel, Houston, 22
Rickover, Admiral Hyman, 250–251
Riley, Ken, his painting *The Whites of Their Eyes*, 260
Roberts, Dennis, 121
Roberts, Emory, 32
Roche, Chuck, 186, 187, 188
Rockefeller, Nelson A., 216, 392
Rockefeller, Nelson A., Jr., 392
Rockefeller, Mrs. Nelson (Happy), 392
Rogers, Edith Nourse, 74
Rogers, William P., 169
Rome, 373–374
Romney, George, 13, 392
Roncalio, Teno, 131
Rooney, Francis X., 62
Roosevelt, Eleanor, 98, 120, 134, 246, 275; JFK's peace meeting with, 202
Roosevelt, Franklin D., 50–51, 58, 83, 104, 155, 165, 179, 210, 213, 217, 251; and 1940 Democratic convention, 43, 120; his Cabinet, 234, 235; and De Gaulle, 290, 291; and German reunification, 295
Roosevelt, Franklin D., Jr., 165, 167, 185, 238, 281, 358
Roosevelt, Theodore, 351
Rose, Alex, 162, 189, 194, 195
Rose, Dr. Earl, 33–34, 35
Roselyn, Earl of, 362
Ross, Barney, 258–260
Ross, Edmund G., 101
Rosse, Earl of, 367
Rostenkowski, Daniel, 175
Rowe, Jim, 161–162, 204, 325–326, 394
Rowley, Jim, 80–81, 226

Ruggieri, Sebastian, 107–108

Rusk, Dean, 9, 15–16, 42, 236, 239, 240, 243, 257, 276, 281–282; and JFK's pre-inaugural briefings with Eisenhower, 244; and Bay of Pigs, 271; and RFK, 281; in Vienna with JFK, 293, 295, 297; and Cuban missile crisis, 311, 312, 321, 322, 324, 327, 332, 334–335; and removal of U.S. missiles from Turkey, 338; and JFK visit to England (1963), 371; attends JFK meeting with Pope Paul VI, 373; at signing of nuclear test ban treaty, 381; final talks with JFK, 388–389; and 1964 campaign, 397

Russell, Francis, 59–60

Russell, Richard B., 327–328

Russia, 4, 23, 414; and Cuban missile crisis, 14–15, 263, 268, 283, 306–343 *passim*; and China, 268, 343; and Bay of Pigs, 271; and Berlin, 278, 291–292, 299–300; and threat of war over Berlin, 297–299; missile strength (1962), 308; U-2 reconnaissance over, 339, 342; and nuclear test ban treaty, 380–381; sale of U.S. wheat to, 381. *See also* Khrushchev, Nikita S.

Russo, Joseph, 62

Ryan, Cornelius, his *The Longest Day*, 248

Ryan, Mary Kennedy, 362–364

Ryan, Matty, 401

Ryan, Robert, 265–266

Saigon, 14, 17. *See also* Vietnam

Saint Lawrence Seaway, 96–97, 101, 141

St. Matthew's Cathedral, 40

Salinger, Pierre, 6, 13, 42, 252, 257, 258, 375, 378; at Los Angeles convention, 182, 185, 186; and JFK's choice of running mate, 191; and post-convention campaign, 208; election night (1960), 224; announcement of birth of John F. Kennedy, Jr., 233; and leaking of Cabinet appointments announcement, 239; and Bay of Pigs, 272; with Kennedy party in Paris, 290; and midterm elections (1962), 320; and Cuban missile crisis, 320–322, 327, 334–335; and White House staff fifty-mile hike, 351; advance arrangements for JFK's trip to Ireland, 362; and JFK's Vatican visit (1963), 373; and Texas trip, 388

Saltonstall, Leverett, 77, 85–86, 97, 384;

and censure of Senator McCarthy, 99

San Antonio, 18, 20–22, 387; Kennedy's reception at, 21

San Cristobal, Cuba, 307, 309. *See also* Cuba, missile crisis

Santamaria, Carlos Sanz de, 263, 266

Santamaria, Mrs. Carlos Sanz de, 263, 266

Santa Monica, California, 409

Saturday Evening Post, 95, 323

Sawyer, Buz, 183, 186

Scali, John, 334–335

Scammon, Richard, 386, 387

Scharf, Adolf, 294

Schine, G. David, 98

Schirra, Walter, 311

Schlesinger, Arthur, 179, 235, 242–243; and Stevenson, 243; and Bay of Pigs, 272–273; his *A Thousand Days*, 273; and rumored "dump Rusk" movement, 282

Schroeder, Dr. Gerhard, 316

Scott, Paul, 320

Scranton, William W., 392

Secret Service, 19, 81, 388, 409–410; in Dallas, 26–30, 33; and President Johnson, 31; and arrival of JFK's body in Washington, 40; and 1960 election day, 225; and President-elect, 226–228, 232; and abortive assassination attempt at Palm Springs, 242; and JFK's disregard for security (1963), 387

Segni, Antonio, 373

Select Committee on Improper Activities in the Labor or Management Field, *see* McClellan committee

Senate, U.S.: Foreign Relations Committee, 129, 140, 236, 271, 294, 327; Rackets Committee, 132–133. *See also* McCarthy, Joseph

Sequoia, cruiser, 270

Shaw, George Bernard, 366

Shepard, Commander Tazewell, 324

Sherwood, Robert E., quoted, 155

Shoup, General David M., 351

Shriver, Eunice Kennedy, 57, 76, 119; and 1960 campaign, 157, 158, 160, 188; on election night, 223; on JFK trip to Ireland, 364, 365

Shriver, Sargent, 20, 121; and JFK's choice of running mate (1960), 192; and recruitment for new administration, 227, 237, 238; and Vice-Presidential possibility (1964), 393–394, 398

Sidey, Hugh, 293–294, 408

Sinatra, Frank, 18, 245, 246, 248; rift with the Kennedys, 380
Sioux City, Iowa, 405–406
Skelton, Byron, 18–19
Skybolt missile, 345–350
Smathers, George, 5, 190, 258
Smith, Al, 158, 159
Smith, Ben, 94; serves out JFK's term in Senate, 243–244
Smith, Bromley, 337
Smith, Jean Kennedy, 115, 139, 157, 158, 164, 188, 371, 387; on election night (1960), 223; accompanies JFK to Ireland, 364, 365; visits Paul VI with Kennedy party, 373
Smith, Steve, 115, 139, 387; and 1960 campaign, 150, 180; and 1964 campaign, 386, 395
Somerville, Massachusetts, 48, 54, 63
Sorensen, Ted, 121, 227, 251; and Cuban missile crisis, 311, 324, 330, 340; and JFK's Vatican visit (1963), 373; and 1964 reelection campaign, 386
South Boston, Massachusetts, 89
South Carolina, 13
South Dakota, 184
Southeast Asia, 13–14, 92, 267–268; and issue of American prestige, 18; and De Gaulle, 269. *See also* Vietnam
South End, Boston, 48
South Vietnam, 15–17, 244, 258, 268; and assassination of Diem and the Nhus, 17; post-Diem leadership, 18; and withdrawal of American advisers, 382. *See also* Vietnam
Soviet Union, *see* Russia
Spalding, Chuck, 94, 351
Sparkman, John, 247
Spellman, Francis Cardinal, 166
Squaw Island, 375, 376, 377, 378
Stalin, Joseph, 291, 295
State Department, 14–15; and RFK, 278, 281–282; and JFK's Vienna summit, 287–288; and Paris talks with De Gaulle, 292; and Berlin Wall, 303–304; and Jupiter missiles in Turkey, 323–324
Staubach, Roger, 388
Stevenson, Adlai E., 10, 19, 90, 92, 119, 202, 265, 266, 310; and 1956 convention, 104; JFK support of, 106, 113, 116; and Truman, 106; and Massachusetts, 108–109, 116, 117; and JFK's rise to national prominence,
117–118; booming of JFK as Vice-Presidential candidate, 117–124; and JFK nominating speech for, 118, 120, 121; JFK's help in campaigning, 126–127; JFK learns from campaign mistakes of, 131; and Hoffa, 133–134; and 1960 elections, 137, 149, 152, 159, 162, 168, 172, 173, 175, 176, 178, 180, 184, 185, 186–187, 236; promise of support to JFK, 178, 183; as Vice-Presidential possibility, 189; his view of LBJ as JFK's running mate, 194–195; his 1956 campaign organization, 214; ambassador to United Nations, 235–236, 240; sidetracked from post of Secretary of State, 235–236, 240; and Schlesinger, 243; and Cuban missile crisis, 311, 322–323, 326, 334; reception in Dallas (October 24, 1963), 388; and 1964 campaign, 397
Stimson, Henry, 235
Stoughton, Cecil, 369
Strategic Air Command, 331
Sullivan, Peter, 108
Sutton, Bill, 46, 51, 52, 53, 62, 76; on JFK's political style, 59; in Bunker Hill Day parade (1946), 70
Sweeney, General Walter C., 326–327, 341
Swindal, Colonel Jim, 34
Symington, Stuart, 7, 10, 148, 149, 152, 162, 168, 178, 184, 192; considered as possible running mate (1960), 189, 190

Taft, Robert, 74, 89, 108; in *Profiles in Courage*, 101
Tague, Peter, 50
Tavern Club, Boston, 126
Taylor, General Maxwell, 17, 278, 283; and Cuban missile crisis, 311, 313, 318
Teamsters' Union, 133–134, 141
Tennessee, 223
Texas, 3–5, 11–13, 18–20, 356; Johnson's waning prestige in (1960), 5–6, 8–9; JFK's hopes to raise campaign money in (1964), 11, 12, 386; enthusiastic reception of Kennedys in, 20–22; JFK campaign in, 204–210, 216; JFK carries in election, 223, 225. *See also* Dallas
Texas Hotel, Fort Worth, 22
Texas School Book Depository, Dallas, 27
Thailand, 268, 269

Thant, U, 306
Thomas, Albert, 11–12, 22, 25–26
Thomas, George, 42, 262, 265, 379
Thompson, Llewellyn, 295, 302; and
    Cuban missile crisis, 311, 318, 336,
    339
Thorneycroft, Peter, 347
Thuan, Nguyen Dinh, 258
Time magazine, 129, 408
Tobin, Maurice, 47, 71
Tower, John G., 4
Tractors for Freedom committee, 275
Trade Mart, Dallas, 26, 27
Traubel, Helen, 246
Travell, Dr. Janet, 102
Treanor, John, 204
Truman, Harry, 9–10, 25, 74, 75, 76, 80,
    104, 113, 217, 234; and election of
    1948, 77, 80; and Stevenson, 106;
    and Mike DiSalle, 148, 151; and Am-
    bassador Kennedy, 151, 202; and
    1960 election, 178–179; JFK makes
    peace with, 202; and Eisenhower's
    first inauguration, 247; JFK's first
    White House visitor after inaugura-
    tion, 251
Truman Diamond Jubilee Dinner, Boston
    (1959), 179
Tuchman, Barbara, her *The Guns of Au-
    gust*, 330–331
Turkey: Jupiter missiles in, 322–324, 328,
    330, 331; removal of missiles from,
    336–340; in Kennedy–Khrushchev
    correspondence during Cuban missile
    crisis, 340
Turnure, Pamela, 37
Twohig, Pat, 164

Udall, Stewart, 272
United Automobile Workers (UAW), 133–
    138, 197, 237, 238
United Mineworkers, 163
United Nations: San Francisco confer-
    ence, 44, 46; Steveson ambassador-
    ship, 235–236, 240; and Berlin, 297,
    302; and Khrushchev troika proposal,
    304–306; and Cuban missile crisis,
    314, 334
United Negro College Fund, 261
United States Conference of Mayors, 357
University of Alabama, 354
University of California, 406
University of Maine, JFK speech at, 384
University of Mississippi, 381
Unruh, Jesse, 178, 227, 392, 394

U.S. Information Agency (USIA), 311

Valenti, Jack, 394, 404
Vandenberg Air Force Base, California,
    349
Vanocur, Sander, 306, 344
Vatican, JFK visits (1963), 373
Vena, Luigi, 38
Veterans of Foreign Wars, Joseph P.
    Kennedy, Jr., Post 5880, 70
Victoria, queen of England, 251
Vienna, 268, 285, 286, 292–298, 300, 302,
    325; O'Donnell makes advance ar-
    rangements for JFK's trip to, 286–
    287; Kennedy and Khrushchev meet
    in, 292–298; welcome of Kennedy
    party in, 294; first official talks, 294;
    JFK's evaluation of talks, 298–299
Vientiane, 268, 269
Viet Cong, 268, 382–383
Vietnam War, 13–16, 267, 269, 350, 374,
    375; and withdrawal of U.S. troops
    and advisers, 13, 16–18, 382; JFK
    seeks solution for, 413–414. See also
    South Vietnam
Voice of America, 358

Waddington Air Force Base, England, 371
Wade, Henry M., 41
Wagner, Robert, 122, 123, 124
Walsh, Dr. John, 233, 375, 376
Walton, Bill, 164, 223, 244, 245, 246
Ward, Mike, 60–61
Ward, Theron, 33, 41
Warren Commission, 37
Washington, Massachusetts, 144–145
Washington Post, 239, 322, 326
Webb, James E., 12
Webster, Daniel, 101
Weirwein, Austin, 155
West, Judge, 231
West Berlin, 291; LBJ mission to, 303;
    JFK's speech in (1963), 357, 360
West End, Boston, 48
West Germany, 291, 296, 299–300, 348;
    and multilateral nuclear force, 350;
    and JFK's European trip (1963),
    357, 358, 359–360
West Virginia, 104; Presidential primary,
    147, 160–172, 174; religious issue, 147,
    148, 159, 160–164, 165–167, 170, 171,
    172; "stop Kennedy" movement, 162,
    168–169; campaign organization, 164–
    165, 203; vote-buying accusations,
    169; Kennedy carries, 171, 172, 176

[433]